I0821665

SHADES OF GREEN

IAN FREDERICK FINSETH

Shades of Green

Visions of Nature in the Literature of American Slavery, 1770–1860

The University of Georgia Press | Athens and London

Athens, Georgia 30602
www.ugapress.org

Set in Sabon by Bookcomp, Inc.
Printed and bound by Thomson-Shore
The paper in this book meets the guidelines for permanence and durability of the Committee on Production Guidelines for Book Longevity of the Council on Library Resources.

Printed in the United States of America
12 11 10 09 08 C 5 4 3 2 1

Library of Congress Cataloging-in-Publication Data

Finseth, Ian Frederick.
Shades of green : visions of nature in the literature of American slavery, 1770–1860 / Ian Frederick Finseth.
p. cm.
Includes bibliographical references and index.
ISBN-13: 978-0-8203-2865-2 (hardcover : alk. paper)
ISBN-10: 0-8203-2865-0 (hardcover : alk. paper)
1. American literature—History and criticism.
2. European literature—18th century—History and criticism.
3. Slavery in literature.
4. Nature in literature.
5. Antislavery movements in literature.
6. American literature—European influences.
7. Slavery—Philosophy.
8. Philosophy of nature. I. Title.
PS186F56 2008
810.9'355—dc22 2008010916

British Library Cataloging-in-Publication Data available

In Memoriam

Frederick Finseth

Gratias ago pro

Audrey Finseth

Contents

Acknowledgments

WHEN I BEGAN this book, in graduate school, I vowed that I wouldn't end up as one of those authors who admit, in their acknowledgments, to having worked on a book for ten years. *Shades of Green* seems to have had a different plan. Its inspiration and nucleus was a term paper I wrote, in 1997, on the representation of nature in Frederick Douglass's *My Bondage and My Freedom*. Since then, oaklike, it has gone through all the slow stages of growth and ramification familiar to anyone who has lived with a project for a long time. Along the way, my good fortune has been the friendship, intellectual companionship, and professional support of an ever-widening cast of characters.

My first and greatest debt is to William L. Andrews, who saw merit in the paper on Douglass and agreed to direct the dissertation that had already germinated in my mind. Throughout the writing process, and in the midst of his own many endeavors, Bill provided indispensable guidance as I struggled to get a handle on the contours of the project and to translate into argument what had begun as intuition. He remains a good friend and mentor, and a model of professionalism.

I am also grateful to the other members of my dissertation committee: Charles Capper, Philip Gura, Trudier Harris, and Joy Kasson. Each provided excellent feedback on the manuscript as it took shape and, during one long Friday afternoon as I "defended" the thing, made a number of cogent and helpful suggestions for how to publish it as a book. Conversations with other friends and colleagues at Chapel Hill also had an impact on my work, and even as some of those conversations recede into the mist I want to call out to Reid Barbour, David Davis, Michael Everton, Alec Ewald, Chris Giordano, Rachel Hall, Dustin Howes, Fiona Mills, Bryan Sinche, and Jessica Wolfe.

During the anxiety-ridden period between the PhD and that first tenure-track job, I obtruded myself upon the attention of a number of scholars who magnanimously agreed to read some of my work, despite never having heard of me and having no particular investment in the project. Gregg Crane commented on my treatment of Emerson; Vincent Carretta read the material on Equiano; and Bryan Wolf, no doubt patiently, read through my early ruminations on American art. Thanks to all.

At the University of Georgia Press, I'm fortunate to have had the help of my editor, Nancy Grayson, who shepherded this book through the whole process; of Jennifer Reichlin and Jon Davies, who oversaw its production; of the eagle-eyed copyeditor Molly Thompson; and of the three anonymous readers, who went the extra mile in providing astute—and sometimes brutally frank—advice for improving the manuscript.

Financial support was forthcoming from several quarters. The University of North Carolina awarded me a Dissertation Completion Fellowship, which provided a crucial year of uninterrupted time. A month-long residential fellowship at the Library Company of Philadelphia allowed me to reinforce the original arguments with substantial archival material. A Rackham Faculty Research Fellowship from the University of Michigan and a Faculty Research Grant from the University of Michigan at Dearborn made possible the hard push to the finish line. More recently, the University of North Texas has chipped in with funding to offset the costs associated with reprinting copyrighted images. Both the University of Michigan at Dearborn and the University of North Texas, finally, provided financial support to help with the costs of production.

Some material in this book appeared, in earlier incarnations, in the following articles and book chapter: "Evolution, Cosmopolitanism, and Emerson's Antislavery Politics," *American Literature* 77, no. 4 (December 2005): 729–60 (copyright 2005; all rights reserved; used by permission of the publisher, Duke University Press); "In Essaka Once: Time and History in Olaudah Equiano's Autobiography," *Arizona Quarterly* 58, no. 1 (Spring 2002): 1–35; "David Walker, Nature's Nation, and Early African American Separatism," *Mississippi Quarterly* 54, no. 3 (Summer 2001): 337–62; and "Geographic Consciousness in the American Slave Narrative," in *American Literary Geographies: Spatial Practice and Cultural Production, 1500–1900*, ed. Martin Brückner and Hsuan L. Hsu (Newark: University of Delaware Press, 2007). Permission to reprint this material is gratefully acknowledged.

Although I had more or less finished *Shades of Green* by the time I arrived at UNT, my colleagues here deserve mention for providing such nourishing friendship, without which a scholar's life can become monastic indeed. Cheers, then, to Deborah Needleman Armintor, Marshall Armintor, Diana Benet, Bruce Bond, Jacqueline Foertsch, David Holdeman, Corey Marks, Ann McCutchan, Walton Muyumba, Jack Peters, Nicole Smith, Robert Upchurch, Luis Velarde, and the rest of the gang.

Well beyond the scope of mere gratitude is my wife, Stephanie Hawkins, whose love has always kept me going, whose determination has always impressed me, and whose intellectual energy has always been an inspiration. Both my life and this book bear her impress in ways that can scarcely be acknowledged.

INTRODUCTION

Nature, Race, Culture

AS THE UNITED STATES lurched toward civil war during the 1850s, the brewing storm loomed in Americans' imaginations in hues of black and white and red—colors suggesting the simplification and polarization of ideological positions, the omnipresence of race as a psychological and social reality, and the contending human impulses toward mingling blood and toward spilling it. Yet Americans also conceived of the impending crisis in shades of green. Nature, in all the senses of that complex term, appeared both vividly and surreptitiously in visual and textual renderings of a social world convulsed. Its central yet protean role in the representational war over racial slavery, and therefore over American national identity, is the subject of this book.

This war of words and images, waged on multiple literary and artistic fronts, developed over many decades and within an international context. The titanic political struggle that shook the transatlantic world from the mid-eighteenth to the late nineteenth century was also, inevitably, a contest over the intertwined meanings of "nature" and "race." Inevitably, because what it means to be "human," and therefore to claim certain privileges or rights as a human being, is closely bound up with cultural perceptions of "nature" and the "nonhuman," while the meanings of "race" depend on social definitions of "humanness" and "the human family." In talking about race or nature, therefore, we are always talking, at some level, about the other, and we are always working within and against the conceptual legacies of the eighteenth and nineteenth centuries. The authors and artists taken up here were important, among other reasons, precisely because, in developing an understanding of how the natural and the racial informed each other, they helped to shape the cultural attitudes and perceptions that we have inherited today.

Late in Herman Melville's *Typee*, the main character, Tommo, complains about "the different senses in which one and the same word is employed" in the Polynesian language, noting that "its various meanings all have a certain connection, which only makes the matter more puzzling. So one brisk, lively little word is obliged, like a servant in a poor family, to perform all sorts of duties."[1] There could be no fitter description of the English word "nature," which, as the last two or three decades of scholarship have made abundantly clear, we should never use without a sharp awareness of its complex history and almost infinite flexibility of signification.[2] Since no hard and fast definition of the term "nature" suffices, we are better off exploring the ambiguities and contradictions that have historically informed the concept, for these are what make the term so slippery and yet endow it with its unique social power. Over the course of this book I will demonstrate how that power operates in specific cultural and literary contexts, and by grounding the abstract in the particular, elicit a better understanding of the theoretical issues involved. For the moment, I simply want to identify a series of polarities or tensions in Western ideas of nature that have made it such a maddeningly imprecise and yet endlessly serviceable concept. Nature has been represented both as something to overcome or transcend and as a source of moral authority. It has been seen both as ontologically independent, beyond our structures of meaning, and as a creature of those structures, a domain of symbolic or linguistic constructs. Nature appears sometimes as a place of order, beauty, and truth, and sometimes as a place of chaos and violence. It may represent freedom and opportunity or constraint and necessity. Nature has been regarded simultaneously as the fount and the byproduct of human history. Human beings imagine themselves as part of nature, subject to its norms, and as separate from and superior to it. Across all these polarities run the cross-hatchings of religion, spirituality, economics, technology, science, and race; no area of human thought or endeavor can be divorced from an understanding of what nature in and of itself means and what it means specifically for us.

The terms "human" and "human being"—and "us," for that matter—are not offered here as hermetic vessels of self-evident truth but as shifting categories within which people work through practical matters of individual ethics and social relations. The question of pressing ethical and political significance that runs throughout the texts that this study examines is What is a human being? (with its corollary, What is race?). That question was as complicated and contested in the revolutionary and antebellum periods as it is today. Writers, artists, and cultural figures answered it in part by turning to natural science and in part through representations of the human being in the physical natural world, and always their work reflected the pressure of historical developments in science, in art and literature, and in cultural politics. Indeed, the openness of the category "human" lay at the center of the struggle over slavery, and the strenuous efforts, across the political spectrum, to conclusively define "humanness" only point up its essential instability.[3]

The almost universally shared philosophical perspective, however, was humanism—or what we might today call anthropocentrism or speciesism—and the problematics of humanism form a recurring theme of this book. In virtually every stripe, humanism makes two fundamental claims. The first is that certain transhistorical and transcultural features of human identity and experience stabilize "humanness" as a distinct, and fundamentally unified, category of being. The second is that the human species not only is a superior species but is deservedly so, and that membership in the human family accordingly confers certain rights not enjoyed by other living beings. Although there has never been a clear, stable consensus on the specifics of either claim—what features of mind or body, and what rights, are we talking about?—our intellectual and popular traditions have tended to define human nature not simply in opposition to nature, or as subject to nature, but through recognizably "human" modes of interaction with the natural world. These ways of relating to nature do not always accord with one another, but that does not really matter; what matters is that they distinguish human beings, or seem to distinguish us, from the "lower" animals. They include a range of individual psychological or experiential responses: an aesthetic appreciation of natural beauty, an emotional sensitivity to nature, a curiosity regarding the meanings of nature, and a spiritual receptiveness to some divine presence behind or informing nature. They also include certain socially embedded practices: the empirical or scientific study of nature; the representation of nature in art; the worship, cultivation, or stewardship of nature; and the manipulation of nature through ingenuity or technology. Animals do not, in this account, have the capacities for such responses and practices, and so these have become defining criteria for membership in the human family. They have also become criteria for defining "civilization" and for comparatively evaluating different human cultures and their historical "progress." In short, highly malleable concepts of nature, and of the relation between nature and humanity, therefore support ideologically potent methods of demarcating the human family and promoting particular forms of social organization and cultural development.

During the era of New World slavery, we find a widespread literary and cultural endeavor to define racial identity and social relations through strategic representations of nature and of human relations to nature. American abolitionism takes center stage in this book because it demonstrated the power of rhetorical adaptability in centralizing what had been a marginal political philosophy, and because the paradoxes and trade-offs of antislavery philosophy have something to teach us about contemporary social movements focused on environmental and racial justice. For the antislavery cause, particularly after the rise of polygenist theory in the late eighteenth century, the imperative was twofold: to assert that people of African descent were members of the human family and, therefore, that they deserved to enjoy the natural right of freedom. As an overarching "racial project" subsuming a variety of representational strategies and political ends, this endeavor had both moral and intellectual sides to it.[4] The basic ethical position seemed clear enough: despite the existence of different "races," and regardless of the histories or perceived capacities of these races, people had a moral responsibility to treat other human beings better than they treated animals—centrally, by not denying them their birthrights of liberty and life. As an intellectual matter, antislavery writers had to make the case that the human species was indeed one species—that all people descended in common from the original biblical pair, or put in the secular terms that became increasingly ascendant in the nineteenth century, that human beings shared a common biological past and future. At a polemical level, this argument led necessarily into the thickets of natural science, in its applications to the human being, and it is a central claim of this book that natural science informed antislavery rhetoric and philosophy more fully than we have recognized. At the level of representational suggestion—in poetry, travel literature, and painting, among other genres—the argument took the form of diverse, subtle, and shifting imagistic patterns in which the depicted relationship between African-descended peoples and the natural world seemed to express distinctive human qualities and experiences. This side of the story, as well, has not received sufficient attention in the scholarly literature.[5]

During the years covered by this study, approximately 1780 to 1860, the antislavery engagement with ideas and images of nature was no well-oiled rhetorical machine. Because the intersecting languages of humanism, race, and nature drew on shifting, arbitrary terminologies, antislavery discourse was shot through with ruptures and inconsistencies. Two main problems stand forth. First, a profound tension subsisted between abolition's impulse toward a universalizing humanism, which tended to fold difference into a sentimentalized and deceptive vision of human sameness, and its habitual invocation of racialist concepts, which worked to divide the human family into multiple subfamilies. Second, we find a contrast between antislavery's dual "green" impulses—on one hand, its celebration of undespoiled nature as an outward manifestation of moral and emotional harmony, and on the other hand, its commitment to capitalist and Christian ideas that subordinated environmental concerns to a larger historical narrative of millennial and economic progress.[6] A major strand of my argument here is that the flexible, catch-all concept of "nature" allowed antislavery writers and thinkers to negotiate these contradictions—even to draw strength from them—but that they did not always do so successfully.

This book is not, however, primarily a history of abolitionism and its rhetorical strategies, but a study of American literature and culture. In fact, the most interesting cultural dynamics take place beneath the level of polemic, on the lower frequencies. In its broader dimensions, *Shades of Green* seeks to identify and explain the energies released at those points where "nature" and "race" converged and clashed in the literature and artwork of American slavery. This is a richer and trickier matter than we might think. Much more was involved than the problems of "naturalizing" racial categories or "denaturalizing" human bondage. Invocations of nature in the cultural fight over the meanings of race entailed a remarkable diversity of representational strategies, responded continuously to shifting cultural circumstances, and drew their power from deeper levels of human thought and feeling. Lorraine Daston and Fernando Vidal have written that the "moral authority" of nature is neither absolute nor unrivalled nor monolithic. Instead, it has specific "jurisdictions and workings" and it "works by paradox and obscurity as well as by the clash of clear-cut positions." Hence the importance not only of reason and argumentation, but also of imagery, suggestion, and figuration in the invocation of nature. Furthermore, to the degree that the ideological contingency of nature's "meanings" remains critically unexamined, nature's authority can "circumvent the discourse of legitimation to penetrate directly into habits, perceptions, judgements, and feelings."[7] This last observation calls for particular emphasis. Not always, or even primarily, did American writers or artists of the antebellum period make explicit appeals per se to nature. Just as frequently, they reveal a vision of the natural world informing their writing, a framework of assumptions, priorities, and beliefs that helped to shape and sustain their views of race.

Examples abound. Anthony Benezet, the Quaker abolitionist, writes that on Africa's Ivory Coast, "indigo and cotton thrive without cultivation and tobacco would be excellent if carefully manufactured." Nat Turner tells Thomas Gray of discovering "drops of blood on the corn" and of his decision to prepare for insurrection when he sees an eclipse. Amy Matilda Cassey, a member of Philadelphia's African American elite, reads a pastoral sonnet that William Lloyd Garrison contributed to her personal album. Frederick Douglass remembers his deceased mother upon seeing the "head of a figure" in James Prichard's *Natural History of Man*. William Sidney Mount, the painter, draws on his childhood memories to produce a landscape, *Eel Spearing at Setauket*, in which economic conflicts are subsumed to racial harmony. Herman Melville imagines the elms of Malvern Hill bearing witness to a Civil War battle. George Lunt, a lawyer and amateur botanist, recounts the African expedition of Mungo Park, whose faith in Providence is renewed by finding "a small moss, of extraordinary beauty, in the process of germination." The anonymous author of *The Tales of Peter Parley about Africa*, a book for children, writes that the Caffrees "inhabit a fruitful country, and are said to be the handsomest Negroes in the world."[8]

Despite their brevity, none of these examples lends itself to quick or easy explanation, and taken together they suggest that elaborating fully on the linkages between "the natural" and "the racial" will require attention to a number of ancillary issues: economics and technology; social class; natural philosophy and the natural sciences; geography; religious belief and spiritual feeling; perception, memory, and desire. Representations of nature and racial identity rarely follow clear ideological patterns, and they have a tendency to transgress the epistemological, professional, and artistic barriers that we imagine for them.

With that cautionary note in mind, the broad unifying argument of *Shades of Green* is twofold: first, that discourses of "nature" both liberated and constrained antislavery and humanitarian philosophy, in ways still relevant to modern social movements, and second, that our understanding of race in early American literature and culture must take the natural world into account, since not doing so is to exclude the very foundation on which ideas of race were grounded. The relation of racial thought and abolitionist rhetoric to concepts of human nature and the natural order figures centrally in this argument. Yet the dynamic relationship between race and nature embraced a number of interconnected issues—theodicy, narrative, biology, historical consciousness, regional identity, aesthetics—and it surfaced in a wide variety of nonpolemical and nonliterary sources: paintings and daguerreotypes, scientific essays, travel writing, personal correspondence, newspaper articles, and more. From this cultural seedbed, in turn, arose the major literature itself, and the canonical writers I consider here—from St. John de Crèvecoeur and Olaudah Equiano to Harriet Beecher Stowe and Frederick Douglass—are interesting to me precisely because they got their hands dirty in wrestling with these issues, and because their writings therefore more vividly reveal the doubts and uncertainties, the working through of ideas, the unspoken fault lines and tensions between different areas of thought.

A number of questions have guided my engagement with their work: How did their attitudes and feelings regarding nature inform their representation of race, and conversely, how did their sense of racial identity inform their treatment of the natural world? How did intersecting representations of race and the natural world reflect broader cultural developments in science, philosophy, economics, religion, and politics? What were the rhetorical and conceptual resources that "nature" provided for the antislavery movement, and what sorts of inconsistencies or historical ironies do we hear in abolitionist discourse? Can we identify patterns of difference in representing the natural world that distinguish African American and European American literature? If so, how might we account for those patterns, and what do they mean? Though necessarily limited, epistemologically, by "representation," can we find within literary and visual texts the *non*representational significances of nature? In other words, what conclusions do these texts seem to support about understanding racial and human identity in terms of the experiential, psychological, and evolutionary power of the living green world?

In addressing such questions, this book starts but does not end with polemics and politics. In the broadest sense, it asks how human identity is formed, defined, represented, and negotiated through "nature"—how nature subtends, and superintends, individual consciousness.

The subject is hydra-headed, and in order to get at how literary or visual representations of nature were ways of simultaneously articulating human experience and racial identity, and of influencing the debate over slavery, this project seeks areas of intersection and forms of synergy between several domains of knowledge: environmental and evolutionary psychology, aesthetics, and phenomenology. Insights from these different fields provide leverage over some of the interpretive problems the argument raises.

The core theoretical positions informing this book do not take long to state, but they do require some defense and elaboration. First, I maintain that racial subjectivity matters to how human beings perceive, narrate, and interact with nature. Second, I posit the natural world (i.e., the terrestrial biosphere) as an ontologically real domain that has powerfully, if not deterministically, shaped human consciousness. Behind both of these claims lies the conviction, certainly not unique to this argument, that "nature" and "culture" inform each other—which is to assert simultaneously that nature exerts a more powerful influence on human culture, and cultures, than many people (especially of the postmodern persuasion) allow for, and that nature (in meaning, process, and form), cannot wholly escape humanity's symbolic and physical appropriation or manipulation of it. As Dana Phillips has observed, "intentionally or unintentionally, human hands have refashioned even the most natural [phenomena], so that they also seem intensely cultural. At the same time, many phenomena that seem fully cultural are bound up and run together with things and events in the natural world. The effect of this multiple causal heritage . . . is the confounding of our basic categories."[9] In the midst of such confounding, however, we need to specify clear distinctions between nature and culture and to understand the limits and peculiarities of their mutual impactedness. Jonathan Levin, writing that "[n]ature and culture are entangled in complex and inherently elusive ways," has clearly articulated the challenge: "To acknowledge this [entanglement] is not to abandon the project of thinking rigorously about their relation but is rather to set that project on an alternative track, one less devoted to resolving once and for all a long-standing sociophilosophical problem than to entering the space of the problem in new ways."[10]

Race represents one of those ways. As a dominant mode of understanding cultural difference, traditionally explained in terms of such "natural" phenomena as biology, climate, and evolution, the category of race provides a means of exploring the relationships between culture and nature, as those relationships are represented in various texts. In a graceful turn of phrase, Robert Young has written: "Race has always been culturally constructed. Culture has always been racially constructed."[11] We can offer a similar formulation in saying that, just as nature is culturally constructed, so is culture in a real sense naturally constructed. To make that claim—more controversial in literary studies than elsewhere—is not to deny that culture diverges from nature in important respects, but to emphasize the complex relation between the two, and to call our attention to the impact of nature on human subjectivity, in both its racial and nonracial dimensions. This does not mean that we have to reify, essentialize, or naturalize race. Quite the contrary: In shuttling between nature and culture, race emerges as a subjective rather than an objective category of analysis. That is precisely because the meanings of nature on which it supposedly rests derive from shifting, competing forms of thought, while the cultural differences that race supposedly marks are, in turn, dissolved or transcended by common human responses to nature.[12] If this sounds self-contradictory, the key lies in recognizing the distinction between, on the one hand, representation and ideology (or "meanings of nature") and, on the other, experience and psychology (or "responses to nature")—a distinction that runs throughout this book, and that provides a method of negotiating the Scylla and Charybdis of racialism and humanism.

Let us start by considering the second major proposition, the claim that nature has "shaped human consciousness." This is an assertion that depends on recent work in environmental and evolutionary psychology, two closely related fields that emphasize the transcultural and transhistorical structures and process of the human mind, while de-emphasizing (but certainly not denying) the role of human "difference." They maintain that human identity is not just *defined* through images and concepts of "nature," but *formed* in and by and through the natural world itself. Evolutionary psychologists argue, in essence, that human consciousness has developed in response to the selection pressures exerted by the natural environment, and that the mind must therefore be understood in terms of its problem-solving capacities and its strategies for making its way in the world.[13] For its part, environmental psychology has tended to concentrate on the emotional or cognitive effects of the physical surroundings in which people live, and therefore gravitates toward such practical issues as architectural design, urban landscape planning, and ecotherapy.[14] Its line of intellectual descent also includes more philosophically oriented explorations of the meanings of "place" and "space" in human life.[15] At root, what these fields offer us is a vision of human life—cognition, feeling, knowledge—as not dissevered from the natural world, not superior to it or independent of it, but as profoundly embedded in it, despite several centuries of industrialization and increasing, self-imposed alienation. And far from representing some kind of mystical romanticism, this understanding is, at its best, methodologically well grounded. Taking this perspective, then, will direct our attention to those aspects of the human relation to nature that cut across cultures and historical epochs. If there are elemental human experiences of nature, or responses to nature, what role might they play in individual and cultural development? How do human beings, having emerged, in a manner of speaking, from nature, encounter the natural world on perceptual, experiential, and emotional levels? In what ways are human memories, desires, impulses, and beliefs shaped through our interaction with the natural world? Posing such questions obliges us to consider nature not only as a realm of symbolic constructs that can be deployed for ideological purposes, but as a real domain from which humans emerged, and in which we inevitably work out our destiny as living beings. Again, this is not a matter of "naturalizing" specific forms of human conduct, thought, or sociality, but of trying to understand what we might call our species' ecological embeddedness—to appreciate the real power of nature in shaping human consciousness and character.

Clearly, environmental and evolutionary psychology are deeply humanist in outlook, but evolutionary psychology is more aggressively so, asserting that "the peoples of the world share an astonishingly detailed universal psychology."[16] Such statements seem almost calculated to provoke allergic reactions among die-hard social constructionists, and evolutionary psychology has predictably encountered fierce resistance from critics who charge its practitioners with everything from misappropriating Darwin's evolutionary theory or subscribing to a pernicious biological determinism to resurrecting in more glamorous form the outmoded ideas of sociobiology and even social Darwinism.[17] At the very least it might seem to advance an all-embracing humanism that accords little or no space to the importance of culture, and racial identity, in human life. Yet as Steven Pinker and others have argued, the claim that human thought has innate structures rooted in the collective experience of the species does not imply that culture makes no difference. Edward Reed, for example, argues that the beginnings of thought lie in "an autonomous ability to represent aspects of the world to oneself" but that the great variety of human circumstances (derived from our ability to inhabit widely dispersed ecosystems) means that culture and history now become paramount in explaining particular patterns of thought. Evolutionary psychology, he concludes, "offers the possibility of genuine cross-cultural and cross-temporal comparisons. These comparisons will be made not against some extra-historical human essence but in terms of the variations in natural human psychological processes that function in any culture."[18] The same might be said for environmental psychology, and both fields thus provide a way of bridging humanist and culturalist, or racialist, perspectives. The innate capacities and structures of the mind that exist prior to culture, so to speak, are always expressed in culturally inflected ways, and that expression is always influenced by an irreducibly particular individual consciousness.

Which brings us to the claim that "racial subjectivity matters to how human beings perceive, narrate, and interact with nature." The term "racial subjectivity," as used here, is meant to refer to the lived experience of identifying with a socially defined racial group, or with more than one group simultaneously, and of "inhabiting" that racial identity in ways that inform one's thoughts, feelings, and relationships. For this definition, it does not matter that race is culturally constructed, or that it has identifiable material and historical bases—that is simply a *donnée* of my argument. The relevant issue, rather, is how an individual's psychology is shaped, over time, by racial identification and racial difference. This latter notion, racial difference, is indispensable. In a society that, for whatever reason, had no concept of racial difference (even if other ideas of difference were operative), it would make no sense to talk of racial identification, and therefore of racial subjectivity. Race only exists in a society that sees itself, or the world, as racially heterogeneous. Race is, in short, radically relational, and although its boundaries and meanings have no "natural" basis, it nonetheless exerts a powerful influence on individual psychology.[19] That much may be fairly straightforward, given the literary and historical record of at least four centuries of Western racial thought, but we should still ask *why* racial subjectivity would matter, in a more than ordinary way, to how people represent and encounter the natural world.

Any answer to that question must begin with the fact that representations of nature, and assertions of what counts as natural, have long formed the arena for racialized contests over membership and status in the human family, and therefore over the allocation of rights and resources. Representations of nature thus not only serve as an index to broad patterns of cultural ideology, but also express what is believed or felt to be personally at stake in particular ideas of nature or modes of interacting with nature. Moreover, to the degree that the very processes of consciousness and our phenomenological awareness of the external world are molded by culture, we should stay alert to how "nature" as depicted in visual or verbal texts may reflect the particular subjectivity of the representer. That is, we can identify two essential modes by which race informs the representation of nature, one involving the deliberate use of images of nature toward specified political or personal ends, the other involving unconscious or prethematic forms of racial awareness that inflect one's perceptions or experiences of nature, and that exist prior to the linguistic or material expression of that awareness.[20] Another way of putting this is that when we talk of the "culturally constructed" status of nature, we need to remain keenly aware of how the racial dimension of "culture," as lived individually, enters into the equation. It is that embeddedness of the individual in culture, and the responsiveness of culture to the nonhuman world, that establishes the link between a psychology of nature and a psychology of race. By the same token, when we talk of the "environmental imagination" or the "environmental unconscious," two of the central terms of modern ecocritical discourse, we must retain a clear sense of both the universal and the culturally particular in these models.

This perspective intersects fruitfully with a phenomenological approach to questions of perception, cognition, and feeling. Most broadly, that approach enables us to speak of common human responses to the natural world while acknowledging the deep influence of culture and history on inner experience and consciousness. Phenomenology—and here I draw principally on adaptations of Edmund Husserl's work by Alfred Schutz, Hans Jonas, Maurice Natanson, and David Carr—does make claims about "the mind," but it remains keenly sensitive to, in fact focuses on, the perceptions, sensations, emotions, and thoughts of the individual, and treats this person as embodying a unique cultural history.[21] Its humanism, in other words, is tempered by a recognition of irreducibly particular subjectivity. In parallel fashion, the phenomenological perspective balances an affirmation of the ontological independence of the *lebenswelt*, or life-world, with a philosophical commitment to the shaping power of consciousness. Consciousness does not exist in a vacuum; in a signature phrase of the field, we always have consciousness *of something*. The world is indeed "out there," but it is "intended" and given meaning by the perceiving mind, and each of us who shares the world intends it in our own way. The various facets of consciousness (perception, memory, imagination, desire) are not purely interior but profoundly bound up with the external world, and in stressing this nonsolipsistic orientation toward the world phenomenology has profound ethical implications, and has been a particularly vital force in environmental philosophy and, to a lesser extent, in race theory.[22] My interest in phenomenology here, as will become apparent, has to do with its relevance for our understanding of human responsiveness to the natural world, and for our understanding of how social ethics can be reimagined.

This is not, however, a study of the human being, but a work of literary and cultural history, in which the central interpretive and methodological problems have to do with representation. These problems involve how we read race in depictions of the natural (even if race seems at first irrelevant or invisible), and conversely, how we read the natural in depictions of race (even if nature seems of a secondary order of concern). The interpenetration of these two categories raises fascinating issues of interpretation. For instance, what are we to make of a conventional landscape by the "black" painter Robert Duncanson? Is there some way in which his racial identity "showed up," so to speak, in his work, despite its ostensibly nonracial subject? Can we read its formal qualities with an eye toward his racial identity, or must we somehow purge race from the act of interpretation? Is the influence of race here operational only in the surrounding cultural contexts in which the painting would have been viewed and interpreted? If so, might the painting bear the impress of the artist's *anticipation* of its racialized reception? Or, consider the following passage by Elias Magoon, a "white" contributor to an 1852 volume titled *The Home Book of the Picturesque*: "A majestic landscape, often scanned and truly loved, imparts much of its greatness to the mind and heart of the spectator. The savage is not too rude, nor the child too infantile, to be either refined or fortified by its lessons." Magoon continues, quoting an unidentified source: "The untutored negro, when he prostrates himself on the reedy bank of his native stream, and adores the Deity of the stream in the shape of the crocodile, or bows before the poison tree, in reverence to the God of poisons, obeys this native impulse of humanity [the 'love of nature'] no less than the disciple of Zoroaster who climbs the highest mountain tops."[23] Here, the racialized representation of nature takes the form not of landscape itself, but of textual commentary upon landscape. Does the crude racialism of this passage outweigh its humanist content? Or, to put the question more gracefully, how do the passage's racialist and humanist ideas cooperate or compete with one another? To what degree do Magoon's obviously class- and culture-bound assumptions vitiate his argument? It is easy to dismiss the man as just another example of mid-nineteenth-century racial false consciousness, but might he actually have a legitimate point?

In addressing such questions—and they proliferate enthusiastically—this study is guided by a number of theoretical precepts or positions. I have sketched them out here, in relatively brief form, to provide an overview of what we might regard as the theoretical nervous system of the argument. In later chapters, they will serve both to anchor and to animate our readings in the primary material.

To start with, I want to suggest that textual and visual representations of the natural world have the potential to stimulate or evoke experiences in the appreciator that approximate but do not duplicate sensorally direct experiences of nature in its nonrepresentational form. This is not simply a question of the mimetic "realism" or verisimilitude of the work, but of its capacity, as an aesthetic object, to arouse the imagination, to spur the memory, to induce sensations phenomenologically analogous to "the real thing." Clearly our responses to art-objects will differ from our responses to the natural world itself, in that the latter can involve all of the senses and provide what might be termed "immersive" experience. In addition, the artwork, as a cultural artifact—conceived and crafted, displayed or distributed, evaluated and commented upon, emulated or resisted, and unchanging in form—will possess a layered ideological and social history that natural scenes, settings, or objects are largely (although not entirely) free of. But experience of the one will necessarily be mediated by experience of the other.[24] Looking at a sunset is not the same as looking at a painting of a sunset, but neither is it entirely different, and just as the painting may conjure up feelings or thoughts associated with previous lived experience, so the real sunset may be seen through many layers of cultural preconditioning. The immediate significance of this experiential reciprocity between "real" and represented nature is that the various forms of representation I consider here—from poetry and landscape to travel writing—would have had psychological or phenomenological effects connected to the appreciator's whole personal history involving the natural world. This is a key point to bear in mind in assessing the different meanings of natural representation for, say, the agricultural slave than for the urban abolitionist or the seafaring trader.

Crucially, our responses to natural imagery will operate on both cognitive or linguistic and subcognitive or sublinguistic levels. This familiar division in aesthetic theory concerns the role of conscious knowledge in the aesthetic experience, and a cognitive approach will emphasize the relative importance of epistemological "objectivity," particularly, in the case of the natural world, as it is grounded in the natural sciences.[25] To properly appreciate nature, goes the argument, we should really have some solid information about it. Noncognitive approaches, by contrast, make room for a wider variety of subjective frameworks in the aesthetic experience, including sensuous response, imagination, religious belief, and memory—while seeking not to merely "subjectivize" it.[26] Appreciating nature, in this view, means perceiving, engaging, and feeling it at deeper levels than we might be consciously aware of. The noncognitive perspective, crucially, loops us back to evolutionary psychology, since we can understand noncognitive responses to nature as shaped, in part, by the structures and processes of consciousness that precede acculturation. Grounding experience in human evolutionary history as well as in cultural and individual histories results in an account of aesthetics that updates and makes more rigorous Kant's seminal idea of "subjective universal validity."[27] That is, it allows us to see individual subjectivity (including conscious knowledge) as the proximate factor in aesthetic experience, while locating that subjectivity within a broader human narrative, and identifying features of its responsiveness that are transhistorical and transcultural. The importance of such an account for this book is that, in the representational war over slavery, both kinds of appeal cooperated. On one level, cultural knowledge about the natural world—including myths, metaphors, and folklore as well as science—formed the basis on which arguments were made or refuted, or on which representations of race sought to establish their authority. On a deeper level, representations of the natural world could bypass conscious thought in order to evoke powerful emotional responses; in many cases, this was precisely the intended effect, quite apart from the question of representational "accuracy." Always these two dynamics flowed into one another, and they help us begin to understand the distinction between polemical and nonpolemical representation.

In literary or visual texts that depict a human being encountering the natural world in some fashion—a category that comprises most of the works discussed in this project—part of the power of natural imagery consists in its potential to evoke an experiential bond between viewer and figure or between reader and character. The experience of the fictional human being is usually of nature in its nonrepresentational, "real" form (Duncanson's fishing boys at Blue Hole on the Little Miami River, for instance), but in certain cases (as with Magoon's "majestic landscape"), nature is encountered in its represented, processed, or artistic form. In both cases the experience of the imaginary character, their awareness of and responses to the natural world, can serve as a template or reference point for the experience of the reader or viewer in "perceiving" the natural world as shown on the page or the canvas. Insofar as these responses, whether of fear, pleasure, curiosity, hostility, awe, reverence, or any other feeling or attitude, extend across cultural and historical boundaries, they have the power to form a circuit of shared meaning embracing those inside and those outside the text.[28] That circuit of shared meaning gives natural imagery its ability to create moments of identification between audience and character, such that the techniques of sentiment and sympathy—so central to antislavery rhetoric—do not merely assert a common experience of nature but work to evoke or stimulate it. It is that imagined or felt experiential bond, I believe, which has the potential to become ethically or ideologically influential in the "real" world of the audience.

Here again aesthetics and phenomenology provide a useful vocabulary for opening up the problem. After a long sojourn on the margins of late twentieth-century scholarship, aesthetics have made something of a comeback—have gotten their "revenge," in one formulation—in literary and cultural studies, where serious consideration of the artistic strategies or properties of a work is no longer regarded with automatic suspicion as ahistorical or apolitical, or more properly, as insidiously concealing a politics of exclusionary cultural chauvinism.[29] Much of the most interesting recent work in aesthetics has considered precisely the question of the power of artistic expression to stimulate the imagination in such a way as to provide a reoriented, potentially more critical, perspective on the public sphere and political ethics.[30] While prompted by the individual's fundamentally private or interior engagement with an aesthetic object or scene, aesthetic experience does not have to amount to solipsistic withdrawal or bourgeois complacency; it can, ideally, initiate a widening circle of awareness, extending outward toward new forms of emotional identification and social renewal.[31]

This perspective enables us to associate the imagination and private contemplation with social renewal, and to understand aesthetic experience not in opposition to but as essential to ethical responsibility and political engagement, and as a way of reapproaching the world in a more engaged, creative, critical way. Still, while aesthetic experience might thus constitute a "source of autonomy and resistance to the status quo," it is worth remembering that such resistance lies in the realm of possibility rather than necessity, and that "aesthetics, like all affective formations, operate within institutional and disciplinary frameworks that seek to orient sense and sensation toward desired outcomes: those framings [are what] make aesthetics either conservative or progressive."[32] In this project, then, aesthetic effects are treated as forming an unpredictable dynamic of autonomous reflection and social reconnection, and as capable of revealing their own cultural contingency. Moreover, and most importantly, I will argue that an aesthetics of nature is capable of revealing the contingency of cultural practice itself. Representations of nature can, perhaps inevitably, influence perceptions of the human sphere, even in those cases where a writer or artist has sought to exclude the human element as much as possible.

Which may sound intuitively sensible, but it still leaves open the question of how that revision of perception might actually take place. This question goes to the heart of this book's argument, and will be addressed in different ways in each of the chapters, but here I want to offer an insight from phenomenology as a crucial part of the answer. Maurice Natanson has written of the ways in which the "current of existence," or that flow of memories and perceptual experiences that we take for granted, as givens, in the ordinary course of daily life, can be interrupted by moments of "irrealization," by which he means "not a 'removal' from reality but rather an abstention from claiming the ordinary as real." In defamiliarizing the real world, such moments of irrealization work to reveal what is possible in addition to what is actual. Taking Husserl's concept of phenomenological "reduction" as a narrowing of focus, as the intentional act by which consciousness brings into relief an object or event in the current of existence, Natanson sees this "abstention from immanent affirmation" as "a way of comprehending the living in terms of fictive possibility."[33] This perspective suggests the opportunity for reconceiving the cultural, and for diminishing its "taken-for-grantedness." It promises, more pointedly, a liberatory recognition of the fictive quality or the contingency of what has been generally agreed upon. Alfred Schutz has observed that "all knowledge taken for granted has a highly socialized structure [that] . . . gives this kind of knowledge an objective and anonymous character: it is conceived as being independent of my personal biographical circumstances."[34] To return the subjective to its rightful place in the creation of knowledge is to pierce through what Husserl termed the "natural attitude," a kind of unexamined realism that tends to elide the importance of history and culture in regarding the surfaces and the meanings of "reality" as congruent.[35]

This perspective gives us a powerful framework for assessing how a human being's encounter with either a representation of nature or nature "itself" can reorient their perception of culture. Throughout the literature I consider here, we find a recurring pattern whose essential structure or dynamic is remarkably consistent: a remove from culture to nature that interrupts the flow of daily existence; an intimate sensory encounter of the perceiving mind with its natural surroundings; the stimulation of self-reflective awareness, particularly of the personal past and future; the reevaluation of social relations and social knowledge prompted by the irrealization of the ordinary; and then the individual's return to the cultural sphere, but in a shifted relation to it. Significantly, the "remove" to nature does not require a physical separation from social space; it can also involve a narrowing of phenomenological awareness to a single "natural" object, such as a rose or a blackbird, whose essential quiddity is thrown into relief when detached from its surroundings. The consciousness that intends the natural thing or scene does not create it, but posits it, builds it up, apprehends its abiding presence through a temporal series of imaginary variations. While this perceiving mind may exhibit—as the evolutionary psychologists would tell us—certain hard-wired responses to nature, it is a mind profoundly shaped by culture, and so brings to bear all of its conditioning and social idiosyncrasies to the intending of the natural object. It is also a mind that, barring total sociopathy, identifies with members of the species and recognizes, at some level, its ethical implication in the affairs of culture; hence the inexorable return of awareness or of the individual to the social sphere. The natural world, then, functions as both agent and slate in the creation of meaning, and this meaning binds all the qualities of personal experience (memory, desire, pain, curiosity, need) to the larger social, ethical, and ideological contexts in which the individual lives. Finally, to the degree that the experience of represented nature approximates that of "real" nature—and as I have suggested, the two are deeply intertwined—this dynamic embraces the audience as well as the characters and thus both, potentially, come to a new and more critical understanding of the human world in which they live. The importance of this dynamic to the representational struggle over race and slavery should become apparent over the course of this book.

One more issue remains to be addressed in this sketch of the book's theoretical orientation, and that concerns the relation between "scientific" and "aesthetic" modes of representing nature. For my purposes, the most important distinction between them has to do not so much with their objective explanatory power (although that distinction in other contexts will be paramount), as with the degree of objectivity *claimed* by the representation. By the "scientific" mode, then, I mean an expressive register that aspires toward the discovery and description of natural "facts," and by the "aesthetic" mode, I refer to an expressive register oriented toward the evocation of particular subjective effects in response to natural imagery. I fully recognize that scientific discourse is often misguided, self-interested, ideologically slanted, or just plain wrong, but I also have no intention of arguing that it is not therefore more self-regulating and self-constraining than nonscientific discourse.

My interest, rather, is in the rhetorical and persuasive strategies of each mode and, more broadly, in the fascinating ways in which they overlap and flow into one another. What kind of artistic tropes or themes do we find in scientific discourse, and conversely, in what ways does science leave its imprint on aesthetically motivated representations of nature? In the first case, an expanding body of scholarship has considered how scientific representations of nature draw upon metaphorical, visual, or literary conventions in ways that not only inform the social meaning of the text but can even influence the process of scientific inquiry itself.[36] This held particularly true, moreover, during and immediately after the Enlightenment, when the sciences had not attained the degree of specialization and professionalization that they enjoy today, and were therefore marked off less rigidly from other forms of expression. At the same time, the reigning scientific knowledge of a period, the scientific episteme, will inevitably influence the representation of nature in art. In a broad sense, it will do so by conditioning the assumptions or beliefs about nature that the writer or artist brings to the act of representation. In a more direct or conscious way, aesthetically motivated representations of nature can serve as opportunities for exploring, challenging, reinforcing, or otherwise articulating scientific understandings of nature.[37] What I want to stress is that these patterns of mutual influence have real-world political significance, particularly during the period covered by this study, for the scientific and aesthetic modes of representing nature were both potent means of defining the human family and describing racial difference.

I offer these ruminations on the entanglements of race, nature, and culture not as definitive answers but as a set of working ideas that will inform the arguments and readings to come. Given the slipperiness of these categories, and their notorious susceptibility to excessive generalization and abstraction, it is especially important to focus on specific usages by specific actors in specific contexts—which, in any event, are all the literary historian has to go on, practically speaking.

A note, first, on the organization and method of this book. It alternates between chapters devoted to cultural history (1, 3, and 5) and chapters devoted to major writers (2, 4, and 6) whose work most imaginatively engages its cultural moment. Not all of the writers discussed here were "abolitionists," or even consistent in their views on slavery and race, but for that very reason they give us a more complete picture of the dynamic role of nature in conceptions of the human and the racial. The book proceeds more or less chronologically, starting with the mid-eighteenth century and ending with the American Civil War, and it follows several relevant historical trajectories: the increasing aggressiveness of Western racial theory; the consolidation of American technological and economic power; the polarization of sectional politics; the liberalization of mainstream religion. Finally, the geographic focus becomes progressively narrower, spiralling inward, so to speak, from the transatlantic scope of chapters 1 and 2, through the treatments of national identity in chapters 3 and 4, to the emphasis on regional difference in chapters 5 and 6. This schema reflects, in a broad sense, the changing concerns of the American polity as the country moved from separation to consolidation to civil war.

In the chapters on literature, I have paired African American and European American writers in order to trace important influences and exchanges between the two literary traditions. Their profound interdependence is a story that merits, in my view, frequent retelling, and the challenge for literary historians is to reconstruct the living web of psychological, aesthetic, and political threads that have linked European American and African American expression from the country's earliest years. That the academy has tended to bifurcate studies in the two literary traditions reflects, in part, simple practicality: we cannot teach everything, nor write about everything, and must make choices. More fundamentally, legitimate concerns exist about the danger of subsuming African American art and writing to a "dominant" white tradition that sets the terms, defines the values, and establishes the conventions. That does not strike me, however, as an inevitable consequence of "intertraditional" scholarship; indeed, critical work that draws on both traditions can do much to demonstrate how "white" American literature, far from standing as a monolithic category, has had to share the stage with, and be responsive to, nonwhite cultural expression. I do not believe, in short, that we can fully appreciate either European American or African

American literature without a solid grounding in both, and without an informed sense of what allies them and what distinguishes them.

In that spirit, in assessing the importance of nature to antislavery thought I hope to provide a fresh perspective both for studies in literature and the environment, which could greatly benefit by more sustained attention to matters of race, and for African American studies, which has only sporadically engaged with the significance of natural imagery. While there has been a growing recognition that these two fields have much to say to one another, the theoretical implications of such dialogue remain in both cases insufficiently elaborated. Ecocriticism, for its part, has struggled to shed a tenaciously "white" reputation, as suggested by heightened attention to African American, Latino/Latina, and Native American authors both in recent "green" scholarship and at recent meetings of the Association for Studies in Literature and the Environment.[38] Yet a tendency persists to assume a kind of transpersonal, deracialized subject position in investigating humanity's changing relationship to the natural world. To the extent that this project brings the question of racial subjectivity toward the center of environmental literary studies, it might assist in the ongoing theoretical self-renovation of ecocriticism.

Conversely, studies in African American culture and history have only recently begun to approach environmental questions with theoretical sophistication and seriousness of purpose. Historically, African Americanist criticism, in showing that race is "culturally constructed," has displayed a theoretical inhibition against considering "the natural" as a category of analysis of human relations. Since "nature" is also socially constructed, the traditional argument goes, to invoke it as a legitimate interpretive framework is to contribute to the mystification of racially discriminatory social practices. If, however, we dispense with the quote marks and try to regard the natural world in its ontological independence, and if we posit a complex relation between nature and culture, then we need to consider how the psychology of race and the psychology of nature are related—without essentializing either one. In undertaking that task, this study joins recent work by Kimberly K. Smith and Dianne D. Glave and Mark Stoll that foregrounds the role of nature in African American thought and history.[39] Where my approach differs is in focusing on the early evolution of African American literature in relation to an Anglo-dominated mainstream; in trying to draw out the affective and phenomenological complexities of the natural world for black authors; and in assessing its importance to the larger world of antislavery politics.

I begin, in chapter 1, with an exploration of how eighteenth-century abolitionism responded to a changing epistemic environment by adapting scientific and aesthetic theories of nature to its own purposes. As the grounds of the debate over slavery shifted during the revolutionary era, with the rise of racial science and Romanticism, the traditional ethical claims of Christian humanitarianism and natural rights theory, while still vitally important for the antislavery movement, began to lose their sufficiency as modes of critique. In seeking to rebut charges of African savagery, and to remove the imprimatur of nature from human bondage, antislavery writers found that the discourses of natural history and natural beauty were conceptually quite fertile, and that they provided a powerful vocabulary for redefining racial identity and delegitimating racial oppression.

In the 1780s, two works appeared that illustrated the remarkable richness of these ideas when refracted through literature, and chapter 2 provides extended readings of J. Hector St. John de Crèvecoeur's *Letters from an American Farmer* (1782) and Olaudah Equiano's *Interesting Narrative of the Life of Gustavus Vassa* (1789), focusing on how these authors imagined personal and social transfiguration in terms of the natural world. As cultural hybrids writing during an era of international exploration and revolutionary upheaval, Crèvecoeur and Equiano were well suited to communicating an optimistic vision of human potential and historical progress. For both men, however, racial slavery posed not only an ideological challenge but a narrative one, as well. The linked problems of temporality, narrative structure, and autodiegesis in *Letters* and the *Interesting Narrative* reveal both the strengths and the weaknesses of postrevolutionary liberal thought. For Crèvecoeur and Equiano, ideas of nature provided a framework for thinking about individual and cultural destiny, but uncertainty about the *meanings* of nature worked to undermine the ideological coherence of each work.

In the following decades, scientific thought moved well beyond eighteenth-century natural history, and chapter 3 turns to the growing influence of race theory on abolitionist and humanitarian literature from the 1820s to the 1840s. During the early antebellum period, American antislavery writers grappled with the claims of ethnology and anthropology more fully and explicitly than they had in previous decades. What were the implications for the country, these writers asked, of the interracial division and conflict that science seemed to locate within the natural order? More broadly, how did the "evils" of slavery and racial violence fit into the narrative of human progress and the scheme of providential history? In working through both the theodicean problem of the existence of evil and the relation between racial, eschatological, and national histories, antislavery writers began to articulate what I term a "natural law of free development." This concept, energized by the intellectual climate of early evolutionary theory, envisioned struggle and conflict as motive forces in human progress, and it provided a way of simultaneously accommodating race as a "natural" category while rendering slavery an "unnatural" block on human development.

Chapter 4 extends this argument by considering how the existence of slavery and, more directly, the prospect of a postslavery United States, stimulated various forms of creative thinking about the relation between racial and national histories. Specifically, I follow the trajectory of a separatist black nationalism stretching from David Walker's *Appeal to the Coloured Citizens of the World* (1829) to Martin Delany's *Blake* (1862), and the development, during roughly the same period, of an integrationist nationalism in the writings of Ralph Waldo Emerson. For all of these authors, the domains of history and nation were deeply imbricated with the natural world and the "natural" relations between races. Their writings seek to coordinate a number of complex issues: the presence of "racial natures" within a common human nature; the processes of racial differentiation, conflict, and evolution; and the role of climate and the natural environment in national and racial development. Yet the tensions in their work among humanist, cosmopolitan, and ethnoculturalist attitudes, and between theory and practicality, reveal the profound difficulties of finding workable alternatives to regnant nineteenth-century models of national identity.

Chapter 5 examines how the themes developed thus far—civilization, human development and human progress, the importance of geography—play out in the antebellum pastoral and landscape traditions, with implications for how Americans understood race on the eve of civil war. At root, these implications had to do with how racial difference could be understood, negotiated, or denied according to the subjective experience of individuals in nature itself or in response to representations of nature. In a variety of genres, including antislavery verse, genre painting, and the slave narrative, we find a concern with the relation of human psychology to the natural world and with the embeddedness of the human organism in its natural environment: precisely the issues that had been developing over decades of natural philosophy and natural history. Concentrating on the visual and phenomenological dimensions of natural imagery, I maintain that racialized landscapes influenced the debate over slavery by appealing to supposedly transhistorical and transcultural human feelings regarding nature, while narrating or imaging these feelings in terms of individual experience.

This argument prepares for chapter 6, which focuses on Harriet Beecher Stowe's *Dred: A Tale of the Great Dismal Swamp* (1856) and Frederick Douglass's *My Bondage and My Freedom* (1855). Building on a growing awareness of the centrality of these texts to their authors' careers, and to the broader relation between African American and Anglo American literature, I examine how their representations of nature enable Stowe and Douglass to reevaluate their involvement with the antislavery cause and to reimagine the nature of psychological and social freedom. In *Dred*, Stowe turns to nature as a source of authority, backed by both revealed religion and natural science, for imagining a revolutionary form of racial "growth" that will burst asunder the oppressive structures of American society. In doing so, she moves far beyond the comparatively superficial (although revealingly superficial) treatment of the natural world in *Uncle Tom's Cabin*. Douglass also engages the pastoral tradition more critically and self-consciously, but the autobiographical form and retrospective mood of *My Bondage and My Freedom* enable him to explore the deeper personal meanings of the genre. Most importantly, he comes to envision vital connections between his search for family and the restorative wholeness of a natural world unpolluted by slavery. In this way, Douglass helped to inaugurate an important strain in later African American literature: the view of rural folk culture, both southern and American, as a source of strength and communal identification, as a form of shared historical rootedness.

The *Value*, or WORTH of a man, is as of all other things, his Price; that is to say, so much as would be given for the use of his Power: and therefore is not absolute; but a thing dependant on the need and judgement of another.
THOMAS HOBBES, *Leviathan* (1651)

[I]t is impossible to make any man a slave, unless he be first reduced to a situation in which he cannot do without the help of others; and, since such a situation does not exist in a state of nature, every one is there his own master, and the law of the strongest is of no effect.
JEAN-JACQUES ROUSSEAU, *Discourse on the Origin of Inequality* (1755)

Mankind being naturally of a social Disposition, and desirous continually to extend their Knowledge, love not only to be acquainted with those among whom they live, but likewise to being informed of the State and Circumstances of their Fellow Creatures, both in the nearest and the most distant Countries.
CLAUDE-FRANÇOIS LAMBERT, *Curious Observations* (1753)

CHAPTER ONE

Nature, Civilization, and the Progress of Antislavery Philosophy

OVER THE COURSE of the eighteenth century, as the practice of forced labor secured its legal and economic footholds in the daily culture and institutional fabric of European nations and their New World colonies, both the conduct and the ideology of slavery faced increasing opposition. Although the seventeenth century had witnessed only sporadic and unorganized opposition to slavery, the eighteenth experienced far-reaching social and philosophical changes that intensified antislavery sentiment and activism on both sides of the Atlantic. The antislavery "movement"—by which I mean a core of political and intellectual leaders, a periphery or secondary circle of less committed or less active participants, and a vast retinue of fellow travellers—emerged from the turbulence of eighteenth-century transatlantic exploration, commerce, and politics, and should be understood as an international phenomenon inflected by nationalist sympathies. It represented one voice—or rather a chorus of voices, growing louder each year—in the domestic struggles of European colonial powers and New World governments as the imperial system, crisscrossed by rivalries and resentments, lurched onward. The instability of this system, despite its profitability, along with the cultural complexities of the circumatlantic world, in which ethnic, national, and religious affiliations were challenged by exposure to difference, required of antislavery, no less than any other political cause, a flexibility of method and discourse. Such flexibility was enabled by a vibrant print culture that facilitated the active circulation of ideas, tropes, perspectives, and information.[1]

My interest here is in the role that natural philosophy, natural history, and literary representations of nature played in the evolution of transatlantic antislavery discourse during the late eighteenth and early nineteenth centuries. This dimension of the history of emancipation in the Western hemisphere has received little sustained attention in the scholarly literature, which has, for understandable reasons, concentrated on the *social* sphere in examining the rise and eventual triumph of British, and then American, abolitionism.[2] In polemical, imaginative, and testimonial writings against slavery, however, we find a persistent grounding of cultural values on ideas of nature, and a recurrent imaging of culture through the discursive lens of nature. From about the mid-eighteenth century to the early 1800s, natural concepts and tropes became increasingly prevalent in the intellectual and artistic traditions of Western Europe, the American colonies, and the various communities of the African diaspora. Concomitantly, across a variety of social, political, and literary contexts, ideas and images of nature acquired a new force and complexity in shaping both popular and elite conceptions of "civilization." Against that background we can discern a gradual but definite shift in antislavery literature toward trying to clarify the "natural" basis of human relations. The supernatural dimension of the antislavery argument—that is, the belief that slavery violated God's will and biblical precept—did not wane in importance, but the traditional claims were supplemented and reinforced by a more secular approach to defining both human ethics and the nature of the human being.

In practical terms, this meant a heightened engagement with the claims of natural science and an expanded range of literary techniques for portraying nature. At the center always lay the question of the human being. Though their epistemologies and representational palettes differed, science and art both promised to *show* nature, and by showing nature promised to reveal the nature of the human being. During the second half of the century, and particularly during the 1780s, a decade of swift acceleration and complication of the debate, science and art came to stand side by side with scriptural exegesis as pillars of abolitionist literature, augmenting both the credibility and the emotional force of the antislavery appeal. The language and the "findings" of natural science provided intellectual resources for the antislavery movement as it grappled with the increasingly complex question of what, if anything, human difference implied about human relations and human ethics. In literature, the classical pastoral tradition—and to a lesser extent the georgic—reemerged in early Romantic literature as modes of representation in which the human experience of nature took center stage. For antislavery writers, creatively reinterpreting that experience represented one of the methods of establishing the meanings of race and culture on ground more favorable to the antislavery argument. Science and art provided representational "affordances" that proved indispensable as antislavery writers, despite their variety of individual agendas, sought to influence public perceptions of race, labor, and liberty—and the boundaries and criteria of "civilization."[3]

This evolution of the antislavery argument did not take place in a historical vacuum, but in the context of great uncertainty over the implications of European, American, and African cultural interaction. Even as the transatlantic trading system extended the colonial frontiers and intensified the economic power of European nations, it also had a destabilizing effect on traditional understandings of "civilization" by bringing European and non-European societies, however unwillingly or unwittingly, into sustained contact with one another. Several recent studies, including those of Philip Gould, Srinivas Aravamudan, Seymour Drescher, Brycchan Carey, and Helen Thomas, have considered how writers associated with antislavery or the Black Atlantic worked within this blurred discursive zone, with its unstable notions of "culture," "savagery," and "enlightenment," in contending for more accurate or more compassionate understandings of African identity.[4] Like these scholars, I am interested in how representations of cultural syncretism and hybrid subjectivity had a kind of solvent effect on dominant racial categories, even as those categories became more entrenched in the public consciousness. My perspective differs, however, in emphasizing that the contest over the origins, forms, and meaning of racial difference always involved ideas of "the natural," and that defining the boundaries and privileges of civilization always entailed particular modes of encountering or representing the natural world. Indeed, the more that "civilization" seemed to require stabilizing, the more that "nature" seemed to represent a stabilizing force, and it was by appealing to nature that antislavery writers could most effectively articulate the values of freedom and justice, while also defending Africans' civilization, or their capacity for civilization.

They did so at a steep price. The costs of this decades-long evolution in abolitionist rhetoric comprised several persistent problems that would work to complicate or even undermine the antislavery argument in the nineteenth century. The first and most significant involved a concession—implicit, scattered across many texts, perhaps unavoidable—to the authority of natural science in resolving fundamentally moral or philosophical questions about the meaning of race in human life. As abolitionists would discover in the antebellum United States, picking and choosing one's science was a tricky game to play. Second, the antislavery attraction to the figure of the "noble African" and to the image of an African paradise tended to run against their commitment to progressive commerce and their claim that African culture or cultures harmonized with the culture of Western modernity. Finally, and most broadly, the whole framework of concepts by which race was accorded a "natural" basis in climate and biology made it more difficult to argue that conflicts of race ran contrary to the natural order of things. In subsequent chapters of this book we will see how the antislavery movement, and individual literary figures, tried mightily to navigate the ethical and intellectual narrows created by these problems.

Natural Science in Early Antislavery Thought

In 1784 in London appeared *An Essay on the Treatment and Conversion of African Slaves in the British Sugar Colonies*, by James Ramsay, an Anglican minister whose fourteen-year sojourn in the West Indies had given him ample firsthand knowledge of the horrors of slavery. Ramsay's essay was one of the major polemical statements that appeared during the fertile, volatile 1780s, a decade that saw the publication of Thomas Clarkson's *An Essay on the Slavery and Commerce of the Human Species, Particularly the African* (1786) and *An Essay on the Impolicy of the African Slave Trade* (1788), John Newton's *Thoughts on the African Slave Trade* (1788), and William Roscoe's *A General View of the African Slave Trade* (1788). These were also the years of several seminal black autobiographies, notably John Marrant's *A Narrative of the Lord's Wonderful Dealings with John Marrant, a Black* (1785), Ottabah Cugoano's *Thoughts and sentiments on the evil and wicked traffic of the slavery and commerce of the human species* (1787) and Olaudah Equiano's *The Interesting Narrative of the Life of Olaudah Equiano* (1789). In its sustained engagement with the "natural science" of race, Ramsay's essay signals that the traditional philosophical positions of antislavery—Christian humanitarianism and natural rights theory—had not quite kept up with the times and needed intellectual reinforcement. Denouncing slavery as, for instance, "so vile a contradiction to the Gospel of the blessed Messiah," or as "Antichristian; for it cannot be of Christ, because contrary to his command; therefore of Antichrist," was fine for the 1710s or the 1730s, respectively, but would not go far toward answering Edward Long's racist aspersions in *The History of Jamaica* (1774).[5] Invoking the Lockean social contract and arguing that members of human society "have not renounced their natural liberty in any greater degree than other good citizens," and that a slaveholder might "find himself degraded by his own folly and wickedness from the rank of a virtuous and good *man*, to that of a brute," might have had some traction in prerevolutionary America, but did little, for instance, to explain African civilization to a skeptical or disinterested public.[6] Indeed, we can fairly link the powering-up of late eighteenth-century antislavery rhetoric to its intensified engagement with natural science.

Ramsay's essay provides an illustrative case. The early sections of the essay proceed as scientific polemic, in which his offstage antagonists are the "curious anatomist" and the "Cartesian, with his audience-hall of perception," who would exaggerate the importance of physical differences in order to argue for European racial superiority. Right off the bat, Ramsay questions the supposed link between phenotype and capacity, or "genius." Skin color, he maintains, is not a binary fact of human life, for "[w]e see colour gradually verging from white to black, through every intermediate degree of tawny and copper," and geography does not determine civilization, for would not history "tell us that arts, sciences, and the immediate capacity for them, are progressive in their nature and objects, visiting sometimes this region, sometimes another?" Although he calls it, somewhat misleadingly, a matter of "innocent disputation" whether the distinguishing physical characteristics of Africans result from climate or from supernatural design intended to fit them for life in the "torrid zone," Ramsay makes his own beliefs clear. The explanations he provides, however, do not always convince. For instance, "[t]he flat noses of negroes, in many cases, may be accounted for from the custom of being constantly tied on their mothers [*sic*] backs when infants, and nature has prepared them for this, by shortening the cartilage of the nose."[7]

In the third section of his essay, devoted to the question of skull capacity and conformation, Ramsay wades further into the brambles of racial science, and finds himself—as would many later antislavery writers—thrashing about in the attempt to settle questions that could not, after all, be settled by science. Indeed, more important for our purposes than his point-by-point response to racist interpretations of skull size and shape is the long paragraph that frames his rebuttal, for it concerns what he considered the right attitude toward scientific knowledge and thus says much about the dilemma confronting antislavery philosophy.

Ramsay starts by echoing the conventional wisdom that physical difference must *mean* something: "we shall first observe, supposing this distinction [in skull conformation] real, that it must have some benevolent and general purpose; which purpose we should search for, and follow out; which purpose we know is not to feed pride, or indulge cruelty, as these notions at present do." The rest of the paragraph is worth quoting at length:

> Matter of fact, or the real agency of nature, where discovered, may be assumed for the foundation of our reasoning; nor should we vainly imagine that she stands in need of our feigned apology, or wants to lie concealed behind the flimsy texture of our conjectures. We may be unacquainted with her workings, or with the particular purpose that she means to carry on. But we need not therefore fear, lest what comes from her hands be found fraught with absurdity, or lead to principles destructive of humanity, or derogatory to wisdom and goodness. Let then the fact be, that negroes are an inferior race; it is a conclusion, that hitherto has lain hid and unobserved, and while it leads only to an abuse of power in the superior race, it is better concealed, than drawn out into notice. Perhaps Providence may keep it doubtful, till men be so far improved, as not to make an ill use of the discovery. I am sure, at present, the power, if it be a right, is delegated to many improper persons. In the mean time, while the superior race continues likely to abuse it, every step that leads to the establishment of a point [African "inferiority"], the good purpose of which lies hid, while the evil purpose is ready at hand, should undergo and stand the severest scrutiny before it receives our approbation.[8]

Ramsay's line of thought prompts a number of observations. First, he invokes the authority of "reasoning" and intellectual "scrutiny" in matters of race, and offers as their foundation and object the "real agency of nature." The Bible makes no appearance, though a naturalized "Providence" does. Evidently Ramsay saw the terms of debate as determined less by scripture than by the science of race, and his careful framing of the issue signals a nascent trend in antislavery literature, in which adopting the putatively analytical, objective mindset of the scientist seemed as rhetorically important as any specific claim or counterclaim. What a fateful concession this was! Even if a writer's specific claims were, comparatively, racially "enlightened," antislavery empiricism inevitably granted epistemological authority to natural science in determining the meaning of race. A strategic compromise of grand proportions (though not necessarily recognized as such), antislavery's embrace of the scientific method could confer polemical advantages in the short term, but it nonetheless participated in the West's elevation of science as a preeminent means of resolving intellectual or social conflicts. Perhaps that embrace was inevitable, perhaps it was even salutary on balance, but certainly it deserves *our* historical scrutiny.

Ramsay, in fact, reveals his misgivings about exactly this issue in his convoluted comments on what science might actually reveal about race, and on how society should make use of scientific knowledge. The key problem, in his view, is that while the providential "purpose" of race could not be otherwise than good, scientific "discoveries" regarding racial difference could lead to evil, to "an abuse of power in the superior race." We can set aside, for the moment, the relatively uninteresting question of whether Ramsay believed in superior and inferior races (almost no abolitionists at this point in history rejected racial hierarchies as such). The more pertinent questions have to do with the uncertainties that ripple through his argument. Does the solution to the problem he has identified lie in better science, less science, or the concealment of science? In his phrase "till men be so far improved," what kind of improvement is Ramsay really talking about? What do we make of the ambiguity between the Hobbesian-sounding "power" and the Lockean-sounding "right" as determinants for who gets to make "use" of the findings of science? What relation does he imagine between the "workings" of nature and the "purposes" of Providence? Such questions run farther afield, of course, than Ramsay intended to go, but they begin to take us into the heart of the problem of antislavery's engagement with natural science.

The intellectual climate in which Ramsay and his antislavery peers worked was one in which the practical and philosophical impact of science was far reaching and deeply felt. In the wake of the seventeenth century's philosophical breakthroughs regarding scientific inquiry and its practical advances in the realms of mathematics and mechanics, eighteenth-century natural science came into its own. Emanating from the metropolitan centers of Western Europe and quickly spreading around the Atlantic world, the ideal of rational, inductive empiricism emerged virtually unchallenged (among the literate classes, at least) as the epistemological foundation upon which any valid scientific inquiry would rest. Championed in periodicals, popular books, the French *Encylcopédie*, and various professional institutions and societies, the scientific method gained a cultural power that in large measure determined the proper fields of investigation and the proper modes of inquiry.[9] In physics, geology, astronomy, botany, meteorology, chemistry, metallurgy, and cartography, the boundaries of knowledge expanded by leaps and bounds. The mysteries of nature at last seemed solvable, capable of being laid open to human sight, and those who could master the epistemology of science had an edge in practicing the art of politics, and in acquiring worldly power. And by promoting a view of human "progress" that emphasized the intellectual and physical mastery of nature, science became both the engine and the sign of "civilization." The history of slavery and abolition cannot be told outside of this framework.

Most directly, the new scientific and technological culture opened the world to exploration, with fateful implications for both the institution of slavery and the development of race theory. By bringing Europeans into sustained contact with other cultures, international exploration forced a reckoning with the realities of human difference, and thus stimulated not only a feverish attention to race, but also new modes of defining racial identity. As the Western obsession with race deepened, two broad patterns of representation emerged across a wide array of writings on race, both of which grounded race in nature—or "naturalized" race, in modern parlance—but in very different ways. One tended to present categories of human difference as fixed, impassable, and static, and to view these categories as a determinative force in human affairs. It naturalized racial categories by basing them in a transcendent natural order; this order could be imagined in religious terms, as God's will manifest through the physical world, or in more secular terms, as the consequence of "Nature" dispensing or withholding certain racial traits. In either case, this model of human difference presented race as static rather than dynamic, as given rather than processual, and it made little room for history as a force in human development. Such biological essentialism could trace its intellectual lineage to the Linnaean taxonomic system, which was premised on the nontransformative nature of the various species that it categorized, which did not take environment into account, and which could only incorporate newly identified plants and animals through an ever more intricate classificatory scheme.[10] The impact of the Linnaean model on eighteenth-century biology, zoology, and anthropology is hard to overstate, and its influence extended well into the nineteenth century, most notably with the natural history of Georges Cuvier. It also anticipated the vicious racial typologies that would prove so destructive in the nineteenth century and beyond, but we should note that believing in European racial superiority did not by itself make one sympathetic to slavery (as in the case of English surgeon Charles White, among others), and that, conversely, one's support for the slave trade did not have to rest on biological essentialism (as in the cases of William Beckford and James Tobin).

Complicating matters, a competing pattern of representation ran across this first, portraying human difference in less static, less rigid terms, as with Ramsay's comment that "[w]e see colour gradually verging from white to black, through every intermediate degree of tawny and copper." It naturalized race by grounding human difference in physical geography: Exposed over time to the pressures of climate, resources, and way of life, the population of a given region developed a set of identifiable physical traits that formed the basis of racial designation. This understanding of racial difference as a function of natural environment necessarily made greater room for historical process and for the possibility of racial change. There was no Linnaeus, no undisputed champion, for this point of view—not until Darwin at least, or arguably the French naturalist Georges Buffon—but rather a slowly growing chorus who asserted long-term, situationally determined biological change as the basis of human development. One of the earliest texts of environmentalist racial thought was John Mitchell's *An Essay on the Causes of the Different Colours of People in Different Climates* (1744), but not until Johann Friedrich Blumenbach's *On the Variety of the Human Species* (1775), with its theory of "degeneration" (i.e., climatically caused racial differentiation), did the environmentalist position become truly influential.[11]

Again, the relation between racial thought and the politics of slavery proved unpredictable. Environmentalism did not necessarily align with humanitarian politics, nor imply that human populations *improved* by virtue of their environment, nor always grant significant agency to human beings in responding to their environment. Environmentalism could be pessimistic (postulating the decline or deterioration of a racial group), deterministic (postulating the inevitability of such decline), and hierarchalist (postulating degrees of racial inferiority and superiority). Yet by opening the door to the influence of circumstances on race—in fact, by identifying circumstance as the cause of human difference—environmentalism, over decades of empirical work and theoretical refinement, would help to erode and finally overthrow the Linnaean system of taxonomic fixity. Ultimately, it would become part of a broader intellectual mindset emphasizing the permeability and contingency of categories, the dynamism of human life, and what we would today call the "hybridity" of cultural identity.

The story of early racial anthropology has been told well and often,[12] and my interest here is not in reviewing the general development of eighteenth-century or Enlightenment race theory, but rather in exploring its ambiguous significance for the antislavery argument, an ambiguity resulting from the discursive instability of the natural science on which race theory based itself. In responding to the new anthropological sciences, early antislavery writers encountered both formidable challenges and unexpected opportunities, but they always sought to keep their eye on the fundamental point: that Africans and their descendants could claim membership in the human family and that they therefore deserved to enjoy the "natural" human birthright of liberty. This proved less straightforward than one might suppose, for abolitionists had to weigh in on a number of subsidiary controversies that the natural science of race generated, including the theory of polygenesis, the fitness of Africans relative to Europeans for tropical labor, and the capacity of blacks to build "civilized" societies. They also faced difficult questions raised by locating race within nature: Is nature a domain of freedom or determinism? Is the state of nature one of harmony and innocence, as Rousseau had imagined, or violence and competition, as Hobbes had warned? If race was natural, to what degree could it be shaped by culture, or altered by natural process? In one form or another, all of the major antislavery writers had to grapple with these questions.

The environmentalist argument became central to antislavery thought for two related reasons. First, it provided a means of attributing the apparent backwardness of Africans or their descendants to circumstances rather than to inherent racial inferiority. What abolitionists argued was inherent, rather, is the natural human capacity for feeling and the desire for liberty, which will call out similar responses to both natural *and* cultural circumstances. Secondly, environmentalism undergirded the humanitarian argument (one that would intensify during the nineteenth century) that a healthy and free environment would allow the black capacity for civilization to express itself fully.

In its embrace of environmentalism, the antislavery movement itself did much to advance a more modern understanding of human origins and human biological development. While abolitionists have received ample credit for making the question of human rights impossible to ignore, their contributions to scientific knowledge have gone essentially unsung. Moreover, although the environmentalist position grew from scientific debates over human development, it took on a much broader significance as the abolitionist campaign grew in scope and coherence. The literal scientific argument about the "causes" of human development represented only one level of communication; more generally, environmentalism had great metaphorical elasticity and transferability. Imagined in the most expansive and optimistic terms, it could help to explain not simply the role of climate in determining skin color, but the role of education in making good citizens, of family in shaping personality, of political systems in fostering virtue—in short, of enculturation. Early environmentalism, in other words, had not only literal but analogical significance for antislavery writers as they sought to voice optimistic narratives of human progress (condescending though such teleologies typically proved). And, as we will see in chapter 3, it would provide the basis for what I term antislavery's "natural law of free development," a crucial contribution to the naturalizing of liberty that had affinities with early evolutionary theory.

More immediately, environmentalism enabled the antislavery movement to confront the new theory of polygenesis, which represented the most literal "scientific" issue that early abolition had to tackle. The claim that the human family might in fact consist of multiple species did not find real traction until the nineteenth century, but as early as the 1770s, the more radical theorizers of race—notably the Jamaican planter Edward Long and the Scottish judge Lord Kames—were asserting the possibility of separate creation.[13] The ideological, and practical, threat posed by the polygenist argument was that it might sanction slavery as a kind of keeping of domestic animals, or at least serve to remove slaves from the spheres of human sympathy and human rights. Since the polygenists' argument ran up against the biblical, or Mosaic, account of unitary creation, it encountered fierce resistance from theologians and from scientists committed to Christian doctrine. For this reason, the theory of multiple creation did not pose a significant problem for antislavery philosophy until the 1830s and 1840s, with the rise of the so-called American School of anthropology and the work of French theorist Joseph Arthur Gobineau. In the eighteenth century polygenesis represented a potent, if unrealized, threat. But the way that the debate was joined from the outset had crucial implications for how people conceptualized race, and the themes that emerged would energize, structure, and challenge antislavery thought in the nineteenth century. As Bruce Dain has demonstrated, the complex dynamics between early racial theory and its humanitarian or liberal critics made race highly malleable both conceptually and politically.[14]

Although extended rebuttals of polygenesis, or involved theoretical expositions of monogenesis, were relatively rare, one challenge already seemed clear. Beyond asserting the scriptural account of creation, and beyond accusing the polygenists of violating the economy of nature, defenders of unitary creation had to explain how a single human type had changed into so many varieties, and to do so while bearing in mind the relatively short period of human history allowed by the Bible. The argument led inevitably to environmentalism of one type or another, all of which held that, following the dispersal of the original human stock across the globe, the forces of climate and history created the racial differences evident in the present. In Europe, one of the more important scientific statements of the monogenist position appeared in Johann Reinhold Forster's *Observations Made During a Voyage Round the World* (1778), based on his work in the South Pacific while serving as a naturalist on the second voyage of James Cook. Forster, attempting to account for the physical and behavioral diversity in the tribes he observed, attributed such racial differentiation to geographic dispersal and the influence of climate. He also offered a concise and powerful summation of the monogenist argument against polygenism: "Some suppose men to be divided into species materially and essentially different from one another . . . which however is inadmissible if we take into consideration the exercises of reason and common sense, the formation of ideas, the language of the heart, the refinement of moral sentiment, with the gifts of speech founded on the variety, power and extent of voice and articulation, and even on the whole structure and mechanism of our bodies."[15] Although Forster did not directly concern himself with the problem of slavery, this passage suggests that antislavery writings that represented African rationality, sensibility, and language—in argument, narrative, character, or image—could ground their humanitarianism in the authority of natural science as well as in the traditional precepts of revealed religion. We will see that as the figure of "the African" becomes more important to Western literature in the early 1800s, the issues of body, speech, and reasoning that Forster raises become likewise vital forms of implicit humanitarian argument—and in the background lay the eighteenth-century antislavery engagement with science.

The humanitarian interweaving of scripture and science approached a rhetorical apogee in Thomas Clarkson's *An Essay on the Slavery and Commerce of the Human Species* (1786), perhaps the central text of eighteenth-century British abolitionism. Clarkson's method is comprehensive, blending history, natural law, civil law, personal testimony, literature, and Christianity in a towering assault on the slave trade. The scientific dimension of his argument comes to the fore in chapter 8 of part 3, in which Clarkson argues that the theory of polygenesis is both unscientific and heretical. The species test he employs, fertile offspring, had been proposed as early as 1704, in John Ray's *Historia Plantarum*, had been updated in Buffon's *Histoire naturelle, générale et particulière*, and proved an enormously difficult obstacle for polygenists to overcome:

> It is an universal law, observable throughout the whole creation, *that if two animals of a different species propagate, their offspring is unable to continue its own species*. By this admirable law, the different species are preserved distinct; every possibility of confusion is prevented, and the world is forbidden to be over-run by a race of monsters. Now, if we apply this law to those of the human kind, who are said to be of a distinct species from each other, it immediately fails. The *mulattoe* is as capable of continuing his own species as his father; a clear and irrefragable proof, that the scripture account of the creation is true, and that "God, who hath made the world, hath made of one blood all the nations of men that dwell on all the face of the earth" (original emphasis).

Given that human beings constitute one species, Clarkson then goes on to ask how they "came to assume so various an appearance." Explaining that the Bible shows such diversity not to have resulted from the "interposition of the Deity," Clarkson instead cites "a co-operation of certain causes, which have an effect upon the human frame, and have the power of changing it more or less from its primitive appearance, as they are more or less numerous or powerful than those, which acted upon the frame of man in the first seat of his habitation."[16] A year later, across the Atlantic, the Presbyterian minister Samuel Stanhope Smith weighed in with his influential *Essay on the Causes of the Variety of Complexion and Figure in the Human Species*, in which he also developed a theory of environmentalism and argued for unitary creation based on fact that racial interbreeding produced fertile offspring.

More common than full-length rebuttals was the appearance of environmental monogenist thought in other genres and situations, by figures less luminary than Forster, Clarkson, and Smith. At Harvard College's 1773 commencement, for instance, two undergraduates engaged in a debate over slavery, subsequently published in Boston as *A Forensic Dispute on the Legality of Enslaving the Africans*. The question on the table was "Whether the slavery, to which Africans are in this province, by the permission of law, subjected be agreable [*sic*] to the law of nature," and most of the debate turned on the definitions and meanings of natural authority, natural (in)equality, and natural liberty, with "application" to the case of African slavery. Theodore Parsons presented the antislavery position, leveling a broadside against subjection in familiar terms of the natural equality and liberty of humankind, but with an emphasis on common descent that reflected the changing contours of the larger argument. He refers to Africans as "descendants . . . from the same common parent with you and me, and between whom and us nature has made no distinction, save what arises from the stronger influence of the sun in the climate whence they originated." His adversary, Eliphalet Pearson, counters by painting Africa as a kind of Hobbesian jungle, asking his listeners to imagine the "condition of perpetual insecurity, arising from the state of hostility and war that forever rages in those inhospitable climes," and concludes that servitude in the civilized world is surely preferable to the "brutality, wretchedness, and misery" of the slaves' homeland. On this point, Parsons admits that "their condition is allowedly not greatly different from a state of nature," but objects that Pearson's "colouring is a little too strong," and asserts that the Africans are "far less savage and barbarous" than commonly supposed. He goes on to express scorn for those who, "to make a gain by this iniquitous practice" of slavery, represent Africans "as nearly upon a level with the brute creation as possible; not to mention the ridiculous attempts that have, in this view, been made to prove them actually of another species."[17]

This theme became a veritable refrain in early African American intellectual and activist discourse. Prince Saunders, reminding his listeners at the Pennsylvania Augustine Society that God "has made of one blood all nations of men who dwell upon the face of the whole earth," translated biblical verse into terms clearly inflected by the language of natural history: "We are formed by nature to unite; we are impelled towards each other by the benevolent instincts in our frames; we are linked by a thousand connexions, founded on common wants." Elsewhere the scientific appeal can be more explicit. Africans, said William Whipper, share "all the sublime qualities of man, differing only in the colour of their skin, which is the natural production of a tropical climate." William Hamilton, similarly, told his audience that "by all the rules laid down by naturalists for determining the species of a creature . . . we have souls, and are men."[18]

What such writings demonstrate—from the essays of Clarkson to the sermons of William Hamilton—is that no one had a monopoly on the intellectual energy in the debate over the natural science of race. We should not think of the early decades of anthropology as wholly given over to the brutal racism of people like Edward Long and Charles White. Abolitionists, despite their all-too-common reflexive belief in the superiority of white Christian culture, actually worked to promote an understanding of race that, in its recognition of the contingency of difference, proved both more humane and more durable than the rigid biological essentialism asserted by their opponents. Moreover, as the exchange between Parsons and Pearson suggests, the debate was reaching into the broader public consciousness, notwithstanding the fact that Harvard was an elite institution. An understanding of natural science, in short, allowed humanitarian activists to confront more effectively the pernicious claims of race theory and to establish the unity of the human family as matter of empirical fact as well as religious doctrine. By the time the polygenist argument significantly geared up in the nineteenth century, the foundation of the antislavery response had already been well established.

The story of natural science and the debate over slavery has another level to it. In a direct sense, as we have seen, science provided a vocabulary for describing, and explaining the meaning of, patterns of physical difference within humankind. At the same time, natural science represented one of the fundamental means of demarcating the human family over and against the nonhuman; everyone acknowledged, after all, that the beasts could not engage in abstract theoretical reasoning. Ergo, the participation of Africans or African Americans in scientific endeavor would go a long way toward proving their membership in the human family. Early antislavery and Black Atlantic writers, therefore, in addition to waxing scientific on such matters as skull size and skin color, began to position blacks not simply as the objects but as the subjects of scientific study. Representing the scientific capacity of African-descended peoples would, by the logic of the Enlightenment, distinguish them from the "brute creation," and more generally rebut Long's charge that "they are void of genius, and seem almost incapable of making any progress in civility or science."[19] The theme of "black science" marked a vital strain of early abolitionist rhetoric, but it proved no less problematic than any other form of "enlightened" racial discourse.

Consider several passages from the early African American context, the first by the mathematician, astronomer, and clockmaker Benjamin Banneker. Banneker, a largely self-taught freeman of Maryland, made his name as the creator of *Benjamin Banneker's Almanack*, a yearly compendium of useful information modeled on Benjamin Franklin's *Poor Richard's Almanack*, but which differed from its predecessor in its freer blending of antislavery commentary with scientific fact. He is also known as the author of a 1791 letter to Thomas Jefferson in which he implored the then–secretary of state to throw his prestige, as the author of the Declaration of Independence, behind the proposition that God "hath not only made us all of one flesh, but that he hath also, without partiality, afforded us all the same sensations and endowed us all with the same faculties." As it goes on, the letter grows more heated, calling Jefferson to account for hypocrisy and mischievously suggesting that if Jefferson would "wean" himself from prejudice, then he would "need neither the direction of myself or others, in what manner to proceed herein." Banneker included with the letter—as a "present" to Jefferson but also as proof of his own scientific prowess—a manuscript of his almanac for the next year, and described "having long had unbounded desires to become acquainted with the secrets of nature."[20]

The *Almanack* is striking not only for its mingling of abolitionism and natural science, but for its self-referential quality, an assertion or embodiment of Banneker's identity quite unlike Franklin's self-effacement and rhetorical disguises. The 1795 edition of the *Almanack*, for example, included a poem "Addressed to Benjamin Banneker" across from a chart titled "The Anatomy of Man's Body as governed by the Twelve Constellations." Signed "G.H.," the panegyric employs science to erase rather than to reinforce distinctions of race:

> How large the field! how wide its vast domain!
> Which doth thy *ideas*, Banneker, contain!
> My muse, to paint it, must to regions soar,
> Where genius', like *Newton's*, do explore!
> What tho' thy skin be of the *blackest* hue,
> Such as the fable sons of *Afric'* shew;
> What tho' descended from that sable race,
> Which nature's *fairer* sons held in *disgrace*;
> . . . .
> The abstruse secrets of great *nature's* plan,
> Like *Newton*, thou presumed hast to scan,
> Nor hast presum'd in *vain*; but hast explor'd
> And o'er the field obscure in *triumph* soar'd . . .[21]

The poem goes on in this vein, as if to match the accumulation of practical scientific knowledge in the *Almanack* with a mountain of praise for the era's most visible African American scientist. Progress, culture, knowledge: the central terms of Banneker's public identity. In every word, the almanac and the poem seek to convey the achievement of selfhood through the mastery of natural science: the transcendence of speechlessness, irrationality, and the state of nature.

Mastery, transcendence—these concepts bring us toward the heart of the problem. For the not-so-submerged worldview informing much of the era's natural philosophy linked divine right, anthropocentric pride, and scientific ability in a single all-conquering union. As Philadelphia ship-maker Joseph Corr put it: "The Creator designed us to be the lords of his creation, to be sole governors of this lower world, and to subject to our service the laws of nature, and so be capable of improving the convenience and gratifications of human life. . . . It is mechanical science which discovers the means of subjecting all things around us to the control of man."[22] Or in the words of the anonymous author of "The Sons of Africans": "[Man's] Maker placed him as head over this lower world, and gave him power and dominion both over the fishes of the sea, the fowls of the air, and the beasts of the field, and all that the earth produced, so that both animal and vegetable creation was for his use and service."[23] The context in each case is racialized; both writers aim to enlist blacks as well as whites in the project of civilization. Both cast natural science in an ongoing drama of spiritual and material progress by which humankind, born into a state of nature and equipped only with reason and a moral sense, is well on the way to recovering some measure of Adam's original grant of mastery of the beasts of Eden.

As suggested above, the complicity of scientific and technological knowledge in racial slavery created unique pressures for black writers of the Atlantic world. Banneker could not simply be a good mathematician, astronomer, and almanac-maker—he evidently felt the burden of representation, the responsibility to put his talents in the service of a racial cause.[24] Whether this was a responsibility gladly taken up, it nonetheless reflected the fact that Banneker did not have the luxury of separating his profession from his racial identity, even as science allowed him to convey his full human identity. But what defined that "human identity"? For Corr and the author of "The Sons of Africans," to be human was to be other than nature, and more importantly, to possess dominion over nature. To be civilized was to exercise that dominion, to extend the distance between humanity and nature. In short, to be a subject meant to make an object, and therefore to buy into, at some level, the essential psychic and ontological structure of objectification: Dominate or be dominated.

I have argued that antislavery's embrace of natural science effectively granted to science the dubious authority to determine the nature and meaning of race, a concession that would haunt humanitarian politics for a long time to come. Moreover, it opens antislavery to a broader critique, one in which Enlightenment science and a liberal ideology of human rights, over a matter of decades, participated jointly in a massive cultural and psychological dislocation whose effects are still playing themselves out. The "triumph" of eighteenth-century science radically altered dominant Western understandings of humanity's relationship to the natural world, consolidating a tidal epistemic shift whereby, in Neil Evernden's words, "the objects of nature [were] vastly diminished, from receptacles of meaning to empty images for inspection."[25] This relentless objectivization of nature, Evernden argues, promoted not only empirical and utilitarian attitudes toward the nonhuman world but also a spiritually debilitating anthropocentrism based on the belief that all subjective meaning resides with humankind: "The increasingly strict division between human and nature provides a sense of secure separateness and assures us that the only apparent path to knowledge of nature will be to gaze across the gulf at the visible surfaces of otherness. But perhaps the most apparent feature of the world has become the gulf itself, which constitutes a kind of moat that appears to protect while actually confining: we may be less besieged by otherness than imprisoned by self-worship."[26] This perceived divide between humanity and nature, also described by Michel Serres, Richard Rorty, and other recent philosophers, worked to produce an actual divide, as the dominance of the human species, "governors of this lower world," claimed a tautologically self-reinforcing authority in the epistemology of natural science. The role of early anthropology in creating such a "gulf" was to operate as a kind of double-ended telescope or microscope, through which both humanity and humanity's environment became objects of study. In a revealing paradox, the *objectivization* of people took as its material human *subjectivity* (which helps to explain why the question of mental "faculties" loomed so large in anthropology), and measured that subjectivity not simply by the capacity to feel or to think, but by the ability to *represent* feelings and thoughts (hence the debate over Africans' contributions to the "arts and sciences"). Anthropology arose, then, as the study of the creature that used symbols and language, or as Michel Foucault has suggested, as a kind of omphaloskeptic metascience whose object of inquiry was nothing less than the creator of science: "The object of the human sciences is not language (though it is spoken by men alone); it is that being which, from the interior of the language by which he is surrounded, represents to himself, by speaking, the sense of the words or propositions he utters, and finally provides himself with a representation of language itself."[27] In this light, the deeper significance of antislavery's engagement with natural science and anthropology becomes clearer. On one level, the very rhetoric of science itself, especially in the hands of black writers, worked to define the human family over and against the natural world, and thus implicitly linked political emancipation to an imaginary ontological liberation from nature into culture. Moreover, it reinforced the status of symbolic representation as the defining action of subjectivity, and thereby cooperated powerfully with the increasingly important role of literacy and autobiography in antislavery discourse. The goal, of course, was to expand the domain of human freedom; the cost was to bind the human being more securely in its cage of self-imposed isolation from nature.

In taking advantage of the representational affordances of natural science, therefore, the antislavery movement was doing what it had to do, but it was also playing with fire. In an era when cultural, national, and geographic boundaries were in flux, nature, for all its "mysteries," seemed to provide a stable set of reference points by which to chart the changing world. Science promised answers to two of the defining questions of the eighteenth century—What is a human being? and What is race?—and it provided a way of simultaneously determining, explaining, and managing the relationship between the natural world and humankind. It also created a conceptual framework, however specious, for describing divisions within the human family and for making sense of those divisions. The material of science may have been "natural," but its aims and uses were cultural, and it behooved anyone with political intentions to speak its language. That science would ultimately prove so problematic for its own purposes did not immediately concern the antislavery movement. What mattered was mobilizing public opinion against slavery and the slave trade, and to the extent that the language of natural science helped to realize that goal, the better.

Natural Aesthetics in Early Antislavery Literature

Intellectually and rhetorically confronting the "latest" in natural-scientific knowledge represented one way in which antislavery writers could represent the natural world as part of their effort to change the cultural world. That mode emphasized factual knowledge, empirical objectivity, and the inner principles or workings of nature that produced, among other perceivable effects in the physical world, human difference. During these same early decades, and not coincidentally, another vital register in antislavery discourse came into prominence, one that focused on the "look" of nature, on its external characteristics and on the lived experience of human beings in their natural environment. In a number of different genres—travel writing, poetry, drama—early antislavery writers drew upon and adapted, at times clumsily and at times artfully, a variety of aesthetic traditions in which nature figured centrally: the sublime, the picturesque, the georgic, the elegy, the pastoral. In complex and not always consistent ways, these artistic forms helped abolitionist writers shape public perceptions of the shifting relations between African, European, and New World cultures.

Emphasizing the sensory textures of nature (primarily visual) and their relation to human consciousness, the aesthetic register appealed less to knowledge, reason, or logic than to the reader's senses and sensibilities, and increasingly, with the rise of Romanticism, to his or her emotions and capacity for sympathetic identification. However, just as scientific discourse never could free itself, even if it wanted to, from tropological and metaphorical language, so did the aesthetic mode reveal a worldview informed by natural science, a structure of epistemological assumptions and perceptual habits, a perspective on what nature *was* that necessarily influenced how nature *looked* and *felt*. Aesthetic practice could no more avoid scientific knowledge than vice versa, even if it meant to repudiate the culture of science or to present a vision of life at odds with the scientific consensus. Most profoundly, eighteenth-century science and art converged and cooperated in their objectification of nature, in approaching the natural world as something that could be apprehended, ordered, re-presented, and re-apprehended by the human mind—and even though Romantic texts, more than most, struggled against this view, the processing and repackaging of nature for public consumption could not, at bottom, get around the philosophical problem of giving bounded linguistic form to what is intrinsically nonlinguistic and nonbounded.

More directly, the scientific and imagistic modes of representing the natural world were, for the antislavery movement, part and parcel of the same project, that of shaping public perceptions of the slave trade, of the human being, and of race. As did natural science, stylized representations of the natural world worked to define human nature and the human family, and therefore had intrinsic significance for how antislavery writers could promote humanitarian understandings of Western and African civilization, and of black subjectivity.

Natural imagery began appearing more explicitly in antislavery and Black Atlantic literature in the 1760s and 1770s, specifically in connection to contemporary debates over African civilization, the morality of the slave trade, the relative fitness of Africans and Europeans for agricultural labor, the political situation in the West Indies, and plans for the settlement or colonization of Africa. In one form or another, all of the major writers of the Black Atlantic, from James Albert Ukawsaw Gronniosaw and Ottabah Cugoano to John Marrant and Venture Smith, along with such widely published abolitionists as James Ramsay, William Roscoe, and Hannah More, employed natural imagery in working through the meanings of race and inveighing against slavery. In doing so they reflected their times, for this expansion of natural imagery in antislavery writing responded to an array of interrelated historical and cultural trends in the West: the rise of literary Romanticism and natural theology; the popularity of travel writing; shifting patterns of economic development resulting in a sharper contrast between rural and urban life; the increasing exposure of Europeans to a variety of climates and terrains; and last but certainly not least, the philosophical impact of scientific inquiry.

Throughout the eighteenth century, travelers' journals, traders' accounts, and editors' compilations largely determined the impressions Europeans formed of Africa and Africans. Though nonfictional in a broad sense, these writings typically presented a highly stylized, even imaginary vision of the continent.[28] Nonetheless, they both responded to and encouraged a public demand for information about the continent and its inhabitants. As we have seen, these writings accelerated the development of eighteenth-century racial theories and formed the unavoidable background for revolutionary-era authors seeking to represent Africa. Competing portrayals of African cultures—ranging from severely derogatory depictions of Africans as lazy, savage, and cruel, to titillating, condescending accounts of such practices as polygamy, to outright defenses of the spiritual and social ways of African societies—centered on the related questions of historical achievement, moral or religious traditions, and the relation of the peoples to the natural environment. Far from constituting an abstract debate, of course, images of Africa had concrete implications for colonial or imperial policy. They conveyed not reality so much as filtered ideological images intended to promote particular political outcomes.

In this context, representations of the African environment, and of Africans or slaves *in* the natural environment, had intrinsic significance for public understandings of race and slavery. Since dominant notions of race, or "national characteristics," were based largely on climate and environment, natural imagery always inflected a writer's implicit or explicit claims about human beings in particular geographic locations. The "literary" uses of nature—as setting, motif, metaphor, plot device, and so forth—therefore represented a way of qualifying or exploring the anthropological importance of nature. Through natural imagery a writer could articulate ideas—without, conveniently, having to argue those ideas—about the sensibilities and "faculties" of human beings, and about the moral orientation of nature, in particular whether it embodied the principles of liberty and justice, as opposed to biological determinism and cruelty.

Travel writing and personal testimonials were the principal genres in which antislavery writers sought to shape public impressions of Africa. Blending anthropological discourse, in its "manners-and-customs" form, with pastoral and georgic themes, antislavery travel narratives tried to provide a vivid, sympathetic picture of West Africa and the cultures there. Yet given the intrinsic volatility of nature as a representational resource, seeking to rehabilitate the international reputation of Africa and Africans through images of the natural world, as well as seeking to promote a non-slave-based economic system through the same means, led the antislavery movement into uncertain territory.

This tension appears vividly in Anthony Benezet's *Some Historical Account of Guinea*, an influential work first published in Philadelphia in 1771.[29] Drawing heavily on the travel narratives of Jean Barbot, Michel Adanson, Willem Bosman, Thomas Phillips, and Francis Moore, and on those accounts collected in Thomas Astley's widely read *Collection of*

Voyages, Benezet's book describes the countries and tribes that constitute "Guinea," extending roughly from the Senegal River in the North to the Portuguese seaport of Benguela in the South. Benezet's pastiche of excerpts from these various accounts, glued together by his own polemical and historical prose, focuses on the natural habitat of the region and the government and laws of the various people who live there.[30]

In the early chapters, we read that African social harmony rests on the broad lap of a bountiful nature; Benezet presents the physical environment of Guinea as exceedingly fertile and fruitful, and at times as explicitly Edenic. Here is Benezet quoting Adanson, for example, on his voyage to Senegal: "Which way soever I turned mine eyes on this pleasant spot, I beheld a perfect image of pure nature; an agreeable solitude, bounded on every side by charming landscapes; the rural situation of cottages in the midst of trees; the ease and indolence of the Negroes, reclined under the shade of the spreading foliage; the simplicity of their dress and manners; the whole revived in my mind the idea of our first parents, and I seemed to contemplate the world in its primitive state" (15–16). The Africa-as-Eden trope, tapping into old European fantasies of a lost Golden Age, fused natural beauty, individual fulfillment, and social innocence into a shining image of the good life, shamelessly eliding the distinction between myth and reality. Consider Henry Smeathman's portrayal of his botanical work on the Banana Islands, just off the coast of what was to become Sierra Leone: "Pleasant scenes of vernal beauty, a tropical luxuriance, where fruits and flowers lavish their fragrance together in the same bough! . . . I contemplate the years I passed in that terrestrial Elysium, as the happiest of my life. The simple food, which my solitude usually afforded, was sweetened with rural labor; and my rest was not broken by those corroding cares and perplexing fears, which pride and folly are ever creating in the ambitious emulations of populous communities."[31] The point of such passages—and they are legion—is not far to seek: by emphasizing the lush natural environment of Africa and the consequent happiness of its native inhabitants, abolitionist writers could intensify the sense of slavery's violation not only of the natural order but of natural innocence and beauty. The Rousseauvian state of nature that these accounts imagine finds its sensory counterpart in the aesthetic generosity of the environment ("pleasant scenes of vernal beauty"), its psychological counterpart in individual fulfillment ("the happiest [years] of my life"), and its social counterpart in communal harmony (freedom from the "ambitious emulations of populous communities"). This image of primitivist bliss helps stack the deck: the slave trade comes to resemble a massive system of cultural rape, the embodiment of the worst impulses of a cruel civilization driven by greed and a warped idea of property.

Trading on the primitivist fantasy, however, came with a significant downside. Not only was the trope of the "noble savage" becoming less potent a force in the public imagination by the 1780s, but the image of a prelapsarian Africa cut across the antislavery movement's practical commitment to progressive economic development. If African nature, in its beauty and bounty, sustained the good life of noncompetitive ease and freedom, how did Africans fit into the scheme of historical progress? If Africa was some kind of "terrestrial Elysium" flowing with milk and honey, how could human achievement and active morality be measured? As Smeathman's reference to "rural labor" suggests, uninterrupted leisure in a tropical setting was not necessarily the prime desideratum. Indeed, most of Benezet's sources make clear that Africa is not, and should not be, a paradise where no one has to work. *Some Historical Account of Guinea* insists that civilization depends upon a society's practical relation to the natural world, and that industriousness and productivity represent hallmarks of an advanced culture. Notwithstanding Adanson's enthusiasm for the "ease and indolence of the Negroes," Benezet's extracts consistently return to the theme of tribal agriculture.

In that respect, the book simply reflected its times, for work had become ever more important to Western social theory, driven largely by John Locke's labor theory of value and its centrality to the writings of Adam Smith. Increasingly, rather than symbolizing (and literally enacting) fallen humanity's sentence of unremitting toil, labor came to be seen as the guarantor of personal virtue and the very engine of civilization. The ideal society, from this view, consisted not in indulgently living off of nature, but in its assiduous cultivation. Accordingly, a number of antislavery writings on Africa similarly envision a kind of agrarian pastoral, or georgic, emphasizing the industriousness of the Africans and their capacity for economic progress. These accounts stressed the happiness of the Africans in their native climes as well as their proper (i.e. productive) relationship to the land, arguing for the actual or potential civilization of African societies based on their cultural relation to nature. John Wesley, for instance, wrote that the Fuli of Senegal "desire no more land than they use, which they cultivate with great care and industry . . . [and] have frequently supplied the necessities of the *Mandingos*, when they were distrest by famine."[32] Similarly, in a 1798 periodical essay titled "The Negro," an anonymous writer attributes the following elegiac soliloquy to a languishing American slave: "'I once was happy. . . . Our hut was in a cool valley, beneath the shade of the lofty palm trees. My labours then were sweet; for I feared neither stripes nor master. My work in the fields provided my father with food, and he repaid with smiles the toil of his sons. All was joy, all was pleasure.'"[33]

More so than most antislavery travel narratives, Benezet's text emphasizes the agricultural stability of tribal societies, portraying a labor system based on voluntary cooperation and well regulated in a framework of contractual relations. Beyond signaling to a European readership that African culture resembled their own more than they might have expected, this theme suggested that the continent would be a good place for Europeans to conduct an honest and profitable trade. Citing Astley's *Collection*, for instance, Benezet stresses the efficient, communitarian nature of the agriculture of the "kingdom of Whidah," where all the neighbors "work in a body for the publick benefit, till every man's ground is tilled and sowed." Few contemporary readers would have missed the contrast between this system, in which all are compensated and none coerced, and New World slavery, in which none were compensated and all coerced. The Lockean social contract is alive and well in Benezet's Guinea, which bears no resemblance at all to the tropical Hobbesian hell figured in much proslavery literature: "'Their markets are so well regulated and governed, that seldom any disorder happens. . . . To keep order the king appoints a judge, who with four officers well armed, inspects the Markets, hear all complaints, and in a summary way decides all differences.'"[34]

The interest in markets here is not accidental. Motivated not only by a humanitarian desire to defend the international reputation of Africans, but also by an interest in promoting financially profitable trade and religiously profitable missionary work, these favorable accounts of Africa sought to cast the continent in the drama of global progress by emphasizing its as-yet unrealized economic and religious potential. In Benezet's text and others, this produced a representational tension between a vision of African cultural history in which change would necessarily signal decline and one in which the forces of modernity—commerce, literacy, religious "enlightenment"—heralded a new and potentially glorious age for Africa.

Thus, when Benezet comes to describe the slave trade itself toward the end of the book, economic as well as moral considerations come to bear. On one level, Benezet's anecdotes of enslavement—the more horrific for our having come to "know" the slaves' homeland—deploy the tried-and-true sentimental strategy of evoking sympathy in the reader by depicting the sufferings of one's fellow human beings. Although tending to the gothic and arguably to the voyeuristic, they nonetheless evoke a sense of nostalgia for a lost way of life and for a violated "innocence." At the same time, Benezet closes on a resounding note of the economic benefits that would follow an abolition of the slave trade. Not until then, Benezet writes, "will Europeans be able to travel with safety into the heat of their country to form and cement such commercial friendships and alliances as might be necessary to introduce the arts and sciences amongst them." And in turn Africa would provide "most of the commodities" Europe and America need, and "the advantages of this trade would soon become so great" that the government must turn its attention there.[35]

Some Historical Account of Guinea quickly became a central, even representative, text of the transatlantic antislavery movement; in 1788, four years after Benezet's death, it was republished in London amidst the roiling debates over whether and how Sierra Leone should be settled as a free colony. This decade also saw the publication of a number of travel narratives describing the western coast of Africa, including Henry Smeathman's *Plan of a Settlement to Be Made near Sierra Leone* (1786), Alexander Falconbridge's *An Account of the Slave Trade on the Coast of Africa* (1788), John Matthews's *A Voyage to the River Sierra-Leone, on the Coast of Africa* (1788), and James Stanfield's *Observations on a Voyage to the Coast of Africa* (1788). These texts did not substantially rework the terms of the argument as laid out by Benezet, but rather added texture, detail, and accumulated force to that argument.

In *Some Historical Account of Guinea*, in the texts it drew upon, and in much antislavery literature to follow, natural realities not only serve as indices to cultural realities, but indeed also give rise to particular forms of cultural development. The "charming landscapes" and "spreading foliage" in Adanson's account serve not merely as scenery, but as natural features enabling the "ease and indolence" of the natives. The rich arable soil described by so many antislavery writers not only produces good crops but good neighbors and social harmony. Natural imagery, that is, makes the environmentalist argument, grounding it in the tangible particularities of a place and time in history. Science hereby operates beneath the surface in texts that do not bill themselves as science, but as more approachable customs-and-manners travel narratives; science has been folded in, plowed under, so to speak, become part of the rhetoric.

Next to polemical treatises, testimonial literature, and travel narratives, poetic verse provided the major expressive outlet for antislavery sentiment. The lines of influence traveled both directions: some figures who were social activists first and foremost, such as Thomas Day and Hannah More, also worked in verse as a potent and popular genre; and conversely, some figures who were primarily poets, such as William Cowper, Samuel Taylor Coleridge, and William Blake, occasionally composed lines on the evils of slavery. As these latter names suggest, antislavery verse owed a significant debt to the Romantic movement, in large part because the Romantic emphasis on emotion accorded with the abolitionists' desire to evoke powerful feelings about a big, dramatic human subject. The Romantic influence also helps to explain the recurring presence of the sublime and the beautiful in antislavery verse, as well as the adaptation of the elegy and the soliloquy to antislavery purposes.

Too often, perhaps, for the tastes of modern readers, abolitionist poetry amounts to little more than argument versified, as in More's influential poem "Slavery," which asked its British readers to "[r]evere affections mingled with our frame, / In every nature, every clime the same," or in Cowper's "The Negro's Complaint," which argues that "[f]leecy locks and black complexion / Cannot forfeit Nature's claim; / Skins may differ, but affection / Dwells in white and black the same."[36] Yet understanding the more complicated functions of natural imagery in antislavery verse—the storms, the jungles, the fragrant boughs and burning sands—requires a different set of reading strategies, for we have moved from one register of polemic and meaning-creation to another. Where the more or less nonfictional genre of travel writing tended toward the documentary and anthropological in representing African nature or Africans in nature, antislavery verse tended toward the imagistic and characterological. And verse is perhaps the preeminently aesthetic genre, meaning that more than any other it calls attention to its formal qualities, seeks to evoke certain responses by virtue of those qualities, and asks that they provide the grounds for readerly judgment—a statement that holds as true for the eighteenth century as for the twenty-first. The proper distinction, then, is not between the polemical force of verse or nonfiction, nor between the emotional impact of the two, but between the kinds of response that different literary techniques can evoke.

Reading antislavery verse returns us to the problem, raised in the Introduction, of the relation between political consciousness and aesthetic experience. As I suggested there, aesthetic experience has the capacity to bring the appreciator of an artwork into a new relation to the cultural world by creating a sense of phenomenological remove, and by occasioning an imaginative space in which social conditions, indeed reality itself, can come to seem contingent rather than natural. At the same time, aesthetic experience does not have to imply a kind of imaginative solipsism, bringing the appreciator merely into communion with self, but can form the basis for a renewal of social bonds and the repair or creation of community. As for the specific question of the role of aesthetic form in shaping perceptions of race and slavery, and the role of natural imagery in abolitionist poetry, we can identify two main avenues of effect. First, a poem will seek to direct the reader toward certain attitudes or feelings regarding the enslavement of Africans, not only through its surface-level "argument" but also through the coordination of natural imagery with other elements of the form, such as the dramatic situation or the speaker's voice. Second, some abolitionist verse operates on what we might call a meta-aesthetic level, whereby imagination and artistic technique become subjects themselves; such meta-aesthetics, especially when linked to the aesthetics of the natural world, proved a vital means of articulating a politics of humanitarian inclusiveness.

As a formal system of knowledge, with different schools of thought and expositors of the proper criteria for "taste" and "judgment," aesthetics arose coevally with eighteenth-century natural science—a historical convergence partially explained by the fact that both disciplines mounted claims about what constituted the truly civilized human being, indeed what constituted any human being. Predictably, the concept of aesthetic sensibility could serve like science to divide race from race, as in Long's slander of Africans that "[t]hey conceive no pleasure from the most beautiful parts of their country, preferring the more sterile."[37] In the face of such aspersions, abolitionist verse commonly sought to humanize its black subjects by portraying their emotional, spiritual, and aesthetic responsiveness to nature, and, beyond that, to make phenomenologically available (i.e., visual and tangible) the principle of natural liberty that lay at the heart of natural rights theory.

These issues surface dramatically in one intriguing poetic variant that sprang up during the 1770s and 1780s, the antislavery eclogue, recast from its Virgilian origins to feature a dialogue between two slaves, typically outdoors, in which the speakers lament their plight and plot some course of action. Prominent examples of this subgenre included Thomas Chatterton's "Heccar and Gaira: An African Eclogue" (1770), Edward Rushton's "West-Indian Eclogues" (1787), and the four eclogues that open Hugh Mulligan's *Poems Chiefly on Slavery and Oppression* (1788), including "The Lovers: An African Eclogue" and "The Slave: An American Eclogue." In their very form as dialogues, the poems communicate the human subjectivity of their African characters; recall that Reinhold Forster cited as evidence for the familialhood of all people "the language of the heart" and "the gifts of speech founded on the variety, power and extent of voice and articulation." And poetry, particularly before the vernacular revolution of the nineteenth century, seemed to provide the best showcase for displaying the "gifts of speech" of its characters, however stilted that speech might sound today. Hearing even a fictionalized, romanticized African character speaking, and speaking in English, rather than simply reading information about "the Negroes," could help to break down the cultural barrier between reader and speaker.

In the eclogues, which can mount just as fierce a polemic against slavery as any work of nonfiction, the natural world appears typically as a backdrop or setting for the slaves' dialogue, or as the African scene from which they were originally kidnapped and sold into slavery. The ideological meaning of this natural imagery is less clear than in nonfictional literature—it operates on less-conscious levels—but it raises the question: Why did the eclogue form appeal to these writers, and how did this poetic form shape their argument against slavery?

Strikingly, these eclogues all explicitly imagine the retribution of Africans against their villainous European tormentors. The aggressiveness of this antislavery stance goes far beyond moral suasion and far beyond the image of black supplication captured in the movement's "Am I Not a Man and a Brother?" medallion. Chatterton's Gaira, for instance, a noble African warrior, does not simply mourn the kidnapping of his wife Cawna but imagines a fierce revenge: "I'll strew the beaches with the mighty dead / And tinge the lily of their features red." Similarly, Mulligan's Bura, upon learning that a rebellion is planned on board the slave ship from which he has just escaped, eagerly waits "for the pointed steel, / To hurl swift vengeance on the pallid foe!" And Rushton's Jumba, after hearing of the whipping of his fellow slave Adoma's wife by an overseer, calls "for the power to bring these monsters low, / And bid them feel the biting tooth of woe!" No gentle idylls, these. Indeed, the assertions of black fury and the startling images of black-on-white violence seem far ahead of their time, more akin to the militancy of Nat Turner and David Walker than to the comparatively nonconfrontational strategies of most eighteenth-century antislavery rhetoric. It is also worth noting that while one of the planned slave uprisings (Jumba's) founders, one is left unresolved (Gaira and Heccar's), and one (aboard ship in "The Lovers") apparently succeeds; the trope of the perishing African martyr, which could evoke sympathy but at the cost of denying agency to blacks, does not hold sway in these poems.

Moreover, as these and other lines suggest, the conflict between the speakers and their antagonists has a starkly racial quality to it. Not just the slave traders themselves but whites generally stand indicted. Bura's "pallid foe" is the same as the "pallid race" that Congo curses, which is the same as Chatterton's "palid race" (sic) and the "pallid shadows of the azure waves" who have sailed from afar and violated Africa. This pattern merits attention because it works subtly, and misleadingly, to cast Western slavery as primarily or originally a racial conflict rather than as fundamentally an economic system, and it attributes such racial thinking to the slaves themselves, which, though plausible, again subtly works to obscure the historical and cultural contingency that attended the rise of racial thought. It is perfectly sensible to think that hatred of the "pallid race" did indeed develop among slave populations; it is not entirely clear, however, whether such thinking would have arisen absent the violent provocation of the slave system. By representing—however inadvertently or however obliquely—racialism as a *human* characteristic rather than a historically conditioned ideology, these three writers make it fractionally more difficult to argue that race conflict and racial oppression run against human nature. While all this might seem like squeezing blood from the turnip of antislavery verse, it points to a persistent theoretical problem that will dog antislavery philosophy in the decades ahead, that of having to work within the consensus framework of naturalized racial difference while still making the argument that slavery violates the natural "liberty" and natural sensibilities of human beings.

In that context, we can evaluate more clearly the problems raised by the eclogues' use of natural imagery. As a general matter, their natural imagery to a degree offsets the psychological thinness or flatness of the speakers. The depicted natural world provides a kind of compensatory backdrop against which the human issues in the poems become more vivid. More specifically, we can identify in the eclogues elements of the sublime and the beautiful—those categories of experience so central to eighteenth-century aesthetic theory—which play a subtle but important role in the poems' antislavery message. Consider the opening lines of Rushton's fourth eclogue, which set the dramatic scene:

> With dreadful darkness, now the Isle is crown'd
> And the fierce northern tempest howl'd around.
> Loud roars the surf; the rocks return the roar,
> And liquid fire seems bursting on the shore.
> Swift darts the light'ning in fantastic guise,
> And bellowing thunder rolls along the skies. (50)

These lines seem intended to evoke a sensation of the sublime, which Edmund Burke in 1757 had described as "astonishment," with "some degree of horror," but also leading to feelings of "admiration, reverence and respect."[38] They also express what Immanuel Kant in 1790, greatly elaborating on Burke's theory, called the "dynamical sublime," in which the perception of sublimity arises from one's apprehension of nature's inherent power or energy (in contrast to the "mathematical sublime," which depends on scale, i.e., the vastness of nature).[39] The paradox Kant identified is that an awestruck or fearful response to the overpowering strength of nature secondarily evokes a liberatory sense of human moral strength, by virtue of our ability to confront that power; not diminishment but triumph results as the human mind realizes that it is not finally mastered by the violent, primal, natural energies of the world.[40] Thus Gaira, for example, in Chatterton's "Heccar and Gaira," tells of tracking and killing the "loud Tyger, pawing in his rage," which "Bids the black Archers of the wilds engage" (2). The sublime elements in the eclogues, then, serve to link the passions of the African characters to the forces of nature and thereby to naturalize the impulse for violent retribution and self-emancipation, while asserting the essential separateness of the human beings from nature and preserving their heroism as moral actors.

Yet the eclogues also seek to show the African characters as cultured as well as savagely heroic, and to suggest that an essential and normative benevolence inheres in nature (because that is what slavery violates), and for these goals the discourse of the "beautiful" proved more useful than that of the sublime. When Zelma calls Bura's attention to "[y]on verdant bank near that palmetto's shade" (28), when Bura promises that "fertile fields and groves shall meet our eyes" (29), and when Congo and Quamina meet "beneath a Tam'rind's cool retreat" (44), the poets situate their black subjects squarely within the extensive contemporary discourse surrounding the concept of beauty, the appreciation of which not only Kant and Burke but Berkeley, Hegel, Hutcheson, Schiller, Shaftesbury and others saw as a defining feature of human consciousness. Significantly, the appreciation of beauty in the eclogues depends on both the objective or intrinsic qualities of the natural world ("verdant," "fertile," "cool") and the subjective responsiveness of the human perceivers, a duality that reflects the eighteenth century's increasing emphasis on the psychological dimension of aesthetic experience. These lines thereby communicate not simply the beauty of nature but the African speakers' capacity for responding to that beauty. Moreover, the discourse of the beautiful counterbalances the violent side of nature imagined by the sublime; it expresses the other side of the moral equation or rift in discourses of nature, figuring the natural world as morally good or at least consonant with moral goodness. This would operate as a vital theme in abolitionist discourse for decades to come, because antislavery philosophy could not admit the possibility that slavery or violent oppression was a "natural" phenomenon or aligned with the "natural" moral order.

For all its suggestiveness, the eclogue itself was not an especially common or important genre in antislavery discourse. That distinction belongs rather to the pastoral, which, of all the great variety of representational wellsprings on which abolitionist rhetoric drew, proved the most salient and the most versatile. Indeed, the pastoral subsumes some of the central themes of the eclogues: the contrast between nature and civilization, the appreciation of rural beauty, a sense of nature's ethical significance. Despite its musty critical reputation, the pastoral is actually one of the richer, and trickier, symbolic modes; it also, in my account, most directly engages the questions of individual experience and psychology that factored into contemporary understandings of racial identity. The following, then, represents a preliminary theory of pastoral and a starting point for this study's recurring engagement with pastoral themes and concepts.

By "pastoral," I refer not simply to the classical tradition and its textual progeny, but to a much broader, more fluid and intense, conception of the role of nature in human life. Through a family of literary tropes, visual images, and thematic motifs, pastoral expresses a complex set of attitudes and feelings regarding the natural world, embracing both the "ideological" postures that have attracted the most scholarly attention, and the different forms of psychic experience that, although much less studied, underlie the ideological potentialities of pastoral. These shared forms of experience—particularly those of loss and longing—give the pastoral its power as a means of articulating and negotiating the racial, the cultural, and the universally human. For that reason the conventionality of much pastoral literature, often taken as an aesthetic weakness of the genre, actually represents one of its great strengths, and it calls for closer attention. We do well to see such conventions as the purling brook or the new-mown hay not as failures of the imagination but as windows into human experience and as vital writerly resources for communicating that experience.

Scholars have shown that a series of cultural pressures, principally population growth, urbanization, and intercultural contact, influenced the shifting patterns of natural imagery in eighteenth-century literature.[41] Of particular importance to the evolution of pastoral was the anxiety generated by rapid scientific and technological advance, which to the Romantics seemed to have deprived humankind of something sacred. In 1750, Rousseau had questioned the fundamental project of natural science, warning that "all the secrets [nature] hides are so many evils from which she protects [humankind], and that the very difficulty they find in acquiring knowledge is not the least of her bounty towards them."[42] By likening the findings of science to the fruit of the tree of knowledge, Rousseau anticipated an entire generation of early Romantics—Goethe, Wordsworth, Blake, Wollstonecraft, among others—who feared that an empirical, analytical approach to nature would destroy the feelings of mystery, wonder, and even reverence that the natural world could inspire. With the wildfire proliferation of Romantic ideas and ideals across the transatlantic world, the theme of the scientific Fall became a veritable refrain and worked to articulate concerns about the social dislocations occasioned by Western modernization. Throughout the late eighteenth and early nineteenth centuries, Romantic literature accordingly offered vivid contrasts between present and past, irreverence and myth, knowledge and innocence, technology and nature. Edgar Allan Poe's 1829 cry against science's epistemological violence captures almost a century of Romantic anxiety: "Hast thou not dragg'd Diana from her car, / And driv'n the Hamadryad from the wood / . . . / The elfin from the green grass? and from me / The summer dream beneath the tamarind tree?"[43] The experience of loss that pastoral typically imagines can be both personal and psychological, as here, and more broadly social and historical, as in Oliver Goldsmith's "The Deserted Village." The unifying theme is dispossession: Through the combined forces of history, social development, and scientific inquiry, some original quality of innocence, harmony, virtue, or fulfillment—representationally embodied in the relationship between human beings and the natural world—has disappeared.

In imagining human decline from a state of nature into a state of culture, pastoral expresses a deep-seated primitivism along Rousseauvian lines. It characteristically resists the passage of time, linking adulthood and social existence with psychic and cultural fragmentation. Yet across this pessimistic vision of history a progressivist ethos often cuts, for in the face of individual or collective dispossession, the pastoral ideal promises recovery. Janus-faced, it looks both backward and forward, toward a life that is past, which reminds the present of its fall, but also toward one yet to come, perhaps one in which the past can be renewed or rebuilt. It expresses a powerful nostalgia for a previous state of happiness, fulfillment, or harmony, even as it looks to the future where these (hopefully) can be recovered. It posits a universal condition of loss or absence, and then offers a redeemed connection to nature as compensation for the grief brought about by this loss or absence. This desire for a closer intimacy with nature—a desire that rests on the assumption that nature, even in its "sublime" or "wild" aspects, has positive moral substance—leads us perpetually toward a distant horizon, all the while reminding us of our various lost Edens: childhood, safety, contentment, primality.

One of the ironies or tragedies of this desire, however, is that it confirms the very thing it means to correct. As suggested earlier, the supposed philosophical opposition between a nature-friendly Romanticism and a nature-hostile science did not really hold up, since art, no less than science, involved a representational objectification of the natural world. It is not clear, for instance, whether or how Poe's imaginary tamarind tree brings us any "closer" to nature than a botanist's detailed drawing of a tamarind leaf. Pastoral can no more reverse the fall into science than Milton can restore Adam and Eve to the Garden. Rather, the pastoral provides a momentary phenomenological release from the psychic pressures of technology and culture, into an imaginary space, the womb of nature, where longing is fulfilled, pain salved, and missing things restored.

Pastoral's concern with loss, transformation, and innocence made it a particularly useful mode for antislavery literature. In the eighteenth century, the typical antislavery adaptation of pastoral involved "Africanizing" it, in ways similar to the Africa-as-Eden trope, but with a greater emphasis on the theme of return. William Lisle Bowles's poem "The African," for instance, starts with the familiar image of the dying slave, whose companions encourage him to imagine a return to Africa after death:

Till thou view those scenes again,
Where thy father's hut was rear'd,
Where thy mother's voice was heard;
Where thy infant brothers play'd
Beneath the fragrant citron's shade;
Where through green savannahs wide
Cooling rivers silent glide,
Or the shrill sigarras sing
Ceaseless to their murmuring;
Where the dance, the festive song,
Of many a friend divided long,
Doom'd through stranger lands to roam,
Shall bid thy spirit welcome home![44]

Note the close intertwining of natural imagery with emotion, memory, family, and community. The poem could have represented the experience of dislocation and diaspora without reference to the natural world, and it could have represented an African landscape without reference to the cultural world, but the poet has carefully linked the balm of imagination to "scenes" in which natural beauty and social harmony reinforce one another in ideal reciprocity. The lines imagine an almost archetypally perfect environment, one in which the people's biological, emotional, and aesthetic needs are profoundly satisfied—an environment that *once was*, and that *can be* again, but only in imagination, in death, or in freedom. To jaded modern readers, such a vision might seem trite or maudlin, but to an eighteenth-century audience less resistant to poetic conventionality, it likely struck deeper chords of sympathy. Certainly, many antislavery poems invoking the pastoral sold quite widely, and helped to create the representational foundation for abolitionist discourse in the nineteenth century.

If pastoral in the hands of white abolitionists commonly sought to evoke sympathy among a white readership for African subjects or speakers, by representing their relation to nature as recognizably "civilized" rather than merely sensual or utilitarian, how did pastoral function in early Black Atlantic texts? By and large, Black Atlantic writers worked within the set of European representational models that they knew, particularly the pastoral, and at this point in history we do not see significant overt differences between "black" and "white" treatments of the natural world. That fact, however, suggests a delicate yet crucial subtext. Reading natural imagery for the expression of racial subjectivity implies reading for its obverse: that is, reading for a more pressing need to express *human* subjectivity, and here Black Atlantic literature proved quite creative. The contours of this problem begin to emerge in the work of Phillis Wheatley and Ignatius Sancho, whose writings, taken together, suggest a growing awareness of the personal and political significance of pastoral.

Wheatley, whose *Poems on Various Subjects, Religious and Moral* (1773) was famously dismissed by Thomas Jefferson, was less famously praised by Thomas Clarkson and the Abbé Henri Grégoire as a living embodiment of black culture. Clarkson, in the seventh section of his *Essay on the Slavery and Commerce of the Human Species*, included portions of three of Wheatley's poems ("An Hymn to the Evening," "An Hymn to the Morning," and "On Imagination"), all of which express pastoral themes, and Grégoire included "On the Death of J.C., an Infant," "An Hymn to the Morning," and "To the Right Hon. William, Earl of Dartmouth" in his *De la Littérature des Nègres* (1808). Wheatley's treatment of pastoral does not address racial subjectivity directly, but discloses a fascinating racial subtext. In "On Imagination" she writes:

> Though *Winter* frowns to *Fancy's* raptur'd eyes
> The fields may flourish, and gay scenes arise;
> The frozen deeps may break their iron bands,
> And bid their waters murmur o'er the sands.
> Fair *Flora* may resume her fragrant reign,
> And with her flow'ry riches deck the plain;
> *Sylvanus* may diffuse his honours round,
> And all the forest may with leaves be crown'd:
> Show'rs may descend, and dews their gems disclose,
> And nectar sparkle on the blooming rose.

Wheatley has long faced charges of derivativeness, and from that perspective, this stanza might at first seem little more than a recasting of the eighteenth century's familiar pastoral images. Viewed, however, as the utterance of a woman facing explicit denials of her race's capacity for culture, the poem serves as one piece of a larger racial project, that of demonstrating a "civilized" relationship between an African American and the natural world. The faculty of imagination, then, has a double importance. In the first place it enacts a phenomenological emancipation that transforms the visible quotidian world, in which "silken fetters all the senses bind, / And soft captivity involves the mind," and it "with new worlds amaze[s] th' unbounded soul." In the second place, the imagination does so by recreating the everyday world as a pastoral landscape, with Aurora's "cheeks all glowing with celestial dies" and "all the mountains tipt with radiant gold," to which the speaker of the poem envisions her escape. Imagination thus reflects and declares her aesthetic sensitivity to nature. At the same time, it is rigorous and rational; as in a hymn to science the speaker celebrates that "We on thy pinions can surpass the wind, / And leave the rolling universe behind: / From star to star the mental optics rove, / Measure the skies, and range the realms above."[45] Imagination here, the ally of reason, underlies the speaker's cognitive relationship to nature: her intellectual ability to transcend the immediate material world and attain a superior vantage point from which to contemplate its secrets. Indeed, the liberatory language in "On Imagination" seems positively Kantian in its association of beauty with the sovereignty of the free mind. "The freedom of the imagination," Kant wrote, "is represented as harmonious with the lawfulness of the understanding in the estimation of the beautiful." Moreover, insofar as the apperception of beauty depends on both the intrinsic qualities of the "lov'd object" and the subjective qualities of the perceiver, the aesthetic experience transcends but does not deny difference, for "the principle of the estimation of the beautiful is represented as universal, i.e., as valid for everyone."[46] Along with Wheatley's other poems, then, "On Imagination" stood as an implicit refutation of the belief that, as Kant put it, the "Negroes of Africa have, by nature, no feeling that rises above the trifling,"[47] and although the poem never mentions race, its entire context—from the frontispiece showing the poet herself, to the other verses with explicitly racial themes, to Wheatley's extraordinary defense of her authorship of the poems at Boston's Town Hall—make the message abundantly clear. Not just literacy but a capacity to master nature cognitively while responding to it aesthetically signal Wheatley's membership in the human community and in civilization.

One of Wheatley's admirers across the Atlantic was Ignatius Sancho, a well-connected, financially independent Afro-Briton who, like Wheatley, well understood the psychological and cultural complexities of living black in a white society, and who was also cited by Clarkson and Grégoire as evidence of black genius. Of Sancho Grégoire wrote: "His writing is lofty when he addresses nature, which reveals to him on all sides the work and the hand of the Creator."[48] Grégoire evidently means to enlist Sancho in the ranks of the romantically sensitive, but it actually proved more complicated than that. In his reflections on the genre's particular aesthetic conventions, Sancho articulated an intriguing shift from art to commentary, from pastoral to metapastoral.

Though nominally the property of the Duke of Montagu, Sancho had enjoyed a fairly privileged service as valet and butler before being set up as a grocer in Westminster, and he had cultivated both a deep knowledge of English literature and an impressive roster of friends and correspondents, including Laurence Sterne, David Garrick, and the Duchess of Queensberry. To one of these correspondents, his friend the amateur artist and government clerk John Meheux, Sancho wrote a 1779 letter playfully disparaging a sketch Meheux had sent:

> And what, in the name of common sense, impelled thee to torment my soul, with thy creative pen drawing of sweet A—r—bn—s? I enjoyed content at least in the vortex of smoak and vice—and lifted my thoughts no higher than the beauties of the park or—gardens.—What have I to do with rural deities? with parterres—fields—groves—terraces—views—buildings—grots [*sic*]—temples—slops—bridges—and meandring streams—cawing rooks—billing turtles—happy swains—the harmony of the woodland shades—the blissful constancy of rustic lovers?—Sir, I say you do wrong to awaken ideas of this sort:—besides, as I hinted largely above—you have no talent—no language—no colouring—you do not groupe well—no relief—false light and shadow—and then your perspective is so false—no blending of tints—thou art a sad fellow, and there is an end of it.[49]

Refracted as they are through his posture of urbane irony, the attitudes toward nature, pastoral, and art that Sancho expresses invite a closer look but resist easy description. Why does the drawing "torment [his] soul" and why does Meheux "do wrong to awaken ideas of this sort"? Why, at the same time, does Sancho seem to dismiss the pastoral life of "groves," "happy swains," and "woodland shades" as irrelevant to his own? What do we make of Sancho's mock-serious critique of Meheux's sketch? And even though it is not overtly broached as a subject, can we read the passage for its implicit racial subjectivity?

The key to the letter lies in the tension between pastoral as a conventional artistic form and pastoral as a means of evoking powerful human emotions, in the contrast between the artificiality of the imagery and the potential reality, however remote or hypothetical, of the rural scene it evokes. Moving from the pose of the modest enjoyer of simple parks and gardens to that of the suave critic, Sancho presents himself as the cultured urbanite, more comfortable in critiquing an artistic representation of nature than in entertaining the ideas or feelings it awakens. Yet perhaps Meheux's rural scene "torments" him not just because it is poorly executed, but because its natural beauty stands as a painful reminder of the "vortex of smoak and vice" in which the city-dweller Sancho lives. Withdrawing into art criticism thus allows him not to confront that contrast, returning from experience to the safer ground of representation. By focusing on such aesthetic criteria as harmony, relief, and compositional balance or "grouping," Sancho diverts attention away from content toward execution; the communicative potential of the sketch is denied on the basis of style.

Of course Sancho is playing around. But in humorously savaging even a bad version of pastoral, he acknowledges as well as resists its psychological power, which would, after all, presumably be greater in the hands of an artist with true "talent," "language," and "perspective." As Paul Shepard has suggested, this power derives from a shared psychology of nature that has developed over the full course of human evolutionary history. The force of the symbolic representation can only approximate or simulate that of the natural world itself, but both speak to fundamental levels of human thought and feeling:

> The artist is not only behaving in a manner similar to but is creating an extension of the nervous system. The art object represents a critical, unified, external part of an internal model—or image, analogue of experience construct, fantasy, or schema. . . . [The object's] abstract qualities [forms, lines, etc.], in contrast to the specific content or subject, are its more generalized organization at once superficial to and deep in the unconscious, the more basic elements of the natural environment.[50]

Sancho's ironic critique works by emphasizing the "superficial" rather than the "deep," but in the ambiguous, playful rebuke of Meheux for "torment[ing] my soul," we can discern another level of possible meaning, a "fantasy" or "analogue of experience" that the irony glosses without canceling. The racial implications of Sancho's rhetorical posture are subtle but intriguing. On one level, his command of the pastoral form—and the archness with which he exercises that command—signal that Sancho, like Wheatley, has attained a "civilized" sensibility hard to imagine for one whose life started as a slave on the Middle Passage itself. At another level, the passage suggests that the idealized rural life Meheux has evoked is so remote from the experience of urban Afro-Britons as to constitute fantasy, but that Sancho can feel its emotional power nonetheless. Beneath the bantering, then, we can discern a double exclusion and a double lament: a mourning, from the perspective of any Englishman, for the loss of "rural deities" and "rustic lovers," and, from the perspective of a *black* Englishman, a feeling of debarment from whatever cultural reality the pastoral might have expressed in the first place.

This is a lot of weight for one passage to carry, but Sancho's letter touches on serious issues that other African, Afro-British, and African American writers of the late eighteenth and nineteenth centuries had to grapple with: the role of nature in their life; the role of *representations* of nature in their life; and their status or recognition as "civilized" commentators on both. The importance of nature as a representational resource would deepen for Black Atlantic and African American writers as more testimony emerged from agricultural slaves, whose day-to-day familiarity with the natural world was so intimate and yet so problematic, and as literary culture continued to plumb the representational possibilities of the living green world.

[I]n the Midst of this great this astonishing Équipoyse Man struggles and Lives.
J. HECTOR ST. JOHN DE CRÈVECOEUR, unpublished Fifth Letter

The tree which moves some to tears of joy is in the Eyes of others only a Green thing that stands in the way. Some See Nature all Ridicule & Deformity . . . & Some Scarce see Nature at all. But to the Eyes of the Man of Imagination, Nature is Imagination itself.
WILLIAM BLAKE to Rev. John Trusler, August 1799

[B]eware of that Scripture, which says, Fools perish for lack of knowledge.
OLAUDAH EQUIANO to Gordon Turnbull, February 1788

CHAPTER TWO

Narrative, Temporality, and the International Traveler

OUT OF THE ROILING CURRENTS of the eighteenth-century transatlantic world, as the antislavery argument sought to assert itself against the forces of public apathy, private interest, and imperial politics, two writers emerged who rendered that argument in unusually complex form. J. Hector St. John de Crèvecoeur and Olaudah Equiano might not, at first intuitive blush, seem the likeliest bedfellows, but reading them in conjunction opens up unusual avenues for assessing liberal literary responses to a volatile historical moment when the West was shaken and transformed by colonization, the slave trade, philosophical ferment, and energetic new forms of cultural syncretism.

In several of the basic categories of selfhood—ancestry, education, religious belief, chosen profession—the two men could hardly have been more dissimilar. In both their public personae and their personal lives, however, Crèvecoeur and Equiano typified some of the qualities we have come to associate with their age: a tolerant cultural sensibility, a steady rationalism punctuated by moments of high feeling, an ironic stance toward the world veiling their deeper philosophical convictions. More fundamentally, both men embraced a classically liberal conception of the individual, which regarded the human being as, ideally, an autonomous agent capable of self-knowledge, moral improvement, rational inquiry, and responsible political engagement. Finally, Crèvecoeur and Equiano were both expatriates and cultural hybrids hoping to reconcile their personal allegiances to different lands. These parallels suggest, first, a measure of overlap in the racial subjectivities of the two men, who occupied anomalous positions, and privileged vantage points, in the contemporary landscape of racial and cultural ideology. Second, they provide crucial context for understanding how and why Crèvecoeur and Equiano portray their textual alter egos as taking charge of their own destiny in a world governed by ever more complex imperial systems and increasingly receptive to the cold economic logic of forced labor.

In their major works—*Letters from an American Farmer* (1782) and *The Interesting Narrative of the Life of Olaudah Equiano, or Gustavus Vassa, The African, Written by Himself* (1787)—Crèvecoeur and Equiano provide striking examples of how literary form could inflect the politics of race and slavery. For unlike the writings we have considered so far, *Letters* and the *Interesting Narrative* are full-length (if selective) treatments of individual lives, which can embody abstract issues in personal experience. Much more so than political rhetoric, whatever its affective or aesthetic strategies, the autobiography of Equiano and the quasi-autobiographical work of Crèvecoeur convey the lived and felt meanings of an institution that was so profoundly shaping their world. At the same time, both men were consummate literary craftsmen, tricksters even, carefully massaging the facts in order to fashion a particular image of themselves.[1] By evaluating their strategies of self-representation side by side, and by considering how these strategies mobilize contemporary discourses of race and nature, we can better assess the power and the limitations of postrevolutionary liberal thought in confronting the threat of slavery.

That threat involved a direct challenge to coherent literary representation. Racial slavery functions in both *Letters* and the *Interesting Narrative* not only as an ideological and moral problem, but also as a narrative problem, and conversely, the language of nature is central to how the problem of slavery is narrativized and—very imperfectly—resolved. In representing individual experience and the broader sociohistorical processes that this experience instantiates, Crèvecoeur and Equiano invoke the Enlightenment ideals of self-determination and self-renewal, and yet slavery looms as the antithetical block: a block both practical, in its stifling of human effort, and philosophical, in its racialized appeal to the authority of natural science. In struggling, therefore, to assimilate racial otherness and racial violence to their own personal histories and to a coherent narrative of human history, Crèvecoeur and Equiano turn to the physical natural world around them and, simultaneously, to an imaginary nature upon which they can project their visions of past and future. Accordingly, *Letters* and the *Interesting Narrative* preoccupy themselves with matters of geography, time, and change—matters that are not only discursively present but also structurally operative. In other words, they provide the narrative energy for both texts as the authors seek to come to terms with the political and economic transformations associated with eighteenth-century "modernity"—and institutionalized racial slavery represented one of the most dramatic of those transformations.

In travelling between cultures, both inter- and intranationally, each narrator has to accommodate himself as best he can to spatial and temporal change. In the process, geographic places and relationships provide a means of navigating and situating hybrid cultural identities. In this respect, however, a crucial difference opens up between *Letters* and the *Interesting Narrative*. For Crèvecoeur's Farmer James, it is rootedness in a particular place that enables the creation of a new and better individual, while for Equiano that self-re-creation depends upon moving through and conquering space, upon the transcendence of merely local situation. Concomitantly, each work expresses a very different sense of history. Historical change in *Letters* is a kind of villain, insofar as Farmer James's idyll in western Pennsylvania needs to exist outside of time; in the *Interesting Narrative* history is an achievement, an act of will. And as the respective titles of the works suggest, each author's attitude toward history finds its due expression in the chosen literary form: a loosely structured epistolary collection in the case of Crèvecoeur, a highly structured, kinetic story in the case of Equiano.

Nature forms what we might call the representational environment for our two sojourners, who each in the midst of turmoil, and in the face of slavery's insult to their deepest convictions, tries to imagine the natural world as a domain of moral order and emotional security. Yet nature proves temporally and spatially dynamic, and instabilities in the discursive domain of nature lead to fissures and paradoxes within the texts as they narrativize the role of race and slavery in an individual life. In *Letters from an American Farmer*, James's anguished response to slavery, during which he questions the universal moral order posited by traditional natural history, displaces the problem of slavery from the realm of political history to that of nature—yet he equivocates as to whether slavery expresses or violates nature, oscillating confusedly between scientific and juridical interpretations of natural law. Combined with the narrative dislinearity of the text, this equivocation robs *Letters* of much of its abolitionist potential. It is nonetheless possible, I will suggest, to recuperate from the book the promise of a natural history, and a political stance, not paralyzed but reinvigorated by the radical independence of nature from human systems of thought.

Equiano, meanwhile, responds to the calamity of enslavement as both a direct victim and one who has subsequently transcended a history of racial violence. His self-portrait, however, is emotionally divided between a cosmopolitan British adulthood and a (possibly imaginary) African childhood. This division complicates the narrative technique of the autobiography by generating a tension between its public status as racialized testimony and its private significance as retrospective memoir. This tension, in turn, manifests as a split in Equiano's representations of the natural world, which appears variously as timeless sanctuary in an African idyll, as the semiotic environment for supernatural meaning, and as the raw material of Christian capitalism. As with *Letters*, this seriously problematizes the text's politics, but in so doing leaves us a vivid record of the energies and internal contradictions of antislavery thought in the age of revolution.

Crèvecoeur's Natural Contract

Readers of *Letters from an American Farmer* have inevitably had to grapple with the work's depiction of human bondage, particularly the narrator's dramatic visit to "Charles Town" (i.e., Charleston, South Carolina) in Letter IX. In this scene, which, according to an anonymous 1782 review in the *Gentleman's Magazine*, "must sensibly affect every mind not absolutely callous to the impression of humanity,"[2] James encounters a slave who has been tortured, caged, and left to die, and he voices a powerful condemnation of slavery, along with passionate despair about human nature and the universal moral order. Critics have taken the scene variously as an early expression of American antislavery sentiment, as metaphysical allegory, as both a critique and an embodiment of the colonialist project, as illuminating contrast to the embryonic national character, and, most commonly, as a fall from innocence which destroys the rhapsodic vision of the early letters and prepares for the final disruption of the idyll by the American Revolution in Letter XII.

This episode will figure centrally in my discussion of *Letters*, but for its thematic rather than its narrative significance. Indeed, the structural chaos of *Letters*—which follows no clear organizational or characterological design—presents fundamental difficulties in evaluating the role of slavery in the work. Many readers of *Letters* have casually assumed that the work's form reflects a deliberate and significant choice on Crèvecoeur's part to create meaning through narrative momentum: through a linear progression of events and through character development.[3] The problem is that Crèvecoeur's London publisher, Davies and Davis, dramatically rearranged the original manuscript, such that what might seem the author's organizational plan really reflects that of the editors, or even, perhaps, such that the final form of the book is little better than accidental.[4] Certainly, the fact that the book took shape in a kind of editorial whirlwind must seriously qualify any interpretation of its ideological purpose or significance. It behooves us, therefore, to understand James's experience in Charles Town in conceptual if not sequential relation to the rest of the work.

Put briefly, his encounter with slavery forces James to fundamentally revise his understanding of "nature" because it defies incorporation into his usual categories of representation and structures of thought. Throughout *Letters*, James has blended the languages of natural history, georgic, and pastoral in his representation of the natural world, and he expresses a good eighteenth-century faith in the consonance of natural law and human purposes. Nature, in this view, is regular, harmonious, intelligible, and comfortable to the human being. Yet natural law in Crèvecoeur's work operates on both juridical and scientific levels, the first imagining the governance of a cosmic moral order, the second focused on the physical properties and processes of nature, and slavery seems to tear open a breach between the two, fundamentally challenging James's deepest assumptions by suggesting that racial violence might instantiate natural law scientifically more than violating it juridically. Here, indeed, we have an early literary instance of how the assumptions and methods of natural history could prove debilitating to the antislavery case when linked to race. However, although this breach seriously undercuts or attenuates the narrowly "antislavery" import of *Letters*, we can nonetheless discern glimmers of a more far-reaching reorientation of vision, one which entails an implicit reevaluation of the customary subject-object dynamic involved in human understandings of nature. That reevaluation does not necessarily enact, but at least opens the door to, a philosophical liberation in Crèvecoeur's treatment of racial slavery.

Crèvecoeur's 1782 dedication to the Abbè Raynal, in which he praises the philosophe's *Histoire philosophique et politique des établissemens et du commerce des Européens dans les deux Indes* (1770), yields a tantalizing clue: "[Y]ou have pleaded the cause of humanity in espousing that of the poor Africans. You viewed these provinces of North America in their true light: as the asylum of freedom, as the cradle of future nations and the refuge of distressed Europeans" (29). It turns out, however, that the Abbè "[pleads] the cause" of the Africans in a most remarkable way: He calls for the emergence of a "Black Spartacus" in the New World who will avenge the rights of nature by leading a righteous slave rebellion against the forces of oppression and stagnation. Raynal certainly does view the provinces of North America as the "asylum of freedom," but his work reflects a deep European ambivalence about the historical significance of America and the position that slavery would occupy in the society developing there. With his collaborators, including Denis Diderot, Raynal attacked the institution of slavery in uncompromising terms that flatly indicted both religious and secular authority, going far beyond the mainstream of antislavery rhetoric. Raynal advocated the amelioration of the conditions of existing slaves, not in any way to prolong the institution, but only until the time arrived for revolution and slavery's final abolition. When this happened, the Americans would grow "drunk with long-awaited blood."

Although it is impossible to determine which edition of the *Histoire Philosophique et Politique* Crèvecoeur knew, or how much of the multivolume work he actually read, it is equally hard to imagine that he was unaware of its antislavery militancy. *Letters from an American Farmer* does not, of course, espouse revolution; its political conservatism consists not only in Crèvecoeur's (and James's) overt opposition to the American Revolution, but in the text's wariness regarding social discord generally. I want to suggest, however, that *Letters* recognizes, even celebrates, another form of revolution, one less physical and political than intellectual and metaphysical. Understood in broad terms, both Crèvecoeur and Raynal describe similar phenomena: the violent explosion of an objectified entity into undeniable subjectivity. Raynal embodies this event in the figure of the Black Spartacus and justifies it by appealing to the "natural" rights of humankind. For Crèvecoeur, nature itself comes to assert its independence, not of physical masters but of human consciousness: of the patterns and systems of thought by which the natural world is perceived and represented. What James's traumatic epiphany in Letter IX ultimately amounts to, however, is unclear, for the narrative incoherence of *Letters* makes it impossible to assess that moment's enduring psychological impact. Its value, therefore, may consist less in a personal or political transformation on the level of the text than, paradoxically, in a recognition on the part of the reader of its unassimilability.

Following this train of reasoning requires first examining more closely the habitual or dominant modes of thought that characterize Crèvecoeur's treatment of nature. These include, most prominently, a contractualist understanding of natural law, a mixture of pastoral and georgic themes, and a natural-historical approach to the physical world. Each relates to the other in complicated ways, and while they all lend creative energy to James's attack against slavery, they also, by reason of their essential instability, elude full authorial control.

The leitmotifs of contract and covenant, rooted primarily in a Lockean conception of individual liberty and managed social concord, run throughout James's manners-and-customs descriptions of various societies, suggesting that although *Letters* most visibly concerns the farmer's relation to his land, it is also a study in social relations deeply influenced by eighteenth-century contract theory.[5] This philosophical tradition, which took shape within the broader context of natural law and natural rights theory, evolved different branches but generally envisioned the social state and civil society as necessary advances over the state of nature. Yet little consensus existed as to what this "state of nature" meant—whether it more closely resembled Hobbes's vision of universal war or Rousseau's of essential compassion and innocence—and Locke himself equivocated on this issue. Consequently a recurring tension arose between imagining nature as a realm of normative moral content or as something that humanity must rise above. This tension surfaces again and again in *Letters from an American Farmer.* In his Rousseauvian moments, James renders nature, or man in the state of nature, as intrinsically peaceful and benevolent. At other times, he imagines humanity as innately violent or rapacious, and invokes the social contract as the indispensable mechanism of civilized society. Recounting a rivalry between two Nantucket tribes, for instance, James first cites the "disposition of man to quarrel and shed blood" (114) and then reports that they achieved a "reciprocal agreement" by which they "settle[d] a partition line" and which is "the only record which seems to entitle them to the denomination of men" (115).

Although contract theory grounded the principles of human liberty and equality in the state of nature, and thereby helped diversify antislavery rhetoric beyond scriptural exegesis, it also tended to support a teleological model of human social development running from "savagery" to "civilization"—an emphasis that, we have already seen, seriously complicated the antislavery argument. Moreover, contractualist thought had built into it a tension between a pessimistic view of human nature (selfish impulses require curbing) and an optimistic view of the ideal society (harmony, peace, and plenitude arise from voluntary social arrangements). Despite its close historical associations, via its emphasis on voluntary trade and social progress, with early capitalism, contract theory also had connections to agrarianism, especially in Locke, whose model for the labor theory of value centered on a farmer tilling his land, and with antihistorical primitivism, especially in Rousseau.

These broad philosophical issues are crucial to an understanding of *Letters* because they inform Crèvecoeur's representation of Farmer James's relationship to the natural world. This relationship displays elements of both georgic, with its characteristic emphasis on practical labor, and pastoral, with its characteristic resistance to intrusion, chaos, or change. These modes do not always comport smoothly with each other, but both counterpose "civilization" to savagery or wildness, and both underlie Crèvecoeur's anguished if highly problematic assault on slavery.

If georgic literature, as Timothy Sweet has argued, constitutes a more mature and practical genre than pastoral because it advances an "understanding of the transformations of [the natural] environment which are necessary to produce human life and culture" (5), an understanding which "has always been directed toward the future, and thus at least implicitly toward questions of environmental capacities and limits" (6), then James, particularly in Letters II and III, seems to embody the georgic ideal.[6] *Letters* presents a particular form of relating to the natural world—freehold agriculture—as a practical blueprint for the creation of an ideal society, and the agrarian existence that Jefferson rather abstractly extols in Query XIX ("Manufactures") of *Notes on the State of Virginia*, James actually lives out, undertaking the hard labor that goes into clearing land, plowing fields, and harvesting crops.[7] The good life in *Letters* is realizable and, Crèvecoeur suggests, imitable; the work's idealism rests on the belief that any American, through hard work and perseverance, can rise to a level of stability and self-sufficiency by owning and improving a piece of land. Although enamored of "the bright idea of property, of exclusive right, of independence" (48), James also recognizes, as Joel Kehler has observed, that "the pull of the land will, in the absence of reasoned property rights, lead to serious disorder and injustice, even as abstract property rights detached from the reality of the land will lead to tyranny and oppression."[8] The ideal society that *Letters* envisions depends not only upon individual freedom and a sufficient amount of land for everybody but upon rational restraint and effective laws, and in this sense, the georgic dimension of *Letters* stands in implicit opposition to slave labor.

The fact that in Letters IX and XII James's idyllic vision suffers profound shocks has tempted narrative-minded readers to argue that the idyll's deterioration constitutes an acknowledgment of the work's, and the country's, unfounded optimism.[9] But James's idyll shows weaknesses or internal contradictions from the beginning, particularly in the paradoxical relationship between two emotional or psychological impulses. On one hand, James feels an almost religious longing for personal transformation, for a transcendence of the hard facts of existence and a re-creation of the individual through a new relationship to the natural world. Farming, traveling, learning, adapting, working: these are the kinetic or dynamic aspects of James's personality and philosophy, and they express themselves primarily in the georgic mode. Yet he also displays a desire for sanctuary, for a retreat from the turbulence of society, from the vicissitudes and sufferings of history, and "from that great combination of mischances which perpetually leads us to diseases, to poverty, etc." (209). This impulse toward refuge is fundamental to the pastoral mood, and it hearkens back to a Rousseauvian primitivism in its fear of historical process and geographic motion. In the pastoral mode, Farmer James imagines an individual's rootedness in time and space, a connection not just to land or the natural world in general but to a *particular* place in nature (say, western Pennsylvania) that is immune to the ravages of time. The paradox running throughout *Letters*, in short, consists in the tension between the sense of temporal and geographic movement inherent in the concept of personal transformation and the necessity of temporal stasis implied by spatial rootedness. That paradox, moreover, expands beyond the individual life to include the course of social history, counterposing a sheltered pastoral community and the desirable historical transformation of a society or nation: "Such is our progress; such is the march of the Europeans toward the interior parts of this continent" (67). And yet in the face of history, James, forced into motion, chooses flight; calculating his future, he imagines a primitivist utopia: "[O]n the shores of a fine river, surrounded with woods, abounding with game, our little society, united in perfect harmony with the new adoptive one, in which we shall be incorporated, shall rest, I hope, from all fatigues" (219).

Despite the conceptual tension between them, both the georgic and pastoral modes in *Letters* rely upon a fairly simplistic understanding of nature as apprehensible, malleable, and representable. By "simplistic" I mean not that James lacks a theoretical or aesthetic appreciation of nature, but that, for most of *Letters*, nature exists for him in objectified form, either as a benevolent, passive, maternal provider or as the raw material that the human hand or mind must shape, literally or metaphorically. Like Thoreau at Walden Pond, James occupies an intermediary space, a middle ground between wild nature and overcomplex civilization, where the former must be "improved" and the latter critiqued. *Walden* actually serves as a revealing touchstone, for Thoreau more clearly, consistently, and self-consciously articulates an ethic of reciprocity whereby he recognizes what we might call the subjectivity of nature—that is, the idea that nature has its own integrity of meaning that transcends human definition or interpretation. In contrast, Farmer James, the practical American, takes what he needs from the natural world and changes those parts of it that resist easy incorporation into the pastoral-agrarian model. Although he is grateful for the opportunity to do both, his sense of ethics involves his obligations to his fellow human beings rather than a reciprocal obligation to nature.

For the morality of nature, from this point of view, will take care of itself. Daniel Boorstin has described the "Jeffersonian cosmology" as grounded in a belief in the "life-giving benevolence of nature" and in its moral simplicity: "Such a universe was singularly undramatic: in it . . .

there was no ultimate conflict between moral forces. But it was singularly dynamic. Efficient, coherent and intricate motion were the be-all and end-all." Given the moral perfection, or pure neutrality, of nature, evil lost its palpable energy, and could be explained as merely one element in the cosmic harmony.[10] Seeming to embrace this Enlightenment theodicy, even on those occasions when Farmer James recognizes violence and apparent injustice in the processes of nature, he does not lose his faith in the infallibility of instinct, for "the whole economy of what we proudly call the brute creation is admirable in every circumstance" (56).[11] Slavery, however, cannot be assimilated to this view of nature, and it thus represents a philosophical as well as a practical challenge to the pastoral-agrarian fantasy of *Letters*. In part, it forms a dark undercurrent to James's boosterism and works to undermine the freehold concept, as early as the first letter, by revealing its partial dependence on black labor.[12] More fundamentally, his encounter with slavery in Charles Town shakes both James's belief in the moral certainties of nature and his intellectual objectification of the natural world. Beyond posing a challenge to James's romantic image of America, the southern institution threatens the pastoral and georgic ideal themselves, insofar as both predicate an essentially benevolent natural economy.

As does James's practice and theory of natural history, which is wholly consistent with the Jeffersonian view of nature as a morally ordered realm that satisfies humanity's various needs in a predictable manner. An archetypal eighteenth-century "scientist," not only does James embody the contemporary interest in useful mechanical science ("Sometimes I delight in inventing and executing machines which simplify my wife's labour" [59]), but in his careful observations of plants and animals he captures the era's fascination with the workings of the natural world and its belief in the discoverability of natural principles through the gathering and analysis of empirical data.[13] And, like that of his peers, James's natural history dovetails with cultural analysis, both in the sense that the principles of natural history could be applied to the scientific study of human society and in the sense that the workings of nature could act as a metaphorical system of reference by which to understand or judge human society. The scientific mindset, then, reinforces a double objectification of the natural world, positioning nature as the object of detached analysis and as fodder for cultural commentary. More broadly, as a default the text fuses two views of natural law, the juridical and the scientific, in an organic, harmonious, stable worldview, one in which the moral and the physical dimensions of nature are in alignment, while the liberal subject stands firmly, rationally in control.

Like the georgic and the pastoral, however, this tidy natural-historical economy reveals internal problems that undermine its philosophical consistency. Specifically, the concept of race introduces perturbations into the system. Just as James's agrarian-pastoral idyll expressed a tension between static fixity and dynamic transformation, so his rendering of race oscillates between the two, and this wavering recapitulates his competing desires for timeless sanctuary and for personal transformation. On one hand, Crèvecoeur suggests that behind the narrator's natural history looms the towering influence of the Linnaean system of classification, with its fixed taxonomic categories and inability to account for geographic or temporal change.[14] On the other hand, James recognizes the developmental capacity of biological organisms and their responsiveness to environment: "We are nothing but what we derive from the air we breathe, the climate we inhabit" (65). Crèvecoeur does not quite envision the transformation of species over time, but he does recognize the potential for racial change. Not surprisingly, James's comments on race show the same tendency to contradiction that characterizes so much of his thinking. Sometimes, as with the frontiersmen who "have degenerated altogether into the hunting state" (72), race seems a matter of manners and customs that have developed over time under the influence of the local social or natural environment. Elsewhere, race equates with blood constitution, and can be intermingled. In his celebratory mood, James welcomes such intermixture; the American "is either an European or the descendant of an European; hence that strange mixture of blood, which you will find in no other country" (63). When James is contemplating heading into Indian territory with his family, however, he recoils at the thought that his children will mix the family blood with that of the natives. Anticipating Jefferson's comment in *Notes on the State of Virginia* that racial difference is "fixed in nature," James writes: "The strongest prejudices would make me abhor any alliance with them in blood, disagreeable no doubt to Nature's intentions, which have strongly divided us by so many indelible characters" (216).[15] Although Pamela Regis has argued that Crèvecoeur "managed . . . the imaginative projection" of transmuting James into an Indian in Letter XII and thus broke free of the fixed categories of natural history, Crèvecoeur's narrator seems ultimately to run up against insurmountable psychological barriers against biological, if not cultural, intermixture.[16] While the "metamorphosis" (219) of James and his family will stop short of biological miscegenation, it will evidently involve linguistic, religious, and behavioral mingling with the "aborigines" (220).

And what, then, of "the poor Africans" in this "asylum of freedom," as Crèvecoeur wrote in his dedication? With the exception of the Charles Town letter, they appear rarely, and then only briefly, in both the published and the unpublished letters. And yet when we closely consider the Charles Town letter itself, in relation to the rest of the book, it becomes no clearer how African Americans, bound or free, will figure into Crèvecoeur's American kaleidoscope. Nor is it evident how James will incorporate his experience in Charles Town into his larger life. The principles or themes of stasis and fixity associated with the work's moments of pastoral sanctuary and its tendency toward moral escapism here become a positive affliction, an aporia, an impasse. If in Letter XII we see James in frantic motion, in Letter IX we seem him in frantic paralysis.

Crèvecoeur opens the Charles Town letter with a description of the sumptuous riches and lush climate of South Carolina, in language that concentrates republican and agrarian fears of the debilitating vice and dissipation associated with idle wealth. He also registers a distinctly Christian-sounding suspicion of those elite classes of society that "have reached the *ne plus ultra* of worldly felicity" (161). Then, characteristically, he turns to the legal customs and structures of the place he is describing, and writes that the three principal classes, the lawyers, planters, and merchants, are "more properly lawgivers than interpreters of the law," and asks, "who can tell where this may lead in a future day?" (162). Even before we get to the question of slavery, Charles Town appears as a place where the social contract has been perverted, in large measure because of the luxury and dissipation associated with its tropical climate.[17]

Crèvecoeur next establishes a contrast between the gay life of the city and the miserable lot of the slaves in the country, fashioning several images that will become—not necessarily because of his text—part of the long-term arsenal of abolitionist rhetoric in the coming decades. He imagines the pastoral-georgic life as corrupted and polluted by a slave society, where "no one thinks with compassion of those showers of sweat and of tears which from the bodies of Africans daily drop and moisten the ground they till." He pictures the innocence of Africa and decries the slave trade's devastating effects on "some harmless, peaceable African neighbourhood where dwelt innocent people who even knew not but that all men were black." And he recoils at the slave auction's violation of the separate ranks of humans and beasts, where "arranged like horses at a fair, they are branded like cattle" (162). These three images—slavery as pollution, Africa as paradise, and the unnatural conflation of species—would appear with increasing frequency in antislavery and humanitarian literature during the early nineteenth century. Crucially, however, James does not leave off at this point; the rest of the letter is an agonized meditation on race and slavery that reveals profound contradictions in Crèvecoeur's thinking and illustrates the philosophical gymnastics that human bondage forced many writers to undertake.

In James's anguished question that frames the rest of the letter—"Oh, Nature, where art thou?"—Crèvecoeur expresses the juridical view of natural law, with its emphasis on the infallibility of a cosmic moral order. This moral order is reflected in an intrinsically benevolent human nature, and slavery therefore stands as a criminal deviation from both. Accordingly, James makes a sentimental appeal to parental affection, lamenting that slave parents cannot "partake of those ineffable sensations with which Nature inspires the hearts of fathers and mothers" (163) and insisting that "those hearts in which such noble dispositions can grow are then like ours" (165). Slavery, in contrast, derives from the master's "interest" and "to that god all the laws of Nature must give way"; insensitivity to the slaves' suffering, for instance, results not from innate depravity but from "force of custom" (164). So far, Crèvecoeur's argument lies squarely within the mainstream of eighteenth-century antislavery rhetoric: Slavery violates both human nature and the natural order, it perverts human relations, and it offends the sensibilities of those people actuated by sympathy rather than mere interest. Crèvecoeur does not stop here, however; the letter takes a strange and dramatic turn away from this relatively safe rhetoric and into unfamiliar territory, as Crèvecoeur offers a dubious defense of northern slavery and as he begins to despair of the benevolence of nature.

If slavery is an "unnatural" phenomenon, it stands to reason that it varies from culture to culture. Ergo, Crèvecoeur attacks southern slavery by comparing it to a more lenient northern variety (as Iwan contrasts it with a more lenient Russian serfdom, where "they are more properly civil than domestic slaves; they are attached to the soil on which they live" [191]). Even as James calls for the eventual emancipation of the slaves, he represents their lot as relatively benign in the northern states, where they "are the companions of our labours, and . . . are not obliged to work more than white people," and where they "participate in many of the benefits of our society without being obliged to bear any of its burthens" (165). Perhaps this helps explain Crèvecoeur's comments elsewhere about the desirability of African labor and his seeming blindness to the contradiction between slavery and both the freehold concept and his own humanitarianism. But by abandoning an outright condemnation of all forms of slavery, Crèvecoeur suggests that an "unnatural" institution might, under certain circumstances, give rise to good, or at least that the moral consequences of violating the natural order are mitigable. He also seems to imply in these passages that the true moral crime of slavery might lie in offending the sensibilities of humanity rather than in violating the law of nature.

This thread once pulled, Crèvecoeur's antislavery argument quickly begins to unravel. The "unnatural" institution of slavery has, seemingly paradoxically, the effect of "naturally" stimulating the feelings of anger and resentment. Slaves "are left in their original and untutored state, that very state wherein the natural propensities of revenge and warm passions are so soon kindled" (166). Yet perhaps we have no paradox at all, for those same passions could have impelled the planters to cruelty and avarice in the first place, and hence the whole system of bondage might result "naturally" from the proclivities of human "nature." Here James broaches an entirely new line of thought in the book: that slavery deserves our condemnation not because it violates nature but because it fails to rise above nature. Contract theory, we have seen, tended to take as its starting point the view that human nature, being naturally acquisitive, needed a system of enforceable agreements in order to bind individuals together into a workable social arrangement; through such an arrangement people could rise above nature. But while it moved ideas of consent and freedom to the center of political theory, it secularized and reinforced the Christian doctrine of the fallen nature of humanity. As James continues to ruminate on the presence of slavery in human society, he begins to despair of human nature, seeing it not as perfectible but evil, not as a tabula rasa but as intrinsically violent and avaricious: "[O]ne would almost believe that principles of action in man, considered as the first agent of this planet, to be poisoned in their most essential parts. . . . [M]an, an animal of prey, seems to have rapine and the love of bloodshed implanted in his heart. . . . [M]en, like the elements, are always at war" (167–68). In the face of such despair, James's earlier efforts to denounce slavery as unnatural prove increasingly untenable.

Yet does not slavery still represent a violation of "Nature" in the cosmic sense? Here James quails as well, asking whether there is "no superintending power who conducts the moral operations of the world, as well as the physical?" Whether that superintending power is a deity manifest in nature or Nature itself, the Jeffersonian theodicy that evil is epiphenomenal collapses, as humanity is abandoned to a senseless chaos, "to all the errors, the follies, and the miseries which their most frantic rage and their most dangerous vices and passions can produce" (167). Far from an absence of moral conflict in the universe, moral conflict rages unchecked, and undirected by any greater purpose. In the absence or abeyance of natural law, on what moral or religious grounds would a person then stand in order to denounce slavery? Moreover, in James's despair, the visible face of Nature—the natural world, its variety of climates, environments, and creatures—seems to lose its aesthetic, emotional, and spiritual goodness. "Look at the poisonous soil of the equator," he tells his reader, "at those putrid slimy tracks, teeming with horrid monsters, the enemies of the human race" (169). Upending the Enlightenment doctrine that various populations or races have been fitted to their particular climates for a reason—namely, happiness and survival—James now observes that "each climate produces . . . vices and miseries peculiar to its latitude" (169). Nature might be more generous in some places, yet even there we find "the poison of slavery" (170). Surveying in imagination the ancient world—Egypt, the fields of the Tigris and Euphrates, the East Indies—James writes that "all these must to the geographical eye seem as if intended for terrestrial paradises . . . yet there in general we find the most wretched people in the world" (170). Will international travel and trade, which James had said "ought to unite" the world, be able to do more than multiply its miseries? Is the pastoral dream which promised a life of timeless felicity a mere will-o-the-wisp, discredited not only by the fact of history but by the moral inadequacy of both Nature and human nature, and practically hindered by the universality of pestilence, famine, and infertility? Does juridical natural law even apply? From the perspective of cold science, James suspects that slavery might represent but one expression of the underlying natural laws of competition, greed, and violence.

These reflections prepare for James's encounter with the caged slave, which closes the Charles Town letter and which inspired his distraught commentary in the first place. He opens the scene on a note at once pastoral and natural-historical: "I resolved to go on foot [to dine with a planter], sheltered in a small path leading through a pleasant wood. I was leisurely travelling along, attentively examining some peculiar plants which I had collected" (171). Since the passage comes on the heels of his despairing comments, the reader, though not James himself, knows this idyllic moment cannot last. Presently he happens upon the cage, in which a slave languishes, birds and insects feeding on his body. The scene, of course, has generated volumes of critical commentary, often in terms of its fablelike style and its ostensible narrative significance. Here I will confine myself to three essential points. First, the animals that devour the slave inhabit, for James, the same moral world as the "ever-raging ocean" off Nantucket (157) and the grasshoppers on the farm, "agents of desolation" that "Eat the substance of y' Good & the wicked indiscriminately."[18] It is a place of moral uncertainty, in which the all-devouring voracity of nature admits of no easy disposition under the usual moral frameworks. Second, this moral condition seems reflected in a sudden diminution or arrest of James's power of moral agency. When he fires at the birds to scare them off, he is "actuated by an involuntary motion of [his] hands more than by any design of [his] mind"; he is "arrested by the power of affright and terror"; he "involuntarily [contemplates] the fate of this Negro"; he is "unable" to commit a mercy-killing even though armed. Finally, at dinner, James learns the cause of the slave's punishment (he supposedly killed an overseer), hears the planter's excuse of "self-preservation" and the other "arguments generally made use of to justify the practice" of slavery, and declines to burden his reader with them. But he has already raised those arguments in their most fundamental form: that slavery expresses rather than transgresses nature.

These observations force a pointed interpretive question: Does James's encounter with slavery *result* in anything other than metaphysical and visceral horror? In his vision of a universe lacking moral foundation, and in his own inability to act for an immediate moral good, has he rendered his own antislavery principles arbitrary and anemic? Such questions reveal how the usual literary relationship between narrative structure and character development is conspicuously inapplicable to *Letters from an American Farmer.* The work's organizational incoherence prevents Crèvecoeur from developing the passages on slavery into something more than a passing anecdote and accompanying meditation, however powerful they may be. James experiences no progressive character growth, letter to letter, that would reveal more about Crèvecoeur's perspective on slavery and enable contemporary readers to witness a model of political and philosophical maturation.

Ordinarily one would look to Letters X, XI, and XII, or to a chronologically subsequent phase of the narrator's life, to assess the impact on him of such a powerful moment. The latter option is not really viable, since James lives in an essentially timeless present, in which even his final decision to head west is a prospective one. But what about the final three letters? Can we make sense of them in terms of the emotional and metaphysical earthquake of Letter IX? Any interpretation beyond their significance in relation to the whole work, but of their specifically *narrative* significance, would have to set aside questions of intention and rely instead on the deconstructive logic of the text, or on the reader's possible experience of them as a kind of aftermath to Letter IX.

In Letter IX, nature imposes itself upon James's consciousness with undeniable force; he comes to recognize it as an independent agent, something to be reckoned with. Acting now in an almost subjective way, it forces him to revise his operative assumptions not only about the existence of a universal moral order but also about its apprehensibility. No longer the benevolent, all-providing maternal figure or the convenient grab bag of raw materials, but an inexplicable, probably indifferent, possibly malevolent force, nature defies the wonted categories of perception and experience. James's very grammar shifts; the subject Nature now takes active, transitive verbs, "refusing" as well as "giving." As erstwhile assets become self-sovereign—as objects become subjects—the principles of property and stewardship at the heart of the freehold agrarian ideal lose much of their power. James's realization of that sovereignty returns us to Raynal's *Histoire Philosophique et Politique*: Both Crèvecoeur and the Abbè envision sudden revolt, one of slaves against masters and one of nature against human control; both are potential sources of resistance and violence to ownership. For James, the challenge to his worldview and self-confidence is more abstract and for that reason more difficult to respond to. We do not exactly witness him recovering from the shock of having his eyes opened to the moral ambiguity of nature, but the following letter, "On Snakes; and on the Humming-bird," gives glimpses of how such a recovery might occur, of the development of a restored relationship to nature that avoids pastoral complacency on one side and disillusioned panic on the other.

Commentators on *Letters from an American Farmer* rarely remark on Letter X but usually pass over it as an anomaly stuck in between the major letters on slavery and the Revolution. It describes the behavior of American copperheads, rattlesnakes, and hummingbirds, and closes with an account of a fierce battle between two snakes, in terms that at first remind us of the natural-historical technique and social commentary of the early letters. The chapter's distinguishing feature, however, is a studied neutrality of perspective: nothing on the satanic associations of snakes, nothing about the use value of nature, no parables drawn from the fauna and flora, and no horror in the face of otherness and violence. In place of the "putrid slimy tracks, teeming with horrid monsters," as James puts it in Letter IX, we have comparatively bland passages drained of moral judgment: "The southern provinces are the countries where Nature has formed the greatest variety of alligators, snakes, serpents, and scorpions from the smallest size up to the pine barren" (174). Similarly, the violent snake-fight—a battle to the death, without apparent meaning—occupies the same order of experience as the "ever-raging ocean," the selfish wren in Letter II (56–57), and the carnivorous birds and insects in Letter IX, but James eschews interpretive commentary and maintains his equipoise, closing the episode reportorially: "The victor no sooner perceived its enemy incapable of farther resistance than, abandoning it to the current, it returned on shore and disappeared" (180). To a degree unequaled in the rest of the book, James experiences in this letter a shift in perception that allows him to see the beauty of natural processes, however violent or inexplicable. The selfishness and "spirit of injustice" of the wren in Letter II is the occasion for a lesson, is "proof that [instinct and reason] border very near on one another" (57). In Letter X, however, even as James poses the same question of the hummingbird's destructive "irascibility" ("Where do passions find room in so diminutive a body?" [178]), he declines to offer an answer or a lesson. Instead, he focuses our attention on the artistry of its creation: "On this little bird Nature has profusely lavished her most splendid colours. . . . [I]t is a miniature work of our Great Parent, who seems to have formed it the smallest, and at the same time the most beautiful of the winged species" (178).

Respect and mutuality, Crèvecoeur implies, should govern the relationship between humanity and nature, with people responsible not only for "improving" the land and reaping its bounty, but understanding nature's subtler meanings and recognizing its ultimate independence. We see glimmers in *Letters*, especially in Letter X, of what Michel Serres has termed "the natural contract," or an ethical reorientation on the part of humankind that "would set aside mastery and possession [of nature] in favor of admiring attention, reciprocity, contemplation, and respect; where knowledge would no longer imply property, nor action mastery."[19] In very similar terms, Neil Everdnen calls for a recognition of the essential ontological otherness of nature but also its expression of "subjectivity, willing, valuation, and meaning," and this recognition obliges us to think, though within inevitable limits, beyond or before the symbolic language we have evolved to describe the natural. "Every question we ask, every solution we devise," writes Evernden, "bespeaks mastery, never mystery: they are incompatible. Yet wildness, otherness, *is* mystery incarnate."[20]

In some such spirit James, with reverence but not naïveté, writes of the lethal black snake: "I admire it much and never kill it, though its formidable length and appearance often get the better of the philosophy of some people, particularly Europeans" (174).[21] And he laments the "open war" on the rattlesnake, which threatens its extinction (177). The possibility of a natural contract, of a redeemed and reciprocal relationship with nature, appears only fitfully in *Letters*, but takes the form of an art that faithfully expresses nature's complex truths and humanity's complex responses. At moments James can see, and creatively balance, the beauty and violence and the meaning and chaos in nature. The natural contract goes a distance toward reconciling the terrifying insights of science (into, say, those climates "where masses of sulphur, bitumen, and electrical fire . . . [hover and burst] over a globe threatened with dissolution" [169–70]) with the emotional and spiritual comforts of the pastoral ideal, the "pleasant farm" (48). It suggests a way of moving beyond self-emancipation, whether from culture "into" nature or vice versa, to arrive at an imaginative emancipation of nature itself—or a recognition that nature has always been and will always remain free.

The political implications of such a renewal of vision are, potentially, far reaching and profound. In Letter X, James—speaking under his breath—almost articulates a theodicy that does not, in Boorstin's words, "[empty] the universe of dramatic conflict" but rests on the principle of taking the violence in nature on its own terms without forsaking one's human, moral responsibility to shun or prevent violence. Yet although

James—for a fleeting moment—can see the beauty in nature's internecine wars and at the same time condemn humanity's violence against nature, he never rises to the level of active, sustained opposition to humanity's violence to humanity. His near paralysis in front of the cage is the last we see of his encounter with slavery, and the topic comes up again only briefly, once during the Russian Iwan's conversation with Bartram, and once in the final letter, when James decides to manumit the people he calls "my Negroes" (213). The former adds nothing of substance to the discussion of slavery in Letter IX, and James's decision to liberate raises some difficult questions: Has the Revolution merely prompted this step, rather than his reflections on slavery? Given the circumstances, how will his former slaves fare in the American "asylum of freedom"? The narrative dislinearity of the book, however, means that we do not get answers; without a structuring arc of experience to follow, we cannot determine how James will assimilate the insights of Letter IX. The dynamics of freedom and progress, those central tenets of the liberal subject, simply dissipate in the formlessness.

Ultimately, slavery emerges as the unassimilable fact of *Letters from an American Farmer*, as it would prove for American society. In Crèvecoeur's treatment, it is transgressive of nature and yet representative of the darkest forces of nature, and this equivocation not only gives the text its puzzling energy but inaugurates a theme of doubt and division in antislavery thought that will run throughout the works taken up in this study. *Letters* offers no brief against slavery, but it exposes the ideological contradictions present at the nation's founding, undermining the American self-image on two levels: as an agrarian Eden, and as a place founded on benevolent natural law. It acts as a springboard for the work's most profound examination of the forces of nature and as a wrench in James's vision of the pastoral-agrarian dream, compelling an inner reorientation toward the meanings of nature. It illustrates the central and intractable problems of theodicy: of recognizing both the evil and the good in nature, of understanding human cruelty and misery as parts of the natural order, and of avoiding the moral debilitation that naturalizing evil potentially entails. And while the work's narrative incoherence signals Crèvecoeur's disinterest in organizing these themes into a coherent political statement, that literary form says more about the nation's collective unwillingness or inability to deal with slavery than would the most outraged antislavery tract.

Olaudah Equiano and the Paradox of History

In 1782, when the first edition of *Letters from an American Farmer* appeared in London, Olaudah Equiano was a thirty-seven-year-old British citizen living in the same city, working as a servant, attending the Church of England, and planning a way to return to Africa as a missionary. Whether Equiano read or knew of Crèvecoeur's work remains an intriguing but unanswerable question. However, while Crèvecoeur adjusted to life after the American Revolution and the loss of his idyll, Equiano set himself to puzzling through the same sorts of questions that *Letters* had addressed, questions involving his relation to slavery, to nature, and to history.

If Crèvecoeur's ideal American farmer embodies geographic rootedness, historical stability, and economic self-sufficiency, the Anglo-African we encounter in the pages of Equiano's *Interesting Narrative* epitomizes the peripatetic, commercially oriented identity formed in the alembic of international trade. Progressivist in mood and ideology, the *Interesting Narrative* charts a network of movements across time, culture, and space: from childhood to adulthood, slavery to freedom, heathenism to Christianity, Guinea to England. All are figured as forward motion, and such momentum carries racial as well as personal significance, for Equiano seeks to embody and represent (in the sense of both sign and spokesman) the capacity of Africans to participate in the onward march of civilization. At the same time, the *Interesting Narrative* registers the personal and psychic loss associated with the passage of time and the course of history. This struggle, at once emotional and intellectual, between progressivism and lament asserts itself as a narrative tension running throughout the text, particularly in Equiano's treatment of the natural world.

Given Equiano's consciously divided cultural identity—he simultaneously claimed membership as an Englishman and as an Ibo—the representation of nature in the *Interesting Narrative* reflects the characteristic rivalry in the text (and in Black Atlantic literature generally) between protest and accommodation, as African and European practices and attitudes toward nature contend for expression. More specifically, in considering the literary technique of the *Narrative* in light of Equiano's ideological and emotional relationship to nature, as both an ex-slave and bourgeois British citizen, I have in mind a series of related questions: To what degree are the contradictions in the text debilitating or energizing? At what cost comes his commitment to economic liberalism? How does Equiano present the relationship between his self-authorized entry into European history and the natural environment of his youth? What are the relationships in the text between nature, religious faith, and narrative technique?

We can approach this last question, and thereby the entire problem I have framed here, by articulating more sharply the phenomenological significance of narrative. David Carr has argued that narrative, far from representing an artificial imposition upon life (as Paul Ricoeur and others have maintained), is a conceptual structure that "pervades our very experience of time and social existence" so that historical and fictional narratives are "extensions and configurations" of reality rather than distortions of it. For both individuals and communities, narrative provides a sense of the coherence of life, of the overarching story and subsidiary stories that people continually tell themselves and others about who they are, what they are doing, where they have been. Carr goes on to identify a "narrative social time" that depends on the acknowledged membership by individuals in a group and consists in the "self-reflective social narration" or collective *besinnung* (Heidegger's term) in which members of the group engage. Two crucial points stand out. The first regards the heightened importance of autobiographical stock-taking during or after periods of crisis: "The most striking occasions for [self-reflection] are those radical conversions, usually religious or political, in which a new view of life, of oneself, and of one's future projects and prospects requires a break with and reinterpretation of one's past." The second is that the narrative character of individual and social experience might not in fact describe a universal human reality but only that of Western culture, particularly beginning in the eighteenth century. Carr warns against considering the narrative conception of time as absolutely valid, or viewing non-Western beliefs regarding time as efforts to deny an objective, narratively structured reality, as this leads naturally to an evaluative dismissal of "peoples without history" and presumes a developmental scheme with "primitive" societies trailing "advanced" ones. The supposed unity of historical existence and historical narrative awareness may only characterize Western thinking, while other societies likely have other ways of confronting the "specter of temporal chaos, the meaninglessness of mere unstructured sequence."[22]

Taken together, these two points raise a fascinating problem. What if the crisis or conversion an individual experiences involves not just politics or religion but also the adoption of a new sense of historical time through assimilation to a previously foreign culture? In the case of a person moving from a nonnarrative to a narrative sense of time, the need for linearly organizational *besinnung* would presumably exist only in the changed self, not the "original" self—how, then, would that person represent the preconversion state? Does Equiano evince a form of double consciousness caused by the clash of two belief systems regarding historical time? Can the wrenching difficulty of his "Europeanization" be attributed not only to his radical religious conversion but also in part to a concomitant new understanding of his relation to time? And if so, how might the natural world, with its complex relation to cultural systems of time and human temporal consciousness, provide a means of charting Equiano's evolving emotional and religious life?

These questions rest on the premise that Equiano had some "original" sense of time as a child that was subsequently challenged, modified, or supplanted by a Western temporal consciousness. But reconstructing African beliefs regarding time and history, particularly those of the eighteenth century from the vantage point of the twenty-first, presents a formidable array of theoretical and methodological difficulties. Not least, the very project of theorizing philosophical systems of time is historically implicated in the imposition of European values and beliefs upon Africa. Additionally, since the eighteenth-century Ibo had not yet developed written records, Ibo beliefs during that period are necessarily the subject of oral, external, or retrospective treatments—all of which create additional layers of mediation between observer and object.[23] These difficulties, moreover, are compounded by the intrinsic uncertainties in trying to assess the influences of culture, even where they can be identified, upon an individual; and any "independent," phenomenologically oriented assessment of Equiano's internalization of African mores and beliefs can have only suggestive rather than probative value. In the final analysis, we stand on the firmest ground in considering how Equiano constructs himself in his autobiography as a historical agent with a particular understanding of the role of time (and nature) in human life. His "Europeanization," I will therefore argue, entailed a conversion (possibly genuine, certainly performed) to an essentially Christian view of history, and yet it also created a countervailing, quite poignant desire to insulate his past from the depredations of time.

At this point, we need to take note of the possibility that Equiano was not born and raised in Africa at all. In his recent biography of Equiano, Vincent Carretta makes the case—a scrupulously documented and highly persuasive case—that Equiano was probably born in South Carolina, based on a baptismal certificate and two ship's musters, on an explication of various discrepancies and problems in the chronology that Equiano gives in the *Interesting Narrative*, and on an absence of any public reference to "Olaudah Equiano" before the publication date of the first edition of his autobiography.[24] Although doubts about Equiano's representation of an African childhood were already in the air, Caretta's detective work promises to exert a seismic influence on studies of Equiano and his autobiography.[25] Notwithstanding certain ambiguities and caesuras in the evidence, the new information should, above all, prevent readers of the *Narrative* from automatically accepting Equiano's claim of African nativity.[26] Clearly, given the charged issue of authenticity that has always surrounded the slave narrative genre, suggesting that both the early chapters of the *Interesting Narrative* and the author's public persona might amount to nothing less than fabrication should not be done lightly, but with an eye toward the unique pressures faced by Equiano and other testifiers to the horrors of slavery. Still, in approaching his autobiography we should regard Equiano's representation of African culture not necessarily as a matter of memory, but of design, and his "Africanness" not necessarily as a psychological and cultural fact, but as an identity assumed for the purpose of heightening his "authority to speak as a victim and eye-witness of slavery."[27] Particularly relevant here are questions of Equiano's relation to an African culture he may have experienced only in its New World form, of the murky distinction between real and represented memory, and of the malleability and usability of the past.

Elaborating these matters of temporality and historical consciousness in the *Interesting Narrative* clarifies our understanding of Equiano's double consciousness, of his self-authorized entry into Western civilization and into an ideological and philosophical framework built around ideas of forward progress. At the same time, this perspective enables us to appreciate more sensitively Equiano's psychological and emotional relationship to his past in general and to his childhood in particular—a relationship which runs against the narrative's progressivist grain. While the *Interesting Narrative* expresses a Christian sense of the linearity of past and present, it becomes clear that Equiano's abiding feeling of attachment to an Africa of which he was dispossessed (whether personally or ancestrally) works against his commitment to irreversible progress. This self-division plays out in the *Interesting Narrative* through a complex interplay of the natural and the cultural, as Equiano's racial project stretches from a pastoral African idyll to a prospective commercial enterprise in Sierra Leone.

The relationship between "history" and "nature" was a central theoretical preoccupation of the eighteenth century, as philosophers and social theorists developed normative models of history that defined forward linear progress as the proper course of human society. Among their other consequences, these schema directly influenced the progressivist ideology that informed antislavery's vision of Africa's future. This Enlightenment progressivism could draw on both religious and secular vocabularies—on the Christian belief that human history unfolds in accordance with providential design and on natural science's revelations of predictable cause-and-effect relationships in the physical world and of the processes of organic growth.[28] Despite the inspiration it could take from natural science, however, social science did not ally human chronology with natural time, for Western thought has long divided nature from history, as from spirit, and assigned them distinct temporal modes, the cyclical and the teleological. This deeply, if not uniquely, Judeo-Christian perspective drew originally on the biblical dynamic of prophecy and fulfillment, and it expresses the belief that divine purpose ultimately guides and governs historical process. Theophanies—those events seen or experienced in the natural world which reveal that purpose to human consciousness—structure time and shed light on the direction of life, enabling interpretation of both the past and the future.[29] Crucially, this understanding of temporality has had very real consequences because it informs people's view of their place in the world, and has therefore conditioned Western attitudes and policies toward other cultures. For progressive historical movement does not, from this perspective, necessarily characterize all human societies; or more precisely, an *awareness* of that movement does not. Accordingly, Western historians and anthropologists have routinely represented non-Christian societies not only as excessively "natural" but also as lying outside of history, perhaps even willfully so.[30]

Equiano's representation of Ibo culture in the first two chapters of the *Interesting Narrative* reflects that philosophical context. Here, he draws upon several antislavery works, specifically, and more broadly, upon the contemporary European portrait of Africa and its inhabitants emerging from travelers' journals, traders' accounts, and the syntheses and interpretations prepared by editors or compilers.[31] As polemic, Equiano's African idyll works in much the same fashion as do his various sources. Coming directly out of the rhetorical tradition outlined in chapter 1, the society described in these chapters amounts to a refutation of proslavery allegations of the chaotic, savage character of African life. Crafting an African pastoral that draws on both agrarian values and the fantasy of a golden age, Equiano invokes the myth of tropical luxuriousness only to the degree that it reinforces his image of an idyllic land, carefully avoiding any suggestion of environmentally determined laziness or savagery.

Equiano makes his own "account of Guinea," however, personal and autobiographical, the originary moment of a life story composed retrospectively yet oriented proleptically toward an envisioned future. Where the era's travel writings and antislavery tracts typically present Africa in a timeless, abstract way, Equiano locates it on a continuum of experience stretching from his childhood to some undetermined point in the future. Stylistically, moreover, in his rendering of African life Equiano slides back and forth between the present and past tense and between the first and third person. Usually combining the third-person and present tense (probably an echo of the travel narratives he knew), Equiano gives an impression on one hand of a living, vibrant society, but on the other hand of his own distance from it. The first-person past tense, in contrast, creates a sense of provincialism or obsolescence but also establishes a more personal connection between the author and his past. This double ambiguity, moreover, establishes a tension between represented memory and present knowledge that will run throughout Equiano's emotional and intellectual relationship to Africa.

Although Equiano, like Benezet, has faith in the future commercial and religious prospects of Africa, he suggests in the early chapters that its present life runs outside the main currents of history. The religion of the biblical patriarchs "appeared to have shed upon us a ray of its glory, though broken and spent in its passage, or eclipsed by the cloud with which time, tradition, and ignorance might have enveloped it"[32] (44). The passage of profane time here implies no upward progression toward a more sacred state; tradition, connoting not just credulity and superstition but a kind of stagnation or slavery to the past, swirls like an eddy, following its own rhythms rather than the grand flowing history of human progress. And temporal and spatial isolation go hand in hand; the geographic situation of the Ibo creates a simplicity not only of customs but of history itself. "The manners and government of a people who have little commerce with other countries are generally very simple; and the history of what passes in one family or village may serve as a specimen of the whole nation" (32). His distinction also appears to involve the undifferentiated history of "primitives" as opposed to civilization's complex history, individual or local history as mere synecdoche rather than as the structuring components of a purposive collective trajectory. In combination, then, Christianity and commerce represent civilizing processes pointing toward a dual historical telos: the salvation of individuals from profane time and the salvation of societies from the backwaters of time.

Equiano's discussion of Ibo religion, which accords fairly closely with the findings of modern anthropology, touches on the people's conceptions of time.[33] Like their belief that the Creator "lives in the sun," Equiano represents Ibo temporal understanding as rooted in the natural world: "We compute the year from the day on which the sun crosses the line, and, on its setting that evening, there is a general shout throughout the land" (40–41). Festivals and rituals are similarly organized around the rhythms of nature: "They have many offerings, particularly at full moons; generally two at harvest, before the fruits are taken out of the ground" (41). These passages correspond roughly with Austin Shelton's division of the temporal organization of Ibo life into "natural time" and "ritual time." The former depends on the solar, lunar, and seasonal cycles and is essentially circular: "Annual life flows cyclically in the alternate seasons of dryness and rains, of dormancy and growth. This is the basic pattern of the northern Igbo worldview, the model of the universe in which dwell the dead, the living, and the unborn." Ritual time, though partly based on natural time, as in harvest festivals, is also governed by spirits and therefore discerned through divination. But in daily life, such ritual time matters less than "the cyclic pattern of human existence conceived broadly, for time becomes in this an endlessness in which one focuses his temporal attention upon that period between attainment of adulthood and death."[34]

Equiano, in short, describes a system of time that does not sharply divide past, present, and future. Significantly, past and future are *available* to the Ibo in a way that they will not be for Equiano during the rest of the narrative. Divination and the interpretation of omens render the future legible; its reading falls to the "priests and magicians, or wise men" who "calculated our time, and foretold events" (42), including Equiano's own good fortune, if we can call it that. As the future is neither the province nor production of an inscrutable Christian god, it yields itself up to human knowledge, at least in its rough outlines. Similarly, the past remains, to a degree, recoverable. Death leads not to a remote and inaccessible Christian afterlife, but to an active form of new life, a participation in the affairs of the material world. Ancestors and others who lived in the past are still temporally and spatially present: the Ibo "believe [those souls that are not transmigrated] always attend them, and guard them from the bad spirits of their foes" (40). The Ibo, moreover, gather up the past into the present through the ritual recreation of bygone or historical events. "[E]very great event, such as a triumphant return from battle, or other cause of public rejoicing, is celebrated in public dances," each of which "represents some interesting scene of real life . . . and as the subject is generally founded on some recent event, it is therefore *ever new*" (34, emphasis added). Such ritual, combined with the rites of sacrifice and marriage that Equiano describes, effects what Mircea Eliade calls "the abolition of time through the imitation of archetypes and the repetition of paradigmatic gestures."[35] In Eliade's terms for describing this worldview, common events acquire meaning and value through their participation in a mythic reality that transcends the passage of time, or that regenerates time. In like fashion, by recreating the acts of an ancestor, hero, or god, an individual can project himself out of profane time into the realm of mythic time.

Eliade's model of "archaic ontology," though theoretically obsolete, nevertheless highlights Equiano's different form of self-projection into time. He does not, after all, see the events of his life as the recreation of a mythical Ibo past. On one hand, he rejects any idea that his willed actions are terribly important: "I offer here the history of neither a saint, a hero, nor a tyrant" (31). On the other hand, what he regards as unique or special about his life occurs precisely because he has left Ibo culture: "[W]hen I compare my lot with that of most of my countrymen, I regard myself as a *particular favourite of Heaven*, and acknowledge the mercies of Providence in every occurrence of my life" (31, original emphasis). Instead, Equiano's self-projection into time will consist in shaping the events of his life into narrative form—a narrative form in which the individual's history is significant insofar as it participates in the progressive history of humanity and the teleological history of ultimate redemption.

He neither willed nor expected, however, his "entry" into Western history, writing instead that history itself has violently intruded upon him, in the form of slave traders who kidnap Equiano and his sister as children. As in *Letters from an American Farmer*, the disruption of the idyll traumatizes the narrator, and as in Benezet's *Some Historical Account of Guinea*, the pastoral-agrarian harmony of African society heightens the sense of violation. This marks not only a fateful personal moment for Equiano, who invests his departure from Africa with profound cultural and emotional significance, but a fateful moment in the text, as these energies—the ideological and the affective—begin to diverge. Narratively, this divergence manifests as a difficult-to-negotiate split between the adult's and the child's perspectives, and congruently between Equiano's representations of Western culture and African nature.

Between the time of Equiano's capture and his first encounter with Europeans, as the traders transport the captives cross-country toward the coast, images and ideas of the natural world proliferate in the text. No longer the rich and yielding farmland tended by the agrarian Ibo, nature now plays different roles and takes on different meanings as the eleven-year-old boy's world changes. New and strange, nature terrifies for the first time: "I was now carried to the left of the sun's rising, through many dreary wastes and dismal woods, amidst the hideous roarings of wild beasts" (50). And yet nature also provides an escape or hideout from an oppressive society, a motif which had already emerged in other slave narratives, including those of John Marrant and James Gronniosaw: "[T]he houses and villages were skirted with woods, or shrubberies, and the bushes were so thick, that a man could readily conceal himself in them, so as to elude the strictest search" (49).[36] In the town of Tinmah, nature grows beautiful again, but now its beauty deceives. As in Crèvecoeur's Charles Town, natural luxuriousness gilds social depravity, and wealth rises from a foundation of slavery. Finally, the practical relation of societies to the natural world begins to change as Equiano approaches the coast. Specifically, the level of technology increases in proportion with the extent of these cultures' dealings with the Europeans; one society, for instance, "cooked . . . in iron pots, and had European cutlasses and cross bows" (53). None of this, however, prepares the young Equiano for his first sight of Europeans. His encounter with the slave vessel moored off the Guinea coast marks the separating moment for Equiano, his simultaneous plunge into Western consciousness and into a bildungsroman he could never have anticipated.

When he boards the slave ship that waits offshore, his shock at the experience—at simply beholding the vessel, the white men who sail it, and the sea itself—parallels Farmer James's shock at stumbling across the caged slave outside Charles Town. In both cases, the narrator comes into sudden, horrifying contact with the other side of the color line, and in both cases his understanding of what is natural and what is unnatural undergoes a profound reworking. If a phenomenological "remove" from culture to nature can reorient a human figure's understanding of the cultural world, the young Equiano seems to undergo two removes: first from Ibo culture to the natural terrain along the coast, and then to the European culture he encounters aboard ship. This sequence matters because Equiano does not simply come to view Ibo culture differently but arrives at nothing less than an understanding of the multiplicity or contingency of the very concept of culture.

In *Letters*, Farmer James's "reorientation" vis-à-vis culture proves uncertain, fleeting, discontinuous. There, the lack of a coherent characterological narrative means that the temporal distance separating the experience from the telling of the experience yields no insight into the larger consequences of James's encounter with slavery. In the *Narrative*, by contrast, Equiano's encounter with the slave ship and Europeans is the rendered object of a parallactic view created by two coexisting perspectives, the child's and the adult's. Throughout the scene Equiano weaves the complementary strands of original experience and retrospective narration; his representation of objects and events is at once the product of youthful wonder and mature interpretation. This parallax enables the author to defamiliarize the slave ship for a European readership—to make it as monstrous and frightening as it would appear to a child—while governing the meaning of the encounter according to adult rhetorical exigencies.

The adult Equiano records his original responses to the novelty of Europeans and sea travel primarily through the category of "nature"—

nature as both the physical nonhuman world and as the spiritual realm that governs the proper behavior of and relations between material objects or beings and that provides the only standard for judging something "unnatural." On one level, the boy reacts to a natural world more vast and complex than he had ever known. The very water of the ocean frightens him for his never having seen it before, and one can only imagine his first impressions of flying fish. Young Equiano also observes how the Europeans have mastered their natural environment through such technological innovations as the quadrant, through the domestication of animals, particularly horses, and through the reduction of human slaves to the rank of animals, "like so many sheep in a fold" (60).

But against this new awareness of the diversity and scope of tangible nature, what accounts for the seeming unnaturalness of the Europeans, who make the boy feel as if he "had gotten into a world of bad spirits"? To what extent does his sense of unnatural whiteness (both physical and behavioral) reflect a child's wide-eyed innocence, and to what extent is it a rhetorical maneuver on the part of an author looking back to, reflecting on, a clash of cultures? Both perspectives are vital, for the incident marks the opening up of a division between "nature" and "culture" that also serves to divide the narrator's mature consciousness from his youthful one. For the child, Ibo culture is "natural" because that is all he knows; he has nothing against which he might judge it as unnatural. The encounter with another culture thus registers as an unnatural experience; the English seem like "spirits," the anchor like "some spell or magic they put in the water" (57). The boy can only assimilate the experience through current understanding, where what is not "natural" must be supernatural, or magical. For the adult Equiano, however, experience with many different societies means that the categories of nature and culture are no longer synonymous. In other words, he knows that what is not natural is only in some cases supernatural (and then it must accord with Christian truth), but that in other cases it is cultural and only *seems* supernatural to the ignorant and superstitious, or to a child. The incident marks the moment when the child's innocent sense of wholeness fractures. In Blakean fashion, the perspective of innocence necessarily informs the scene, and yet can only be represented from the perspective of experience; the two modes of consciousness coexist and reinforce one another, and in that way create the parallax necessary to convey the encounter's full meaning for Equiano's life.

That full meaning begins to emerge when we consider that Equiano's doubleness of perspective is both temporal and individual on one level, as are all acts of memory, and cultural and geographic on another, as are the memories of exiles. The adult man looks back to a younger self, and the cosmopolitan British citizen looks back to his fall from pastoral security into the knowledge of cultural and geographic multiplicity. And given the inseparable intertwining of culture, race, and geography, an initiation into the awareness of different peoples posed a threat to the doctrine of human unity—a threat already evidenced by the contemporary development of radical race theory and polygenesis. Under two imperatives, then, one aimed at an integration of old and young self across the divide of time, and one directed toward an integration of peoples across the divide of space, Equiano will seek to embody in himself the unity of separate cultures.

Whereas Farmer James, in response to intrusion from the outside world, flies from history, confused by chaos, Equiano's story creates a sense of order achieved through the active seizure of history. Where in Letter XII we find James fleeing panic-stricken into the woods and the uncertain future, in the *Narrative* we follow Equiano's deliberate organization of equally, if not more, chaotic experience into a coherent autodiegetic trajectory.

At once geographic, racial, intellectual, and soteriological, the narrative momentum of the *Interesting Narrative* has two major implications for our understanding of the ideological and psychological consequences of Equiano's separation from African culture. First, it reminds us that the author of the *Narrative* is a believer in Providence, a man severed from his childhood, an advocate of progress—for whom past, present, and future are indeed divided, as both a cognitive and an experiential matter. This is the Equiano who advocates the commercial development of Africa, and who believes that progressive history, both individual and social, implies a separation from nature and from people identified as "natural." Even, then, as the narrative gestures toward a reconstruction of the childhood idyll in the final pages—"May the time come" when the slave trade is abolished; "[i]n a short time" will justice, humanity and interest combine to civilize Africa (232, 234)—Equiano's new Africa will bear little resemblance to the old. In some measure may he recover the loss occasioned by "all the adversity and variety of fortune," but the "paradise" he has in mind involves a wholly new relation to the natural world, one of mining and manufacturing rather than agriculture.[37] Conceived in these terms, nature represents the commodified raw material in a system of global exchange that enables the political and spiritual reunification of the people of the earth.

Readers of the *Interesting Narrative* have understandably concentrated on the ideological and economic issues involved in Equiano's relationship to and representation of Africa. We should not lose sight, however, of the emotional and psychological power of his memory of it, or what he represents as his memory of it, for part of him undeniably remains, and the idyll is never quite effaced. Even if Equiano was born in South Carolina rather than in Africa, we hear a genuine sense of loss in his memories of childhood: "They had been implanted in me with great care, and made an impression on my mind, which time could not erase, and which all the adversity and variety of fortune I have since experienced served only to rivet and record: for, whether the love of one's country be real or imaginary, or a lesson of reason, or an instinct of nature, I still look back with pleasure on the first scenes of my life, though that pleasure has been for the most part mingled with sorrow" (46). Whether his African idyll is indeed "real or imaginary," whether he was born to the Ibo nobility or to South Carolina parents whose identity might never come to light, Equiano suffers the disruptions and dislocations of history, and we have no good reason to question the validity of his emotional response. He has lost home and parents, and Africa, which he regards as an originary racial homeland, still beckons, irrespective of any intervening generations or transplantings in the diaspora. If not literally true as described, his separation from Africa nonetheless carries metaphorical and psychological authenticity.

Two illuminating passages convey both the separation of Equiano's past and present and the affective and intellectual dimensions of his relationship to time. The first comes toward the end of the narrative, as Equiano relates the climax of his conversion experience, when the "Scriptures became an unsealed book" and "Christ was revealed to my soul as the chiefest among ten thousand." He describes his spiritual vision in temporally specific but still puzzling terms: "Now every leading providential circumstance that happened to me, *from the day I was taken from my parents to that hour*, was then, in my view, as if it had but just then occurred. I was sensible of the invisible hand of God, which guided and protected me, when in truth I knew it not" (190, emphasis added). Why does he mark Providence from that particular day? Parsed carefully, his language yields an interesting meaning. He could not mean that Providence only operated in the life of a believing Christian, because he did not convert until years after the day of his capture; indeed, he would believe that Providence operated at all times, even in the lives of heathens. And it's not even that his *apprehension* of Providence dates from that day, for his awareness—visual, conscious, cognitive—is clearly described as the gift of grace. Rather, it seems that his exposure to Western consciousness, no matter that it came about through kidnapping, signaled his entry not into providential time per se, nor into an awareness of providential time, but into a life which could be the *object* of temporal awareness, in which the workings of Providence could take coherent, visible shape. It is as if the retrospective gaze of *besinnung* meets a barrier defined temporally and culturally, beyond which his vision cannot see, or more precisely, which delimits an era of experience available to another part of his being.

For Equiano's past remains with him emotionally, even if its providential workings are not "in [his] view." Pierre Nora has written of "the difference between true memory, which has taken refuge in gestures and habits, in skills passed down by unspoken traditions, in the body's inherent self-knowledge, in unstudied reflexes and ingrained memories, and memory transformed by its passage through history, which is nearly the opposite: voluntary and deliberate, experienced as a duty, no longer spontaneous; psychological, individual, and subjective; but never social, collective, or all encompassing."[38] Nora laments what he regards as a casualty of modernity, an unfortunate corollary of social and technological "advance": the supplanting of communal forms of memory by a dissective history that preserves the past, datalike, in official archives and commemorative sites rather than in the organic fibers of human existence. The *Interesting Narrative* appeared when this transition was well under way, and Equiano himself—the "Black Jack," the roving mariner of a culturally hybrid Black Atlantic—lives at the juncture of old and new.[39] His relationship to his past operates on both registers that Nora describes, that of visceral remembrance and that of intellectual reconstruction. Approaching Africa as both ethnologist and African, Equiano bases his representation of the Ibo partly on formal historical re-creation and partly on memory. That memory, however, is not only cognitive but also instinctive, and thus at the same time that it underwrites Equiano's historical reconstruction of Africa, it remains immune to history itself.

The second illuminating passage comes as Equiano describes his separation from his sister, who was captured along with Equiano but sold to a different buyer: "Though you were early forced from my arms, your image has been always rivetted in my heart, from which neither *time nor fortune* have been able to remove it" (51–52, original emphasis). His choice of words here echoes the passage quoted above, in which he writes that his memories of Africa "made an impression on my mind, which time could not erase, and which all the adversity and variety of fortune I have since experienced served only to rivet and record." The emotional force of these memories is suggested by his description of his mother's oblations at her mother's tomb: "I have been often extremely terrified on these occasions," he writes, using the present tense, as if the memory were sensorally present to him (40). In each case, the powerful feeling that accompanies an adult's recollection of a lost family member is deepened by the exile's memory of a lost culture—yet also complicated, for the exile might not want to recover that culture. His childhood and Africa exist, in a sense, outside of history, impervious to the normal depredations of time, and that may be just how he wants it. Equiano's emotional relationship to "irreversible" time entails a heightened desire to resist, through force of memory, the loss it has brought him.

The tension between the preservative, antihistorical function of memory and the prospective orientation of a belief in providential history runs throughout the *Interesting Narrative.* Time is woven into the very fabric of Equiano's narrative, in a dense interstitching of past, present, and future; the text is shot through with an awareness of transience, and of the intimacy of temporality and consciousness. At one level, Equiano attends closely to the passage of time in his recollection of events; he tries carefully to indicate the year, month, date, or duration of various happenings. In the course of just one paragraph, for instance, he makes the following references to time: "the next morning, the 30th of December"; "in one day's time"; "for six weeks, till February, when one morning"; "till it was day-light"; "[o]n the 13th of February 1763" (97–98). Such attentiveness reflects, in part, the simple act of keeping a sailor's log and dutifully marking the date of each entry. But it takes on greater import in the context of Equiano's emotional and cognitive relationship to time. Like almost all autobiographers, Equiano tries to fit the events of his life into a coherent scheme, to give them a meaningful trajectory. As the narrative perspective shifts between that of the perceiving consciousness experiencing events as they occur and the retrospective view of the author interpreting those events after the fact, Equiano structures his story around the passage of time. Not unusual, that; following the soul's unfolding over time lies at the heart of spiritual autobiography. Equiano's variation on the theme, however, becomes more interesting because of the racial and cultural issues involved, as his past, present, and future refract through the prism of exile, diaspora, and civilization.

The past, for Equiano, embraces both a complicated emotional relationship to Africa and a sense of the providential meaning of his post-African life. From the perspective of the slave (or exile) whose past has been shorn from him, finding value and significance in that past, and even to reconstruct its most ordinary details, becomes vitally important. When Equiano writes that "[i]t was about the beginning of the spring 1757 when I arrived in England, and I was near twelve years of age at that time" (67), the statement assumes a deeper meaning than were it to appear in, say, Benjamin Franklin's autobiography. In similar fashion, the narrative's present (i.e., the envelope of time enclosing the perceiving consciousness of the younger Equiano, rather than the adult author's present) appears as a series of moments or events participating in a greater story, a story that fuses personal and providential history in the idea of destiny ("I thought my case singular" [191]). Those moments and events he ordinarily interprets literally, as the acts of an interventionist God making his will manifest, as theophanic revelation. Reading the book of nature thus becomes vitally important for Equiano. At times he renders the natural world as an unassimilated, even unholy, realm of monsters and chaos, and some passages sound like a secular eighteenth-century adventure novel: "When it was dark, we made a fire around us for fear of the wild beasts, as the place was an entire thick wood, and we took it by turns to watch" (153). At other times, Equiano invests the natural world with transcendent meaning, as natural events come to represent boon, warning, or punishment: "There was also a large rock on the beach, about ten feet high, which was in the form of a punch-bowl at the top; this we could not help thinking Providence had ordained to supply us with rain-water" (152). In these natural hieroglyphics Equiano tries to read God's will and to determine his own standing in the design of Providence.

The events of Equiano's life seem, to him, to organize themselves temporally and irreversibly toward some future culmination, and together they constitute the propulsive narrative structure of the autobiography. As an epistemological and spiritual matter, however, Equiano does not know for certain what the future holds, whether liberty and salvation or something worse. Much of the urgency with which Equiano tries to read the hieroglyphics of nature, after all, derives from the sheer precariousness of his life as a slave. In one typical passage, Equiano voices his shock at having been sold, apparently without reason, by his owner Pascal: "Thus, at the moment I expected all my toils to end, was I plunged, as I supposed, in a new slavery: in comparison of which all my service hitherto had been perfect freedom" (95). The desire for progression, for a life heading toward something, seems unjustly thwarted by such intrusions, and it seems likely, if impossible to demonstrate, that the constant reversals of fortune which Equiano cannot predict, much less avoid, had a profound influence on his phenomenological consciousness of time. Equiano's "conversion" to a Western belief in teleological time could therefore be partly a matter of deliberate, willed adoption of its values and religion, and partly the brute result of the vicissitudes of slave life.

In the final analysis, the instability of Equiano's present, and the murkiness of his immediate future, are gathered up and annihilated by his faith in providential design. As Equiano's own spiritual destiny unfolds, his belief in the design of Providence promises, without quite guaranteeing, that the uncertainties of human existence will be transcended, and given meaning by, the ultimate certainty of judgment day and glorification for the elect. Much like a belief in the cyclical regeneration of time, faith in Providence is a way of coping with the sufferings of history, for it envisions the final obliteration of history in a single act of regeneration. Equiano's visceral sense of loss and vulnerability, in other words, may find compensation in a cognitive understanding of historical time that envisions the future as accessible and meaningfully directed, and as culminating in union—the union of believers with Christ, and the reunion of a geographically dispersed human family.

Forced into a new posture toward history by events beyond his control, Equiano responds by seizing history as well as he can. He might not perceive time in a new way, but certainly his experience of his past and his apprehension of his future have been radically altered by enslavement and subsequent acculturation to Britain and Christianity. Yet his participation in the drama of historical and spiritual progress carries more significance than his own salvation; he also wrote as the most visible representative of a cultural and racial group that seemed to many Europeans to be lagging in the race of history, or perhaps to be out of the race altogether. Equiano's assertive historical consciousness thus inevitably mingles the personal and the political. In an implicitly and explicitly progressivist narrative, Equiano seeks to create of himself a living, speaking, acting testament to the human capacity for transformation, through both individual agency and divine grace. That strategy aims toward a reorientation of the European reader's attitude toward Africa and Africans, namely the inclusion of the continent and its inhabitants in the course of history that embraces all the peoples of the globe: "Let the polished and haughty European recollect," Equiano writes, "that his ancestors were once, like the Africans, uncivilized, and even barbarous" (45).

Equiano's racial optimism depends fundamentally on the principle of individual and social transformation through time. Externally, environment and grace can bring about that transformation; internally, individuals and social groups can shape their lives into a meaningful story aimed toward a higher end. As a polemical matter, Equiano joins other antislavery writers in emphasizing the role of environment and climate in human development, thus not only buttressing the monogenist argument, but removing the presumed inferiority or backwardness of Africans from the category of transcendent fact and placing it on a social-historical continuum along which no race is barred from advancing. In turn, a race's present location on that continuum depends partly on the relation it sustains to nature, and moving upward on the scale of civilization involves achieving a greater mastery over the natural world. Accordingly, as Equiano seeks to embody in himself Africa's capacity for historical civilization, he comes to advocate a relation to the natural world of Africa that is commercial and Christian rather than heathen and agricultural.

And that is where the *Narrative* ends, ironically cyclic, with an envisioned return to Equiano's place of origin. At the time of publication and for several years afterward, Equiano was deeply involved in the movement to colonize Sierra Leone, one of a variety of contemporary efforts at settlement in Africa. The settlement at Sierra Leone, the upshot of a variety of different schemes, was generally intended as a way to repatriate poor blacks, provide Britain new access to natural resources, challenge the West Indies system, and introduce the arts, sciences, and religion into Africa. From the outset, however, the colony was beset with problems, and Equiano's own participation in the project became embroiled in controversy and animosity, eventually resulting in his dismissal.[40] Closing the circle of Equiano's life by linking England and Africa in honest and godly trade was proving more difficult than he had imagined.

Despite such obstacles, Equiano continued to agitate for African colonization and against the slave trade during the early 1790s, while working on revised editions of the *Narrative*—which met generally favorable reviews and found a wide readership. The specter of French Jacobinism, however, created a fear of revolution in Britain, tended to discourage "the publication of radical or reformist sentiments in general, and very probably account[ed] for Equiano's apparent public silence after 1794."[41] When Equiano died in 1797, across the English Channel Crèvecoeur had retired from his position as French consul to the United States in order to lead a life of provincial obscurity in Normandy and work on his *Voyage dans la Haute Pennsylvanie et dans l'Etat de New-York*. In 1813, Crèvecoeur joined Equiano in ultimate tranquility, and both men were freed from history at last.

Everywhere we see the arrangements for the species perfect; the individual is left, as it were, to take his chance amidst the *mêlée* of the various laws affecting him.

ROBERT CHAMBERS, *Vestiges of the Natural History of Creation* (1844)

Order will emerge from disorder; and, as it were, a new creation will rise out of the chaos of a moral state.

REV. C. L. HEQUEMBOURG, *Plan of the Creation* (1859)

Certain it is that no individual was ever cleared of sin by development.

HORACE BUSHNELL, *Nature and the Supernatural* (1858)

CHAPTER THREE

Natural Evil and Human Development

UNDER THE PRESSURES of history, the eighteenth-century transatlantic antislavery movement rapidly became skillful at turning the languages of natural science and natural aesthetics to the purposes of denouncing the slave trade and defending African civilization. As they matured philosophically and politically, early antislavery writers established representational traditions that would continue to inform the debate as, in the nineteenth century, it came to center primarily on slavery in the United States. In the American context, the essential antislavery claims remained the same—that slavery violated the natural order and sullied natural beauty—but they had evolved and taken on different emphases as the intellectual and cultural milieu shifted. In particular, the issues of race and bondage got linked to the question of national identity, with disputants on all sides fiercely contending for their own ideas of what kind of country the United States should be and how race should function in the American experiment. Moreover, antislavery had to contend not only with a proliferation of antihumanitarian racial theories and texts, but also with an array of advances in natural science that bore on popular understandings of race. There was, finally, the uniquely charged importance of nature in both the nation's mythology and its lived history, and this presented unexpected opportunities and challenges to American abolitionists as they intensified their campaign for political and moral influence.

In various ways each of these issues runs throughout the rest of this book, but in this chapter I want to focus on a cluster of interconnected themes that began appearing in the literature of slavery in the 1820s and helped to shape the antebellum debate. These themes include evil and violence as philosophical problems, the idea of supernatural or natural design, and the phenomena of biological hybridity and racial amalgamation. As the dispute over slavery became more polarized during the 1830s and 1840s, traditional beliefs in the workings of nature and the identity of the human species faced increasing pressure from developments in natural science and anthropology. Very few people abandoned the idea that the processes of nature were orderly and harmonious, and that they furthered an underlying divine design, but increasingly they appeared unstable, kinetic, unpredictable—what William Ellery Channing perceived as "these awful forces" and "this fearful stir."[1] The scale of geological time, the history of extinctions, the relation between anatomy and environment—these and other areas of research revealed a world more complex and more dynamic than most people had previously reckoned. In the human sciences, with their obsessive preoccupation with race, a similar image of restless agitation took hold, and the building consensus in anthropology, shared even by those on the left of the political spectrum, held that the various populations of the globe necessarily competed against one another in the rough jostle of existence. At the same time, a longing for social harmony ran urgently through many writings on race and slavery, and was frequently linked to pastoral aesthetics, since natural beauty seemed but to make visible an underlying moral goodness to the world. The difficulty arose in figuring out how a state of "social beauty" would come about and what, exactly, it would look like.

In incorporating the new thinking in natural philosophy, and in seeking to clarify the relation between race and nation, antislavery writers began to develop what I call a "natural law of free development," which held that growth and liberty are inborn qualities of living organisms and structure the destiny of populations. This doctrine of free development forwarded two important goals. It articulated a kind of "natural theodicy" that envisioned the disappearance of evil through the processes of nature, and thus complemented traditional theodicean arguments. Moreover, it enabled antislavery writers to continue to represent slavery as unnatural, as a block on free development, while accommodating the scientific "facts" of natural racial division and struggle. Ultimately, however, this strain of American abolitionist discourse was limited by its inability to productively integrate two vital ingredients: the nascent theory of developmentalism and the reality of racial intermixture. And yet this represented no major liability in the short term, for antislavery writers, to be effective in renarrating the national story, had to work within religiously and politically sanctioned bounds.

The Problem of Theodicy

In 1808, in Lexington, Kentucky, there appeared a small book by an obscure author that lucidly and efficiently explained why slavery violated the laws of God and nature, if not, unfortunately, of man. It is worth noting that southern opinion had not yet coalesced and hardened in reaction to northern agitation on the slavery question; in fact, a good number of early American antislavery figures hailed from the South.[2] It is also significant that in the title of David Barrow's book—*Involuntary, unmerited, perpetual, absolute, hereditary slavery, examined on the principles of nature, reason, justice, policy, and scripture*—"nature" gets top billing among the principles: a sign, even at this relatively early stage, of the shifting parameters of the debate. Yet Barrow's rendering of nature reveals as well, in retrospect, how dramatically those parameters would change in the coming decades.

A good polemicist, Barrow starts by defining his terms, in a flatly and fittingly declarative rather than exploratory tone: "I intend by the word *nature*, those *laws* impressed on, and the fitness of the different parts of matter and spirit contrived by the *great Creator*, that were not only necessary to produce and perpetuate action and re-action, through the vast body of *nature*, collectively considered; but also to preserve union and harmony throughout the great whole." This union and harmony expresses itself in the animate world as a universal "sociability" among creatures and in the inanimate world as gravitation. On this basis Barrow condemns slavery as unnatural:

> Therefore whatsoever breaks those laws imposed on *nature*, by her *alwise Creator*, must in itself be a great evil, and as far as it operates, destroys union and harmony through all creation. The great parent when he had finished the fabrick of nature, pronounced it "very good"; not only good as originating from himself, but capable to do and produce good reciprocally. . . . Conformity to the laws of nature, would diffuse peace, love, joy, order, and harmony, through all parts of our world; under nature's dictates, *involuntary, unmerited, perpetual, hereditary, slavery* could not possibly exist.

Barrow acknowledges that a different view of nature exists, but argues that all deviation from order and harmony is a form of sin, and points out that the animals do not share humanity's propensity for making war on and enslaving each other. Learning to do so could not have come from the "brutal parts of creation," he maintains, nor from "the first dictates of our own nature," nor of course from the angels or Christ, but from an external villainous agency to which our human nature is susceptible: "Upon the whole it should seem, we have learned to enslave one another, from satan's conduct toward ourselves—He having enslaved our whole race, we in imitation thereof, turn in [*sic*] and enslave one another."[3]

If one accepts Barrow's premises, here and elsewhere, one should accept his conclusions—and many Americans had reasoned similarly. Yet those sequential premises—that nature is orderly and harmonious; that disorder and disharmony are therefore "unnatural"; and that slavery is therefore a distortion, a deviance, an "evil"—would face increasing pressure in the years ahead. Even those who believed that slavery was evil did not always know how to understand the source or the purpose of such evil, and the image of a nature suffused with harmonious benevolence had to compete with the image of a natural world torn by strife, and red in tooth and claw.

If we jump ahead to 1851, when John Campbell published his virulently racist *Negro-Mania*, we can appreciate the fierceness of the assault on the premises of Barrow (and others). Campbell, a member of something called the Social Improvement Society of Philadelphia, composed his book almost entirely of extracts from such writers as Charles Hamilton Smith, Peter A. Browne, and others who wrote on the "natural history" of race. Campbell, for his part, lends to the production a flair for dramatic overstatement and a willingness to offend, and *Negro-Mania* stands as a monument to how hysterical proslavery rhetoric had become by the 1850s. After a section on Robert Knox and his own racial determinism ("With me, race, or hereditary descent, is every thing; it stamps the man"), Campbell makes the following observation: "[B]e he savage or boor, citizen or man, colored or fair, war to the knife is the cry with Nature's Fauna and Nature's Flora; destroy and live, spare and perish, is the stern law of man's destiny." For those sentimentalists who recoil at such a Hobbesian vision he has no patience: he will leave to the philosophers, Jews, and crackpots the "jesuitical task of discovering in physical and moral suffering a benefit and a pleasure." Instead, Campbell sees all creation as an eternal cycle of destruction and renewal, with man and nature locked in perpetual combat: "To this life, as produced by nature, clothed with the forms necessitated by development in time, or by time (for this has not yet been fully resolved) man, also a part of Nature's plan, else he could not be present, is the perpetual antagonist. . . . [H]is destiny is . . . to extrude and destroy, if he can, all that is wonderful and beautiful on the globe as it came from Nature's hands." After ruminating on the extinction of species, from the mammoth in the past to the antelope in the future and possibly to the "colored man" some time after that, Campbell delivers a striking image: "The destroying angel walks abroad unseen, striking even at the races of men. But nature dies not; ever young; ever returning; ever reviving; she is eternal. The form is immaterial; the essence is the same; first and last."[4] Like a dark obverse of transcendental idealism, this vision of continual creative destructiveness in nature subordinates embodied materiality (especially, in context, black bodies) to the supreme realm of spirit—which was, in fact, always the problem with transcendentalism when not securely ethically moored. Campbell's vision is certainly a far cry from the "peace, love, joy, order, and harmony" that Barrow imagined as inherent principles of the natural, not just the supernatural, world. It suggests, powerfully, that Americans could no longer take for granted early-century assumptions about the benevolence of the natural order, and that this shift had vital implications for the debate over race.

Yet underlying their incompatible racial politics, Barrow and Campbell do share two crucial assumptions. They agree, first, on the basic intelligibility and internal logic of nature. They believe that nature is governed by laws or principles, that organisms have their place in the system, and that the mind can apprehend all this—in short, that it makes sense. When Barrow speaks of the "fitness of the different parts of matter and spirit" and Campbell speaks of "Nature's plan" and the "destiny" of humankind, they express the almost universally held belief that natural events and processes have some rationale, some purpose, in the greater scheme of things. They agree, secondly, that humanity somehow exists both inside and outside nature; that we are natural beings, certainly, but that our actions can affront, violate, or sully nature. In Barrow's view, sin represents a perversion of the natural order itself, a breach of God's natural laws. For Campbell, what humanity "destroy[s]" lies on the material plane: "all that is wonderful and beautiful on the globe."

In exactly what, then, does their disagreement consist, specifically in regard to slavery? They diverge in conceiving of the place of violence, broadly conceived, in the natural system. Barrow acknowledges that violence exists and has a purpose, but he condemns a particular kind of violence—the kind required for one human being to enslave another—as unnatural and therefore "evil." Campbell, by contrast, offers no moral judgment about racial violence, seeing it rather as part of the natural order: the strongest racial essence survives the whirlwind of "natural" destruction while others do not. This divergence, in turn, manifests a larger philosophical incompatibility involving the entire structure of relation between natural law and moral law. For Barrow, natural law and moral law express the same cosmic benevolence, and both are backed up by a superintendent God whose will expresses itself as "peace, love, joy, order, and harmony." In Campbell, the moral dimension of natural law has dissolved away, and the operations of nature, violent or otherwise, go forward quite independently of any divine intention. A "plan" exists, certainly, but it proceeds deterministically, and the concept of "evil" has no place: violence, suffering, extermination enter in merely as facts of the natural order.

This juxtaposition of two relatively obscure, but highly revealing, texts helps to illustrate a central problem for antebellum antislavery philosophy. That problem centered on the place, the purpose, and the provenance of "evil" in the natural and divine orders. Slavery, after all, represented not just a political controversy but, ultimately, a profound spiritual and religious crisis in Western societies. For ordinary people brought face to face with it, slavery presented a spectacle of human suffering that, at the very least, proved difficult to assimilate to a belief in either divine justice or divine mercy and that, for many, challenged their sense of human nature, of the natural order, and of God's purposes. "Speculation leads on to speculation," observed Edward Pringle in 1852, "until we are brought up at last by the hard question of the origin of evil. . . . This power that slavery gives to one man over another is met with everywhere in society."[5] Crèvecoeur, when confronted with the sight of slavery, questioned the existence of a "superintending power who conducts the moral operations of the world, as well as the physical." During the nineteenth century, as American slavery grew more widespread, more virulent, and more publicly visible, an increasing number of people were asking that question, along with a number of others that arose in its wake: If there is such a "superintending power," if there is a benevolent God, why would he allow for the manifest evil of slavery to exist? Was it of Satan, as Barrow believed, or was it of God himself? If the latter, how did it fit into the pattern of human redemption? For that matter, what part did race—with all the conflict surrounding it—play in the divine scheme?

The antebellum debate over racial slavery, in short, waded deep into the murky waters of Christian theodicy, and it did so at a time when the sciences were forcing a revision in dominant understandings of the operations of the natural world and its relation to the supernatural. Increasingly, nature appeared more complex in its internal arrangements, more kinetic in its action, more dynamic in the relation between small-scale and large-scale events, and more unpredictable in its consequences than had been recognized. In addition, more aggressive forms of anthropological and ethnological theory postulated that racial conflict and racial oppression inhered in the natural order, and at the far extreme asserted that such violence actually furthered the divine plan. Amid this epistemological and religious flux the American antislavery movement, from the early years of the nineteenth century, found itself navigating the overlapping complexities of religious doctrine, natural science, and social politics.

Across several centuries and many interlocking branches of theological argument, one basic form of Christian theodicy emerged as the most common: the argument that out of evil came good. In both natural time and providential time, in the lives of individuals and in the sweep of human history, the phenomena of sin and suffering would contribute to God's good purposes, of which personal redemption and the ultimate reunion of believers with Christ stand foremost. Affliction, from this point of view, can make people aware of their dependence on Christ's mercy; evil can bring the good into vivid relief; and these new forms of awareness can lead individuals to repent and to return to God.[6] Just as Adam's disobedience gave rise to the possibility of redemption, the exercise of Christ's mercy, and the entire human experience of struggling back toward God, so worldly sin gives rise to penitence and thence to salvation. And just as the Passion served as both prerequisite to the resurrection and a display of Christ's suffering for human sinfulness, so human pain can ennoble and transfigure the sufferer. On a larger scale, theodicy provides a kind of narrative structure for human history, a framework within which social or natural events and processes, however agonizing, can be understood as participating in the divine plan. At the center of all theodicies, finally, lies the question of human agency. The crucial distinction is between "natural evil" and "moral evil," or between forms of evil or suffering that exist independently of human agency, such as disease, and those authored by human beings themselves, such as murder.[7] Human agency also mattered in terms of the role that people themselves could play in working good out of evil. These were fundamental ethical considerations, and they made all the difference for how Americans understood the place of the "evil" of slavery in society and in the providential design.

To the degree that "good" equates with "beauty"—and most nineteenth-century writers took such an equation for granted—theodicy necessarily has an aesthetic dimension to it. In theodicies that strive to go beyond the abstract, the goodness of God commonly appears as natural beauty, while the "evils" of the world often appear as natural ugliness—which begs the question, needless to say, of what natural beauty and ugliness consist of. It also raises the problem of whether the directional and temporal quality of theodicy, which posits the emergence of good out of evil in human and providential time, applies as well to the natural world: that is, whether the "defects" or "monstrosities" in nature can or will give way to more aesthetically pleasing forms that body forth the triumph of divine law and love. As to the former question—the nature of beauty, so to speak—the irresistible temptation was to fall back on convention and imagine beauty in terms drawn from literary tradition, particularly the pastoral tradition. In Thomas Branagan's 1808 treatise *The Beauties of Philanthropy*, for instance, Branagan discourses on the goodness of God and laments the fact that humankind does not universally reciprocate God's love. In a passage that helps to frame the climactic denunciation of slavery to which his argument is building, Branagan offers this self-chastising paean: "Can I look upon thy sovereign beauty, without being enamoured with the transporting sight. Every time the sun rises majestically grand, he chides me for my insensibility; every time the lark mounts upon the wings of the wind, she accuses me of ingratitude; when the rain descends, when the silver queen of night, and the golden stars appear, when the vernal flowers of spring, and the blushing fruits of autumn appear, all, all seem to chide me for my ingratitude; and say, in reasons [*sic*] ear, what more can God do to win your love" (197–98).

To justify the ways of God, in Branagan's telling, is to call men to an awareness of the natural "beauty" that surrounds them and that serves as recompense for the evils of life and as a promise of ultimate harmony and redemption. When properly read, the signs of nature communicate divine meaning, and the perfect goodness of God appears as a variety of essentially stock images drawn from the pastoral literary tradition.

This homology between divine goodness and natural beauty had its counterpart in an imagined homology between sin and natural ugliness, and both share the basic assumption that natural phenomena possess interpretable moral meaning. Horace Bushnell, working through the same theological problems as Branagan half a century later, also posited a fundamental distinction between the natural and the divine—"God is expressed but not measured by his works; least of all, by the substances and laws included under the general term, nature"—but insisted on the fallenness of nature and warned against being led astray by its outward forms. Arguing that sin begets an "ever-widening circle of disturbance" in nature, Bushnell rails against a sentimental natural theology, and one hears his impatience with fifty-plus years of literary Romanticism: "Not only do the poets and poetasters in prose go the round of nature, sentimentalizing among her dews and flowers, and paying their worship at her shrine, as if the world were a gospel even of beauty; but our philosophers often teach it as a first principle, and our natural theologians assume it also in their arguments, that the forms of things must represent the perfect forms of the Divine thought, by which they were fashioned." For Bushnell, the "imperfections" and "deformities" of nature belie the fact of universal sin and make it more difficult to believe in an innocent state of nature. Where Branagan saw larks and sunrises, Bushnell turns his attention to the unpleasant face of nature:

> The earth itself displays vast deserts swept by the horrid simoom; muddy rivers, with their fenny shores, tenanted by hideous alligators; swamps and morasses, spreading out in provinces of quagmire, and reeking in the steam of death. In the kingdom of life, disgusting and loathsome objects appear, too numerous to be recounted; such as worms and the myriads of base vermin, deformed animals, dwarfs, idiots, leprosies, and the rot of cities swept by the

> plague; history itself depicting the mushrooms sprouting in the bodies of the unburied dead, and the jackals howling in the chambers, at their dreadful repast.

Crucially, Bushnell maintains that such disfigurements in nature appeared before humankind came into existence, as revealed by geological science, and that this pre-Adamite imperfection serves as evidence of divine premeditation (since it prefigured Adam's disobedience). In turn, the recent increase in natural deformities, Bushnell argues, serves as a powerful lesson regarding humanity's moral development, because it shows that, in fact, no such development has taken place. Only God himself, not Nature, can repair or surmount the catastrophe of sin and "unnature," whatever the natural-theologians would have us believe. Mere natural process will not regenerate the world, and no amount of human "development" will substitute for divine grace: "It is even a fair subject of doubt whether any nation, or race of men, was ever advanced in civilization by inherent laws of progress. Certain it is that no individual was ever cleared of sin by development."[8] Bushnell had in mind, specifically, the rise of pre-Darwinist evolutionary theory, or developmentalism, and more generally, the belief in some quarters that not just divine intervention but also natural processes could be efficacious in remedying the moral state of humankind, in righting the wrongs of the world, in bringing good out of evil both natural and moral.

This brief prècis of Branagan and Bushnell opens up several vital avenues into exploring the role of theodicean argument in antebellum antislavery literature. The general issue, again, had to do with the function, if any, of the "evil" of slavery in both human history and American history. As the above passages suggest, however, there was more to addressing that issue than simply denouncing slavery as an evil that should be restricted or abolished. A belief in the aesthetic visibility of moral goodness or wickedness *in the natural world* implied that certain representational practices—especially pastoral, with its characteristic attempt to body forth the qualities of "peace, love, joy, order, and harmony"—could inflect or intensify literary treatments of slavery or, conversely, of the virtue of non-slave-based economics. As we saw in the contrast between David Barrow and John Campbell, representations of nature articulated not only one's religious beliefs but one's sense of ethics, and as the American antislavery movement geared up, its writers became increasingly sensitive to the implications of natural imagery for their representation of evil. In addition, the question arose as to whether Nature possessed within itself the means of cleansing itself of the aberration of slavery, and if so, what this means consisted of. Would the natural progressive development of the human species ultimately make slavery obsolescent? Were biological, social, and moral progress really all connected? And what of race, that "natural" phenomenon that was somehow connected to the "unnatural" condition of slavery? Where did it fit in the grand design, given the evils of division and conflict that it seemed to engender? Even when not explicitly raised, or answered, these questions underlay and energized much antislavery rhetoric during the antebellum years, prompting a deeper engagement with contemporary natural science and encouraging an expanded range of representational strategies. To get there, however, we need to back up for a moment and consider some of the distinctive emphases that theodicy acquired in the American context.

In the British colonies and subsequently the United States, the core concepts of Western theodicy were linked both to the Calvinist belief that God dealt more strictly with his chosen people and to the related belief that America had a special role to play in the course of world history. In the covenantal theology of the Puritans, suffering marked divine reproval, and divine wrath marked (possibly) elect status, as God sought to bring the flock to order; the evils of human life served to punish transgression and to restore man's sense of dependence on divinity. "When God gives a speciall commission," John Winthrop pointed out, "he lookes to have it strictly observed in every article," and the fear or conviction that the colonists had not lived up to their special commission, had deviated from the righteous path, formed the basis for the innumerable jeremiads that Sacvan Bercovitch long ago identified as a central force in the development of American literature.[9] More recently, Richard Forrer has traced a gradual shift from the orthodox Calvinist theodicy, in which the theological covenant implied some restriction on divine arbitrariness, to a more liberal, rationalistic conception in which a benevolent God provided the free human soul a "model for the morally impeccable use of sovereign power."[10] As the Calvinist orthodoxy began to break apart in the eighteenth and early nineteenth centuries, the newer conception of evil made greater room for the exercise of human agency in the achievement of good on earth. Significantly, both theodicean traditions, when linked to nationalist sentiment, rendered the country's sins and sufferings as part of its not always evident but certainly unique, possibly divine, mission on earth. Of those sins and sufferings, slavery quickly became, during the early national period, the most ominous, and more Americans began expressing the fear that slavery represented not just a human evil but a national sin. This fear can be traced in a historical arc stretching from Jefferson's comment "I tremble for my country when I reflect that God is just" to Lincoln's portrayal of "this terrible war" as "the woe due to those by whom the offense came."

The popularization of theodicean thought owed much to the early American evangelical tradition, which also provided indispensable energy for the spread of antislavery sentiment—even if the evangelical legacy regarding slavery proved ultimately a mixed one. During the late eighteenth century and early decades of the nineteenth century, evangelical Protestant ministers—including the populist Methodist Bishop Francis Asbury, the iconoclastic Virginia Baptist John Leland, the eccentric preacher Lorenzo Dow, and the Presbyterian lawyer Charles G. Finney, among others—made slavery increasingly a matter of religious concern, turning the public consciousness toward the moral issues involved in human bondage.[11] The Second Great Awakening was not only a socially but a conceptually organizing process,[12] and it played a central role in connecting theological questions of evil to individual behavior and free will, to people's private judgment and personal lives, and to their sense of the communities and society they were building. In turn, although the issue of slavery bitterly divided denominations and congregations, and although many white evangelicals would back off their early antislavery assertiveness, the populist-revivalist tradition indissolubly linked slavery and evil in many Americans' imaginations, a link that remained even as once-revolutionary churches sought to rejoin the fold of mainstream respectability.

The strain of theodicy that held that slavery would occasion a purging or purification of the national soul, its violent extirpation allowing the light of freedom to shine more powerfully, represented a recurrent theme throughout American antislavery discourse. In *The Beauties of Philanthropy*, an unusually fierce text for the year in which it appeared, Branagan laments that many people "do not remember that God has permitted the partial reign of evil, in order to draw from it an everlasting good," and then asks his readers to ponder the immediate question at hand: "[W]hat shall we, or, indeed what can we say in favour of our gratitude or philanthropy, our national rectitude, justice or morality, while there are at least one million of our fellow-worms, in the most ignoble and tormenting slavery, in the bowels of our country, though we at the same time profess to be the votaries of liberty?" Branagan goes on to denounce the unexampled wickedness of modern Christians, with their fashion, materialism, sensuality, and so forth, and warns that "the awful period has arrived, when God is determined . . . to purge his church by unparalleled persecution, and scourge the Christian nations with terrible severity; and if that will not reform them, extirpate them from the face of the earth." If we "forego our national crimes," he writes, "we need not fear either men or devils," because the covenant will have been observed. He does not make it entirely explicit, however, what "good" will come out of the evil of slavery, other than a rigorous collective self-examination and self-correction, which might redeem a sinful nation.[13]

Next to the theodicean narrative of purgation other, less apocalyptic, ways of understanding the "purpose" of slavery also began appearing. Through its vivid horrors, for example, it could stimulate unbelievers to conversion. In an early fictionalized narrative titled *The Devil Let Loose*, the writer "L.M." tells the story of a cruel slaveholder whose terrifying vision of retribution brings his fellows around to an awareness of goodness, and concludes with this moral: "Thus you see how easy it is for God to bring good out of evil. The wickedness of this K. perhaps was the means of converting his sinful companions to God."[14] The focus here on supernatural power was characteristic of the more traditional form of theodicy, while the focus on individual conversion reflected a more limited conception, at least on the part of "L.M.," of the scope of the problem of slavery. Later years witnessed a diversification of theodicean responses to slavery, with a decreased emphasis on the supernatural, an increased emphasis on the cultural, and even a sense of positive good arising from the institution. A common claim was that slavery would provide Africans with a salutary, if rigorous, education in Western or American civilization—a claim that would reach its pithiest postbellum articulation in Booker T. Washington's image of the "school of slavery." This claim often led to its corollary: that American slaves or freedmen, when colonized, could help discharge the "fearful responsibility resting upon our land" by bringing the light of civilization to "benighted Africa"—and thus "God can educe good from this master-evil."[15] This idea, in fact, developed into something of a consensus on both sides of the Atlantic, even among those who were not "activists" in the antislavery cause. The British geological engineer David Thomas Ansted, for example, wrote that freed slaves "may found a republic or an empire in Western tropical Africa, which, by encouraging commercial enterprise, might soon occupy an important position among nations; and then, bringing good out of evil, the institution of slavery might be the means of elevating the vast population of an almost unknown continent to rival their former masters."[16]

Theodicean responses to slavery presented two philosophical problems for antislavery thinkers. First, in the tradition emphasizing supernatural power in "bringing good out of evil," the danger consisted in diminishing the role of human moral agency in overthrowing the institution. Second, insofar as the evil of slavery was acknowledged to lead to certain good effects, the silver lining (Western civilization!) threatened to become more visible than the cloud itself (bondage for some). Antislavery writers therefore had to maintain a vigorous ethics and a clarity of vision when discussing the nature of evil, and usually the argument was unwavering: God had nothing to do with slavery, and its cessation would serve God's good purposes. Yet natural science, in conjunction with the gradually waning authority of religious orthodoxy, was complicating the problem of evil and making moral clarity a somewhat more difficult thing to achieve. The confounding factors had to do with notions of biological "progress," the question of the relation between different "races," the place of violence in the natural order, and—most broadly—with *how* and *whether* the divine will expressed itself through natural process. The specific issue that antislavery thinkers had to contend with was whether slavery expressed some more generalized form of racial conflict that inhered in nature. Traditional theodicy, with its orientation toward the supernatural, did not provide adequate resources for addressing that issue, but the new natural and human sciences helped to fill the breach. Just as in the eighteenth century antislavery's traditional scriptural arguments had to be supplemented by a more "scientific" polemics, so in the nineteenth the argument about racial histories and futures had to be waged on a broader foundation. What natural science gave antislavery philosophy, I would suggest, was a language for identifying the emergence of good as a natural process, a dynamic working-out of the inner principles of nature, which, as long as they accorded with divine purpose, could only be salutary. Even if the "evil" of racial division and racial oppression inhered within nature, therefore, so did its antithesis.

Antebellum Natural Science

Whether they welcomed it, feared it, or tried to ignore it, Americans of the early nineteenth century recognized that the work of geologists, botanists, astronomers, physicists, chemists, engineers, and anthropologists was exerting a profound influence on their society. Science had a transformative impact both theoretically and practically, dramatically altering Americans' relation to the natural environment, their attitudes toward each other, and nothing less than their understanding of society and reality—much the role that it plays today. The challenge centered on how to represent and manage scientific knowledge in relation to longstanding and deeply held cultural values. In many ways science yielded easily to nationalist interpretations, providing evidence of the uniquely rich natural history of America, buttressing claims of the innovative genius and progressive temperament of Americans, and in general feeding into millennialist narratives of the "redeemer nation." In its most attractive guises, science promised nothing less than union, democracy, and freedom. Lee Rust Brown has argued that natural history came to represent a form of knowledge in keeping with republican ideals of equality, liberty, and individual merit, and a kind of social tonic that would alleviate a variety of ills: "[I]ts very technical sophistication made natural history not only a path for spiritual recovery, but also a way of indexing other social and intellectual 'symptoms,' a means of exposing, laying open to public speculation, the disturbingly opaque conditions of contemporary life."[17] At the same time, despite its "technical sophistication" natural science had a distinctly democratic appeal. In a seemingly paradoxical process, between the turn of the century and the Civil War scientific knowledge became both more abstruse and more popularly exciting, both a rigorous inductive undertaking requiring advanced education and a kind of publicly owned stock that allowed people to feel they could participate in expanding the frontiers of human achievement.[18] As Edward Everett, a man unusually attuned to the spirit of his age, observed, "[p]opular treatises and works of reference have made the great principles of natural science generally accessible," but "actual instruction in the principles of natural science is confined to the colleges; and the colleges are, for the most part, frequented only by those intended for professional life."[19] These coeval trends—the diffusion of scientific knowledge sideways through the culture and its upward institutional ascent—had implications for how and where the approaching cultural skirmishes over science would be fought.

The waxing epistemological authority of science had profound, if multivalent, implications for traditional philosophical and religious beliefs. When Benjamin Silliman, the first editor of the *American Journal of Science*, and an antislavery figure in his own right, assured his readers that natural science "demonstrates both supreme intelligence, and harmony and benificence [*sic*] of design in THE CREATOR," he expressed a widely held belief in the compatibility of natural order as revealed by science and divine design as revealed by scripture or described by religion.[20] Or as William H. Furness put it: Christianity is "a fact in nature and a fact of nature. . . . It does not lead us away from nature, but leads us into it, into the very centre and heart of it, whence all its light radiates."[21] In his discussion of the intellectual climate in which Darwin formulated his early ideas, Dov Ospovat has lucidly summarized the dominant "way of seeing nature" in the early nineteenth century. This perspective orchestrated a number of core concepts: "[the idea] that the adaptation of organisms to their environment is perfect, that nature is a well-adjusted mechanism, that there is a harmony among organisms and between them and the inorganic world; the idea that the laws of nature were established by God to achieve his ends; and the idea that all natural phenomena serve purposes relative to the whole economy of nature."[22] We should recognize, first, the implicit harmony between these scientific ideals, the aesthetic assumptions of pastoral, and the theodicean vision of ultimate good. In this worldview, the findings of geologists, botanists, and anthropologists, even if difficult to reconcile with established doctrine, served nonetheless to reveal the ever-more beautiful complexity in the natural world, a complexity that bespoke God's benevolent design. When scientific findings could not be assimilated to existing theories, or when gaps remained in the scientific picture of the world, it redounded not to the fundamental principles of natural harmony and purpose, but to the imperfections of human endeavor. And when science revealed violence in the processes of nature (the "turbulence of conflict and mutual destruction as we now see"), it revealed not evil but an elaborate working-out of a greater good.[23]

However, although religious faith worked, with variable success, to guide and circumscribe scientific interpretation, undeniable tensions had arisen between Christian and naturalistic explanations of the world. Coming at a time when the traditional cultural power of the clergy was already in decline, naturalistic explanations of physical phenomena had grown increasingly self-confident, and advances in such areas as geology and astronomy had forced changes in conventional scriptural exegesis.[24] And although the antebellum period witnessed a widespread cultural and intellectual effort to reconcile the findings of science with the teachings of the church, conservative religious sensibilities felt increasingly besieged both by the findings of science that ran counter to church teachings and by a climate of evident skepticism and irreverence fostered by the scientific mindset.[25] By 1858, things had gotten so bad, at least in the eyes of Bushnell, that this venerable dean of the New England Congregationalist establishment charged the new "infidelity" with explaining everything "on the level of mere nature, without miracle, or incarnation, or resurrection, or new-creation, or any thing above nature," and warned, ominously, that the "current is this way, and the multitudes or masses of the age are falling into it."[26]

Even among religious liberals, the creeping advance of secular or materialistic thought seemed troubling. In his essay "The Present Age" (1841), the Unitarian minister William Ellery Channing captured a widespread unease about the scientific endeavor, which seemed at times to portend ill things for the moral condition of human society. Although science, Channing writes, "is conferring on us that dominion over earth, sea, and air, which was prophesied in the first command given to man by his Maker," in a postlapsarian age that dominion seemed to have taken on an almost satanic quality: "Men forget the limits of their powers. They question the infinite, the unsearchable, with an audacious self-reliance." Channing acknowledges the capacity of science to alleviate "human burdens" and to renew a sense of national vigor and promise, but he expresses a deeper concern for its spiritual implications, and from here begins to articulate an important line of theodicy. Noting that the scientific spirit of inquiry has "stirred up a fierce competition" and an "insatiable cupidity," Channing maintains that the jostle of life can produce good, as long as it expresses not merely greed but a healthy sense of competition. "God intends us . . . for effort, conflict, and progress. . . . If we look at outward nature, we find ourselves surrounded with vast and fearful elements, air, sea, and fire, which sometimes burst all bounds, and overwhelm man and his labors in ruin. But who of us would annihilate these awful forces, would make the ocean a standing pool and put to silence the loud blast, in order that life may escape every peril?" As does Farmer James in *Letters from an American Farmer*, Channing imagines a world of turbulent energies and violent processes, but he seems more secure in his faith than Crèvecoeur's narrator: "Let us never forget, that, amidst this fearful stir, there is a paternal Providence, under which the education of our race has gone on, and a higher condition of humanity has been achieved." And science, the record of that education, provides a narrative of passing through these dangers, of overcoming them, in a way that moves the human race spiritually and materially forward, in accordance with the principles of a transcendent design. The alternative is too horrible to contemplate: "Were I to look on the world, as many do, were I to see in it a maze without a plan, a whirl of changes without aim . . . I should turn from it with sickness of heart, and care not how soon the sentence of its destruction were fulfilled."[27]

"The Present Age" marks an historical moment when a seam began to open up between those who retained a traditional belief in the meaningfulness, legibility, and divine benevolence of natural process and those who wondered how much Providence really had to do with such matters as extinction, dispersal of species, geological formation, and so forth. Not far beneath Channing's determination to turn away from a (delicately hypothetical) world without meaning lurks an awareness—given life by the subjunctive mood—of the contingency and fragility of belief, and his comment that "many" already see the world as purposeless reveals what was at stake for Channing: the fear that science was creating knowledge that would defy assimilation under the old certainties. Take away the belief that science but advances a general, progressive spiritual movement, that it reveals rather than disrupts providential order, and it becomes terrifying—and science itself is what threatens to take away that faith.

Antebellum science challenged traditional religious beliefs (and natural-philosophical assumptions) in two particularly relevant ways that provide the context for understanding American antislavery's engagement with the interlocking claims of natural history and race theory. One was the gradually maturing developmental hypothesis, or transmutationism, whose adherents continued to gather biological and geological evidence and to refine their structure of ideas for explaining the appearance and development of different species. The hypothesis seemed to be catching on. "[O]ne can scarce travel by railway or in a steamboat, or encounter a group of intelligent mechanics, without finding decided trace of its ravages," lamented the Scottish geologist Hugh Miller in 1849.[28] Miller overstated the case, but developmentalism did pose a growing challenge both to orthodox creationism and to the Cuvierian taxonomy, which managed to hold sway in most quarters until the late 1850s. Concurrently, the polygenist school of thought had grown more assertive in its claims and, because it rejected the biblical account of creation, faced growing opposition among both religious authorities and humanitarians, who hated and feared its proslavery applications. The concurrency of developmentalism and aggressive polygenesis was not coincidental, for each field had implications for the other; their claims were incompatible, and all they shared was a willingness to dissent from scientific consensus.

Developmentalism arose as part of a larger debate surrounding the relation of humankind to the natural world, and specifically to animals. Most accounts of this relation, not surprisingly, adhered to a rigidly hierarchical and inviolable anthropocentrism: human beings not only occupied the apex of creation, but by virtue of their spiritual and intellectual nature were (almost) as distinct from the "lower orders" of life as spirit from matter. In a fair sample of this view, the Maryland educator N. C. (Nathan Covington) Brooks argued in 1843 that mankind "stands immeasurably above the brute creation—the incarnate image of his God," and that where the actions of animals reflect not "design" but instinct, "which they blindly and irresistibly follow," the mind of man "controls at once both matter and instinct." In keeping with this view, and logically consistent, granting the premise, Brooks argues against developmentalism, which renders humanity "a mere gradation of the animal, a higher species of ape . . . that in their transition, have cast their tails."[29] Yet some people, even if acknowledging the mental and technical superiority of the human species, saw a much more intimate relation between humanity and nature, saw humanity as embedded, as it were, in the natural world and in natural processes. As early as 1772, the radical French philosophe Baron Holbach had inveighed against the "haughty pretensions" of those who believed that only human beings had souls, reason, and "sublime faculties," and insisted that humanity differs from the animals "only in his organization, which enables him to produce effects, of which they are not capable." In keeping with *this* view, Holbach articulated a prototypical theory of biological transformism, maintaining in *The System of Nature* that "man is a production formed in the course of time" and that if the planet were to "change position," humankind would have to adapt, for in such an event "there would not be that with which man could co-order himself with the whole, or connect himself with the whole, or connect himself with that which can enable him to subsist."[30] The idea that humankind existed in "connection" with the rest of creation was certainly not limited to eighteenth-century French materialists; it surfaced in more popular literature as well. In 1831, for example, the same year as the third American edition of Holbach's *Good Sense*, Robert Jameson published his *Narrative of Discovery and Adventure in Africa*, an entertaining travelogue, in which he speculated that the "orang-outang appears to constitute the link between man and the lower orders of living things. . . . It seems even to make a nearer approach than any other animal to the exercise of reason."[31] None of this means that anthropocentrism faced any danger of being overthrown by a new and humble ecological awareness, or that those people who emphasized human connection with nature subscribed to protoevolutionary or evolutionary theories, but that people had different ways of thinking about the relation of human beings to the natural world and the animal kingdom.

More specifically, the Cuvierian biological paradigm—a hugely influential orchestration of comparative anatomy, classification, zoology, and paleontology—was slowly eroding under pressure from a new generation of natural historians. In *Le règne animal* (1817), along with two previous works—*Leçons d'anatomie comparée* (1800–1805) and *Recherches sur les ossemens fossiles* (1812)—Georges Cuvier had transformed the field of natural history by developing a system of analysis and classification that radically expanded and reworked its Linnaean predecessors. This system stood on the principle of teleological adaptation—that is, that organisms were perfectly adapted, or designed, for their environments—and on the principle of functionalism, which held that a creature's organs or structures all had a specific function in relation to its "conditions of existence." Crucially, the Cuvierian paradigm made no room for the possibility that structural similarities between organisms or species represented any challenge to the insuperable taxonomic divisions that his system posited.[32]

The developmental hypothesis fundamentally challenged this latter assumption by suggesting that structural affinities between creatures might indicate closer relationships than were dreamed of in Cuvier's system. The story of the rise of protoevolutionary theory—with the overlapping, mutually enabling contributions of such scientists as Jean-Baptiste Lamarck, Lyell, Geoffroy, and others—has received ample attention, but a few salient points deserve emphasis.[33] First, while developmentalism asserted the possibility of taxonomic fluidity, of biological transmutation in species themselves, it still adhered to a teleological view of nature, to the principle of perfect adaptation, and to a developmental model of upward ascent that embodied some kind of meaningful divine plan. Not until Darwin's *Origin of Species* would the teleological assumption be seriously undermined. Second, one of the intellectual dividing lines between those who entertained the developmental hypothesis and those who did not involved the validity of analogical reasoning. Since the evidence for development was fragmentary, literally as well as figuratively, its adherents had to make the fragments cohere by detecting or asserting meaningful relationships among them: precisely the analogical leap that Cuvierian orthodoxy ruled out. In the hands of those unconstrained by the technicalities of professional science, developmentalism thus acquired a remarkable plasticity of application, and readily lent itself to the idea that progressive development might occur in the moral as well as the biological world. Third, the developmental hypothesis represented a uniquely powerful extension of the environmentalist argument. While the orthodox view held that nature and species had been "fitted" for one another in an essentially static way, the concept of development rested on the dynamic influence of environment on successive generations, which over long periods of time will undergo effectively permanent biological changes. In this way it encouraged, at a deep level, the idea that human beings existed not outside of nature but in a profound and intimate relation to natural process. Fourth, this application of the idea of development to humanity—despite the anthropocentric assumptions of its proponents—had begun the long ontological destabilization of the concept of the human being (later to reach its apogee in Darwin's *The Descent of Man*), as it undercut the argument for favored creation, linked human beings to other forms of life, and even raised the prospect that human development had not yet concluded. In all of these ways, developmentalism showed that the principles of natural law, perfect adaptation, and teleology—principles that few people questioned—did not have to mean what traditional biology said they meant.

In doing so, early forms of evolutionary or transmutationist theory irreversibly complicated the questions of supernatural design and of humanity's relation to the rest of the animate world. In *The Phenomenon of Life*, Hans Jonas identified several major paradigm shifts stemming from the evolutionist conception of life. Although Jonas focuses on post-Darwinist evolutionary theory, the philosophical changes he describes began stirring as early as the 1830s and 1840s. Foremost among these, as suggested above, is the rise of a post-Linnaean, post-Cuvierian view of the organism as relationally situated rather than isolated and independent: "Organism is seen as primarily determined by the conditions of its existence, and life is understood in terms of the organism-environment situation rather than in terms of the exercise of an autonomous nature." Thus divesting life "to an unprecedented degree of original and inherent determinations" gives priority to process over essence in the notion of species: "Species, a relatively stable, temporarily self-perpetuating structure, is an incidental result of life's history with no terminal status in creation and no indication where it may lead next. The flux of dynamism replaces essence and qualifies what appears as such with a radical contingency." Accordingly, the existence of more advanced or more complicated biological structures implies no superiority of origins: "If higher levels happen to emerge in the dynamics of the primitive, their quality as levels is wholly contingent, though their factuality is necessary."[34] In Jonas's account, as in later accounts by Stephen Jay Gould, Ernst Mayr, and Elisabeth Lloyd, evolutionary theory tends to support antiessentialist, antiplatonic, and antinecessarian conceptions of the world.[35]

The evidence (the textual fossil record, so to speak) shows that the basic insight of pre-Darwinist evolutionary theory—that existing species had developed over time and would continue to do so—influenced the thinking of a lot of people besides professional naturalists, whether they acknowledged it or not. The developmental hypothesis remained scientifically heterodox, certainly, but already by the late 1830s it had filtered into popular conceptions of natural process and the human being, and after 1844, when Robert Chambers anonymously published *Vestiges of the Natural History of Creation*, it had grown into a fierce controversy that irrevocably changed the public debate.[36] Eventually, it would exert a powerful influence on the artistic imagination, providing, in a variety of genres, a rich conceptual lexicon for addressing problems involving narrative structure, dynamic characterization, and the resolution of social and moral conflicts.[37]

Among those who rose up to denounce developmentalism, the advocates of the theory of polygenesis proved unusually vociferous. The polygenists did not, as a general matter, reject developmentalism because it ran counter to established doctrine, since they themselves put forward heterodox ideas and on occasion made explicitly anticlerical or antiscriptural statements. Rather, they resisted developmentalism because it provided implicit support to the monogenist argument by accounting for the appearance, in historical time, of different human races within a single human family. This helps to explain why George Gliddon, for example, the Egyptologist who collaborated with Josiah Nott on the polygenist *Types of Mankind* (1854), dismissed the developmental hypothesis as "transcendental anatomy." Nott himself identified more closely the link between developmentalism and monogenesis: "Those who contend that all the races of men are of common origin, must, in spite of themselves, fall into these heterodox opinions of Lamarck, Oken, and St. Hilaire. . . . The climatic influences now at work, it is supposed, will be changed, and *development* take up its line of march and carry on the great plan of the Creator."[38] Polygenism took the idea of race as spiritual essence to its extreme, denying the power of environment to create, sharpen, or minimize racial difference. Like developmentalism, polygenism had filtered down to a popular level of understanding, and despite its theological offensiveness to many, it made some headway in promoting the belief that natural science had revealed the existence of distinct human species and that distinctions between the races were essential and insuperable.[39] In philosophical terms, polygenism—even if given a Christian moral gloss—tended toward an essentially Hobbesian view of nature as a place of fragmentation, strife, and destruction. It still adhered to concepts of law and design, but as John Campbell maintained in *Negro-Mania*, the workings of that design could easily involve violence, competition, and extinction.

The polygenist argument had two major conceptual vulnerabilities (beyond the obvious): one to the idea of nature as process, and the other to the phenomenon of "interbreeding." We see these weaknesses vividly illustrated, but totally unacknowledged, in *Natural History of the Negro Race* (1837) by J. H. Guenebault, a lawyer by training, a *bachelier-es-lettres* at the Academy of Paris and a member of the Literary and Philosophical Society of Charleston. Right out of the gate, Guenebault calls into question the principles of liberty and equality, reasoning that: "If in nature are seen summits and abysses, if uniformity is contrary to its laws, if every thing must constantly change, rise or fall, increase or decrease, if in its kingdoms all is progression and amelioration, who can affirm that the differences remarked among the various species of men are contrary to the order of nature?" Yet this rhetorical question is not nearly as ironclad, or as rhetorically effective, as Guenebault seems to assume. In the first place, the conclusion that "natural" differences separate the "various species of men" does not logically require the premise of universal change that he articulates. In the second place, one could easily reply that, if everything "must constantly change" and "all is progression and amelioration," then natural process could work over time to erode whatever differences might exist among the "various species of men." As if in response to such an objection, Guenebault goes on to argue that "negroes, or blacks," form a distinct and permanent "species" that "does not undergo a peculiar change as long as it is not mixed with any other races."[40] Yet not only does Guenebault elide the distinction between "species" and "race," but the phrase "as long as" introduces a condition that entirely undercuts his point, since racial "mixing" was already, by 1837, recognized as a widespread fact, and since it could provide the mechanism of "natural process" that would undermine racial distinctions. These related flaws in the polygenist argument—its reliance on a static model of nature and its rigidly taxonomic approach to race—presented ample opportunity for monogenists to join the fray.

These debates did not proceed at the level of pure abstraction, but with an acute awareness of the direct implications of scientific discovery for social life and political fortunes. In particular, the questions of human origins, human development, and human destiny seemed ever more pressing, because they bore directly on the very real problems of race that science undertook to explain. The relation between race, as a "natural" category, and a controlling or teleological design either natural or supernatural, became a matter of increasing interest during the first half of the nineteenth century because the future of American society, with its undeniable and intensifying racial conflict, seemed largely to hinge upon it. Where did race come from and where was it leading? Asking that question necessarily brought the temporal dimension of racial and social development to the fore, and the major branches of natural science, especially anthropology and geology, had directed attention toward such temporal issues as the age of the earth, the forces guiding human development, and the appearance and disappearance of species. When conceived of less as a static than as a dynamic manifestation of an unfolding transcendent plan, race invited a new kind of scientific scrutiny, one oriented toward change—whether such change appeared as shifting interracial relations or intraracial growth or decline. The political controversy, then, turned on the function of race, assuming it had one, in furthering the purposes of nature or God.

The Natural Law of Free Development

The simultaneous professionalization and popularization of natural science meant that the antislavery movement had to make its case across a wider rhetorical and ideological front. Certainly, the supernatural argument—that slavery contravened God's will—remained central, but appeals to nature grew in frequency and power. Indeed, the necessity of grounding ethical arguments in natural authority led some antislavery writers actually to demote the power of scriptural or supernatural revelation. "What is Man?" asked the radical clergyman Henry Clarke Wright, in calling for a truly humanitarian understanding of anthropology: "Shall we go to God, or to man for an answer? To discover the nature of a rose, we go to the flower itself; so, to learn the nature, relations and duties, of man, we must go to man, and no where else. . . . [T]he only way to inquire of God about man, is to investigate the fixed laws of his body and soul, and the relations which he bears to his fellow beings, and the duties that grow out of such relations. God communicates with men, *only* through the nature he has given them" (original emphasis).[41] Wright's point here reflected a changed intellectual climate in which natural science challenged religion for epistemological authority, and in which race theory had become more theoretical and, in the hands of proslavery polemicists, more belligerent. In addition to "advances" in racial biometrics, the natural science of race found a congenial vocabulary in the social science of Adolphe Quételet, Charles Fourier, Comte de Saint-Simon, and others, a science geared toward describing human populations in mathematical and statistical terms.[42] Accordingly, the antislavery engagement with the natural history of race continued to build on its eighteenth-century foundations, growing more explicit and sustained in the decades leading up to civil war. Even though white abolitionists, as we well know, frequently held paternalistic and hierarchical racial views, they held to the same basic tenets: an unshakeable belief in the familialhood of all people and, concomitantly, an environmentalist concept of racial differentiation. Far from rejecting the natural science that buttressed or informed race theory, antislavery writers tried to get a purchase on it, to work within it, and to adapt it to humanitarian purposes. The intellectual energies involved in racial science certainly did not run all in one direction, and as the above passage from Wright suggests, the fields of anthropology and ethnology formed the primary battleground.

In his 1849 essay "Ethnology," James Russell Lowell glosses the core antislavery response to the polygenists, arguing that "[t]he instances hitherto collected by ethnological students seem to put beyond question the fact that differences of physical structure, and of the color of the skin, may all be referred to climatic causes, and do not in the least countenance the theory of essential diversity of race." Rather more interesting, however, is Lowell's sense of the broader importance of natural science in antebellum antislavery thought. In light of the rise of polygenesis,

> the researches of ethnologists become particularly interesting to Abolitionists, and furnish them with arguments more generally appreciable by the mass of mankind than those appealing exclusively to the principles of abstract justice and right. It is worth remarking from how varying and unexpected sources the quiver of the reformer is constantly recruited with fresh arrows, and how the investigations of science, prosecuted in directions which seem the farthest removed from every day interests, have yet a practical bearing, more or less decided, upon the humanitary questions of the time.[43]

Lowell's image of the replenished quiver provides an apt metaphor for the concept of representational affordances spelled out in chapter 1. More significantly, however, in describing the usefulness of ethnological arguments to the antislavery cause, Lowell contrasts them not with *divine* justice and right, but with "abstract" justice and right—a mark not necessarily of a decline in religious sentiment but of an ever-more influential empiricism impatient with "abstractions."

A fuller response to the proslavery co-optation of anthropology came in 1854, in Frederick Douglass's "The Claims of the Negro Ethnologically Considered," an address delivered at Western Reserve College on July 12, 1854, and printed in pamphlet form in Rochester, New York, in 1854. Into this address Douglass compressed the full range of argument that could be brought against polygenism, without, however, wandering too far into the weeds of anatomical or physiological analysis. He maintains, first, that the Negro is a man and, second, that the Negro shares a common ancestry with the rest of the human family—both in response, of course, to assertions to the contrary. In defense of the first claim, Douglass offers both a moral and psychological definition of humanness (the Negro's "innocence and his guilt, his joys and his sorrows, proclaim his manhood in speech that all mankind practically and readily understand[s]"), and a functional definition based on practical superiority to the animals ("The horse bears him on his back—admits his mastery and dominion"). In defense of the second, Douglass names the opposition (Gliddon, Nott, Morton, and Agassiz), denounces them as a group who "speaking in the name of *science* . . . forbid the magnificent reunion of mankind in one brotherhood," and decries the "reasoning of men who reason from *prejudice* rather than from *facts*." He does assert that "the credit of the Bible is at stake" in the dispute, but rather than making a scriptural argument, cites the "geography of the world" (which accounts for physical differences) and the "intercourse of nations" (which reflects a shared human nature) as evidence of common origin. As Douglass recognizes, however, the real issue in all of this is slavery, "[f]or, let it be once granted that the human race are of multitudinous origin . . . and a chance is left for slavery, as a necessary institution"; and by the same token, even if the case for unity did not hold up, he argues, slavery would be unjust and unwise.[44] Douglass's essay is significant not only in relation to *My Bondage and My Freedom*, published the following year, but as a high-water mark in the collective antislavery rejoinder to polygenesis.

Yet the "findings" of anthropology and ethnology generated a problematic tension within antislavery discourse. That tension lay between an *a priori*, usually religious commitment to an optimistic historical narrative oriented toward universal harmony (in Douglass's words, "the advancement of human welfare, happiness and perfection"[45]), and an inductive, *a posteriori* approach to scientific race theory, which seemed, with each passing year, to run more strongly against the ideal of human spiritual unity, quite apart from the question of common biological origin. No one saw race as simply a social construct, and everyone recognized that race generated violent conflict, and therefore certain difficult questions arose. What were the broader implications of the interracial division and strife that contemporary science seemed to locate within the natural order? In theodicean terms, was the "moral evil" of slavery, *pace* Douglass, really a "natural evil," a manifestation of an underlying natural fact, and if so, how could this evil be remedied, and what part did it play in the grand scheme of human progress? More specifically, what part would it play in American history? It is in light of the issues of theodicy and human development that we can begin to address the problems raised by these questions.

The unwavering adherence in antislavery philosophy to monogenesis and environmentalism might seem likely to have led abolitionists to embrace the developmental hypothesis, since it interacted so powerfully with both of these biological-historical models. As an explicit matter, however, they generally did not do so (with the notable exception of Emerson, as will we see in the next chapter), and we can identify three probable reasons for this. First, for all the attention it generated, developmentalism still ran contrary to the religious beliefs of most abolitionists, whose case against slavery depended so centrally on the belief that man is a *created* being beloved of God. Second, even those who might have accepted the developmental hypothesis in one form or another probably wanted to avoid any suggestion of eccentricity; the goal, after all, was to influence public opinion, and intellectual respectability represented an important asset. Third, and most simply, developmentalism per se did not have a natural place in antislavery rhetoric, in contrast to environmentalism, which, as we have seen, proved indispensable to accounting for racial difference in the most humanitarian way possible. However—and this is a significant "however"—while antislavery writers did not embrace evolutionary theory outright, I believe that its core concepts, and the whole climate of intense discussion surrounding the question of human development, helped to structure or condition a certain attitude toward human progress and race relations that had a bearing on antislavery thought.

Undeniably, the language of human development, in the broadest sense, became much more pervasive in antebellum antislavery discourse during the 1840s and 1850s. This language reflected a maturing understanding of nature, and biology in particular, as process rather than essence, as a dynamic working-out of inner principles or potentialities that, as long as they accorded with divine purpose, could only be for the good. "The *first* law of the human constitution to which I would advert, is its *tendency to develop itself*," declared Rev. George Bassett in 1858, in perhaps the least controversial statement in an otherwise highly radical antislavery sermon (original emphasis). "It is the result of the instinctive desires of our common humanity. From the dawn of existence these primary tendencies prompt a man to aim at his legitimate destiny." The rhetorical value of this claim becomes clear when the other shoe drops: "Now it cannot be disputed that slavery lays the iron hand of compulsion upon the whole nature of man, and precludes its appropriate development."[46]

Bassett articulates what I termed earlier a "natural law of free development," which draws upon the era's interest in human development generally and its more specific interest in organismal growth, and which surfaces in one form or another throughout antebellum antislavery literature. This coinage is meant to express certain internal tensions and ambiguities in the concept. In the first place, a natural law of free development is "natural" because it is not immediately impelled by supernatural force, even if it accords with divine design; it is natural because it admits of study by the methods of natural science, without recourse to scripture or revelation. It is a "law" because it is not anomalous but universal and invariable, not incidental but intrinsic to the organism, not aimless in its manifestation but orderly and purposeful. And as a law, it is capable of violation, with the implied penalties that such violation can incur. ("Man is an empire in himself," wrote Wright, "whose laws can never be justly infringed by any being, not even by him who established them, unless he changes our nature and relations."[47]) At the same time, it is a law whose central principle, paradoxically, is the free agency of the organism; in contrast to the severe biological determinism of the polygenist variety, it envisions creatures determining their own lives in keeping with their inner nature, an ambiguity that Bassett described as "primary tendencies prompt[ing] a man to aim at his legitimate destiny." It is a law of development, finally, because it sees growth, somewhat tautologically, as progressive, as the inborn qualities or propensities of a creature germinate, sprout, and gradually become more advanced, more complex, and more expressive of the creature's place in the world.

The idea of a natural law of free development gave antislavery writers of all stripes—from polemicists to slave narrators, from ministers to freethinkers—a vital way of locating a principle of liberty within the natural world while accommodating the image of a kinetic, even violent, struggle for life that natural science, particularly anthropology, had created. A natural law of free development differed from environmentalism in that, rather than passive adjustment to climate or circumstances, it envisioned active, forward growth and the outer-directed exercise of the inner will. While the principle of adaptation at the center of environmental thought remained indispensable in accounting for racial differentiation, there still had to be a way of talking about the energetic confrontation of human beings with their surroundings and their self-impelled upward path in life. Free development thus stood antithetical to both environmental determinism and nonenvironmentalist essentialism. As Ospovat has pointed out, a growing number of biologists during the 1830s and 1840s, including such comparatively conservative thinkers as Louis Agassiz, maintained that "organisms exhibit an extraordinary independence from the influence of physical agents,"[48] and this sense of independence ("Man is an empire in himself") rendered the influence of climate and environmental conditions as contingent rather than deterministic, and temporary rather than permanent. At the same time, the organism, or population, was seen in processual terms, as developing within the context of natural settings and natural laws, rather than as expressing an unchanging ancestral or spiritual essence. In this way, early developmentalist theory, in both its "professional" and literal form and its popular and metaphorical variants, provided crucial intellectual support for the concepts of freedom *in* nature and freedom *from* nature.

Most importantly, therefore, the natural law of free development served to denaturalize slavery, to render it a "moral evil," while making room for the concept of the rough jostle of life and the "natural evils" that that might occasion. "God gave us intellectual power, that it should be cultivated," wrote William Ellery Channing, invoking one of the organic metaphors that often signal the language of free development, "and a system which degrades it, and can only be upheld by its depression, opposes one of his most benevolent designs."[49] The concept had other important implications as well. It could refer not only to the individual creature, but to populations; in this view, the self-determined growth of the individual radiates outward, in a manner of speaking, to encompass the social group. In this sense the concept of free development provided a vocabulary for describing racial progress or "improvement" over historical time as scientific fact, in contrast to, and in response to, pessimistic charges of racial stagnation or decline. Such pessimism was everywhere. Take the following passage from Frederick Rauch's *Psychology; or, A view of the human soul*, based on a series of lectures he delivered at Upham College in 1840:

> With man, *reason* and *will* are to be unfolded in all their riches. Both, in the savage, are sunk in the life of nature, which by its energy, and by the fullness of its sensual enjoyments, keeps him in bondage. Reason and will ought to break loose from this life, but being satisfied with their state, they would act against themselves in doing so. Hence the savage has no history, for he is what he always has been. Civilization is connected with many struggles, all of which form the theme of history.[50]

Even though Rauch invokes the language of development, and sees the unfolding of human nature as the font of history, his concept differs from the natural law of free development in two fundamental respects: it does not treat development as a universal and invariable law, but as the privilege of only a portion of the human family, and it identifies "bondage" rather than freedom as an intrinsic operating principle of nature.

Of the variety of genres in which antislavery writers worked, the slave narrative proved perhaps the richest territory for these ideas. As we saw in the case of Equiano, the slave narrative, from its early decades, held up the individual life as an exemplum of the potentialities of the racial group. In the antebellum American slave narrative, we find an increasing emphasis on the active and adaptable character of the narrator, and a more pervasive language of growth, development, and cultivation. "The growth of a young and unbroken spirit is rapid when the weight that crushed it is taken off," wrote the amanuensis for Jermain (Jarm) Loguen, in an emblematic statement of one of the genre's central tenets.[51] Since many American slave narrators had worked on farms or plantations, they often establish a pattern of thematic analogies between agricultural, individual, and social growth, drawing a contrast between the natural growth of crops and the unnaturally stunted intellectual and moral development of the slaves. Jarm Loguen, in another quintessential phrase, "had been bred in darkness, and his faculties were all undeveloped."[52] The *physical* development of slaves, however, was often remarked upon, for it had economic significance for the owners; like crops, properly "cultivated" slaves could grow into marketable commodities. John Brown, who devotes a large portion of his narrative to the proper cultivation of cotton, recounts that his mistress "used to call us children up to the big house every morning, and give us a dose of garlic and rue to keep us 'wholesome,' as she said, and make us 'grow likely for market.'"[53] Moreover, as many slaves, both male and female, discovered, their physical development had sexual significance for the owners as well; female slaves were vulnerable to coercion and rape, while the "manhood" of male slaves represented competition or a psychic threat to white male sexuality.[54] The sexual dimension of the theme of development, both individual and social, was particularly important, we will see, because it touched on fundamental questions about the relation between races, and whether and how the development of one population interdependently twined with the development of another.

The natural law of free development also raised the prospect of improvement in the *moral* universe, and thus had clear theodicean implications. Given that the processes of nature expressed a meaningful, purposeful design—as everyone agreed until Darwin broke the news in 1859—there seemed reason to think that natural and spiritual development would go hand in hand. Just as the body grew strong through exertion, so struggle and strife would strengthen the moral character, and this would hold true for the whole human species—recall Channing's comment that "God intends us . . . for effort, conflict, and progress." The natural laws of harmony, economy, and benevolence, when seen as governing human development over the long term, would imply that conflict and disorder were temporary, or at least productive, conditions. Perhaps the violence and cruelty in nature, which manifested itself at times as conflict between the races, might represent not simply sin, but natural processes in a larger historical narrative whose raison d'etre was, in Douglass's words, "the advancement of human welfare, happiness and perfection." For those skeptical of the traditional theodicean argument that God brought good out of evil, particularly in its application to slavery (since that would seem to imply divine sanction for the institution), identifying the emergence of good as a natural process, a matter of natural law, represented a complementary or alternative line of theodicy.

And what, then, did such goodness *look* like in antislavery literature? Not surprisingly, it often looked a lot like a peaceful New England countryside, in which bountiful natural beauty not only provided the most appropriate setting for but actually fostered social harmony. In Whittier's "Hymn," for example, the natural world embosoms a gathering of antislavery activists, and by implication embraces their cause:

> We thank Thee, Father! hill and plain
> Around us wave their fruits once more,
> And clustered vine, and blossomed grain,
> Are bending round each cottage door.
>
> And peace is here; and hope and love
> Are round us as a mantle thrown,
> And unto Thee, supreme above,
> The knee of prayer is bowed alone.[55]

In this and many other examples from the abolitionist press, the moral semiotics leave little room for misinterpretation: traditional pastoral images serve as evidence of divine goodness and love—and favor. In perfect converse, the evil of slavery is linked to southern decay, ugliness, or rank luxuriousness, with the same implication that natural and social conditions not only reflect but reinforce each other. Now Whittier imagines the farewell of a slave mother to her daughters, who are

> Gone, gone,—sold and gone,
> To the rice-swamp dank and lone.
> Where the slave-whip ceaseless swings,
> Where the noisome insect stings,
> Where the fever demon strews
> Poison with the falling dews,
> Where the sickly sunbeams glare
> Through the hot and misty air.[56]

The underlying, unstated warrant for such highly morally inflected representations of nature is the belief that the visible, tangible exterior of nature reliably communicates something about its moral essence—that nature does, in fact, take sides in human affairs.

The pastoral tradition, however, posed two significant problems for antislavery literature. First, since natural science continued to reveal the apparently indifferent destructiveness inherent in natural process ("[t]he destroying angel walks abroad unseen,") pastoral had to pick and choose; it had to emphasize those features of the natural world that comported with its aesthetic-moral agenda while suppressing others. While recent research in evolutionary psychology suggests that our sense of natural aesthetics depends in part on hardwired preferences (there are good reasons, after all, why cockroaches, for instance, appear less frequently than birds in representations of natural "beauty"), geographically defined cultural background or allegiance fundamentally shapes our perception of what counts as beautiful in the natural world. In other words, a representational tradition closely associated with one geographic region, as antislavery pastoral increasingly was, shares a deep philosophical affiliation with climatism, which as we know is historically complicit in the theorization of racial hierarchies—while, moreover, refusing to acknowledge its partial or provincial character.

A second thorn in antislavery pastoral was that it ran somewhat at odds with the principle of historical and cultural development that the movement championed. In envisioning a state of natural and social harmony, whether on Crèvecoeur's farm in western Pennsylvania or in Equiano's Essaka, pastoral often implied a kind of stasis or timelessness, which made sense insofar as it meant to communicate an unchanging quality of divine goodness. Change, or development, would seem to perturb this blissful condition, threatening to unsettle its carefully crafted harmony; Whittier's fruits and vines and "blossomed grain" are seasonal, certainly, but they exist in an eternal present, and the cottages they environ are in no danger of decay, abandonment, or absorption into a city. At the same time, southern pastoral envisioned the same kind of peaceful harmony, usually on the plantation, as at John Pendleton Kennedy's fictional Swallow Barn, in the countryside, where "[t]he skies have a deeper blue than common, the clouds rest upon them like paintings," and "[t]he soft flutter of the groves hushes one into silence."[57] For both of these reasons—to acknowledge historical change and to distinguish itself from its southern counterpart—antislavery pastoral had to accommodate the principle of development, and during the 1840s and 1850s it did so both by representing southern nature as a place of stagnation rather than concord, where slavery stymied the natural development of both society and individuals, and by representing northern nature, or free soil, as ideal for the cultivation of human souls. These issues will reappear in chapter 5, but here they begin to outline the challenges faced by the antislavery movement in articulating a vision of goodness as a natural state or as a natural process.

Antislavery writers, in any case, by the nature of their cause, sought above all to represent goodness as a *social* state, and they did so both negatively, as the absence of bondage, oppression, and cruelty, and positively, as the rule of law, the reign of freedom, and racial harmony. Yet in practical terms people themselves had to bring about that state, in historical time and in a defined geopolitical space, and this raises a problem that bedeviled antislavery rhetoric throughout the years leading up to civil war. That problem centered on the respective roles of contingent political action and of self-actuated natural process in leading humanity to a higher stage of being. As we have seen, natural theodicy (i.e., the emergence of good through natural processes that can entail violence or destruction) seems to require either the application of the principle of development to humanity's moral condition, or, less grandly, the disappearance in historical time of particular evils such as slavery (and race too?) through natural social evolution. But the actual natural mechanisms by which the evil of racial conflict would give way to the good of racial harmony proved less than entirely clear. Would the conflicts generated by race simply wither away? Would race itself disappear? How might the biological processes of human development contribute to the formation of a better society? Or to put a finer point on it: What role would intermixture, amalgamation, and hybridity play? To a greater degree than one might expect, antislavery writers did wade into these waters, for the issues of population and reproduction were in fact very much in the air, very much part of the antebellum debate.

Beginning in the 1830s and accelerating in the 1840s, the popular press, including such antislavery periodicals as *Frederick Douglass' Paper*, the *Liberator*, and the *National Anti-Slavery Standard*, witnessed a running series of exchanges about the meaning of race in general, and more specifically, about the existing, potential, and/or desirable relations between racial populations—all in the context of national identity and history. The antislavery movement, not surprisingly, never spoke with one voice. When it came to the unavoidable issue of whether and how blacks and whites could coexist in the United States—an issue that fractured into enormously difficult political, practical, and moral questions involving such matters as assimilation, colonization, amalgamation, intermarriage, and racial "fitness" or "destiny"—individual writers were all over the map. In a sense, however, they had painted themselves into a corner by their decades-long insistence on human biological unity, on the consanguinity of the species. The logical extension of their literal interpretation of Acts 17:26 (God "hath made of One Blood, all Nations of Men, for to dwell on all the face of the Earth") was that different human "races" could interbreed, were interbreeding, and would continue to do so; indeed, many of their political opponents acknowledged as much. This may appear less surprising if we consider that many antebellum Americans regarded miscegenation as an open secret, or a fait accompli.[58] The fundamental disputes arose along the fault lines this reality exposed: whether intermixture was a good thing, where it was leading, and what it portended for the national experiment.

In large measure the issue turned on whether one believed intermixture led to racial degeneration or improvement. Proslavery writers, of course, usually argued that degeneration inevitably resulted, and they pointed to the supposed sterility of hybrid offspring, the "pollution" of white blood, or the general dilution of the different bloods involved. Some antislavery writers, hoping against hope, saw intermixture as portending the inexorable demise of slavery, while others deemed it an unworkable "solution" to racial difference, given the intensity of interracial antagonism. A few regarded it as a natural, normal fact, not deserving scorn: "All animals or beings in our world possessed of the procreative nature, which are of the same species, kind and blood, will mix in all conceivable degrees without producing a single unproductive grade, no matter how dissimilar the individuals may appear; and . . . there is no local truth more generally known and believed than the indiscriminate mixing of the races."[59] A common belief held that biological intermingling would produce cultural intermingling—that nonphysical "racial characteristics" could be transmitted or blended through miscegenation—and even some African American leaders thought this might contribute to the "elevation" of blacks.[60] Most importantly, in the context of the developmental hypothesis and the debate over polygenesis, intermixture was beginning to appear as the mechanism by which human progress, as a single human family, occurred. The centrist-conservative Presbyterian minister Thomas Smyth, for example, arguing that there is "a gradual and imperceptible transition from one [human] variety to another," suggested that racial characteristics emerge "through a long series of generations," yet saw this as a process of exchange rather than of increasing isolation. The usual pattern, he wrote, involves "the springing up in [a tribe] of some new congenital peculiarity, which is afterwards propagated, and becomes a character more or less constant in the progeny of the individuals in whom it first appeared, and is perhaps gradually communicated by intermarriages to a whole stock or tribe."[61]

Soon, antislavery activists, both black and white, found themselves in the position of cultivating a northern public not eager to think about intermixture while simultaneously trying to accommodate the undeniable fact of intermixture to a positive vision of the country's future. That proved an almost impossibly difficult task, because in an age when heritability and hybridity had become central anthropological concepts, one could not talk about populations without talking about reproduction, and in the nineteenth-century United States, this was perilous territory indeed. Interracial sex was like the elephant in the room: Everybody knew it took place, but nobody really wanted to address it squarely or constructively, and so the literature that does touch on intermixture has conspicuous fissures and contradictions, and figures of ruin: tragic mulattoes, rapacious slave owners, degenerate libertines, the invisibly "tainted." Tellingly, one of the more erotically charged treatments of black-white relations actually turns out to be political metaphor. In an 1855 editorial discussing the breakdown of good feeling between the Garrisonian abolitionists and their African American allies, the New York black intellectual James McCune Smith wrote that "the twain ought to be, but are not, one flesh." Extending the marital metaphor, Smith describes the early rapport and then the falling-out between the two antislavery camps in sexually charged terms:

> "All went merrily as a marriage bell" in this honeymoon of the Anti-Slavery movement, the smiles, caresses, blandishments, and terms of fondness were tossed backwards and forwards—reciprocally—so assiduously that although Mr. Garrison sometimes "blushed" at an unusually warm hug, it was hard to tell which loved the other most, Mr. Garrison the Colored People, or the Colored People Mr. Garrison. . . . But all at once . . . [o]n this good, warm soil the Liberator had grown beyond the measure of colordom.[62]

More commonly, however, antislavery writers handled the literal issues presented by actual or potential intermixture clumsily, or with dread, rather than gracefully and with humor. "We are heartily disgusted with the ridiculous cry of amalgamation! amalgamation!!" wrote the African American activist Samuel Cornish in a June 30, 1838, editorial for the *Colored American*. "It is a mean, dishonest, ungodly resort of colonizationists, knaves, and fools, and seems to be the only argument they are capable of using in defence of their corrupt system of slavery, their oppression and tyranny." Fair enough, yet in taking this position Cornish seems to leave himself but two possible responses, both inadequate to his purposes: either defend amalgamation against the "ridiculous cry" against it, or argue that it is not really occurring. As if sensing this conundrum, Cornish rejoins that amalgamation is only taking place in certain areas:

> Why do not these "eagle eyed" beings, who have set themselves up to prevent amalgamation, turn their attention to the south? Are they not aware of the mixing up, bleaching process of amalgamation carried on in that ill-fated region, where the slaves are fastly growing as white as their masters? And why do not these little minded "amalgamation trumpeters," draw aside the curtain in New York, Philadelphia and other cities, and reform the houses of assignation which are kept, *wholly*, for the amalgamation of white males and colored females—if driven to it, we can give volumes with names and numbers on this subject. Yet all these things are overlooked—nobody gives the alarm.[63]

Cornish argues that by crying "amalgamation!" proslavery southerners mean to scare the public into opposing emancipation, and he implies that free blacks want no more than to go about their honest Christian business. Yet Cornish's rejoinder does not quite amount to a logical refutation of the "amalgamation trumpeters," since he neither defends amalgamation nor denies its prevalence. Rather, he seeks rhetorical traction by subtly invoking class, suggesting that intermixture only takes place in whorehouses and slave quarters, and not in the respectable areas of the North. Yet given the evident popularity of such "mixing up," in both regions, respectability would seem a pretty shaky bulwark against rampant intermixture.

Cornish's reference to the "whitening" of southern slaves through the "bleaching process of amalgamation" directs our attention to a related, equally fundamental, problem in antislavery thought. That problem centered on the implications of intermixture for widely accepted patterns and meanings of racial difference, and for its very validity as a concept. Since, as everyone recognized, intermixture between blacks and whites resulted in a visible lightening of the offspring relative to the black parent, and since over generations this process was known to produce very light-skinned people, some writers raised the possibility that the "black race" might disappear in the course of time. The fact that they did not imagine, or admit to imagining, the disappearance of the "white race" through the same process we may ascribe in part to the assumption, not always tacit, that whites were "stronger."[64] Yet the prospect of a "whitening" of the country's African American population, as opposed to a "darkening" of its white population, also intersected powerfully with the prospect of widespread passing. In a letter to Horace Greeley, reprinted in the *National Anti-Slavery Standard*, James McCune Smith described "the facility with which colored men and women turn white at the North," and dramatically expanded the scope of amalgamation into reputable society, giving agency in the process to African Americans themselves: "[H]ere at the North, the boundary line is less distinct; the colored white has merely to change his place of abode, cut his old associates, and courtesy will do the rest—he is a white. There is not a path in literature or science in our State, in which I could not point out very distinguished colored men. Of one hundred boys who attended with me the New York African Free School in 1826–7, I could name six now living—all white."[65] Some commentators rejected the notion that amalgamation would ever lead to the complete "absorption" of blacks by whites; simple prejudice, in their eyes, would provide the bulwark against that eventuality. "No amalgamation producing an unity of feeling and identity of interest, can take place," reasoned Ebenezer Baldwin, "until difference of complexion is obliterated by intermarriages. It need hardly be said that this plan is not feasible, even if it were desirable."[66] Perhaps, then, an intermediary stage of racial amalgamation would need to occur. In Central and South America, wrote the anonymous author of a tract titled *Spermaceti for Inward Bruises*, the "black" and "yellow" races will intermix, and "by a cross between this improved stock and the white race, between which there exists no antipathy, will emanate a mixture, by means of which the black race will gradually disappear." In this way, the "progressive movement" of history will naturally bring about the end of slavery, and thus "[a]ll will work together for good. Human nature is human nature! Its lights and shadows will, like kindred drops, soon mingle into one."[67]

At hand, seemingly, was a convenient means for antislavery writers to envision both the inevitable decline of the institution of slavery and the gradual disappearance of racial conflict—through natural biological process, in conjunction with, although ultimately independent of, political action. The natural law of free development, applied to populations as well as to individuals, would imply that these populations developed toward a higher plane of being, morally as well as biologically, since development comported with the grand design. "All will work together for good," and the "lights and shadows" of human nature will "soon mingle into one"—in context, a statement of what we might term racial theodicy, whose shining telos resembled Barrow's "peace, love, joy, order, and harmony" or Douglass's "advancement of human welfare, happiness and perfection." From fragmentation would emerge unity; from racial division, human fulfillment. Such utopianism linked racial theodicy to the pastoral ideal, since both posited a final condition of natural and social harmony, aesthetically pleasing and morally sound. And was this not a good thing, this racial theodicy? It was certainly tempting to think of the evil of slavery as a partial and temporary flaw in the scheme of national and human history, while still allowing for the "natural" basis of race. If slavery withered away through the simple but relentless pressure of population dynamics, the nation could avoid the purgative trauma of civil war.

The underlying assumption of racial theodicy, of course, was that the direction of human development would be away from blackness, toward whiteness, or toward some vague condition of racelessness. A Manichaean logic operated in this fantasy—that out of blackness would come whiteness, as out of evil would come good—and the image of a bleached America liberated from its violent racial history (the same image that inspired the dreams of most colonizationists) coursed through a good deal of antislavery rhetoric. The biblical doctrine that God "hath created of One Blood, all Nations of Men" provided the humanitarian, egalitarian core of antislavery racial philosophy, but it could easily be turned to imagining the disappearance of racial difference altogether. We should receive with a measure of caution, therefore, critical celebrations of antislavery's commitment to racial equality. Paul Goodman, for example, has written that "[a]bolitionists expected those who joined their movement to accept and advance the principle of racial equality, regardless of the walk of life, social stratum, and religious background from which they came," and he argues that "never before had so many white Americans labored with black Americans to lessen the distance between the races."[68] The challenge for antislavery, I believe, was to acknowledge racial difference in constructive ways while striving to achieve equality for all people under the law. That it proved difficult for antislavery writers to imagine a state in which racial difference would not lead to pervasive violence or deception attests not only to their historical experience but also to the degree to which they had unconsciously adopted the perspective of contemporary racial science. The doctrine of natural human development showed the path out of this difficulty, but its envisioned outcome was too often imagined in terms of the denial of racial difference, and its animating principle, the reproductive interaction of populations, could not, as a general practical matter, be openly or fruitfully discussed in nineteenth-century America. It presented, in the end, yet another theodicean problem.

He hath made of One Blood, all Nations of Men, for to dwell on all the face of the Earth.
Acts 17:26

This land which we have watered with our tears and our blood, is now our mother country.
RICHARD ALLEN

It is the result of science that the highest simplicity of structure is produced, not by few elements, but by the highest complexity.
RALPH WALDO EMERSON

CHAPTER FOUR

Nations of Blood

THE CONCEPTUAL PROBLEM described at the end of chapter 3—the function of race in human development—erupted, in more specifically political terms, as a dilemma of liberal nationalism during the antebellum years. Philosophically, the antislavery movement embraced the doctrine of human unity, but what this commitment entailed vis-à-vis the actual racial character of the United States proved a trickier proposition. God may have created "of One Blood, all Nations of Men," but this did not quite solve certain practical issues confronting abolitionists. For the most part, antislavery authors, both black and white, worked within the dominant mythologies of American national identity,[1] and they tended to elide the tension between a vision of social cohesion and a belief in the naturalness of racial difference. This philosophical centrism helped to moor antislavery expressions of discontent with the United

States and its racial politics to a more or less recognizable, reassuring base of nationalist identification. Yet the antislavery movement's stated goals created an imperative to think seriously about questions of national and racial identity. Would the union survive the sectional crisis and the attempt to end or limit slavery, and should it even survive? If so, what kind of union would emerge? If not, what were the alternatives? Assuming that general emancipation came about, what could be the future relation of two "races" whose shared history contained so much blood? How could white American society incorporate millions of slaves, or anywhere from 12 to 15 percent of the total population?[2] More concretely, what policies regarding citizenship, civil rights, and reconciliation should the country pursue?

With increasing urgency as the United States headed toward civil war, such questions stimulated various lines of creative thought about the future of the nation and, for some, about the very concept of "nation" itself. Some writers concluded that the races could not or should not coexist within the same geographic and political space, and came to advocate one or another version of physical separation. Others saw racial assimilation or even amalgamation as not just possible but desirable, or even as a destined part of the order of things. Both positions reflected a desire to get beyond the comparatively inert belief that the United States could eliminate slavery without having to seriously address questions of racial hatred, racial mixture, racial competition, and racial reconciliation. At stake, in other words, was not just political freedom but the racial character of the nation, and whether a writer came down for separation or assimilation, he or she posed a challenge to the complacent mainstream assumption that the country could avoid such unpleasant difficulties.

In this chapter, I examine the trajectory of a problematic form of black nationalism stretching from David Walker's *Appeal to the Coloured Citizens of the World* (1829) to Martin Delany's *Blake; or, The Huts of America* (1859–62), and the development, during roughly the same period, of an equally problematic amalgamationism, drawing on proto-evolutionary thought, in the writings of Ralph Waldo Emerson. For all of these authors, the language of "nature" provided powerful rhetorical energy for the articulation of alternative narratives of national identity, and it served as a stabilizing theoretical substrate as they sought to re-imagine the future of the nation in terms of the violent history of two races.

At one level, they each envisioned some form of social utopia, hovering in the obscure future, that echoed, and would embody, the pastoral ideals of peace and harmony—authorized, as always, by natural law. This social aesthetic had also a corollary rhetorical function: It helped to "package" the claims of natural history by linking them to theodicean process and the general moral advancement of humankind. In turn, to invoke the epistemological and moral authority of natural history functioned, in part, to normalize controversial or unfamiliar racial ideas. In exploring the social risks and possibilities their historical moment presented, Walker, Delany, and Emerson drew on scientific concepts of human and nonhuman "nature" and they espoused two basic principles: first, that the future of racial and national development would be governed by "natural" processes (themselves governed by divine will), and second, that the observable biological traits and cultural practices of different human populations held the key for understanding how those natural processes worked. They diverged, however, in how they imagined the biologization of race. For the black "separatists" (a vexed term elaborated on below), the concepts of "natural" racial difference and distinct racial "bloods" generated a theoretical resistance to hybridity or assimilation and underwrote a call for Africanist political solidarity. For Emerson, racial blood seemed less an insuperable barrier than an opportunity for exchange, amalgamation, and, ultimately, collective human improvement. This political and intellectual divergence undoubtedly reflects their differing racial subjectivities, the black writers proving far less sanguine than their privileged counterpart as to the possibilities of transracial reconciliation in the United States.

Yet the appeal to nature in these authors' writings also revealed the practical and conceptual horizons of otherwise quite innovative, even audacious, political responses to the American crisis of race. Unintentional compromises, unavoidable entanglements, and unacknowledged conservative impulses qualify the oppositional tenor of Emerson's writings, Walker's *Appeal*, and *Blake*. Practically speaking, neither Emerson's assimilationist vision of an "alliance of men of one stock" nor Delany's separatist vision of an independent black state in South America was feasible.[3] Political, social, and psychological forces that defy complete assessment prevented then, as they do now, both complete intermixture and black independence, the result being, at best, an uneasy coexistence, or as Frederick Douglass put it, "a nation in the midst of a nation."

Moreover, serious ideological and philosophical complications ripple through their work. In the case of the black nationalists, we find a reactive ethnoculturalism and a de facto American expansionism, by which the cultural values of the society they repudiated entailed themselves on the language and the projects of racial separatism. In the case of Emerson, his model of assimilation threatens to erase the distinctive identities of racial or ethnic groups under the all-inclusive banner of (white) American nationalism. Together, these weaknesses represent flip sides of the central tension within American liberal thought—a tension that has descended, in various strains, to the present day, as the competing impulses toward identitarian politics on the one hand and inclusive humanist politics on the other play out in various moments or contexts.

Undeniably, however, these authors' reimagining of national identity took root in the desire for a more racially just society. We should see their writings, then, as advancing other kinds of cultural work than either the utopian assimilation of African Americans within the United States or the utopian transnational union of blacks in some other country or across territorial boundaries. Rather than setting forth avenues of public policy, they offered rhetorical and intellectual positions regarding the meaning of American civic identity. These positions had ethical instrumentality for themselves and for their readers, in exerting some measure of influence over the course of American politics, in insisting on the importance of African American pride and uplift, and in reminding whites of their responsibility to help overthrow the system of slavery.

The Separatist Impulse, from David Walker to Martin Delany

In February 1829, Robert Alexander Young, a preacher in New York City, published his *Ethiopian Manifesto*, one of the earliest texts of black militancy to appear in this country and one that presaged some of the central issues of later, more theorized articulations of black nationalism. We know next to nothing about Young himself, but his militant pamphlet came on the heels of a series of events that likely contributed to the radicalization of some free northern blacks: the founding of the American Colonization Society in 1816, the Missouri debates in 1819 and 1820, the Denmark Vesey rebellion of 1822, and the advent of the African American newspaper *Freedom's Journal* in 1827 (to which Walker himself contributed essays). Although students of American cultural history have long underestimated the role of the 1810s and 1820s in the emergence of a major black intellectual tradition in the United States, the innovative or militant thought of more well-known African American writers of the 1840s and 1850s took root in this fertile soil.[4] Centered primarily in Philadelphia, Boston, and New York, these writers—including, among others, William Hamilton, William Whipper, Joseph Corr, Peter Williams, James Forten, Paul Cuffee, Prince Saunders, and Russell Parrott—disseminated their ideas through newspapers owned and operated by African Americans and through addresses or sermons to black audiences at churches or other institutions. Operating in a virtual wilderness of white apathy or obliviousness—the years before the advent of Garrison's *Liberator* in 1831 and the founding of the American Anti-Slavery Society in 1833—they nonetheless managed to apply pressure against slavery and against northern silence and complicity, contributing in vital ways to a polarization of public attitudes regarding slavery and ultimately to the outbreak of civil war.[5]

In the *Ethiopian Manifesto*, in place of the mild, integrationist Christianity espoused by many of his contemporaries, Young gives voice to an apocalyptic rage and a vision of an African messiah who will avenge the wrongs of slavery. Telling his readers that "many signs shall appear" of the coming deliverance, Young writes that the messiah will be known by a physical monstrousness: "[P]rovidence decreed he should appear peculiar in his make. . . [T]he two middle toes on each of his feet were, in his conception, webbed and bearded."[6] Two years later Nat Turner would describe seeing "drops of blood on the corn as though it were dew from heaven" signaling that "the Savior was about to lay down the yoke he had borne for the sins of men."[7] Both "revelations" locate transcendent meaning in the physical world, but whereas Turner focuses on external nature, Young sees divinity as expressed in the human organism. His vision is one of anatomical theophany, and its principal importance, in my view, consists in what we might term the hyperbiologization of racial difference. Whether Young knew of the "findings" of his era's racial science remains conjectural, but he does express a similar concern with the bodily and biological features of racial difference. If "epidermalization," in Frantz Fanon's apt phrase, describes the psychohistorical process by which racial identity became associated with skin color, Young seeks to reclaim the tenacious notion of black monstrousness, and to celebrate it by identifying its most dramatic manifestation as the mark of the savior.[8] And he turns this to advantage by asserting that Africans throughout the world are united by common bloodlines and identified by their skin color. The epidermal marker of racial affinity thus acts as a prolepsis for the anatomical theophany by which the African messiah will be known. Finally, then, Young takes the step that defines the separatist position, asserting that people of different descent, of separate bloods, should not intermix (36).

The *Ethiopian Manifesto* embodies a number of principles that have important but problematic implications for the theories and movements of black nationalism that it anticipated. Most importantly, far from making apologies for blackness, Young figures it as a sign of membership in the holy remnant that will emerge triumphant on the day of reckoning. This and other separatist expressions of racial pride, although representing a creative and aggressive response to white oppression and enabling the emergence of an invigorating Africanist ethos in the New World, do raise inevitable, difficult questions about the future relationship, both biological and political, between European-descended and African-descended Americans. In addition, Young makes no reference to a forgiving Jesus, invoking instead an avenging deity who we are left to assume is the Christian God, but could as easily be Allah. The text, in other words, points to the coming reaction against an integrationist strain of African American Christianity. Finally, the *Ethiopian Manifesto* has a programmatic vagueness to it, a cloudiness regarding what course of action, exactly, Young advocates. But that does not necessarily constitute a weakness. The text seems directed less at achieving a particular result than expanding the conceptual horizons of its reader. Young seems to aspire for the material object—the pamphlet itself—to galvanize a change in consciousness by illuminating and celebrating a common identity that transcends time and place.

Certainly, the persistence of an intrinsic African identity, or more to the point, the claiming and celebrating of such, was an indispensable precondition for the rise of nineteenth-century black nationalism. But nationalist aspirations as articulated in African American texts drew on European and "white" American ideologies of race, nation, and nature as well as on a common African heritage. At the most fundamental level, the very language of African American nationalism—English—carried the ineffaceable imprint of the accumulated history of Western thought, and meant that militant and even separatist discourses operated within as well as against the conceptual structures of European American culture. Moreover, few African American nationalists wanted to repudiate or to leave the United States altogether; more common was the black jeremiah who lamented the nation's fall from its ideals, and perhaps even condemned the Constitution as a proslavery document, but who nonetheless affirmed the essential value of those ideals. Others saw in the United States the best opportunity for moral and material uplift that could enable the emergence of a vanguard of pan-African civilization. In these ways, African American nationalist texts could combine the revolutionary rhetoric of Thomas Jefferson and Thomas Paine with that of Toussaint L'Ouverture, the promise of Christian salvation with the image of a black messiah, the language of capitalism with West African values of communal land ownership. This discursive hybridity, as we might term it, had both a circumscribing and an energizing effect on African American nationalist texts, enabling visions of a shared destiny and pointing out vital avenues of critique, but also reproducing within these texts ideas and attitudes that ran against a purely Africanist ethos.

More specifically, the emphasis in some early African American literature on physically defined racial identity, as in the *Ethiopian Manifesto*, reminds us that European and American race theory cast a long shadow over black nationalist texts, since the category of "African" or "Ethiopian" derived not just from detribalization in the New World but from a series of white texts dating to the eighteenth century. Echoing the paradox of inclusion and exclusion at the heart of democratic political theory, black nationalist authors affirmed those phenotypic or "essential" bonds that defined the community while at the same time separating the community from outsiders. In pursuing a highly identitarian activism, however, they greatly complicated their political and social relationships to the antislavery community in particular and to the American mainstream in general. Next to the optimistic narratives of reconciliation and mutual progress informing much integrationist rhetoric, militant and separatist texts ran the risk of alienating even their intended readers by seeming to encourage a vision of perpetual racial division and conflict. The specter of ceaseless racial violence also preoccupied Emerson, who would find a way out of this philosophical problem by turning to the insights of early evolutionary theory, eventually understanding blood exchange as a corollary to blood conflict, and as the engine of collective human progress.

Yet militant African American literature had much less luxury than Emerson for speculative philosophy, given the immediate political pressures under which this writing appeared—and even Emerson confined his more intrepid thoughts to his private journals. As for the practical issue of results, African American literature that sought to influence American political life had obvious disadvantages. Fundamentally, early Africanist or "black nationalist" literature—from Young to Marcus Garvey—sought to further the welfare of African-descended people around the world by reorienting readers' minds toward the necessity of some kind of reorganization of political structures and reallocation of social and economic resources. But by what program or course of action? What is the actual entity to be brought into being? What, in essence, do the words "national" and "nationalism" mean? Is the goal an independent political state in Africa along the lines of Liberia or Sierra Leone? A separate nation or community within the boundaries of the United States? Both of these possibilities present difficult ideological issues involving the values and laws that will govern membership in the community, and difficult practical issues revolving around location (whose land is to be used for settlement?) and around the future (what are the realistic chances of success?). Or is the goal a kind of supranational community that embraces all peoples of African descent but does not depend on the formation of a geographically and politically discrete state? Perhaps the goal is more modest, though still ambitious: the full extension of the benefits and rights of American citizenship to slaves and free blacks; in this case, do we have nationalist rhetoric directed toward essentially assimilationist ends? These questions define the central dilemma of nineteenth-century African American nationalist writings, and even when taken up explicitly, they often reveal the tangle of concepts and ideologies that can enmesh a writer. I am not, of course, the first person to remark this dilemma, but I hope to provide a better sense of how discourses of nature in the work of militant or separatist African American authors can help us understand both the opportunities and the challenges they faced in articulating a black nationalist ethos.

By the time David Walker's *Appeal* appeared, in September 1829, or about seven months after the *Ethiopian Manifesto*, a number of common themes regarding nature had developed in African American writing: a rejection of the notion of a natural racial hierarchy; an emphasis on the scientific study, and technological mastery, of nature; the depiction of slavery as a disordering or pollution of nature; the assumed dependence of social forms on the natural environment; the representation of Africa as either luxuriously Edenic or agriculturally fertile; and an affection for American nature and a sense of connection to the land.[9] These themes, in turn, operated within a larger pattern of nationalist and antinationalist rhetoric by which northern African American intellectuals positioned their arguments in relation to the master narrative of American exceptionalism. We should understand the *Appeal* against that background, for Walker could not have written his incendiary call-to-arms outside of the rich social and discursive world in which he lived and moved. More elaborately than previous African American writing, however, Walker's text attempts to authorize an aggressively identitarian politics by invoking and reworking the natural law tradition—which proves a slippery undertaking, given the intrinsic instability in the term "nature."

As the operator of a used-clothing store in Boston, Walker managed to distribute his fiery pamphlet clandestinely, relying on sympathetic or unwitting sailors to get it into circulation among the southern black population.[10] Intended to spur black resistance to oppression, the *Appeal* more visibly ignited white paranoia about servile insurrection and provoked repressive measures across the South—for good reason. In its fiercely elenctic relation to the major texts and personages of white America, the *Appeal* represents a milestone in African American militancy. Refuting Jefferson's comments on race in *Notes on the State of Virginia*, satirizing the Constitution, invoking the spirit of Thomas Paine, arguing with Henry Clay, and quoting the Declaration of Independence at length, David Walker talks back as few others had done, and none in print. Yet Walker—as would Henry Highland Garnet and others in his wake—also levels sharp criticisms against what he sees as black weakness, tantamount to complicity, in the face of oppression. He therefore calls for blacks to unite and demands that they work for their own liberation; as suggested by the title, Walker takes a global view of the plight of African-descended peoples, a view that identifies him as a black nationalist as well as a militant. Whether Walker was a "separatist" remains open to debate—Peter Hinks has argued the contrary—but certainly he employed the language of separatism, connecting it to the language of natural race and natural law, for rhetorical purposes.[11]

Walker establishes his empirical frame in the first sentence of the *Appeal*; he writes that his argument will be based on "having, in the course of my travels, taken the most accurate observations of things as they exist."[12] Later in the "Preamble," he writes that his goal is to awaken "a spirit of inquiry and investigation" (2) in his readers by endeavoring "to penetrate, search out, and lay [the sources of oppression] open for your inspection" (3). The word "penetrate" appears on several other occasions, as does its cousin "expose," and recalls the whole tradition of antislavery empiricism extending from James Ramsay's call for the "severest scrutiny" of racial science to William Watkins's comment that "Man, with his wonderfully penetrating and comprehensive powers, has, with singular success, explored the arcana of nature."[13] In the final pages of the *Appeal*, Walker closes the frame: "I do not speak from hear say—what I have written, is what I have seen and heard myself. No man may think that my book is made up of conjecture" (76). From start to finish, then, the reader knows that Walker means to offer not simply an impassioned screed but a rational investigation that observes high standards of evidence, induction, and analysis. Although the European Romantics and early American "transcendentalists" had begun to emphasize intuition rather than "penetration" as the path to truth, Walker saw his imperative as analysis rather than prophecy—as did, with such notable exceptions as Young and Nat Turner, most early African American writers, laboring under the racialized epistemological standards of the "Age of Reason."

Walker's empiricism has a specific purpose. It undergirds his rhetorical method, whereby logical argumentation is grounded in "natural" law, which in turn is grounded in biblical truth. The gestures toward empiricism in his text heighten his rhetorical authority in designating certain social practices unnatural or ungodly. Since he saw no intrinsic conflict between the findings of science and the revelations of the Bible—both point toward the same absolute truth—Walker collapses the realm of nature into that of divinity and assigns to human reason the responsibility of searching out both. He agrees with Jefferson that some truths are "self-evident," but insists that a scientific (i.e., skeptical and inquisitive) approach to history and human society is necessary in order to uncover white society's crimes. An analytical, inductive approach to the plight of both free and enslaved blacks, working backward from the available evidence to the causes and principles at work, would expose the hidden forces, the springs of oppression, the secrets of racial identity, in a manner perfectly analogous to the slave narratives' collective exposé of the realities of the southern institution.

This rhetorical objective helps to account for the insistent historical orientation of the *Appeal*, particularly in the first three sections, in which Walker explains his people's "wretchedness in consequence of" slavery, ignorance, and hypocritical Christian preachers. Having "for years troubl[ed] the pages of historians" (14), Walker writes for "unprejudiced men, who have taken the trouble to read histories" (7), and for those who have taken the trouble to understand the Bible, for just as science and religion ultimately harmonize, so do religion and history: "All persons who are acquainted with history, and particularly the Bible" will recognize, for instance, God's coming judgment against the Spaniards (4). Explicitly, Walker's historicism works to demonstrate the virulence of American slavery in comparison to other forms the world has seen, in contradiction both to proslavery myth and to Jefferson's claim that the southern system could not wholly account for black "inferiority." Implicitly, it enables Walker to trace the causes of racial "degradation" to sociohistorical rather than natural forces.

In that sense, the *Appeal* participated in what John Ernest has termed an African American "counterhistory," a collective endeavor aimed at repairing and reconstituting a story of the past more inclusive of black experience. This "*mode* of representing history," Ernest argues, incorporated both secular and sacred dimensions, and it enabled early "African American communities in the North [to create] consistent patterns of communal discourse that spoke of continuity over time and space, an imagined community drawn from biblical pages and involved in providential journeys."[14] Walker, significantly, concerns himself not only with social history and divine history but also with the history of nature, all of which flow into one another, and although precious little evidence exists as to Walker's direct familiarity with the field of natural history, its intellectual pressures make themselves felt in his text.

Polygenesis posed the most pressing threat. Measuring the racial claims of Jefferson and others against the facts of sacred and profane history, and finding them wanting, Walker mounts one of the most aggressive and sustained responses to the theory in pre-1840 African American writing. Insisting that African Americans themselves must make the case—"for unless we try to refute Mr. Jefferson's arguments respecting us, we will only establish them" (15)—he argues that the Bible irrefutably demonstrates the common humanity of the descendants of Noah, including Ham. Since he must still explain the current "abject" state of his people, Walker turns to the established environmentalist position of antislavery and insists that racial situation derives from historical and social process. Since environmentalism, however, could support the barely compatible notions of racial degeneration in the tropics and of the natural fitness of Africans for hard physical labor, Walker must also counter such proslavery climatism. He therefore predicates his environmentalist argument on an original standard of African greatness, turning like many other African American writers to Egypt, the supposed apex and archetype of black civilization, which only European avarice and cruelty could destroy.[15] The greatness of their civilization, Walker writes, consisted largely in scientific and technological achievements: "the wise legislators, the Pyramids, and other magnificent buildings—the turning of the channel of the river Nile, by the sons of Africa or of Ham, among whom learning originated" (19). While allowing for a degree of intermixture among the Egyptians—"some of them yellow and others dark—a mixture of Ethiopians and the natives of Egypt—about the same as you see the coloured people of the United States at the present day" (8)—like Robert Alexander Young he champions blackness because "it pleased [God] to make us black" (12).

That phrasing, though, would seem to locate racial distinctions in an original and divine plan, and touches on the central paradox of the *Appeal*: If race relations are the product of history, why does Walker suggest on numerous occasions that whites and blacks are "natural enemies," italicizing the phrase every time? Such aggressive identitarian rhetoric runs against the antislavery doctrine of the unity of humankind, in the sense that racial degradation or racial self-interest are presented as sociohistorical products of *intrinsic* racial difference and *natural* racial conflict. Arguing that "whites have always been an unjust, jealous, unmerciful, avaricious and blood-thirsty set of beings" (16), he writes that "I therefore . . . advance my suspicion of them, whether they are *as good by nature* as we are or not" (17, original emphasis). In this parodic inversion of Jefferson's "suspicion" regarding blacks' inferiority in *Notes on the State of Virginia*, Walker substitutes morality for intellect as the criterion of natural superiority. "Natural observations have taught me," he continues, that "there is a solemn awe in the hearts of the blacks, as it respects *murdering* men: whereas the whites . . . murder all before them" (24). Perhaps, then, it is not in human nature, but in *white* nature, that racial oppression originates. For that reason, Walker scorns intermarriage ("the black man, or man of colour, who will leave his own colour . . . and marry a white woman . . . ought to be treated by her as he surely will be, viz: as a NIGGER!" [9]), even as he cites it as a sign of liberality in ancient Egypt. While unabashedly reversing the terms of the Jeffersonian position may be a rhetorically and psychologically effective strategy, Walker does not rebut the essential core of that position, namely, that racial difference and conflict are part of the natural order.

Though in part parodying Jefferson, Walker turns serious in explaining what he means by "natural enemies" in Article IV of the *Appeal.* In the beginning, he writes, the races were not natural enemies, since "[m]an, in all ages and all nations of the earth, is the same" (61). After the flood, only Noah and his wives and sons survived to people the earth, and these eight "were not natural enemies to each other" (60). Through the greed and violence of the whites in later ages, however, through the "natural love in them, to be called master" (61), "they, themselves, (and not us) render themselves our natural enemies, by treating us so cruel" (62). Confronted with the corner that Walker seems to have painted himself into, Stuckey makes the debatable claim that "Walker apparently did not mean literally that whites were the natural enemies of his people."[16] But without defining what "literally" might mean in this context, Stuckey misses the central paradox of Walker's argument: the tension between a universal human nature and divergent racial natures. Walker *does* mean it literally, because he plays on a crucial ambiguity in the relation between history and nature. On one hand, "nature" is grounded absolutely and immutably in biblical truth and thus transcends historical time; on the other hand, human nature is responsive to history, and can be changed, for better or worse, through human agency. In dancing between humanism and racialism, then, Walker suggests that slaves and freedmen face the ongoing challenge—authorized by a standard of natural law that religion and science both affirm—of fighting prejudice and oppression and restoring society, especially white society, to a state of natural harmony that the history of racial nature has clouded but not fundamentally altered.

Walker's doubts, like Jefferson's, as to whether "natural enemies" can peacefully coexist would seem to militate in favor of colonization or voluntary emigration to Africa. Walker, however, denounces the former policy on both practical and ethical grounds. He calls Henry Clay's advocacy of colonization a transparent ploy designed to remove free blacks from the United States, and argues that Elias B. Caldwell's seemingly innocuous procolonization arguments require "close examination and deep penetration" to be revealed as pernicious (52). On slightly different grounds, and echoing a common anticolonizationist argument, he maintains that slaves and freedmen have earned the right to stay in America because they have laid down cultural and psychological roots in the land. He quotes a *Freedom's Journal* essay by Richard Allen in which the founder of the AME Church writes that "[t]his land which we have watered with our *tears* and *our blood*, is now our *mother country*" (58). For the same reason Walker criticizes those African Americans who choose to emigrate, but he suggests that if they must, the logical destinations would be England, with "the best friends the coloured people have upon earth" (41); Haiti, home of "our brethren" (56); or the "hospitable shores of Canada" (49). Africa, however, he calls a land of "Pagans and blood" (50). Although Walker admires what he sees as the natural moral virtue of Africans, and their slumbering martial courage, he likewise did not regard African countries as civilized or African cultures as truly enriching. The *Appeal*, rather, offers an epidermalized Africanist ethos uniting the people he collectively calls "my colour," but detached from the actual geographical and cultural realities of Africa. Walker insists on the need for "Africans" in the diaspora to unite, but he is *not* talking about reversing the process of spatial dislocation.

When the historical weight of Walker's argument, therefore, moves from an analysis of the past to a vision of the future, his comments take on an oracular vagueness. "Our sufferings will come to an *end*, in spite of all the Americans this side of *eternity*" (15); glory and happiness will not come "but with the entire emancipation of your enslaved brethren all over the world" (29); "our greatest happiness shall consist in working for the salvation of our whole body" (29); the "enslaved children of Africa will have, in spite of all their enemies, to take their stand among the *nations* of the earth."[17] In the terms he has set up, however, the obstacles to such a non-African Africanist nationalism are formidable. They involve having to overcome the laws and structures of white society, the now depraved "nature" of whites, and the very burden of history itself, for only at a time when "the whole of the past will be sunk into oblivion" will they be able to become a "united and happy people" (70).

The power to unmake history, Walker makes clear, belongs fundamentally to God, but people can participate in the divine plan. Here as well, however, the programmatic dimension of Walker's argument grows dim. He consistently advocates doing *something*, but he just as often equivocates as to what, oscillating between representing violence as morally justified and advocating nonviolent means of resistance. On one hand, vengeance belongs to God: "although the destruction of the oppressors God may not effect by the oppressed, yet the Lord our God will bring other destructions upon them" (3); on the other hand, God "will give you a Hannibal" (20), an avenging leader reminiscent of Young's black messiah and Abbé Raynal's "Black Spartacus." In one of the text's most richly ambiguous passages, Walker conflates agency and inevitability, divine mercy and divinely sanctioned vengeance:

> As true as the sun ever shone in its meridian splendor, my colour will root some of them out of the very face of the earth. . . . No doubt some may say that I write with a bad spirit, and that I being a black, wish these things to occur. Whether I write with a bad or a good spirit, I say if these things do occur in their proper time, it is because the world in which we live does not exist, and we are deceived with regard to its existence.—It is immaterial however to me, who believe, or who refuse—though I should like to see the whites repent peradventure God may have mercy on them, some however, have gone so far that their cup must be filled. (20)

Here Walker seems to aim for a stylized, studied ambiguity, perhaps to fray the nerves of his white readers, or perhaps, out of fear for his own life, to avoid the charge that he was advocating anything more radical than a faith in God's justice. The latter possibility runs up against his stated willingness to risk his own life in the interests of publication, and the former fails to take into account that he needed his white readers. A more compelling explanation is that Walker really was not certain in his own mind what he envisioned—that the ambiguity in the text is heartfelt but not deliberate, a product of the horizons he descried in his own argument.

The utility of violence represented one horizon; the future relationship of blacks and whites represented another. Opposed to both colonization and emigration, Walker insists that blacks should stay in the United States, which "is more our country than it is the whites [*sic*]" (65), but could these "natural enemies" coexist even after slaves and freed blacks obtain their due freedom and rights? Can they form one nation under God? Significantly, Walker frequently refers to "Americans" and the "American people" collectively as the enemy; consistent with his comments on the racial nature of whites, he desectionalizes the causes of oppression. The goal, we know, is not an independent black nation outside of the United States, and several statements in the *Appeal* suggest that Walker does not advocate a kind of internal separatism. If his people achieve full liberty, he writes, "we will love and respect [the whites], and protect our country" (66); if they are treated "like men, . . . there is no danger but we will all live in peace and happiness together" (70). Witnessing that day would require a reversal of history and the historical transmutation of human nature, but the clearly emotional longing for inclusion in "America" and for interracial harmony among Americans must qualify our common perception of David Walker as a militant black nationalist.

Stripped down, his real aims seem to be that African Americans should "prove to the Americans and the world, that we are MEN and not *brutes*" by assuming responsibility for their situation and undertaking the "dissemination of education and religion" (30), while whites should "repent and reform" (40). (Walker, incidentally, addresses his white readers fully as often and as urgently as he does the "coloured citizens of the world.") Modeled, ironically, on the U.S. Constitution, David Walker's *Appeal* represents a blueprint not for a governmental system but for racial *and* human consciousness. It is a black nationalist text in the sense of calling for, and seeking to create, unity, self-respect, and self-help among all people of African descent, but it nonetheless points up the complications and limits of black nationalism as the ideology could be articulated in 1829. History, geography, human nature, divine nature—these represented the coordinates of the *Appeal*, and they defined both the center and the circumference of the text. In the coming years, Emerson would grapple with precisely these issues in trying to formulate a vision of human history and American civic identity that accommodated racial difference and conflict. But Emerson had the advantage of working on this problem for decades. Walker, however, died less than a year after the publication of the *Appeal*, apparently of natural causes, leaving us to wonder where his thinking, and writings, would have taken him.

In the decades following, as the national conflict over slavery grew more entrenched and divisive, radical African American politics attained increased visibility both inside and outside the antislavery movement. While black nationalism or black militancy did not, predictably, prevail over the generally integrationist strategies of mainstream abolitionism, they did push the rhetorical envelope. Indeed, such radicalism found inspiration, and justification, in the continuing failure of moral suasion and accommodationist politics to accomplish real results in limiting the growth of slavery, let alone abolishing it. The abiding questions centered on which strategies would best serve the interests of American blacks, and how those interests might or might not align with the American polity at large or with other African-descended peoples in the world. Among the black activists and leaders who emerged during the 1830s, 1840s, and 1850s, including Henry Highland Garnet, Samuel Ringgold Ward, Robert Purvis, Frederick Douglass, and others, these questions gave rise to a wide spectrum of responses, and generated considerable debate, at times curdling into rancor, within both black and white antislavery circles.

Rather than tracing the evolving contours of militant African American thought during this period, I want to leap ahead to the work of Martin Delany, particularly his novel *Blake*, in order to assess a revealing expression of that thought on the brink of civil war. In concentrating on the endpoints of an ideological trajectory stretching from the late 1820s to the early 1860s, I hope to suggest the ways in which antebellum black nationalism acquired new strengths, encountered new challenges, and faced many of the same internal problems as it had in the 1820s. Delany's work in particular creatively orchestrates scientific and aesthetic languages of nature, linking ideas of human nature and the natural world to a shifting understanding of both national and transnational communities.

The late 1840s were a frustrating, embittering time for Delany, and they provide crucial context for understanding his turn to more aggressive, emigrationist politics during the 1850s. The Mexican War of 1846–48, the subsequent annexation of Texas as a slave state, the evident hypocrisy of the Free-Soil Party, which Delany regarded as working "not for the extension of liberty to the black man, but for the protection of the liberty of the white,"[18] his own dismissal from Harvard Medical School on account of race, and then the hated Compromise of 1850—all these, among other reverses, made it increasingly clear to Delany that the usual antislavery strategies were not succeeding and that the racial climate of the United States might never allow black people freely to work out their own destiny. During the brief period in 1848 and 1849 when he collaborated with Douglass as coeditor of the *North Star*, Delany did pursue a generally integrationist line, but it was getting harder to maintain one's optimism about the prospects for African American uplift. During his "Western Tour for the North Star," a year-long sojourn through the mid-Atlantic and mid-West, Delany wrote a series of letters to Douglass for publication in which he shared his thoughts and observations about American society. The signs were not good. In an April 1848 letter, for instance, he railed against "the miserable truckling to the slave-power, and low servility manifested at most every house upon the road, and in every town through which I passed."[19] The extent, the toxicity, and, perhaps more importantly, the unexamined character of northern racism seemed to Delany an insurmountable obstacle to the achievement of black freedom in the United States.

Beyond the toxicities of the cultural world, however, the natural world provided Delany some relief, and a much-needed morale boost. A letter he wrote to Douglass in February 1849, describing the mountains of eastern Pennsylvania, is worth quoting at length:

> Many are the scenes throughout the whole course of these vast mountains and valleys—beautiful, picturesque, grand and sublime, well worthy the pen-

> cil of the most accomplished artist. In summer, when clothed with foliage and verdure, the scenery is beyond the most graphic description. . . . The soul may here expand in the magnitude of its nature and soar to the extent of human susceptibility. Indeed it is only in the mountains that I can fully appreciate my existence as a man in America, my own native land. It is then and there my soul is lifted up, my bosom caused to swell with emotion, and I am lost in wonder at the dignity of my own nature. I see in the works of nature around me, the wisdom and goodness of God. I contemplate them, and conscious that he has endowed me with faculties to comprehend them, I then perceive the likeness I bear to him. What a being is man!—of how much importance!—created in the impress image of his Maker; and how debased is God, and outraged his divinity in the person of the oppressed colored people of America! The thunders of his mighty wrath must sooner or later break forth, with all of the terrible consequences and scourge this guilty nation for the endless outrages and cruelty committed upon an innocent and unoffending people.[20]

Not its fairly commonplace Romantic rhetoric but the arc of its ideas makes this passage particularly interesting. The natural world first appears a collection of scenes understood through the usual aesthetic categories and providing the raw material for artistic representation. Then, since Delany finds it "beyond" objective description, the focus shifts to subjective experience, Emersonian in its intensity, by which temporary immersion in the surroundings (being "lost in wonder") stimulates both active knowledge, prompting him to "contemplate" and "comprehend" nature, and self-knowledge, in perceiving his likeness to God. The moral and emotional renewal this experience brings about leads, in turn, to the ideological and political aggression figured in his jeremiadic call for divine vengeance against an unjust society. The trajectory of this passage, wherein nature appears sequentially as aesthetic challenge, as phenomenological life-world, and as the face of divine authority, nicely illustrates our recurring theme of how an experiential turn to nature can occasion a more critical stance toward culture.

During the 1850s, the pressing question for Delany centered on whether African Americans could achieve meaningful and long-lasting uplift within the United States or would need to emigrate, perhaps to Africa, perhaps somewhere else, in order to establish a racially just society. As Robert Levine has demonstrated, Delany's thinking about the issues of emigration and assimilation intersected with his ambitions to "representative identity," and evolved as part of a complex dialogue with the writings of Douglass, Garnet, Lewis Woodson, Henry Bibb, Samuel Ward, and other black leaders.[21] Though generally occupying the separatist and emigrationist end of the spectrum, Delany revealed a high level of ambivalence and even contradiction in his views of the potential for interracial coexistence, of the respective value of racial as opposed to national allegiance, of the best location for a new Africanist state, and even of the desirability or feasibility of such a state.[22] In his major works of nonfiction—*The Condition, Elevation, Emigration and Destiny of the Colored People of the United States* (1852), *Origin and Objects of Ancient Freemasonry* (1853), and *Official Report of the Niger Valley Exploring Party* (1861)—Delany worked toward the position of advocating the Christian and commercial civilization of Africa, an undertaking that American blacks themselves would lead. Although his vision of a renewed Africa proceeded, in Basil Davidson's words, "on entirely non-African lines," that vision was based on an enduring belief in the value of "black blood," which would ultimately unify people of African descent.[23] Delany, however, seems never to have quite resolved in his own mind how to imagine the future relation of that blood to the American polity. As in David Walker's *Appeal*, this irresolution resulted partly from the inevitable entanglement of his writings in American values and ideologies and partly from his own uncertainty; a more immediate and commanding intrusion came in the form of the Civil War, which radically altered the historical and conceptual landscape for all ideologies of African American nationalism.

These issues converge dramatically in Delany's novel *Blake; or, The Huts of America*, serialized in the *Weekly Anglo-African* from 1859 to 1862 and first published in book form in 1970.[24] The novel, the first full-length fictional treatment of black nationalism to appear in the United States, follows the insurrectionary plans of Henry Blake, born free as Henrico Blacus in Cuba but sold into American slavery while still a child. The narrative covers nearly as much geographic territory as does Equiano's autobiography, but it tends to meander. In part 1, Blake travels throughout the southern states, planting the seeds of conspiracy and rebellion among rural slaves, and then escapes with several companions to Canada. In part 2, he heads for Cuba to rescue his wife from slavery, becomes involved with the movement to overthrow Spanish colonial rule, travels to Africa as a stowaway spy aboard a slave ship, and finally returns to Havana, where the rebellion haltingly approaches a climax, having become embroiled with the local forces of proslavery countersubversion. The international scope of the novel reflects Delany's determination to expose the complex geopolitical forces at work in sustaining the slave system, and Delany's attention to the economic interdependence of North and South works, as in the *Appeal*, to desectionalize the problem of slavery and thereby establish the rationale for separatism as opposed to assimilationist reform.[25] Despite *Blake*'s explicit separatism, however, it cannot escape the concept and reality of "America," largely because the discourses of nature on which Delany draws, to great effect, remain implicated in the same ideological and cultural system he seeks to repudiate.

Consistent with the Lockean line of natural law theory (particularly as adapted to the American context), *Blake* presents the right of revolution as a right authorized by nature. The novel goes beyond mere polemic, however, by illustrating that the processes of nature themselves participate in the course of liberation, and that to impede them is as futile an endeavor, ultimately, as to dam the Mississippi. Where eighteenth-century natural law theorists had posited a quasi-historical "state of nature" in which people enjoyed an elemental freedom, Delany imagines a much closer relationship between the course of human society and the course of nature. Turning to organic metaphors to describe Blake's planned uprising, he compares the conspiracy to a harvest ("little time is required to mature the crop for the sickle of the reaper" [241]), and to an infection ("it will spread like smallpox among them" [41]). The concept of historical inevitability underlies the entire argument: "Nature being exact and regular in all her fixed laws, suspended nor altered them to suit no person, circumstance, or thing. . . . [The time to strike] would overtake them whether or not they desired it, though in accordance with its own economy, would be harmless and unfelt in its action and progress" (292). Framing the rebellion in these terms places on all people (and on the readers directly) the responsibility of aligning themselves with the forward motion of nature, which entails the advance of universal freedom, which entails in turn the destruction of the international slave system.

Clear that the course of nature and history tends toward rebellion and freedom, Delany seems less clear as to the relationship between human history and human "blood." As does Walker's *Appeal*, *Blake* expresses a tension between human unity and racial division, a simultaneous assertion of a common human nature, eternally unchanging, which entitles all people to natural rights, and of the existence of multiple racial bloods that have emerged over time and in various places. Not bothering with Walker's gestures toward reconciliation, Delany, who claimed full African blood himself, insists that "pure-blooded" blacks have the right to their own land, not only in Africa but in the New World as well:

> The colored races . . . were by nature adapted to the tropical regions of this part of the world as to all other similar climates, it being a scientific fact that they increased and progressed whilst the whites decreased and continually retrograded, their offspring becoming enervated and imbecile. . . . [The colored races] had inherited those regions by birth, paid for the soil by toil, irrigated it with their sweat, enriched it with their blood, nothing remaining to be done but by a dependence in Divine aid, a reliance in their own ability, and strength of their own arms, but to claim and take possession. (287)

Inverting the proslavery argument that the tropical climate of Africa had destined Africans for hard labor, the revolutionaries argue from the same premise but for the purpose of asserting a right to the land they worked, a right to a humanity and a subjectivity defined by their relationship to the natural world. Charged with Delany's scorn for European and American imperialists, this sharply ironic moment of racialist pride nonetheless bears the stamp of a colonialist outlook, not only in the appeal to "scientific fact," but in the vocabularies of Christianity, of Emersonian self-reliance, and of private property.

When all is said and done, however, nothing much happens at the end of the novel. No broad revolution or even local rebellion takes place, and Henry Blake himself has faded into the background. The characters stand poised at the edge of insurrection, their plans for a general uprising at the point of fruition, but the expected climax never comes. The final line of the book, "'Woe be unto those devils of whites, I say!'" is spoken by the minor character Gofer Gondolier as "an authentic statement of [the Afro-Cubans'] outrage" (313)—but this is essentially the same outrage with which the book began, notwithstanding its sharper edge. Over the years, critics of the novel have attempted to explain its curiously open-ended conclusion, or nonconclusion, or what T. Douglas Doyle has called its stance of "paralyzed resistance."[26] Eric Sundquist links the incompleteness of *Blake* to the uncertain future of the struggle against slavery in 1862, and goes on to suggest that "perhaps, like Melville [in *Benito Cereno*], Delany took proslavery countersubversion to be more potent than black rebellion; or, perhaps the most interesting possibility, he saw that such a surprising eclipse of the novel's revolutionary import augmented its threat."[27] Robert Levine points out, however, that the extant text ends with chapter 74 while the original reputedly had eighty chapters, and speculates that in these missing six chapters Delany might have "written a series of relatively nonviolent scenes that enabled Blake to emerge at the helm of a regenerated society in which blackness is seen not as an exclusive or essential good but as equally worthy (or unworthy) as whiteness." Levine therefore suggests that, in the context of Delany's ongoing struggle with Douglass for political stature and influence, this hypothetical ending would represent an effort to temper the novel's message and widen its appeal by drawing back from a depiction of widespread bloodshed. Blake's ascent "would . . . provide U.S. whites with an image not of black homicidal fury but of responsible black leadership" and would thus "contribute to the emancipation and elevation of blacks in the United States."[28]

Or we might downplay the role of intention and suggest that Delany encountered a horizon of vision when approaching the end of his novel. From this perspective, the force of black nationalist rhetoric in *Blake* reveals the same programmatic limitations as did the *Appeal*. The novel's final chapters cannot quite answer how to translate inevitability into actuality, natural providence into concrete realities, for even if nature authorizes revolution, people still have the responsibility to create new political and social circumstances within historical time. The inevitability of the future, that is, runs up against the difficulty of imagining what, exactly, the future will entail—a difficulty the more striking in a work of fiction, where we might expect a greater imaginative freedom. As does the *Appeal*, *Blake* accomplishes other kinds of cultural work, shaping perceptions rather than offering a blueprint for a new society. Separating from the United States as a political and geographical entity evidently proves harder to accomplish than the work's revolutionary optimism might suggest.

Even when Delany does get down to the real business of separatism and emigration, leaving America proves easier than leaving "America." In his 1861 *Official Report of the Niger Valley Exploring Party*, Delany makes very specific recommendations about emigration to Africa, discussing everything from the best season to travel and the necessary precautions against disease to the importance of clearing land and the possibilities for expanding commodities production and trade. Yet although he writes that "I have outgrown, long since, the boundaries of North America, and with them have also outgrown the boundaries of their claims," he can sound much like any other nineteenth-century colonialist seeking to bring "civilization" to the benighted regions of the world: "Africa for the African race and black men to rule them."[29] Just as he separates the concept of Africanism from geographic place in *Blake*, so he separates "America" from the United States in the Niger Valley report, recommending for Liberia and Yoruba civilization on essentially American terms, including a Christian view of nature and a utilitarian attitude toward the natural world. No less eagerly than Equiano seventy years earlier, Delany imagines a future for Africa that involves the expansion of free trade and free labor, the growth of manufactures and technology, the taming of the wilderness ("wild beasts are driven back before the march of civilization" [102]), and the inculcation of a spiritual worldview at odds with local religious traditions—all in the service, understandably enough, of promoting antislavery and making

Africa more competitive on the world stage. Nonetheless, the project essentially recapitulates the founding of "America," and suggests that, despite the importance of blood identity in Delany's thinking, national identity, as an ideological and cultural, if not political or geographical, matter, proves more tangibly and durably effective as a unifying force. Separatism and expansionism, it becomes clear, are near allied.

At this point in Delany's life—the simultaneous publication of the Niger Valley report and of *Blake*—the South undertook precisely the step of political separation that Delany fantasized about for American blacks. The outbreak of war, of course, fundamentally changed the equation for all abolitionists, particularly in terms of their thinking about their relation to the union. Certainly the war enabled the antislavery movement to coalesce around a nationalistic core that represented their apotheosis into the mainstream, and for some abolitionists, including Delany, that represented an ironic reversal of long-standing, radically oppositional commitments. The militant emigrationist, author of some of the era's most aggressively anti–United States texts, accepted a commission as a major in the Union army and ended up fighting not only for the values but for the political and geographic integrity of the nation he once advocated leaving.

Of Men and Mollusks: Emerson's Providential Biology

In 1829, when the *Ethiopian Manifesto* and David Walker's *Appeal* appeared, Ralph Waldo Emerson was a twenty-six-year-old Unitarian minister whose views of race involved more or less unreconstructed stereotypes passed down within the insular class structure of Boston's professional and social elite. By 1862, the year of Delany's *Blake*, Emerson had become a convert to abolitionism and an active supporter of the Union cause—a personal odyssey that entailed, on his part, a thoroughgoing reassessment of the meanings of race and nation.

Like his African American counterparts, Emerson struggled with imagining the possibilities and forms of racial coexistence in the United States, and he faced similar challenges in developing a political and philosophical position that was both sufficiently creative and sufficiently practical—sufficient, that is, to govern the transition to a postslavery society. And like them, Emerson faced a difficult conceptual conundrum. His spiritual philosophy had always rested on an unshakeable faith in the absolute unity, interconnectedness, and goodness of a universe that embodied on every hand the spirit of the Deity. His nationalism had been built on a determination to unify his countrymen under the banner of Americanism, even as he insisted that individuals obey their own genius, and to have them see that the "thousand various threads of national descent and employment [are bound] fast in one web."[30] But Emerson's understanding of race—powerfully influenced by his reading of contemporary scientific and ethnological literature—both presupposed and posited the inevitability of interracial conflict. No less than Walker and Delany, he suspected that "whites" and "blacks" might be "natural" enemies. Yet Emerson reached conclusions very different from theirs.

To extricate himself from a logical cul-de-sac, Emerson would assert that racial competition enabled a more perfect union, that the conflict of parts strengthened the whole, and that a vital pluralism undergirded a healthy American state. Drawing on and transforming contemporary theories of race, history, and natural science, Emerson developed an understanding of national destiny that envisioned racial struggle as integral to the upward progress and inevitable union of America. As the sectional crisis deteriorated, Emerson came to believe that the volatile energy of racial conflict, like that of individual dissent, would serve not to disrupt the union but to provide the creative dialectic necessary to its well-being.

Emerson also drew on different conceptual resources than did Walker and Delany. In working toward an optimistic interpretation of "facts on the ground" that seemed to leave very little room for optimism, Emerson found crucial assistance in early evolutionary theory, which gave him a model for reconceiving racial and national history, indeed for reconceiving the very categories of race and nation. Translating his long-held belief in the importance of individual spiritual transfiguration into scientific, literal, and collective terms, Emerson came to understand the ongoing ascent of the human species as a natural biological process that embodied, advanced, and partially revealed the divine plan. To this extent, he occupied the scientific mainstream—the mainstream, at least, of those scientists who accepted the proposition that species could change over time in accordance with God's will. Yet when it came to the racial dimensions of early evolutionary theory, Emerson proved much more unorthodox. Interpreting racial competition and evolutionary progress in highly metaphorical ways, and incorporating them into a vision of transcendent design, Emerson began to articulate a concept of racial developmentalism that enabled him to see the classifications of race as mutable and the conflicts of race as purposefully directed. From here Emerson drew two striking corollaries: first, that collective human ascent would involve the mingling and eventual unification of racial "stocks," and secondly, that racial union superseded national union as a means of realizing humanity's full potential. In his writings and addresses on slavery and race, dating from roughly the mid-1840s to the outbreak of civil war, Emerson seems to have arrived at the conclusion that the motto *e pluribus unum* must apply to racial pluralism, and that national vigor, even survival, depended on racial assimilation and amalgamation. This pointed, ultimately, toward what I will call a "cosmopolitanism of blood" that recognized different racial identities even as it sought to merge them, and to submerge the violence they occasioned. The *sine qua non* of this cosmopolitanism was Emerson's irreducibly humanist belief that the biological and spiritual bonds linking humanity into one whole were more important, more fundamental, than national allegiance, cultural background, or environmental circumstance.

While much recent work on Emerson has, implicitly or explicitly, divorced his reformist activities from his spiritual philosophy, during the intensifying crisis over slavery Emerson sought to develop an ethics informed by rather than disjunct from transcendental insight.[31] And its most important area of influence, he came to believe, would be race. For a long time, however, scholarship on Emerson has adhered to a simplified analytical binary in which he appears as either a "racist" who betrayed his faith in human equality, or a kind of "recovering racist" who managed to overcome his retrograde views and take his place on the right side of history. More recent work, however, has begun to liberate Emerson from this restrictive framework, and from the anachronistic judgments of his racial thought that it tends to promote, and we can now appreciate more clearly Emerson's shifting, subtle responses to contemporaneous debates regarding race. At stake are both our full understanding of the history of racial thought in the United States and Emerson's reputation as a writer who has something important to say to modern readers, even if they reach different conclusions as to where he stands on the key issues.

Put broadly, Emerson's vision of natural design informed, and greatly complicated, his understanding of all things racial. Through his reading in natural history and natural philosophy, Emerson came to regard human biology and racial differentiation as part of the process whereby Nature manifests itself in the affairs of people. Throughout the 1840s and 1850s, he sought in professional science answers to the mysteries of both racial identity and providential design, for these he deemed inseparable; providence worked, in part, *through* the existence of race as an element of the natural order, and natural science worked, ideally, to reveal that order. Yet because this order revealed itself over the course of time, in visible transformations in the natural and human worlds, people could only apprehend it within the inevitable limits of their historical, social, and cognitive circumstances. Accordingly, race constitutes both a natural and a historical category in Emerson's writings; it derives from such physical circumstances as climate and biological inheritance, and yet remains a matter for social definition and manipulation. As Emerson recognized, however, "naturalizing" race to any degree posed the danger of undermining or compromising his antislavery activism by seeming to reinscribe the hard-line position that racial inequality was both ordained and eternal. This resembled, indeed, the very problem that confronted aggressively identitarian African American writers. Somehow, Emerson believed, he had to find within nature, or natural process, a recuperative vision of racial harmony. The challenge was to accommodate theories that posited the "natural" origin of racial division and conflict with his conviction that slavery violated natural law and the divine will, and with his belief in the ultimate goodness of eschatological history.

The philosophical flexibility demanded by such a challenge manifests in the complex exchanges between the natural and the cultural that run throughout Emerson's writings. These exchanges appear, on the one hand, in his awareness of how culture can, if not fundamentally alter Nature itself, then largely govern its role in human life, and in his belief that distinct forms of social development can generate potentially self-replicating variations within "human nature"—an idea similar to Walker's concept of racial natures. On the other hand, they appear in Emerson's belief that natural environments and dynamic natural processes will give rise to a variety of cultural practices. This lemniscate relationship between nature and culture implies that in "naturalizing" race, Emerson did more than simply locate human difference in some unchanging, transcendent biological order. Within the limits of his time and place, Emerson undertook a rediscovery of the meaning of race precisely because he appreciated the dangers of ideological obscurantism, and because he saw more rhetorical and political maneuverability within "nature" than he has been given credit for. Characteristically, he found that maneuverability, aimed toward establishing a more humane social truth, by reconstructing on his own terms the languages of natural science.

Take one of his more well-known comments on race. In his 1844 anniversary address on West Indian emancipation, Emerson offered a rather grim tribute to the colony's former slaves by applauding their capacity for racial self-reliance: "When at last in a race, a new principle appears, an idea;—*that* conserves it; ideas only save races. If the black man is feeble, and not important to the existing races, not on a parity with the best race, the black man must serve, and be exterminated. . . . I say to you, you must save yourselves, black or white, man or woman; other help is none. I esteem the occasion of this jubilee to be the proud discovery that the black race can contend with the white" (*EAW* 31). Over the coming years Emerson would tone down the rhetoric, but his essential belief in the inescapability of racial competition never significantly changed, and this passage, along with many others, can readily be construed as evidence of a blithe acquiescence to the "naturalness" of racial domination, or at least to the concept of "natural enemies."[32] However, it also reveals one of the master keys that would help Emerson out of the ethical and intellectual jailhouse of biological determinism and everlasting race war. That key is the tension subsisting between his Hegelian fetishizing of "ideas" and "principles," which he believed defined a racial group's metaphysical identity, and his evident acceptance of the physical or phenotypic characteristics that defined a racial group in the first place.

For it was in the conceptual and rhetorical field defined by the poles of biology and spirit and culture where Emerson's love of metaphor and metamorphosis found its revitalizing power, enabling him to develop a workable philosophical response to the dilemma he faced. That response depended on a particular attitude toward scientific "facts," one that incorporated them into a more subjective epistemological framework by passing them through a kind of analogical filter. Though sharing Walker's respect for empirical method, Emerson blended it with a transcendentalist's love of internal vision. Accordingly, the "findings" of racial and evolutionary science prompted Emerson, in the late 1840s and 1850s, to revisit and reevaluate his earlier views of natural process—not so much to reject the assumptions he had made as to shift the ground of subjective understanding.

In the same year as the West Indies address, Emerson jotted down a problem that had preoccupied him: "The two Histories [line break] The question whether the trilobites or whether the gods are our grandfathers; and whether the actually existing men are an amelioration or a degradation, depends on the contingence whether we look from the material, or from the poetic side."[33] Three years later, the problem still intrigued him: "History. [line break] It is not determined of man whether he came up or down; Cherubim or Chimpanzee." For Emerson, who saw human origins as a kind of Rosetta stone to human destiny, this apparent indeterminacy represented one of the ambiguities of midcentury natural science. Some of the big questions that he had been asking since at least the late 1830s—"Whence came the negro? . . . What is the genealogy of languages? & When & What is the Genesis of Man?"—seemed to call for determinate answers, but part of Emerson's intellectual evolution lay in recognizing that determinacy was a subjective as much as an objective state.[34] It represented one of the means by which culture created nature, and by which scientific and historical languages would seek to settle the question of human origins. Cherubim or chimpanzee, trilobites or gods?

Any answer, Emerson came to believe, lay within as well as without, and this belief reflected not just transcendental rapture but also a deeply conflicted response to the scientific project.

Throughout the 1840s and 1850s, the very literal claims of anthropology, zoology, and geology (the "material" side of the question) exerted increasing pressure on Emerson's metaphoric (or "poetic") turn of mind. Although he rejected an absolutist conception of higher law or natural law, and although he insisted on the sanctity of human agency and consent, Emerson's reading in natural science seemed to intimate that a network of deterministic principles operated everywhere in nature, generating an almost infinite web of causal relationships that he sometimes designated by the term "necessity." Together, these higher laws, in the plural, constituted the material side of existence that could not in good faith be explained away, and they had, in Emerson's view, a direct bearing on the course of racial and social history.

Yet because it posed a threat to the heavenly gifts of human liberty and even human individuality, scientific materialism seems to have stimulated in Emerson new and fruitful avenues of metaphorical reasoning. The literal "facts" uncovered by professional science, he believed, were but shards of divine Fact, and even if objectively true only acquired real (i.e., spiritual) meaning in the kaleidoscope of human consciousness. Throughout the 1850s this impulse toward analogy and perspective would serve as a bulwark for Emerson against the increasingly insistent literalism and narrowness of focus that characterized the scientific establishment. In a notebook entry from the early 1850s, Emerson criticized the epistemology of an undifferentiated realm of "science": "Science false by being unpoetical. It assumes to explain a reptile or mollusk, & isolates it, which is hunting for life in graveyards. Reptile or mollusk, as man, or angel, only exists in system, in relation. The metaphysicist, the poet, only sees it as an inevitable step in the path of the Creator."[35] To see men and mollusks in their infinite relationality—to read the world metaphorically—meant removing the self from too close an association with its objects of attention. While not allowing us to deny scientific facts, a poetic or philosophical perspective would enable us to regard them from a more favorable angle of vision. Among its other benefits, such as limiting humanity's implication in "lower" biological realities, it would provide psychological insulation against the ceaseless violence of natural process: "The whole circle of animal life, internecine war, a yelp of pain & a grunt of triumph, until, at last, the whole mass is mellowed & refined for higher use,—pleases at a sufficient perspective."[36] If modern natural science had made vivid a "ferocity in the interiors of nature," Emerson instinctively longed for a vantage point outside the abattoir.

For all its harrowing revelations, however, natural science also yielded important spiritual resources. In the pages of botanists and biologists, paleontologists and entomologists, Emerson found not just a pattern of isolation, constraint, violence, and destruction but one of seemingly universal melioration—a process of correction and improvement in natural forms that went forward in all places and at all times.[37] Good fortune! Here was a material "fact" that accorded very neatly with a belief in divine design and human progress. Since "[w]hatever he pretend, naturalist means you & me," it would require but little effort for the mind to achieve the poetic perspective, and to grasp that biological melioration implied both spiritual and sociohistorical progress, that the corrective principle radiated outward from cells to societies. The "moral of science," after all, "is the transference of our trust in Nature's admired arrangements to the sphere of personal & social life."[38] This idea presented one way of seeing past the horizon that confronted Walker, and it reappears as a fictional principle in *Blake*'s natural economy of progressive freedom. Emerson pushed it a bit further, however. Crucially, it was his predilection for metaphorizing the findings of science that encouraged Emerson—as it did others of an analogical turn of mind—to seize on the developmental hypothesis as a theoretical template for meliorative social growth.[39] As suggested in chapter 3, not many antislavery writers engaged with early evolutionary theory in a serious and sustained fashion. Emerson was one of those who did.

In the broadest sense, developmentalism enabled Emerson to move from a synchronic and radial model of human existence ("[man] is placed in the centre of beings") to a linear and diachronic one ("finer to finest").[40] More specifically, the theory gave Emerson a method for conceiving of human progress in terms that bridged the scientific and the spiritual. It helped to discipline and strengthen his long-standing belief that only through a temporally situated process of transfiguration (as opposed to instantaneous grace) could the potential in any human being be fully realized. In identifying human biological development as one of the essential forms of universal, natural melioration, Emerson added a vital literal dimension to a concept of spiritual metamorphosis that had tended toward the vagueness and contingency of "self-culture" or toward the extravagance of transparent-eyeball metaphors. If purposeful metamorphosis occurred at the levels of cell and organism, the rhetoric of human spiritual capacity would carry the imprimatur of modern empirical science as well as the stability of a received and optimistic faith. And if organismal transfiguration, through the principle of heritability, both instantiated and produced meliorative changes within the human species, spiritual progress became a collective and necessary rather than a contingent and individual phenomenon. In this vision of what we might call "providential biology," moral evil—whether active or privative—would become vestigial.

To argue, as most adherents of the developmental hypothesis did, that moral growth and increasing biological complexity were not merely parallel but cooperative phenomena required one to predicate the concepts of transcendent order, economy, and meaning. Something *had* to link the two, else life were monstrous. However, even before the publication of *On the Origin of Species* in 1859, developmentalism had already begun its ontological destabilization of the "human being," and of "life" itself. Although few people posed the question publicly, or in print, anyone who thought seriously about the developmental hypothesis probably wondered, however fleetingly, whether development had in fact stopped with human beings, or rather pointed the way to some higher species. Assuming that we descended (that is, ascended) from trilobites or chimpanzees, did we stand at the end of the line, the closest that evolution would come to making angels of us? Emerson had his moments of doubt. "Culminate we do not," he wrote in 1843, "but that point of imperfection which we occupy—is it on the way up, or down?" Usually, however, Emerson does locate humanity at the apex of the animate world, a place where we have arrived rather than been placed:

> *Consolation for readers of Darwin.*
> Why is Man the head of Creation the power of all, but because his education has been so longaeval & immense? he has taken all the degrees; he began in the beginning, & has passed through all the steps through radiate, *articulate mollusk* ~~articulate~~ vertebrate, through all the forms to the mammal, & now holds in essence the virtues or powers of all, though *in him all the~~i~~ exaggeration of each* subdued ~~into harmony & their~~ *through the* antagonism of their opposites, & is at last the harmony, the flower & top of all their being,—their honored representative.

We should first note Emerson's acknowledgment, in his afterthought heading, of the threat to traditional faith (and to emotional comfort) that evolutionary theory posed. By the same token, this passage is a good example of his ongoing effort to do justice to scientific fact while enfolding it within a reassuring narrative; he repositions "articulate" so as to get the order right, and adds "through" the "antagonism of their opposites" in order to suggest the purposefulness of competition, a process that has culminated in the human species. Providential biology thus recapitulates traditional theodicy: out of conflict, harmony; out of chaos, order; from the primordial slime, the race of Achilles.[41]

In such terms, anthropocentric developmentalism could "console" those who believed that human beings, uniquely beloved by God, represented the telos of the evolutionary process. Yet evolutionary theory depended on the existence of "varieties" within a given species, and this greatly complicated the question, particularly when it came to antislavery ideology, although the complications ran in both directions. On one hand, as we have seen, a natural conceptual affinity obtained between development, racial "improvement," and monogenesis. At the same time, the existence of different human varieties raised more challenging questions. If a species consisted of multiple varieties, did these varieties develop unevenly, and if so, what did that imply? If the varieties, or races, of the human species, through the forces of environment and hermetic reproductive history, developed unevenly, might they not represent incipient species themselves? To be consistent, monogenists had to assert that all races developed within a single human species, and that this species itself was continuously improving, without actually becoming another species. For decades, mainstream antislavery racial thought had derived from Acts 17:26: God "hath made of One Blood, all Nations of Men, for to dwell on all the face of the Earth." Developmentalism required a more dynamic, though not less ethically binding, concept of human family.

As we saw in chapter 3, evolutionist theory, broadly speaking, argues for the importance to life of openness, interaction, and interrelation, as opposed to enclosure and isolation—and if we blur the distinction between "species" and "varieties" (a distinction, in fact, that has always been blurry and disputed), these principles transfer readily to racial thought. In the case of Emerson, we find, if not complete acceptance of the full implications of the evolutionary hypothesis, then distinct motion in that direction, as he sought to clarify for himself the science of race.

Clearly, Emerson attributed nonphysical qualities to phenotypically defined racial groups in a way that today we would call "essentialist," "racist," or "racialist." Yet he also went much further than most of his contemporaries in imagining the arbitrariness of racial categories and the mutability of racial "characteristics." In the first instance, he came to an understanding of the *metaphorical* nature of racial categorization, seeing the established dividing lines not as literal or transcendent but as products of the human impulse to affirm relationality where none might exist, and to deny it where it might: "I believe, the races, as Celtic, Norman, Saxon, must be used hypothetically or temporarily, as we do by the Linnaean classification, for convenience simply, & not as true & ultimate. For, otherwise, we are perpetually confounded by finding the best settled traits of one race, claimed by some more acute or ingenious partisan as precisely characteristic of the other & antagonistic."[42] Emerson, who in 1834 had thrilled at the Cuvierian spectacle of the natural history cabinets in Paris, in the 1850s doubted the validity of a biotaxonomic approach to human difference. Though not questioning the existence of "race," he believed that it defied static systems of organization, for the ostensibly permanent traits of a physically defined racial group will undergo, over eons, perpetual change: "The fixity or unpassableness or inconvertibility of races, as we see them, is a feeble argument, since all the historical period is but a point to the duration in which Nature was wrought. Any the least and solitariest fact in our natural history has the worth of a power in the opportunity of geologic periods. All our apples came from the little crab."[43] A recognition of such universal mutability leads Emerson to the conclusion that "[t]he foundations of race are not in anatomy, but in metaphysics."[44] As in his comment, cited above, that "ideas only save races," he again subordinates biology to the all-encompassing domain of metaphysics. But he does not mean to deny the importance of biology. His point, rather, is twofold: first, that a common human biology transcends whatever physical distinctions may exist between races, and second, that as the divine essence flows through all transient forms, so through a constant process of racial flux will the truths of nature exert themselves. The concepts of anatomical change and permeability underlying the developmental hypothesis aided Emerson in imagining racial transformativity as an essential component of human evolution and spiritual progress.

To get from point A (racial fluidity) to point B (human evolution), Emerson suggests that the grand narrative of human ascent will necessarily entail racial amalgamation, and that this intermixture will proceed both culturally and biologically—precisely the move that most antislavery writers would not or could not make. A veritable refrain for Emerson is his observation that "Nature loves the crossing of stocks." Close variations on that phrase occur in no fewer than nine journal or notebook entries and published essays.[45] At times, Emerson uses the idea metaphorically, as when he writes that "Milton, Bacon, Gray, are crosses of the Greek & Saxon geniuses."[46] But he also refers to intermixture among human "varieties." This intermixture, in his view, entails the exchange and mingling of "blood," an image that expressed, in a conveniently oblique way, both the violent and the sexual dimensions of interracial contact. For the crossing of human stocks, in Emerson's conception, did not go forward harmoniously, equitably, or even voluntarily. Rather, he imagined an aggressive, competitive process, in which blood—along with the "ideas" or "qualities" that it carried—survived, circulated, and thrived according to the strength of the participants. Racial competition did not amount to an amoral Hobbesian free-for-all, but a process by which the rough-and-tumble of amalgamation produces collective uplift.

The concepts of "blood" and "stock" *are* metaphorical for Emerson, as Gregg Crane has argued, but they are more than that; they function centrally in his racial thought precisely because they did bridge the literal and the figurative, the bodily and the cultural, the physical and the metaphysical.[47] Yet by the same token, this does not mean, as Laura Dassow Walls has suggested, that for Emerson "[u]ltimately the concept of race was a convenient fabrication—a social construction."[48] Biological inheritance represented one of the determinisms of identity that Emerson could not fully sever from political concerns by transmuting it into a "trope." Rather, the term "blood" has for Emerson slippery referential value, seeming to shuttle indeterminately between "material" and "poetic" usages. We need not posit a deconstructionist Emerson and clear him of the charge of "naturalizing" race, because both nature and human nature, in his understanding, accommodated cultural process. From this perspective, Emerson sought not only to expose the theoretical fraudulence of much racial discourse, but also to reinterpret the factuality of race in ways that accorded with humanitarian politics. Specifically, the reality of intermixture provoked more than just a passing acknowledgement on Emerson's part; it seemed to represent one of the ways in which nature, abetted by culture, could repair the destructive divisions that history had introduced into the human species.

Antebellum Americans recognized, even if they denounced, the reality of widespread racial intermixture. This cultural awareness advises us to see Emerson both as advocating a deracialized moral and political consensus, *and* as seeking to create a usable, proactive narrative of the undeniable fact of human miscegenation. That narrative, as I have suggested, points toward a cosmopolitanism of blood that stands opposed to the cultural and biological solipsism implied by a "pure blood . . . marrying in & in."[49] "Like all living organisms," writes Timothy Reiss, "cultures need interweavings and exchanges with others, in and through their very differences." Although Emerson is clearly premodern in seeing cross-cultural transmission as correlative to cross-biological transmission, his belief in the salutary effects of blood intermixture actually closely resembles the consensus of modern genetic science that a population's genetic health is well served by reproductive crossing with outsiders.

"In America, fusion," he wrote, in a tersely evocative statement that one can take in a number of ways. Horace Bushnell, always a useful foil for the more freethinking Emerson, would likely have waxed abstract: "The system will be one that systematizes the caprices and discords of innumerable wills, and works results of order, through endless complications of disorder." Yet when Emerson wrote "abstractions are not for me," he may have had that sort of abstraction in mind, for his idea of "fusion" was deeply political and undeniably racial. Where he could, a few years earlier, refer almost reflexively to "this dynasty of the Caucasians & Saxons," such ethnoculturalism—the very kind that provoked a reactive ethnoculturalism in Walker and Delany—began to give way to his belief that the strength of the union would depend on the vigor of its ethnic pluralism. In the fall of 1845, in a journal entry criticizing the "narrowness of the Native American Party," Emerson took the image of the American "melting pot" and recast it in terms drawn from developmentalist theory:

> It is the result of science that the highest simplicity of structure is produced, not by few elements, but by the highest complexity. Man is the most composite of all creatures, the wheel-insect, *volvox globator*, is at the beginning. Well, as in the old burning of the Temple at Corinth, by the melting & intermixture of silver & gold & other metals, a new compound more precious than any, called the Corinthian Brass, was formed so in this Continent,—asylum of all nations, the energy of Irish, Germans, Swedes, Poles, & Cossacks, & all the European tribes,—of the Africans, & of the Polynesians, will construct a new race, a new religion, a new State, a new literature, which will be as vigorous as the new Europe which came out of the smelting pot of the Dark Ages, or that which earlier emerged from the Pelasgic & Etruscan barbarism.
>
> La Nature aime les croisements.

This model of pluralism, significantly, does not hold that the various subsets of the population will coexist as discrete entities composing a variegated whole, but that they will "cross" and give rise to an entirely "new" and "more precious" whole. In 1864, in a lecture encouraging postwar immigration, Emerson reprised the theme, telling the Parker Fraternity in Boston, "The capital advantage of our republic is that by the organic hospitality of its institutions it is drawing the health and strength of all nations into its territory, and promises by perpetual intermixture to yield the most vigorous qualities and accomplishments of all." Similarly, in "Progress of Culture" (1867), he observed that "[m]en come hither by nations" and cited the "fusion of races and religions" as one of the "advantages" of postbellum American life.[50]

The contributions of different races would depend on the "ideas" they carried in their blood, and these ideas were evolutionarily competitive to the degree that they expressed divine truth (a theme to which Emerson returns repeatedly in his antislavery addresses). As these racial qualities sorted themselves out, the composition of "America" would gradually approach the amalgamated state of Corinthian Brass, and insofar as African Americans embodied an "indispensable element of a new and coming civilization," they could not be excluded from the country's racial-historical narrative. In terms drawn from Adolphe Quetelet, the influential social theorist whom Emerson was reading at this time, the "new race" Emerson imagines might be considered nothing less than a statistical inevitability, and its "average man" (the individual, in Quetelet's model, who most closely typifies the social body) as a representative bodily locus of transracial, or panracial, fusion—as darker, certainly, than the "pale diluted stream" that American blood seemed at midcentury.[51]

But Emerson had more than the United States on his mind. For all his vaunted "nationalism," he did not regard nationhood as a permanent, immutable fact, or as the primary category of social reality. On one level, his commitment to the American project was tempered by a political cosmopolitanism, which held that sound judgment and social justice depend on emancipation from ethnoculturalist habits of thought.[52] On a more theoretical level, Emerson went much further than that. Influenced both by his reading in history and by his travels through England in 1847–48, Emerson developed an understanding of the artificial and temporary nature of national identity, and came to believe, following Hegel, that individual nation-states obey the law of organic decline. More than the boundaries, documents, and systems that regulate a nation-state, and even more than the shared history and mutual imagining that create a national community, it is the qualities of a people, the "ideas" they embody, their spiritual haecceity, that matter to Emerson—for these give the measure of a nation's value to the larger human family that transcends political divisions.[53] In the grand upward flow of humanity, the systems and institutions of any given society would inevitably crumble and perish, he felt, but the people would live on in their ideas and in their biological natures. To preserve the teleological optimism of this national-historical concept, Emerson had to imagine that the internal qualities of a people—their values, beliefs, virtues, their "blood"—would somehow leap the barriers of political and social circumstance to achieve immortality in the realm of spirit. Biological cosmopolitanism thus represented a spiritual counterbalance to the breakdown of nations.

He did not philosophize in a vacuum, however; immediate political considerations motivated him as much as did the joys of speculation. After passage of the Fugitive Slave Law in 1850, Emerson began to express a willingness to see the nation come apart if that's what it took to root out slavery (or at least to protect the moral integrity of the North). As he contemplated, without exactly advocating, the possibility of disintegration, racial developmentalism and blood cosmopolitanism enabled Emerson to understand "America" in less narrowly political terms. While the United States, as a political and cultural entity, clearly had an important role to play in the progress of world history, its permanent contribution would consist in the character of the people, in the *type* of Americans that this temporary nation-state produced. And this type was defined by freedom, by progressive energy, and by an enduring hematologic bond: "America is the idea of emancipation. . . . All proceeds on the belief that as the people have made a gov.t [*sic*] they can make another, that their Union & law is not in their memory but in their blood."[54]

From this perspective, Emerson appears both more and less politically oppositional than the conventional wisdom allows. Where a number of recent readers have taken Emerson as relatively enlightened on questions of race, he actually proved more intellectually bold than that, not only in holding up interracial amity as a pragmatic approach to questions of identity differences within the social body, but in naming biological intermixture as the principal dynamic of American progress—as more important, in fact, than the continuance of the United States as a geopolitical entity. This was not a position around which many Americans in the 1850s were prepared to rally. By the same token, however, Emerson can seem much less avant-garde: in proffering a totalistic narrative of social and historical process, in working within rather than rejecting scientific approaches to race, and in regarding racial identity as "naturally" determined as well as culturally conditioned. Moreover, the inclusive egalitarianism that Emerson, along with many later Americans in the liberal grain, imagined as a cure for the country's racial ills has the potential for erasing minority difference by folding it into a myth of social unity that works to justify what amounts to a tyranny of the majority.

Among the numerous accounts of how liberalism's specious "nonracial" or "race-neutral" ideal operates in law, literature, and culture, David Theo Goldberg's formulation is particularly cogent: "[T]his standard nonracialism is imposed upon the body politic at the cost of the self-defined subjectivity of the traditionally dominated. Liberalism's response to matters of race in the face of the fact that race matters amounts to denying or ignoring race, paternalistically effacing a self-determined social subjectivity from those who would define themselves thus without imposing it on others."[55] In the United States, with its deeply conflicted history of immigration, slavery, and westward expansion, this liberalism—alongside, although not always in tandem with, the major political traditions of republicanism and ethnoculturalism—has been instrumental in fashioning the national mythology. It is a mythology that, as Russ Castronovo reminds us, has tended to promote images of hierarchy, homogeneity, and stable lineage over those of racial disruption, guilt, and miscegenation: "national narrative has been able to present an ossified story of unity, sameness, and order—a definition that necessarily precludes the possibility that national narrative might be something other, such as an utterance of difference or heterogeneity."[56] In these terms, a narrative of panracial amalgamation, particularly when claiming the imprimatur of "science," can work to subsume a whole range of divergent identities, memories, and actual lives to a transcendent but deceptive vision of human unity.

Race, as Emerson conceived it in the 1850s, does have a certain self-dissolving quality; it is central to the *process* of godly civilization, American or otherwise, but absent from the result; it is a fundamental means of achieving a social condition of racelessness. For that reason, his rather sanguine model of amalgamation lies open to the charge that it functions ultimately to consign nonwhites to a mere supporting role in the drama of Anglo-American progress. In one form or another, this indictment links recent discussions by John Carlos Rowe, Anita Patterson, and Christopher Newfield, who see Emerson as participating at least rhetorically in an imperialist or quasi-imperialist erasure of nondominant, nonwhite populations from his picture of America.[57] On the other hand, offering a vision of history that prioritizes racial union over national union can be seen as a creative response to a national story that has served the interests of white supremacist ideology. We can read Emerson favorably, as exposing and challenging the doctrine of "Anglo-Saxon" purity by suggesting that African Americans, along with other nonwhites, will play a culturally and biologically integral role in the nation's future. The principle of *croisement* would seem to dictate that although the Anglo-Saxon race had already proven its capacity for historical achievement, it would face the bleak fate of what Robert Chambers termed an "arrested undertype" if it isolated itself from the reservoir of cultural and biological value in other races.[58] In practical terms, this implied that American society had to be reconstituted on a basis more receptive to the contributions of nonwhites—a position reflected in Emerson's public postwar advocacy of foreign immigration and radical Reconstruction.

To break out of the interpretive binary into which this issue can quickly devolve—is Emerson undermining or reinforcing the ideology of "whiteness"?—it helps to see racial developmentalism and blood cosmopolitanism as themselves amalgamated narratives that reweave multiple ideological and discursive traditions in American political life. The fundamental question has to do with how civic identity is defined and civic participation enabled, and as Rogers M. Smith writes, "American political actors have always promoted civic ideologies that blend liberal, democratic republican, and inegalitarian ascriptive elements in various combinations designed to be politically popular." Smith goes on to argue that much of ascriptivism's enduring force lies in the "inability of egalitarian liberal republican views to provide an understanding of why Americans should see themselves as loyal members of this society in preference to all others, a task that ascriptive myths perform well."[59]

This last observation is crucial, because we see Emerson, during the years of his antislavery activism, trying to find a way of speaking of "the people" that celebrated a cohesive identity without grounding that identity in either racial purity or geopolitical circumstance. The polity Emerson imagined emerging from the sectional conflict would be a distinctive polity not because it was white and Protestant, or because it happened to share a particular government and homeland, but because it embodied particular values (e.g., "the idea of emancipation"). To that degree it was a nonidentitarian concept. Yet Emerson's understanding of history and of racial science led him to the conclusion—shared by many—that the racial constitution of a people is an unavoidable determining factor in its national identity. In order to avoid the destructive ethnoculturalism to which so many of his countrymen were given over, he had to imagine a cosmopolitan community inclusive of divergent racial identities—an "asylum of all nations." Were these identities divergent solely because of different histories and circumstances, the inclusive cosmopolitan project could proceed relatively smoothly. However, Emerson's abiding belief in heritable racial "characteristics," both physical and nonphysical, posed a threat to such cosmopolitanism—as did, in less abstract terms, the omnipresent fact of interracial conflict. How would the essential values of the polity, or the polity itself, survive in the face of the viciously identitarian politics playing out every day, and in the face of the racial science that white supremacists routinely invoked?

The answer, riskily enough, also lay in science, but for Emerson's purposes in the principles of biological flux, permeability, and openness that undergirded the developmental hypothesis. Racial developmentalism and blood cosmopolitanism can thus be seen as an effort to formulate an optimistic narrative of American identity that avoids inegalitarian ascriptivism without jettisoning a concept of biological racial difference, and without, on the other hand, acquiescing to the malignant claims of racial science. They helped Emerson move beyond a deracialized liberal model of the polity to one that acknowledges the centrality of race while seeking to accommodate racial difference and racial conflict to a larger, utopian historical narrative. In this light, Emerson can seem unusually forward-looking—in developing a theorized response to essentialist racial categories, and simultaneously in seeking common ground between racial identity and human community. Nonetheless, the "realness" of race for Emerson remained grounded in natural science, and his cosmopolitan vision entailed a quasi-mystical blending of identities rather than a negotiated political pluralism.

Amidst all the philosophy and rhetoric, it is essential to remember that antebellum slavery—even for those who preferred not to think about it—represented an immediate ethical and political crisis, and that it threatened, in reality as well as in perception, the character and destiny of the United States as people understood it. What did the future hold for the country? How would race figure in to that future? What did natural science reveal about the relation between different races? In addressing these questions, in very different genres or modes of writing, Emerson and the militant African American authors pushed different sides of the same envelope, not in order to stay out on the edge but in the interest of exploring what could be thought and said in a climate of violence, fear, and agitation, and in the interest of bracing the nation ethically for what had to come. Considered in toto, their work embodies the basic and continuing dilemma of American liberal thought: its fundamental commitment to the intrinsic worth of the individual, and yet its conflicting impulses toward identitarian racialism on one side and inclusive humanism on the other.

Memory is telling me of my childhood's home, the dearest and most lovely spot on the face of the earth, and I regret that I can visit it only in my dreams.
CHARLES LANMAN, *Letters from a Landscape Painter* (1845)

In the literary effort, as in the pictorial effort, it is important to transcribe, not the obvious details of events and characters, but the ensemble of their relationships and dependencies; that is to say, their logical arrangement.
HIPPOLYTE TAINE, *The Philosophy of Art* (1865)

When what we have *done* is added to what we have *seen* and *felt*, the history of self is complete.
ALEXANDER BAIN, *The Senses and the Intellect* (1855)

CHAPTER FIVE

Race in the Landscape

IN 1851, SHORTLY BEFORE the first installment of *Uncle Tom's Cabin* appeared in the *National Era*, Harriet Beecher Stowe described her literary technique in a remarkably candid letter to editor Gamaliel Bailey. "My vocation is simply that of a painter," she wrote, "and my object will be to hold up in the most lifelike and graphic manner possible Slavery, its reverses, changes, and the negro character, which I have had ample opportunities for studying. There is no arguing with *pictures*, and everybody is impressed by them, whether they mean to be or not" (original emphasis).[1] Few southerners, of course, were favorably "impressed." In one of the first extended southern responses to *Uncle Tom's Cabin* (published, ironically, in Cambridge, Massachusetts), Edward J. Pringle condemned the novel for stirring up sectional animosity, and called for "calmer thought on the subject of slavery than is likely to be the result of pictorial writing." As Pringle recognized, literary "pictorialism" dovetailed nicely with abolitionists' efforts to make the institution of slavery as imaginatively visible as possible, to as wide an audience as possible. For that reason, he writes, the South "has been led very naturally to turn to the bright side of the picture by way of relief from the many exaggerated horrors" of northern antislavery propaganda.[2]

We have grown accustomed to understanding the grand debate over slavery as having been waged primarily on a polemical and intellectual, or at least verbal, level. David Walker and Ralph Waldo Emerson stand as preeminent examples of this. Yet in the increasingly rich visual culture of the antebellum United States, pictures, as well as words, shaped the public ethics of race and slavery. In the era's many forms of iconographic representation—from lithography and wood printing to sculpture, painting, and daguerreotype—Americans' core preoccupations, assumptions, and values were both reflected and formed. Enjoying improved methods of production and distribution, given cultural authority by a middle-class ethos of consumerist respectability, and supported by a broader trend toward cultural differentiation from Europe, American pictorial art became a primary means of shaping and embodying public attitudes toward the salient issues of the day. Moreover, images, as both Stowe and Pringle recognized, had the power to motivate people on subconscious or subrational levels, since there is "no arguing" with them.

Next to political rhetoric, then, visual images of race and the natural world constituted an equally important, if less frequently remarked, kind of representational currency in the political crisis surrounding slavery. In particular, antebellum landscape art and depictions of African Americans in painting (not to mention statuary, daguerreotypes, political cartoons, and other forms of representation), provide a remarkable visual record of the psychological and ideological differentiation of North and South, charting a deepening regional schism in which economic and political conflicts got articulated through competing images of racial identity and the natural world.[3] Some of the era's artwork blended these two representational traditions and their distinctive visual idioms to produce what I will call "racial landscapes," which portray African Americans, or an interaction involving whites and blacks, in a natural setting or scene, and which invite us to try to read race in the landscape: to discern and to excavate the racial meanings encoded within the natural iconography or imagery. Enacting, on a visual field, both subject/object and nature/culture dynamics, racial landscapes stage complex phenomenological dramas of human experience in the natural world. Crucially, this dramatized experience has the potential either to disrupt or to reinforce dominant patterns of cultural power, or more commonly, to work ambiguously within and against those patterns.

The basic interpretive question will sound familiar to any student of visual culture: How does the image work, and what does it accomplish? Yet given the tremendous elasticity and social volatility of natural and racial imagery, other more charged and far-ranging questions come to bear. What are some of the broad connections between sensory experience and cognition, and more specifically, how does the faculty of sight condition (limiting, filtering, perhaps intensifying) one's apprehension of a natural or artistic scene, in contrast to the immersive, three-dimensional, fully sensory experience of being "in" a natural setting? What happens, phenomenologically, when nature is literally brought inside, displayed in a living room, a museum, or a book? How do the pressures of culture (artistic norms, economic values, religious beliefs) mediate the subject-object relation between human perceiver and natural thing or image? How do these artists (visual or verbal) imagine the responsiveness of human psychology to the natural world, and the embeddedness of the human organism in its natural environment? Bringing all these to a somewhat sharper, more historically specific point, what was the particular power of visual experience when it came to defining race through images of nature? This last question gets to the main quarry of this chapter—the function of visual culture in the debate over slavery—and requires looking both at the psychology of pastoral, georgic, and landscape, and at the ideological conflicts operative in these traditions. Landscapes, natural settings, and natural objects served as encoded terrains or sites for thinking about race precisely because they had the capacity to speak, plausibly and with authenticity, to universal human responses to the natural world. Yet underneath the calm surface of rural landscapes, behind the cultured refinement of pastoral words and images, and within the georgic scene of pleasant labor, ran fault lines of social division, and currents of uncertainty, threat, and violence.

Pastoral, Race, and the Visual Imagination

As in literature, we can read painting for those moments when an encounter with nature breaks the circuit—when it interrupts the current of existence, heightening phenomenological awareness by temporarily bracketing the cultural as an unfamiliar or contingent domain. Through some present experience in the natural world—the perception and contemplation of a given object, perhaps, or the simple excitation of the senses—the horizon of past and future are brought into perspective in such a way as to denaturalize social experience. Memories can take on new significance, unforeseen avenues of future action can present themselves, and one's ordinary life can come to seem strange indeed. Such reassessment has ethical force, and can serve as prelude to political action, upon the return of awareness to cultural matters, or on the physical return of the individual to the social sphere. Moreover, beyond the represented remove to nature, we have an analogous motion on the part of the reader or viewer, whose encounter with a landscape has likewise the potential to bring about a new awareness of cultural context. That the sensory and cognitive experience differs from written description to two-dimensional scene to three-dimensional environment means only that the contemplation of "nature" is efficacious in different ways. Imagining and seeking to evoke, through aesthetic technique, an experiential turn toward nature, racial landscapes have the power of subtly shaping perceptions of the place of race in the social order. Their natural aesthetics, however, are not, and could never be, an unmediated representation of the natural, not only because the artist's personal vision is deeply conditioned by cultural knowledge, but more simply because the paintings show culture and nature as already intertwined.

Two closely related axioms of recent landscape studies hold that all representations of the land or of natural scenery assert some vision of social existence, and that what we see in a landscape always depends, to a high degree, on what we bring to it. Despite frequently imagining an opposition between nature and society, landscape presents a natural world suffused with culture, not only in terms of the introjection of human things, such as covered wagons, into the natural scene, but in terms of the richly layered strata of religious attitudes, political beliefs, moral values, and emotional dispositions that inform both the choice and the treatment of a natural subject. Landscape meditates on civilization, and on the relation between human beings and the environment, and it expresses dominant configurations of power.[4] But the question that particularly intrigues me is, in essence, the reverse of the usual approach; that is, how might our encounter with a landscape influence our perception of the social order, especially in regard to race relations and racial identity? If we see in a landscape what we bring from society, does the obverse also hold true, that we see in society what we bring back from a landscape? That a confrontation with a two-dimensional natural scene might redound to cultural perception in nondeterministic ways accords with what Robert Abrams has discerned in American Renaissance literature's treatment of landscape. In resisting or questioning "artfully mediated" representations of wildness, Abrams observes, "midcentury American writers begin to develop an alternative, less escapist aesthetic whose liberating power lies immediately *within* rather than *beyond* culture and history." By virtue of this alternative aesthetic, he argues, "[a] mobile and fluxional history opens up in the depth of the false steadiness of culturally constructed objects and named events."[5] Not all landscape, of course, works to denaturalize cultural norms, but it possesses within itself the power to do so. It has the potential to break the viewer out of the circuit of ideologically determined responses to nature, and therefore the potential to call into question cultural definitions of what is natural. That circuit, to put it schematically, runs as follows: socially generated preconceptions inform perception; perception then shapes and directs experience; experience in turn informs representation; and representation finally reinforces socially generated preconceptions. We can define the conservatism of a racial landscape, then, as its tendency to affirm the existing social and economic order and, conversely, the oppositionalism of a racial landscape as its tendency to dissent from that order.

These issues find vivid illustration in William Sidney Mount's *Eel Spearing at Setauket* (1845; fig. 1), a racial landscape whose ideological ambiguity merits close scrutiny. Reading this painting in conjunction with two contemporaneous cultural artifacts—a public address by a Boston lawyer and the personal album of a young African American woman in Philadelphia—we can see the power and the slipperiness of natural and racial imagery when fused. Together, these artifacts support an important conclusion about antebellum American culture specifically and the place of nature in human art more broadly. They demonstrate that despite the intensity of its investment in the transcendent symbology of nature, American pastoral could not entirely conceal its own cultural fractures, or transcend its theoretical vulnerability and its implication in social conflict. Pastoral affirms human commonality and promises a renewal of human community, yet to do so it must subsume or sublimate its ideological, and particularly its economic, presuppositions. Like myth, it seeks to direct our vision in one direction only. Resisting its lure, therefore, means reading it critically, with an eye toward understanding its semiographic mechanisms.

In Mount's painting, a young white boy, perhaps 10 to 12 years old, maneuvers a shallow skiff while his companion, an older African American woman, stands at its prow, preparing to dart her spear into the water. Yet the general impression is of activity suspended, not because the painting cannot convey motion, but because of the glassy smoothness of the water, and the lazy, hazy heat that seems to have settled on the summer landscape. A somnolent peacefulness reigns, hallmark of the pastoral mood. It looks forward to Huck Finn's contentment on the Mississippi, when there's "[n]ot a sound, anywheres—perfectly still—just like the whole world was asleep, only sometimes the bull-frogs a-cluttering, maybe." And the cooperation depicted here, the mutuality of labor, looks forward to Huck's ethical cry that "what you want, above all things, on a raft, is for everybody to be satisfied, and feel right and kind towards the others."[6] Indeed, Mount's vision of natural and social felicity, of a moment in which the pastoral life seems to transcend the harsh realities of race, is strangely prescient of Twain's treatment of the same theme. Essential to both works is the difference in age between the characters, which positions the black adult in a tutelary role, instructing the white child in the ways of the river, both technically and philosophically. This relationship implies, on one level, that the African American is more attuned to the natural world, and has important

FIGURE 1

William Sidney Mount, *Eel Spearing at Setauket*, 1845. Oil on canvas, 28½ × 36 in. Fenimore Art Museum, Cooperstown, New York, N-395.55.

FIGURE 2

William Sidney Mount, *Farmers Nooning*, 1836. Oil on canvas, 20¼ × 24½ in. The Long Island Museum of American Art, History, and Carriages, Gift of Frederick Sturges Jr., 1954.

FIGURE 3

James Goodwyn Clonney (American, born in England, 1812–67), *In the Cornfield*, 1844. Oil on canvas, 14 × 16 7/8 in. Museum of Fine Arts, Boston, Gift of Martha C. Karolik for the M. and M. Karolik Collection of American Paintings, 1815–1865. 47.1263. Photograph © 2008 Museum of Fine Arts, Boston.

FIGURE 4

Edward Troye (American, 1808–74), *Richard Singleton*, ca. 1835. Oil on canvas, 24½ × 29½ in. Virginia Museum of Fine Arts, Richmond, the Paul Mellon Collection. Photograph © Virginia Museum of Fine Arts.

FIGURE 5
William Sidney Mount, *Dance of the Haymakers*, 1845. Oil on canvas, 24 × 29¾ in. The Long Island Museum of American Art, History, and Carriages, Gift of Mr. and Mrs. Ward Melville, 1950.

FIGURE 6

Eastman Johnson, *Old Kentucky Home—Life in the South (Negro Life at the South)*, 1859. Oil on canvas, 36 × 45¼ in. Collection of The New-York Historical Society, the Robert L. Stuart Collection, accession no. S-225.

FIGURE 7

John Antrobus, *Plantation Burial*, 1860. The Historic New Orleans Collection, accession no. 1960.46.

FIGURE 8
John William Hill, *View of Richmond, Virginia*, 1847. Virginia Historical Society, Richmond, Virginia.

wisdom to share with the young companion. On another level, the black character's willingness, even eagerness, to undertake this tutelage serves to obscure the racial and economic complexities involved in the relationship, by subsuming any feelings of resentment, envy, or disloyalty in a fantasy of social harmony where such troublesome matters have little place.

Eel Spearing at Setauket displays the qualities of pastoral outlined in chapter 1. There, I offered a highly expansive definition of pastoral, including under that umbrella term both the classical tradition and a wide range of aesthetic practice in which natural beauty is meant to communicate social harmony, spiritual certitude, and emotional comfort. More than a convenience, the expansiveness of this definition reflects the fact that pastoral itself aspired to a radical inclusiveness, postulating a fundamental human responsiveness to natural beauty and a common capacity for individual and social rejuvenation through certain experiences of nature. What people consider "beautiful" varies, of course, from culture to culture and epoch to epoch, but we would err in regarding the universalism of pastoral as purely spurious; it actually accords with the basic perspective of environmental and evolutionary psychology that the human mind displays certain patterns or structures of thought that do not substantially differ from person to person or from population to population. A belief in the psychically regenerative power of nature, a power that pastoral art attempts to recreate, reflects nothing less than humanity's ancestral dependence on the life-sustaining bounty of the natural world. It is the residuum of this dependence that links pastoral both to reverential feeling and to childhood, and that energizes pastoral at those times when industrial or social existence seems to have compromised the human relation to nature. The ideological significance of pastoral, therefore, goes beyond a mere rhetorical opposition of city and country. Its engagement of subconscious and emotional material represents pastoral's most potent method of putting forth an all-embracing vision of human life, a vision we do not have to share in order to recognize its cultural and rhetorical power.

Mount's own comments about *Eel Spearing at Setauket*, which identify the painting as essentially an act of memorial reconstruction, help to reveal the centrality of memory and idealism to pastoral, along with the genre's vexed relation to racial identity. "Recollections of early days," he noted. "Fishing along shore—with a view of the Hon Selah B. Strong's residence in the distance during a drought at Setauket, Long Island." In a letter to Charles Lanman, dated November 17, 1847, Mount elaborated:

> An old Negro by the name of Hector gave me the first lesson in spearing flat-fish & eels. Early one morning we were along shore according to appointment, it was calm, and the water was as clear as a mirror, every object perfectly distinct to the depth from one to twelve feet, now and then could be seen an eel darting through the seaweed or a flatfish shifting his place and throwing the sand over his body for safty [*sic*]. "Steady there at the stern," said Hector, as he stood on the bow (with his spear held ready) looking into the element with all the philosophy of a Crane, while I would watch his motions, and move the boat according to the direction of his spear. . . . "Stop the boat," shouts Hector, "shove a little back, more to the left, the sun bothers me, that will do—now young Master step this way. I will learn you to see and catch flat-fish."[7]

Mount evidently savors the memory of being so competently coached, but we should ask whether the memory pleases the adult artist because he knows he does not really have to face any similar lack of power—perceived or substantive—in his dealings with African Americans. If racial subjectivity matters to how people narrate or represent their experience of nature, in *Eel Spearing at Setauket* Mount's racialized nostalgia fundamentally underlies the pastoral mood of the painting.

As Mount seeks to recreate and preserve in visual form a pleasant memory from his childhood, the painting's visual harmonies support the theme, or the fantasy, of racial harmony. Like other realist-luminist paintings, *Eel Spearing at Setauket* asks us to believe in it; the painting grounds its authority and authenticity in its fidelity to detail and its concern with everyday experience. Yet all realisms pick and choose their concepts of reality, and we would do well to note the unusual geometrical symmetry of the painting. This symmetry appears in the almost perfect equilateral triangle formed by the boat, the spear, and the oar, and in the almost perfect watery reflections organized around two horizontal seams: the shoreline and the bottom of the skiff. Such insistent regularity invokes two fundamental (if not entirely compatible) attitudes toward Nature. The first, suggested by the dominant triangularity of boat, oar, and spear, envisions the imposition of cultural order on a natural background, and serves to create an analogy between labor (the spearing of eels) and aesthetics (the drawing of triangles) as acts of definition and civilization. The visual grammar encoding this attitude tends to involve straight lines and rigid patterns laid across a landscape, as in Robert Salmon's *View of Palermo* (1845). By contrast, the second attitude, suggested by the horizontally organized reflections, envisions a state of moral and physical order *within* or *behind* Nature. From this essentially neo-Platonist perspective, the outward appearances of nature act as images or indices of an invisible world of ideal forms, conceived in either traditional Christian or natural-theological terms. In this case the artwork communicates the spiritual comfort that nature, as the embodiment of supernatural truth, can provide, as in Jasper Cropsey's *View near Sherburne* (1853) or Robert Duncanson's *Uncle Tom and Little Eva* (1853).

Linking these seemingly incompatible attitudes toward Nature, the order Mount envisions—whether manmade or preexistent—does not emerge out of natural process, but is *given* to nature, either from on high, or from the hand of man. Crucially, this reflects the fact that Mount created this painting before the Darwinist revolution forced a rethinking of the centrality of temporal process in human life, and in all life. Among its other shocks to human conceptual systems, evolutionary theory worked to deprive people of an imagined refuge of timelessness. And this sea change had profound implications for the domain of painting. In the words of John Berger: "The language of [nineteenth-century] pictorial art, because it was static, became the language of such timelessness. Yet what it spoke about . . . was the sensuous, the particular and the ephemeral. Its mediation between the realm of the timeless and the visible and tangible was more total and poignant than that of any other art. Hence its iconic function, and special power."[8] The hypnotic regularity of *Eel Spearing at Setauket* suggests something of this desire to live outside of time, to avoid the depredations of time. Despite its representation of action, despite the active verb in its title, the painting is antinarrativist and antiprocessual, and it seeks to lull the viewer into a mood of abstract and pleasant contemplation. Perhaps it is this quality in Mount's paintings, not just *Eel Spearing*, that prompted landscape artist Charles Lanman to observe that they "are stamped with an entirely American character, and so comically conceived, that they always cause the beholder to smile, whatever may be his troubles."[9] At a deep level, certainly, *Eel Spearing* serves a conservative function by directing attention away from the inequalities implicit in the scene and toward the fantasy of racial harmony. The landscape setting, in this light, is indispensable, for nature—whether transcendent or transcended—draws us, lures us, away from the divisions of culture.

Yet society and time inevitably encroach on the pastoral, both as it exists for the two depicted figures and as it exists for the viewer, despite the vertiginous distinction between our *actual* experience of *imaginary* nature and their *imagined* experience of *actual* nature. As our eyes wander over the canvas, and as we speculate on the relationship between boy, woman, and landed estate, the possibility arises that he will inherit the estate where the woman might presently work as a servant—or at least that he will have, as an adult, immeasurably greater opportunities than she to acquire such land. We know that the boy will grow up, and that his maturation will transform or supplant the innocent felicity that the painting so carefully depicts. As in *Adventures of Huckleberry Finn*, the characters' lives will lead inexorably *away* from the present moment, and from each other. Just as much of the charm and power of Twain's novel derives from the fact that Huck never grows up within its pages, so the painting depends for its pastoral vision on suppressing the larger social context that its characters inhabit. But it can never perfectly succeed at doing so.

To read the painting this way, to weigh the scene's emotional idealism against the material realities it cannot wholly efface, is to resist the lure of narcissism. In his reflections on the figure of Narcissus, Gaston Bachelard has written that "[t]he image contemplated in the water appears as the contour of an entirely visual caress that has no need for a caressing hand. Narcissus takes pleasure in a linear, virtual, formalized caress.

Nothing of the material remains in this delicate, fragile image."[10] Observed carelessly, *Eel Spearing at Setauket* puts us at the same risk of forgetting the material, as if we were, along with the boy and the woman, gazing into the water ourselves. Yet the inescapably tangible, ephemeral elements of the painting are like a stone tossed in. For the painting's saving imperfections—the ever-so-slight deviations in geometry and symmetry, the unsettling gravity of its subject matter—hold the potential of disrupting our gaze. It might then return to us an image of our cultural past rather than our own egos, and the smile Lanman predicted might fade to a troubled frown.

In its subtle, ambiguous navigation of the relation between nature and culture, *Eel Spearing at Setauket* is a revealing, even an emblematic, painting. It imagines a turn from society to nature, an enriching encounter with the natural world, and the characters seem absorbed by their immediate environment, immersed in their shared experience, in such a way that difficult conflicts have fallen away. The painting's formal aesthetics seem designed to absorb the viewer similarly, creating a phenomenological analogy between our viewing of the happy scene and the characters' concentrated gazes; in both cases abandonment in nature threatens to overwhelm cultural ideology. Yet whereas the characters' remove is timeless and static, the viewer's is necessarily temporary, and it heralds a return to culture, on which the painting's fantasy of racial harmony may become all the more powerful as a reminder of real-world racial division. While other commentators on *Eel Spearing* have cited the painting's representation of a strong, active African American woman as its racially liberal element, the real counterbalance to the painting's general conservatism consists in its disconcerting tension between reality and ideality. Although Stowe wrote that there is "no arguing" with pictures, the faculty of vision proves a bit more independent than that. The affective strategies of pastoral depend on directing our vision in predetermined ways, but, even as recognized at the time, the relation between images, reason, and emotion is unpredictably complex.

In 1845, the same year as *Eel Spearing at Setauket*, a Boston lawyer and Whig politician named George Lunt gave a public address that suggests the importance of the visual imagination to the pastoral experience.

At the dedication of Horticultural Hall, in the merry month of May, Lunt delivered his rhapsodic oration on the beauties of the natural world. Freely blending spiritual, aesthetic, and scientific vocabularies, Lunt rejected both "cold philosophy" and utilitarianism, and sought to harness natural history to his deeply emotional Romanticism. He had neither the intellectualism of Emerson nor the irony of Thoreau, but like them he regarded natural beauty as a stimulus to faith and the imagination, and as a tonic against the corrupting, conventionalizing influences of social life. Lunt's address stands as one of the era's most concentrated distillations of pastoral thought, and as an object lesson in the genre's Protean flexibility.

Lunt opens his address with an anecdote about the Scottish explorer Mungo Park, whose widely reported expedition into West Africa in the 1790s seized the public's imagination. Lunt first pictures Park struggling amidst the "vast deserts of a barbarous clime . . . hundreds of miles away from the very outskirts of civilization, and surrounded on every side by the beasts of the wilderness, and by men scarcely less ferocious." Suddenly, "an object caught his eye . . . a small moss, of extraordinary beauty," reminding him that "the same bountiful and eternal Providence, which protected this minute but lovely object in obscurity so complete . . . could not be unmindful of one of his intelligent beings, the highest in the order of intellectual creation." The scalar reduction is striking: Once Lunt has provided the barest sketch of the setting, the focus narrows sharply to the delicate moss, which immediately fills both Mungo Park's vision and our own. Every other natural phenomenon—insects, hot gritty sand, unfamiliar sounds or smells—is relegated to the margins, or removed from the picture altogether, in order for the beautiful moss to work its magic, to minister to Park's emotional and spiritual comfort. This constriction of focus, indeed, characterizes what we might call the "pastoral moment": that moment when a person's confrontation with a natural object or experience in a natural setting has an interruptive quality to it, a bracketing of social context and intensification of perceptual and phenomenological response. It is in this state that the "pastoralized" subject can experience, potentially, new forms of awareness and emotional regeneration. The pastoral moment does not, however, represent an exit from culture, but a temporary detour. In Mungo Park's case, "[i]t was the reflection thus suggested which banished his despair, and nerved his heart to those renewed efforts which secured his eventual return to his native land."[11]

The pastoral moment requires the subject to be *in* nature or *with* nature, but not *of* nature. It depends on the mind's faculty of abstraction, its ability to assimilate natural objects or scenes to preexisting psychological and cultural frameworks. As Lunt goes on to make clear: "To fulfil their highest ministry, [flowers] must have become blended with their kindred associations. They must have linked themselves, as they have done, with the domestic, and public and religious story of the world. Their sweet and gentle names must have floated upon the voice of song."[12] To facilitate such abstraction, and the subsequent narrativization of nature, pastoral works to remove its natural objects from a confusing context, and to "cleanse" its natural landscapes of disorderly or contaminating material. Thus Mount clears away the distracting contexts in *Eel Spearing*, enabling the experience of abstraction on the part of both viewer and characters. Emotional or religious sensitivity to nature requires, in these terms, an intellectual or aesthetic distance from it. The alternative is to be in nature as an animal is in nature—that is, to sense it and interact with it, but not to transcend it. Transcendence, however, implies repression, or a denial of real experience, which we might regard as the psychological correlative to pastoral's occlusion of its economic and ideological commitments.

Significantly, Mungo Park's "reflection" on Providence follows on an act of sight; his epiphany and emotional restoration attend his *visual* contemplation of the tiny moss. This hints, more broadly, at the highly visual nature of pastoral experience and pastoral literary strategy. While we might expect the pastoral moment to depend on the greater intimacy with nature that the other senses provide, it is precisely the detachment provided by visual experience that forestalls a total phenomenological immersion in nature, an abandonment that threatens to animalize or even annihilate the subject. Hans Jonas has written that, as seeing does not necessitate physical contact with, or even proximity to, an object, it allows us to regard "the thing as it is in itself as distinct from the thing as it affects me," and that this heightened objectivity makes possible theory, imagination, and free thought, even as it comes at the cost of offering a "becalmed abstract of reality denuded of its raw power."[13] To a much greater degree than the other senses, vision confers a remarkable cognitive power over one's natural surroundings, and one of its primary capacities is the composition of numerous discrete elements into a coherent whole, into a scene, landscape, or prospect. Antebellum Americans recognized this fact; by virtue of the faculty of sight, wrote Thomas Upham, a professor of "mental and moral philosophy" at Bowdoin College, man "is in a moment possessed of all the beauties of a wide and variegated landscape."[14] The language of possession here has more than metaphorical significance. Paul Shepard has identified in our remarkable ocular abilities a possible source of the human sense of dominion over nature: As an observer "moves through an actual terrain the sense of being at the center of a three-dimensional world falls upon him with the delight of a continuous unfolding revelation. Perhaps this suggests to him that he is the center and therefore the master of all the world."[15] At the same time, the visual coordination of discrete elements into a coherent landscape suggests the longing for harmony, unity, and permanence that underlies all pastoral. The Scottish philosopher Alexander Bain, in his 1855 treatise *The Senses and the Intellect*, associated the faculty of sight with our awareness of temporal flow and, from there, nothing less than the integrity of the self. First identifying the mind's long-term retention of emotionally charged visual images as fundamental to psychological coherence, he writes that personality and self-knowledge entail the same harmonization of parts as does the perceptual organization of a heterogeneous landscape: "Our individual history [is] broken up into sections and partial narratives; and to recover the total current, we should find it requisite to collect these into one great combination upon the thread of strict succession in order of time."[16] Vision thus underwrites pastoral's characteristic theme of memory, or rather selective memory, particularly in relation to childhood, as it calls up to the mind's eye remembered scenes or events that stand as a beautiful counterpart to the present. "Hills, valleys, brooks, trees—our first and fondest friends beyond the domestic hearth—are never forgotten," wrote the American art enthusiast and collector Elias Magoon, in an echo of Mount's recollections of his experience on the river. "Memory recalls the sunny days of childhood and youth; and, like the green spot in the desert . . . we love to ramble again amidst the scenes of earliest emotion and purest thought."[17] Sight, we could say, helps to satisfy the emotional desire for harmony or fulfillment by enabling people to imaginatively project themselves into a living green space, to see themselves in the scene, while nonetheless ensuring that it remains just that: a *scene*. Given this tension between subjective experience and objective perception, the visuality of pastoral remains always ambiguous or divided, speaking to the longing of the "lonely species" to find communion with nature while reaffirming the dissevering, objectivizing power of vision.

As an artistic form, pastoral itself does not, of course, bring anyone into contact with the natural world per se, but with nature as represented on page or canvas. Or more precisely, pastoral brings only its fictional characters into some manner of rejuvenative contact with an imaginatively filtered, processed, and repackaged version of the natural world. Ordinarily pastoral texts hold up the depicted experience as exemplary, or even try to elicit some echo or approximation of that experience in the audience. But to what degree can they succeed in doing so? The immediacy and visceral force of sensory perception might suggest that images or simulacra of nature, no matter how realistic or compelling, are a pale, inadequate substitute for the real thing, and that pastoral remains permanently, tragically trapped within the prison of mere representation. To this claim two objections or caveats appear. First, while nature and art make different "appreciative demands" on us aesthetically, in Emily Brady's phrase, they cooperate in shaping our experience of both, such that neither nature nor art exists independently of the other.[18] "When [an] observer looks now at the forest and then at a painting of the forest," Shepard argues, "a feedback is turned on, a circuit of constant comparison, discovery, and modification. The sensory input from the painting and from the trees interact so that the perception of each is affected. Recurrent cycles are initiated with the production of a succeeding painting."[19] In other words, it is a blurred and shifting line that divides the subject-object relation involved in the appreciation of art and that is involved in the appreciation of nature. Secondly, the claim that representation is radically inadequate next to the "real thing" implies that the physical senses are, by virtue of their biological immediacy, more important than mental reflection or reasoning in the development of experience. That is not a self-evident proposition. We can as easily regard the psychological potency of nature as its ability to refer us to something else, something not present in space or time, which affects us more deeply. Such is the power of a memento, which enables the mind to turn from the present to the absent, and from the present to the eternal. And herein lies a possible explanation of the psychological power of the pastoral moment, a transitive move from the intellectual, analytical quality of visual aesthetics to a place where emotion enters in. This psychological power speaks both to the transhistorical and transcultural appeal of pastoral, but by the same token to the capacity of pastoral to evade questions of human difference.

Pastoral texts frequently invoke an inclusive egalitarianism, suggesting that all people respond to nature in fundamentally the same way, regardless of their particular historical circumstance or social identity. As Lunt rather crudely puts it, "[t]he very savage, indeed, must derive some moral elevation from the contemplation of external nature."[20] Clearly, even explicitly egalitarian texts make powerful assumptions about class and "civilization," assumptions that underlie a normative ideological framework in which human sensitivity to the beautiful or the sublime helps to raise people out of "degradation" or "ignorance" or "savagery." Yet pastoral attempts to submerge patterns of difference in the human response to nature, particularly the interlinked problems of race and social class. Lunt addresses himself, imaginatively and probably actually, to the sensibilities of the well-heeled: "You wander into the fresh fields and gather the flowers of spring. In crystal vases, resting, it may be, upon sculptured marble, you cherish these frail children of the sun and showers." He then goes on to picture "the humble dwelling-place of the poorest laborer, in some crowded city's dim alley," where the poor man yet rejoices in discovering "some simple flower, which indicates the longing of our more spiritual being, [and] recalls to the mind's eye of the wearied man the green fields of his boyish days."[21] In effect, Lunt makes no distinction between bourgeois and proletarian responses to natural beauty, conscripting the laborer into an extrinsic model of understanding or experiencing nature, one that even seems to suggest that the poor man is not that bad off, as long as he can contemplate a flower now and then. But what if there *are* no flowers, or only dead flowers, or simply weeds, in the laborer's "dim alley"? Far from whimsical, this question gets to a problematic issue in pastoral usages that link spiritual and emotional regeneration to the presence of nature. If natural beauty ennobles the mind, it follows that they who enjoy frequent contact with nature, or with certain kinds of nature, have greater opportunities for mental and moral elevation, and for the attainment of culture. A flower in the alley may suffice, but is not a bouquet on the mantle superior, or an entire walled garden, well stocked and well tended? In short, antebellum pastoral is riven between a humanist ideal of nonracialized sensitivity to natural beauty and a belief that different natural settings or environments will produce different levels or qualities of civilization. More pointedly: By valuing some natural forms over others (flower over weed, glade over desert), Western pastoral inevitably allies itself with the assertions of climatism, and climatism easily grades into national and racial hierarchies.

This ideological bias in pastoral represented one of the major challenges for antebellum African American literature and culture. That challenge subtly but powerfully informs the personal album of Amy Matilda Cassey, a young African American woman living in Philadelphia. Amy and her husband Joseph Cassey were members of the black elite, and they participated actively in intellectual and abolitionist circles.[22] Amy's album, manufactured in London in the early 1830s and bound in embossed black morocco, would not have cost very much, but it nonetheless signalled its owner's culture and refinement.[23] While such personal albums typically included expressions of affection and esteem from friends and family, what distinguishes this particular one was that a number of well-known figures in African American history contributed to it: William Whipper, William Lloyd Garrison, James McCune Smith, Wendell Phillips, and Frederick Douglass, among others. The material product of a wide network of individuals, the album provides a rare view of pastoral in the private sphere, of how representations of nature actually appeared in people's daily lives. It also underscores the vital importance of mutual assistance, and class identification, for this community of activists. If class identification, as recent critics have stressed, arises not simply from common interests, but from the iteration and circulation of in-group narratives, we should see Amy Cassey's personal album as participating in one of the competing sociological narratives of antebellum African American culture.[24]

The specific contributions to the album—primarily poetry, calligraphy, watercolors, pressed flowers, and written sketches—resemble fragments that collectively establish that narrative of middle-class acculturation. Taken together, these fragments convey something of the pervasive social power of Western, and specifically American, ideas of economic progress, Protestant millennialism, and aesthetic refinement. All these ideas cooperated to sustain a widespread ideological hegemony regarding civilization, or Culture, and all worked to define Culture by defining Nature, by authorizing particular forms of relation between humanity and the natural world.

The women's contributions to Amy Cassey's album consistently employ pastoral gestures that reflect the era's discourses of sentimental domesticity. The following poem by Margaretta Forten, for example, accompanied by a watercolor depicting a bouquet of flowers in a vase, contrasts the permanence of memory with the transience of manufactured things:

> Long, long be my heart with your memory fill'd!—
> Like the vase, in which roses have once been distill'd—
> You may break, you may ruin the vase if you will;
> But the scent of the roses will hang round it still.

If pastoral attributes human loss and psychic fragmentation not only to time but to society and technology as well, it follows that in the domestic space the unities of life can be better preserved, and in the antebellum period it fell, or was supposed to fall, to virtuous women to oversee and protect this domestic space.[25] Sentimentalizing nature therefore required its interiorization and domestication. Rescued from the corruption and violence of the public world, and brought indoors, nature could exert its emotional and spiritual influence in the form of, say, floral arrangements or gentle landscape paintings. And, predictably, class once again obtrudes—for the civilizing influence of domesticated nature will correlate with the possession of domestic space, and with the nonutilitarian consumption of nature, or of representations of nature.

By contrast, the men's contributions to the album, typically one-paragraph essays, tend toward self-consciously "masculine" representations of nature, emphasizing the exterior world, often in terms of the power and grandeur of sublime natural prospects, or the conquering of wilderness and the improving of open land as civilization advances. In William Whipper's essay "Moral Reform," for example, the speaker seeks his destiny and freedom outdoors, without the social gestures toward friendship and feeling in the Forten poem. "There [at the "immutable temple of truth"] planting our standard, on the great foundation . . . of first causes, we survey from that bold, that sublime eminence, the works of creation, and the boundaries of universal worlds. We look to God as the author of all, while we contemplate for our dominion, the surface of our globe."[26] In the album's most significant entry, from the perspective of literary history, Frederick Douglass himself contributed a brief untitled essay dated "Jan. 1850." Here Douglass fashions himself as the rough-hewn man doing battle in the public arena—as too rough hewn, in fact, for signing personal albums:

> I never feel more entirely out of my sphere, than when presuming to write in an Album. It is suggestive of beauty, elegance and refinement—whilst my habits of life [&] passed history—& present occupation—have called into exercise all the sterner qualities of my head and heart—so that I walk upon uneven, uncultivated and stony ground—gazing upon huge rocks with far more pleasure, than I experience, while promonading the most richly cultivated garden and gazing upon the most luxurious flowers. It is mine to grapple with huge wrong—with gigantic tyranny—to launch the fiery denunciation of outraged and indignant man at the hoary headed oppressor!—This my dear friend is my apology for not writing something becoming the pages of your precious Album.

Seeming to criticize or resist the album's feminized pastoral, perhaps out of a recognition of its class pretensions, Douglass asserts, in response, the masculinist posture of his 1845 *Narrative of the Life of Frederick Douglass*. In 1850, when Douglass wrote these lines, he was in the process of reassessing his relationship to the African American community and to the women in his life, but he had not yet reached the more mature perspective of *My Bondage and My Freedom*.

Despite their differences, both the "masculine" and the "feminine" representations of nature in Amy Cassey's album draw on well-established European American conventions. Their conventionality, as in sentimental literature, functions as a kind of shortcut to readerly sympathy. Moreover, as we have already seen in the cases of Wheatley, Sancho, and Equiano, both the pastoral and the sublime signal the writer's command of a "civilized" literary genre, and, by extension, their participation in the entire course of human civilization. And again, the racial implications cut both ways. On one hand, pastoral and the sublime availed themselves for humanitarian purposes. A psychological universalism, however specious, can communicate a narrator's or character's seemingly unique human traits: an aesthetic and spiritual responsiveness to natural beauty and a simultaneous capacity for shaping or dominating nature. On the other hand, conventional representations of nature came at a high cost for nineteenth-century African American writers. That cost involved, as it did for Martin Delany and others, the replication of ideological and discursive patterns that were interwoven with the oppressive system: material acquisitiveness, the separation of spheres, hyperindividualism, religious dualism. In other words, challenging or redefining the role of "race" in Western civilization required in the first place various forms and degrees of acquiescence to Western notions of civilization. Antislavery and humanitarian writers, after all, were asserting not simply African Americans' membership in the human family, but the fitness of African Americans for a dominantly Christian and capitalist culture.

Eel Spearing at Setauket, George Lunt's public address, and Amy Cassey's personal album each reveal something of the complex psychology at work in pastoral, and of pastoral's suppression of the broader economic forces shaping class identity and race relations. Yet the problematics of natural imagery cannot be abstracted from real-world economic realities. Specifically, regionalized patterns of economic development played a crucial role in how this suppressive dynamic operated in antebellum pastoral and landscape. In both North and South, as actual landscapes became, in rhetoric and literature, mythical landscapes, pastoral worked to displace the problems and weaknesses of their respective economic systems, diverting attention from the different forms of exploitation on which economic growth depended.

In the South, fictional works such as John Pendleton Kennedy's *Swallow Barn* (1832) and Augustus Baldwin Longstreet's *Georgia Scenes* (1835) had popularized the myth of the pastoral plantation landscape—a myth that fed on other ideologies, values, and psychological needs, such as deference to aristocratic order, a wish to escape the inexorable march of time, a reverence for nature, and, predictably, a belief in the supposedly docile nature of African Americans.[27] As an increasingly cohesive regional identity began to form around a romantic image of the plantation, southern pastoral had either to erase the black presence or to harness it securely to proslavery ideology by invoking the dream of familial harmony—in either case denying the racial exploitation at the heart of the southern agrarian system. In the North, as antislavery writers responded to the increasing aggressiveness of their southern counterparts, we find a continuation, from its eighteenth-century roots, of the uneasy marriage between free-labor capitalism and green rhetoric. In an 1838 essay in the *Liberator*, for example, William Lloyd Garrison imagined the benefits that would accrue to an industrialized, slave-free South:

> We will remove from them all source of alarm, and the cause of all insurrection—increase the value of their estates tenfold—give an Eden-like fertility to their perishing soil—build up the old waste places, and repair all breaches—make their laborers contented, grateful and happy—wake up the entombed genius of invention, and the dormant spirit of enterprise—open to them new sources of affluence—multiply their branches of industry—erect manufactories, build railroads, dig canals—establish schools, academies, colleges, and all beneficent institutions.[28]

This attempt to elide the inherent contradiction between the urban and the rural, however, tended to obscure not only the long-term incompatibility between "manufactories" and "an Eden-like" landscape, but also the forces at work in the wage labor system that left workers far from "contented, grateful and happy." Generally speaking, the problematic tension in antebellum northern pastoral was not that it effaced the brutalities of slave economics, as did its southern counterpart, but that images of natural beauty coexisted with a commitment to scientific and technological development. To the degree that pastoral depended on scenes of rural simplicity, or on an undespoiled natural environment, northern industrialization proved antithetical to the pastoral ethic—as a growing number of Americans recognized, and as history has amply proved. Yet antislavery rhetoric needed to walk on both sides of the street, celebrating industrial capitalism as superior to slavery while trading on the cultural currency of richly fertile gardens and bucolic landscapes.

As Angela Miller has demonstrated, the United States' decades-long breakdown of national unity manifested itself in antebellum landscape painting, in which the symbolic power of nature to "gloss over political contradictions" gave way to the use of natural imagery to articulate regional and local attachments, as these contradictions "broke through the surface, clamoring for recognition."[29] If anything, the destabilization of natural imagery proved even more far reaching than that. In the antebellum climate of disintegrating political consensus, American pastoral revealed deep strains in its ambivalent relationship to "civilization," a many-layered concept structured around ideas of economics and technology; region and climate; race and family. How nimbly or awkwardly they managed these strains gives pastoral texts their continuing interest, since their cultural force depended on invoking common human feelings and experiences while simultaneously negotiating or redefining human difference. None of the cultural artifacts considered in this section are "about" slavery directly, but they all contributed to a shifting ideological and intellectual landscape on which the great struggle over human bondage went forward.

Toward an African American Georgic

As *Eel Spearing at Setauket* suggests, in both its action and its title, the symbolic potential of racial landscapes has at its center the African American relation to the natural world. The practical dimensions of that relation, including economic productivity, collaborative work, and the role of the market, now deserve greater attention. Paintings that imagine African American labor in the natural world raise a number of ancillary issues: the role of animals in these images, the establishment of a viable African American community on the land, and the representation of black leisure. No predictable patterns of meaning emerge from these images. Rather, antebellum visual depictions of African American labor and family prove complex and problematic, charged with racial significance and implicitly weighing in on the central political crisis of the union.

The georgic tradition, which emphasizes the moral and social value of agricultural work, presents itself here as the more fruitful interpretive framework than the pastoral. In its pragmatic orientation, georgic represents an arguably more "realistic" genre than pastoral, one that not only acknowledges work as inevitable but also celebrates its vitality, and imagines the geographic places of work as sites of collaborative human effort. Despite its idealism, georgic usually manages to avoid the tendency toward fantasy that can afflict pastoral. Moreover, given the rich, foundational, and vexed role of agricultural labor in African American cultural history, the georgic represents a vital literary or artistic reference point for black literary studies. If georgic, in Anthony Low's account, "differs from epic because it emphasizes planting and building instead of killing and destruction; and that it is preeminently the mode suited to the establishment of civilization and the founding of nations," it provides a powerful source of meaning in the semiotic war over slavery and African American identity, one especially well suited to the twin challenges of redefining the significance of work and of providing a basis for communal renewal.[30] Yet it remains a regrettably underexplored theme in African American literary history.[31] What the images in this chapter suggest is that white representations of black labor during the antebellum period tended to inhibit or warp the development of an independent African American georgic by severing black labor from community and future. It would take several decades to get to Booker T. Washington's championing of physical work in *Up From Slavery*, and as we will see in the next chapter, Frederick Douglass played a pivotal if subtle role in that movement in African American literature.

We can approach the question of how black labor appears in antebellum artwork by considering first the representation of black leisure. The trope of black lassitude appears throughout the era's artwork, and it is usually inflected negatively, as sloth, in paintings that depict African Americans sleeping or loafing outdoors while their work goes unattended. Mount's *Farmers Nooning* (1836; fig. 2) is a well-known example, and James Goodwyn Clonney practically specialized in the theme, in such works as *Sleeping Negro* (1835), *Fishing Party on Long Island Sound Off New Rochelle* (1847), and *Waking Up* (1851). With the exception of *Sleeping Negro*, each painting portrays a white child or children surreptitiously teasing a sleeping African American adult, and would seem at first glance not only to affirm the racist stereotype of black sloth but to infantilize the black character by making him the butt of kids' pranks. From that perspective, both the progress of culture and the cultivation of personal virtue depended on the imposition of human reason and productive labor on the "unimproved" natural world, and against that background, the trope of African American lassitude would seem to express a hostile, hypocritical attitude toward the capacity of blacks to participate in the advance of civilization. Yet physical exertion is not—and was not—the only way of conceiving of humanity's ideal relation to the natural world. If we adjust our angle of vision, so to speak, and take a longer look at these paintings, we can see drowsiness or sleep as restorative immersion in the natural surroundings, as a deep responsiveness to or pastoral communion with nature. The Hegelian-minded philosopher Frederick Rauch, for instance, wrote that while the "eye is cold, dwelling only on the surface of things, . . . the ear listens to every sound of nature, and makes us feel with all that lives."[32] In almost identical terms, Josef Pieper has more recently suggested that leisure involves a "listening to the essence of things," and we can link this receptivity to the natural world to an alternative philosophy of civilization, one that regards culture as a matter of reflection and contemplation, with the spirit ennobled and made wise through sensory and moral acceptance of natural being.[33] Nor did one have to be a transcendentalist to believe this; to one degree or another this ethos runs through Jeffersonian agrarianism, early British Romanticism, and even eighteenth-century natural history. Moreover, while an undeniable elitism clings to the notion that leisure underwrites culture, in the context of nineteenth-century American slavery we can regard African American leisure as a subtle form of resistance to the dominant labor regime. Indeed, the subversive power of laziness constitutes a recurring theme in antislavery literature, and in the slave narrative particularly. Mount and Clonney probably did not intend such a reading, but it does not take too strenuous a leap of the imagination to see their dozing African American figures as essentially opting out of culture in favor of nature—of preferring, like Bartleby, not to participate, at least for the moment, in an economic system (whether southern or northern) that routinely denied them the fruits of their labor.

The fact that neither Mount nor Clonney were southerners suggests that the tropes of black leisure and labor, and the ideological freight they carried, operated widely in American culture. Yet the national debate over the nature of labor increasingly split along regional lines, and any depiction of African Americans at work or at ease necessarily entered into a charged political atmosphere. At the center of intensifying debates over economic development—debates that played out in periodicals as well as in political and educational institutions—lay the question of the respective value of free and slave labor. For many northerners (the number grew with each passing year) free labor represented not only the most moral but also the most practical and progressive form of economic organization. In Olaudah Equiano's day, Western political philosophy and economic theory had begun redefining the value of physical labor, even as the slave system delegated much of that labor to non-Westerners. In the nineteenth century, northern free-labor ideology extended the earlier assault on the long-standing stigma attached to wage labor as a form of bondage by associating the principle of voluntary exchange with the values of individual freedom and personal responsibility. Increasingly, the wage laborer in a capitalist system was seen as a full agent in his work, making a voluntary contract for his labor and receiving in return the full compensation to which he has agreed. Although the term "free labor" tended to obscure the ways in which wage labor was not free in practice, the ideology derived energy from its rhetorical association with the national rhetoric of freedom and from its rhetorical opposition to its putative antithesis, slave labor.[34] The concept of free labor was, furthermore, a cardinal tenet in the era's middle-class faith in the virtuousness of hard work. As Daniel T. Rodgers has argued, the social valuation of the work ethic in nineteenth-century America depended on identifying labor with moral fiber and seeing it as a means of personal and social regeneration.[35]

If idleness represented, for the mainstream North, a failure to exercise virtue by undertaking the hard work of life, slavery represented the *impossibility* of exercising virtue because moral exertion required freedom of will. And in a climate of moral irresponsibility, antislavery writers argued, stagnation inevitably resulted. Free labor advocates presented slave-based economics not only as an immoral system depending on violence and coercion, but as a backwater from the healthy circulations of commerce and as isolated from the world and from history. In a congressional debate during the Missouri Crisis, William Plumer of New Hampshire emphasized slavery's detrimental effect on agriculture in hyperbolic rhetoric: "The slave and his task-master, placed in a land flowing with milk and honey, would convert even the garden of Eden into a desert and a waste."[36] Plumer voiced a crucial line of the free-labor argument—the depiction of slavery as a blight on the region's natural productivity—that would later become a recurrent theme in the work of northern travelers in and commentators on the South.[37]

In response, some southerners began portraying slave-based agriculture as superior to freehold agriculture, based primarily on the efficiency of the system and on the "natural fitness" of African Americans for field labor—as demonstrated, ostensibly, by science. Introducing the first edition of the *Southern Agriculturist* in 1828, the journal's editors lamented that "whilst every other Science has had her votaries, AGRICULTURE has been neglected and despised." After citing recent improvements in technology and method, they granted that "much remains to be accomplished. The thick veil which has been spread over the operations of Nature, has not been removed. A few, only, of those things which were hid from us have been made known as inducements for us to persevere in our attempts to establish the SCIENCE OF AGRICULTURE on a surer foundation."[38] This rhetorical effort to present agriculture as a genuine science, supported by the journal's staple reports on new findings and techniques, reflects the extent to which the scientific ideal had permeated American culture and set the standard for what constituted modernity. Yet the defensive tone of this and a number of subsequent articles suggests the degree to which southerners as well as northerners perceived a growing split between the regions' economies and identities.[39] One response, on the part of southern advocates, involved the defense of agriculture not so much by accommodating it to northern standards as by aligning it against free-labor capitalism and with the nationalistic agrarian tradition associated with Jeffersonian republicanism.[40] Mounting a counterattack that gathered steam during the 1830s and 1840s, proslavery writers developed a more self-conscious ideology of slave labor that wove together notions of the racial identity of Africans and of the ideal role of the natural world in southern society. At times they echoed free-labor northern rhetoric, but always with a difference. For example, Thomas Kettell, a proslavery economist from New York who had written frequently for the popular southern periodical *De Bow's Review*, invoked the work ethic in defending slavery, for "even a large mixture of white blood . . . never suffices to impart energy or enterprise to the black descendant."[41] Some such attitude or belief, even if not recognized or embraced as such, seems to lie behind, and to have been reinforced by, the era's "comic" portrayals of sleeping African Americans.

Paintings imagining African American labor in the natural world, therefore, necessarily participated in a widely dispersed, ideologically fluid cultural discussion. Yet they characteristically occluded a broader social context in imagining that labor. In *Eel Spearing at Setauket*, Mount created an image of black-white cooperation that obscured, or even reversed, the inequality inherent in the labor relation; in fact, it removed the characters' productive activity from the economic sphere altogether. Similarly, James Goodwyn Clonney, in such works as *In the Woodshed* (1838), *In the Cornfield* (1844), *Which Way Shall We Go?* (1850), and *What a Catch!* (1855), depoliticizes and deracializes labor, rendering it instead a matter of friendly, even intimate, cooperation. *In the Cornfield* (fig. 3), for example, anticipates *Eel Spearing at Setauket* in portraying not just interracial collaboration but black leadership and white assistance. There is nothing intrinsically wrong, of course, with such themes, except the fact that the ideal of interracial harmony (assuming Clonney even intended it as such) works subtly to obscure the reality of lopsided racial power. It is difficult, moreover, to read Clonney's paintings as undertaking an ironic deconstruction of that ideal in order to critique the real; rather, they seem to express a kind of sentimentalized free-labor ideology, almost premodern in its eschewal of system, context, and complication.

A related problem arises in visual representations of black labor. As "culture" was defined largely in opposition to nature, the achievement of culture required the transcendence or domination of the natural. Insofar as African or African American characters in painting, therefore, undertake the work of improving, managing, or shaping nature to human ends, they act as agents of culture, extending or maintaining the domain of civilization: the essence of georgic. Again, there is nothing inherently objectionable to this theme, but we should ask *which* culture these characters are agents of, or what cultural values and practices they bring to their encounter with the natural world. Asking that question directs attention to the complex forms of acculturation experienced by diasporic communities, and helps us gauge more sensitively the costs associated with that acculturation. Those costs have to do not only with the "de-Africanization" of New World black communities as they had to accommodate themselves to either slave-based or trade-based economics, but also with the perpetuation of a restrictive representational axis on which a "black" relation to nature could be depicted, an axis running from primitive, unreflecting simplicity (i.e., unacculturated) to appropriative mastery (i.e., acculturated). The ideological field created by these two poles—blacks as natural force or blacks as vectors of Western culture—allowed little space for alternative ways of understanding the place of nature in human life, and served primarily to reinforce the belief that nature had to be suppressed or overcome to allow for the advance of civilization.

European American painters often navigated this problem through the representation of animals, which in racial landscapes often serve as vital symbolic elements mediating the relation between the cultural and natural worlds. The three most common include fish, horses, and dogs, each of which plays a distinctive role in the broader iconography of the work. Fish, which appear in Mount's *Eel Spearing*, Clonney's *What a Catch!* and Clonney's *Fishing Party*, among others, usually simply represent prey, the bounty of nature, food or commodity, and are not objects of fascination or appreciation so much as targets of human ingenuity and exertion. The horse, by contrast, by virtue of its greater integration into the sphere of human activity and its unique psychological resonance, particularly in nineteenth-century American society, appears as a more charged and complex mediator between culture and nature. As a beast of burden, it serves as the immediate or proximate object of human labor, with the tilled field, typically, standing as the secondary object; this is the basic role the horse plays in Clonney's *In the Cornfield*, for example. Horses appear more evocatively in Charles Deas's *The Devil and Tom Walker* (1838) and Edward Troye's *Richard Singleton* (ca. 1835; fig. 4), where they help to articulate the relation between blackness and culture that each painting envisions.

Deas depicts the scene from Washington Irving's 1824 story in which the devil, enforcing his contract with Tom Walker, has the usurer borne away on a black horse "gallop[ing] like mad across the fields, over the hills and down into the black hemlock swamp."[42] In the painting, Walker, illuminated by a flash of lightning during a thunderstorm in the wilderness, is carried away on this black horse while pursued by the devil, a pitch-black imp brandishing an axe and a stick while chasing and tormenting his victim. Irving's tale, a fusion of folklore and allegory set in and around early eighteenth-century Boston, associates the rise of Anglo-American capitalism with the destruction of nonwhite culture, the energy and history of which persist only in the swampy forest outside the city, an area "full of pits and quagmires, partly covered with weeds and mosses; where the green surface often betrayed the traveller into a gulf of black smothering mud." White economic culture, Irving warns, has raised itself out of the muck of nature only imperfectly, and in its greed has made itself vulnerable to being dragged back down. In Irving's story, despite its suspicion of the swamp, we can see distinct motion toward associating the swamp with "alternative versions of America," with blackness, and with resistance to patriarchal and capitalist values.[43]

Few commentators have focused on the complex racial dimension to the story, but race matters centrally to its meaning.[44] In Irving's ambiguous coding, the devil is "neither negro nor Indian," but he is described repeatedly as "the black man," and he exacts revenge on the "white savages" on behalf of the dispossessed "red men." The phrase "the black man" is of course a traditional nickname for the devil, but it nonetheless invokes the Manichean cosmogony associating blackness with evil, and a cruel irony thus subsists in the devil's self-characterization as "the great patron and prompter of slave dealers."[45] At a superficial level, Deas's representation of the scene echoes Irving's racial Manicheanism, giving us a distinctly negroid Satan, but both story and painting reveals more complex layers of meaning. In particular, far from celebrating Anglo culture, they decry its perilous moral bankruptcy, and although the black characters are problematically identified with the primal, destructive forces of nature, the common narrative is one that upends the social hierarchy through explicit black-on-white violence: the allegorical revolt of nature against culture. And what, then, of the horses? Two of the beasts feature in the story, Tom Walker's and the devil's. According to "probably a mere old wives fable," Irving coyly writes, the newly zealous Walker "had his horse new shod, saddled and bridled, and buried with his feet uppermost; because he supposed that at the last day the world would be turned upside down; in which case he should find his horse standing ready for mounting." Here the beast figures as a mere appendage or servant, the equivalent of a slave, perhaps, and might put us in mind of Jefferson's "palpable truth" that "the mass of mankind has not been born, with saddles on their backs, nor a favored few booted and spurred, ready to ride them."[46] The devil's black steed, then, appears as the agent of oppressed nature's revenge against an avaricious culture, bearing the latter across a nightmare landscape utterly at odds with the pastoral glades and glens of New England lore. The return to nature, in this case, is a violent event, but one of justice.

Edward Troye's *Richard Singleton* provides a striking contrast, not least in terms of its style. Troye, a native of France who spent most of his professional life in Philadelphia, Alabama, and Kentucky, specialized in realistic paintings of thoroughbred racehorses, and his works concentrated as fondly and formally on the animal as did portraiture on human subjects. Here, Troye shows Richard Singleton, a prize-winning thoroughbred, standing tall and majestic, accompanied by three African American men: the well-dressed handsome trainer, the groom, and the jockey. Behind all of these figures runs a wooden fence, and the background consists of a grassy field and trees. Clearly the racial and social context matters here, but as in Deas's painting its meaning seems ambiguous. At first glance, Troye represents his black characters as forceful cultural agents, as shapers or commanders of natural force as embodied in the horse; they have trained the beast for a specific cultural purpose, that of competitive racing, and will act directly as his human masters in the event. Yet despite their proud bearing in the painting, the actual cultural power of the black characters is severely circumscribed; none of them, after all, is actually the horse's owner. Moreover, they have trained the horse not for a productive activity such as farming, but for gambling, a leisure activity from which African Americans were, for the most part, legally barred.[47] The work undertaken by the black characters, then, feeds back into a speculative economy whose rewards lie beyond their reach, while their formal clothes, their uniforms, communicate social status only in the most problematic way, because that status is defined, limited, and enforced extrinsically—yet internalized nonetheless.[48] Finally, we might note the subterranean significance of the sport's preference for thoroughbred horses—for the pure or, more pointedly, the *unmiscegenated* specimen. This subtle analogy between race and breed, in conjunction with the parallel roles of horse and trainers as performers in an economic spectacle controlled by others, suggests that while the painting envisions the black characters' human superiority to nature, it inevitably reveals their restricted place in the social and racial hierarchy. The painting takes no particular political stand, however, and the background landscape does not naturalize the situation so much as frame it. What matters more is the fence that divides the landscape, the physical symbol of the theme of cultural partition that suffuses the painting at a deep level.

Similar issues arise in Mount's *Dance of the Haymakers* (1845; fig. 5), which strategically portrays a dog near the center of the action. As the most acculturated of animals, the most deeply absorbed into human society, dogs tend to carry the greatest symbolic and psychological weight. They appear regularly in slave narratives, as trackers of fugitives—in essence, as enforcers of the social order—and in the accompanying woodprints usually appear as terrifying extensions of white power. Yet dogs in paintings can also mediate between race, culture, and nature in more nuanced, complicated ways. In *Dance of the Haymakers*, for instance, a small group of farm laborers are making music and dancing in a barn, while outside a young African American man watches them while drumming along with a pair of sticks; this character is watched in turn by a small brown dog, perhaps a puppy, lying on the ground in front of the open barn door. Compositionally, and through the rising sequence of gazes, the painting creates an implied narrative leading from animal to culture, positioning the black man in an intermediary stage. Culture reaches its apex in the barn, the built structure, where community and art thrive, while outside the dog and the young African American character are linked not only by their exclusion but also by color. At the same time, the humanness of the black character is signalled by his apparent ownership of the dog, who pays attention to him rather than to the inviting plate of meat nearby, and by his participation, even though marginal, in the music-making. Although the built landscape takes center stage, the surrounding rural landscape (implied by the pitchfork resting against the barn) helps establish the painting's allegory of the hierarchical development of civilization. By circumstancing the cultural scene, this unseen natural domain, from which the dog and the African American character emerge in ascending order, provides an important reference point for understanding the social vision underlying the painting's "comically conceived" (in Lanman's words) surface.

Significantly, all of these paintings, with the exception of *Richard Singleton*, depict a solitary African American character. In fact, excluding those paintings that depict fugitive slaves, such as Eastman Johnson's *A Ride for Liberty* (1862), or slave auctions, such as the anonymous *The Slave Market* (ca. 1850), antebellum American painting seems almost incapable of imagining other than a lone black figure, cut off from family and community, and this deficiency, whether consciously intended or not, represents the deeper ideological hazard posed by racial landscapes. Even representations of black heroism or agency such as Nathaniel Jocelyn's *Portrait of Cinqué* (1840) or Thomas Waterman Wood's *Moses, the Baltimore News Vendor* (1858) fail to envision a healthy, self-sufficient black community on the land, or the expression and development of black culture outside the confines of Anglo society. Like much of the rest of the culture, American artists evidently had trouble imagining the free, healthy, independent African American family. In addition, the work undertaken by the black characters simply gets folded back into the white-dominated economic system, rather than serving as the basis for collaborative racial uplift.

The cultural context for this phenomenon involved the highly racialized discourses surrounding "the family." In the era's domestic fiction, in its popular periodicals, in its political debates, and in its human sciences, the image of the family circulated endlessly. As with representations of labor, we find a divergence between northern and southern conceptions of the family—most intensively, of course, when it came to the African American family and the relation between slavery and the family. The extreme proslavery position appears, passionately if eccentrically, in the major works of George Fitzhugh, *Sociology for the South* and *Cannibals All!*, which represent society as an organic familial hierarchy, given by God and not to be remade according to any utopian philosophical or social system. In Fitzhugh's conception of a divinely ordained social hierarchy, the necessary adhesives, the bonds that stabilize society, are love and benevolence. Accordingly he tries to emphasize the selfless side of human nature uncorrupted by competition—especially competition in a capitalist economic system. Whether sincere or disingenuous, Fitzhugh's utopian vision centers on "the family," which, by regulating selfishness and fulfilling the need for sociality, would enable the fullest, healthiest expression of human nature, and which, as the "first and most natural" form of human organization, provided the proper model for society and government. Closely echoing southern plantation fiction, Fitzhugh's pastoral fantasy of patriarchal order imagined a dangerously specious harmony that embraced whites and blacks, flora and fauna, in a virtual commune of happiness:

> Within the family there is little room, opportunity, or temptation to selfishness—and slavery leaves but little of the world without the family. . . . [Man] feels deeply for the sufferings of domestic animals, and is rendered happy by witnessing the enjoyments of the flocks, and herds, and caroling birds that surround him. He sympathizes with all external nature. A parched field distresses him, and he rejoices as he sees the groves, and the gardens, and the plains flourishing, and blooming and smiling about him. All men are philanthropists, and would benefit their fellow-men if they could. But we cannot be sure of benefitting those whom we cannot control.

Such idealized depictions of the slaveholding family circulated widely in southern literature, and by effacing all trace of racial conflict in a pastoral utopia they represented not simply an affront to truth but a formidable threat to antislavery philosophy. That threat involved not simply denying the reality of black suffering, but enfolding blackness unresistingly into the white family's zone of control. Fitzhugh does not, of course, imagine a free and independent black family, but neither does he imagine blacks integrated into the southern family; the slaves, rather, are simultaneously absent and present, ancillary and integral. In fact, on the basis of the assumed dependence of the slaveholding family on slaves—a logical, even definitional, assumption—he accuses abolitionists of seeking "the destruction of the family."[49] Fitzhugh's pastoral vision of southern life represented the logical extension, the theorized outgrowth, of the myth of plantation felicity that had already arisen in southern fiction.

In reaction, therefore, both to the actual and pervasive smashing of slave families, and to southern pastoral's perversion of the otherwise healthy human longing for community, slave narratives and sentimental antislavery texts began to concentrate much of their emotional energy in images of the family—the intact and happy family, the violated family, the reunited family, newlyweds in the blush of love—and they broke ground, crucially, in foregrounding the experience of African American families. The politics of this were vitally important, for people across the political spectrum in midcentury Victorian America regarded the nuclear family as the best hope for human happiness and social stability. But until antislavery writers began calling attention to the black experience, "the family" remained for most of the reading public an implicitly white or deracialized entity. To the degree then, that the nation represented the family writ large, racializing the family in antislavery literature had important implications for how people could understand the composition of the American polity. Yet even the most important writers encountered imaginative limitations in this respect. Harriet Beecher Stowe famously racialized the family in *Uncle Tom's Cabin*, but just as famously failed to imagine the integration of blacks into American society. Emerson had the opposite problem; he could imagine, in the abstract, a national family amalgamated like "Corinthian brass," but never really broke through to consider actual human relationships or the emotional and psychological dimensions of racial pluralism. The crucial challenge—one that the country still wrestles with today—is to understand "the black family" both on its own terms and as an integral part of the American polity at large.

Antebellum paintings, therefore, that depict a vibrant black community were ahead of their time. Eastman Johnson's iconic *Old Kentucky Home—Life in the South (Negro Life at the South)* (1859; fig. 6), for example, imagines the vitality of African American life in the midst of poverty. Intriguingly, it does so not only at the overt level of showing us a range of social activities—work, music, courtship—but also at a subtextual level on which images of cultural, even biological, intermingling operate. And again, an animal provides a crucial symbolic reference point. As in *Dance of the Haymakers*, a dog figures prominently in Johnson's painting, also appearing in the lower central foreground and playing a similarly subtle role in a complex social scene. In contrast to *Dance of the Haymakers*, however, the primary visual plane of Johnson's work is horizontal; almost the entirety of the action takes place in a social panorama running from left to right, and with the exception of a mother and child at an upper window, the people all occupy the same spatial stratum. These characters, moreover, display a full range of skin color, from a very dark brown, through several medium and lighter hues, to the pale complexion of the woman entering at stage right. This woman's appearance on the scene, indeed, alerts us to the furtive subplot afoot in this picturesque tableau of "Negro life." The woman, whose clothes clearly mark her as upper class, is followed by another woman in a bonnet, and seems herself to follow after a young "white" boy (clad in blue) who, in turn, has apparently followed the dog into this scene, gesturing for the women to come along. Meanwhile, the dog's playful stance, as if barking for attention, suggests that he has mischievously led the white characters into this otherwise unseen space, where the black community now becomes visible to their eyes, and to the viewer's. The dog, indeed, occupies a privileged place in the painting, with no distracting clutter immediately around him, and with a number of gazes directed toward him. In this light, Johnson's decision to give the dog a coat of brown and white, mixed in about equal proportion and yet unblended, takes on pointed significance, efficiently encapsulating the contrapuntal themes of intermingling and separation that inform the rest of the painting. Johnson has actually balanced these themes masterfully, and neither can claim a preponderance of the visual evidence. The spectrum of skin color invokes a history of biological intermixture, and yet the extreme poles of the racial binary remain as visible as ever, in the glaring white of the man's shirt and the cavernous blackness of the fireplace or upper window. The unalarming presence of the white characters in this "old Kentucky home" suggests a degree of social familiarity, and yet the white woman's finery dispels any notion that economic equality exists. The two buildings—one ramshackle and the other magnificent—are simultaneously separate and adjoined. The banjo, even, captures the uneasy balance between assimilation and segregation, with African and European musical traditions both present, and yet distinct, in a single instrument. And finally, the natural and the cultural coexist easily in the painting, the tree seeming to embrace or preside over the human activity, which goes on more happily outdoors, evidently, than indoors. This pattern of balance renders *Negro Life at the South* more suggestive than polemical, and the "miscegenated" dog, so vital to the scene, comes to resemble a kind of living Rorschach blot, a mischievous test for how the viewer will regard this slice of "Negro life." This ambiguity may help to explain why contemporary reviewers of the painting could arrive at no consensus as to its political stance vis-à-vis slavery.[50]

Notwithstanding its title, Johnson's painting depicts African American life in an urban setting. What of images of the black family or black community on the land or in a rural setting or natural scene? These images, such as John Antrobus's *A Plantation Burial* (1860; fig. 7) or John William Hill's *View of Richmond, Virginia* (1847; fig. 8), raise more directly the question of the role of the natural world in African American life, and they remind us that the psychological and ideological potency of racial landscapes should be viewed in terms of the real communities, in real locations, that actually drew on nature as a vital—and liberatory—resource. In the former painting, Antrobus depicts a gathering of slaves in a stylized, even gothic forest clearing, for a funeral at which the white characters (evidently the master, mistress, and overseer) are barely visible, lurking off to the side among the trees and observing the proceedings. Culture, and specifically American Christian culture, is figured in the dress and ritual, and yet nature provides the context where the African American community, at least temporarily, can find a measure of independence from white society. In *View of Richmond*, similarly, Hill shows a black family in the foreground, on the near shore of the James River, which seems to cut them off from the city and American culture, to symbolize their exclusion, and the figures are casting their gazes in that direction. Yet the land the family stands on represents a stable present, *safely* distant from culture, and perhaps the site of a current or future home.

Hill's painting also returns us to the importance of the georgic tradition, with its characteristic themes of finding a place on the land, of working the land, and of cultivating the black family or community there. In a fashion reminiscent of *Letters from an American Farmer*, the African American georgic functions as a kind of antidote to southern pastoral, indeed to the escapist undertow of all pastoral, in that it offers a practical blueprint for rebuilding community by redefining the place of work and the natural world in African American culture. In African American literature, an agrarian or rural ethos, in which the working of the land provides crucial economic and spiritual strength, had begun to surface, fitfully, in the antebellum slave narrative—as Frederick Douglass's *My Bondage and My Freedom*, discussed in the next chapter, attests. Given the history of agricultural slavery, such an ethos came burdened with pain, but it represented nothing less than an indispensable strategy of survival. A rich aesthetic component, drawing on the pastoral tradition and its suggestions of cultured refinement, provided a measure of rurality's power—an aesthetic one can hear, for instance, in Martha Browne's description of a Sunday "pleasure-walk": "The patriarchal trees and the delicate sward, the wind-music and the almost ceaseless miserere of the grove, elevate the heart, and to the cultivated mind speak with a power to which that of books is but poor and tame."[51] At the heart of the rural ethos, however, lay an assertion of the dignity of physical labor. "I am what is called a 'handy fellow,'" wrote the ex-slave John Brown. "I am a good carpenter, and can make just what machinery I want, give me only tools. I understand all about the growth of cotton, from the time of preparing the land to receive the seed, till the wool is jinned and packed. I am a good judge of its quality, too, and know what is the best kind of jin for the various sorts."[52]

Nonetheless, before the Civil War, the georgic tradition had not yet asserted itself powerfully in African American literature or visual art. In antislavery travel literature of the eighteenth century, such as Anthony Benezet's *Some Historical Account of Guinea*, an African agrarian pastoral played an important role in shaping public perceptions of African societies, but in the antebellum United States, the possibilities for such mythmaking proved less robust. The pressures of slavery and the immediate exigencies of abolitionist politics meant that a wide-ranging and realistic redefinition of rural black labor would have to wait until the late nineteenth century—and even then it never fully sloughed off its negative connotations. Moreover, the representation of black labor in white literature and artwork tended to separate it from the long-term communal uplift of African American society. This delay or denial of a healthy valuation of agricultural work in black culture, combined with the destructive legacy of slavery in the post-Reconstruction white labor regime, cast a long shadow of ambivalence or doubt over African Americans' connection with the land. In the late nineteenth century it provoked such responses as Booker T. Washington's wish that "by some power of magic I might remove the great bulk of [urban blacks] into the country districts and plant them upon the soil, upon the solid and never deceptive foundation of Mother Nature, where all nations and races that have ever succeeded have gotten their start,—a start that at first may be slow and toilsome, but one that nevertheless is real."[53] W. E. B. Du Bois, too, imagined the "Black Belt" of the South as a land "full of untold story, of tragedy and laughter, and the rich legacy of human life; shadowed with a tragic past, and big with future promise," and as a "land of rapid contrasts and of curiously mingled hope and pain." Yet he also described the "hard ruthless rape of the land" under slavery, and detailed the social pathologies that arose in southern black districts because of the continued exploitation and disempowerment of tenant farmers, landowners, and laborers, many of whom eventually decided simply to join "that long procession" of migration to northern cities. So the georgic tradition, more realistic, forward looking, and constructive than pastoral, nonetheless confronted in American history more powerful forces than it could easily harness to a literary vision of communal black renewal. Yet it remained indispensable to that vision.

Coda: Antislavery Pictorialism

As suggested at the outset of this chapter, the story of the great struggle over American slavery included the impact of visual culture on antislavery literature. Recognizing, as did Harriet Beecher Stowe, the power of "word-pictures" to motivate people on subconscious levels—even if this recognition itself operated subconsciously—some antislavery writers began employing "pictorial" strategies or techniques. Although the finely wrought images and carefully staged tableaux characteristic of high literary pictorialism had their place, antislavery pictorialism generally involved not a highly technical method, but a general effort to use text to stimulate visual images in the mind of the reader.[54] Its dominant modes, in Marianna Torgovnick's terms, were the ideological and hermeneutic. The former "embodies major themes of the [work]—especially its views of politics, history, society or, more generally, of 'reality'—in descriptions, objects, metaphors, artist figures, or scenes based upon the historical visual arts or in the same aspects of fiction conceived and experienced pictorially." Hermeneutic pictorialism, by contrast, comprises "the ways in which references to the visual arts or objects and scenes experienced pictorially stimulate the interpretive processes of the reader's mind and cause him to arrive at an understanding of the [work's] methods and meanings."[55] These two modes had particular relevance for antislavery literature because they aligned its political orientation with its psychological, and specifically affective, rhetorical strategies.

Antislavery pictorialism emerged in dialogic, symbiotic relation to antebellum painting, with novelists and poets drawing on a common cultural vocabulary of visual images, and painters, conversely, often taking their subject matter from the slavery debate. In S. Sanford's "Poem, suggested by A. F. Biard's picture of a slave market," for example, Sanford refers to Francois-Auguste Biard's painting *The Slave Trade* (1840), which depicts a violent, lurid trading scene on the West Coast of Africa (a scene itself "suggested" by antislavery literature), and which was displayed at the Twelfth National Anti-Slavery Bazaar, held at Faneuil Hall in Boston in 1845. (Antislavery bazaars, or fairs, were annual events at which activists would gather to raise money for the cause by selling household goods, books, periodicals, and so forth, and they did much to involve antislavery in the broader symbolic economy of antebellum America.) Similarly, Robert Duncanson's *Uncle Tom and Little Eva* (1853), which renders Stowe's heroine as a kind of literal link between the earthly Tom and the spiritual beauty of the heavenly sky, does not unilaterally translate the text into image, but takes its very cues from Stowe's pictorial description: "It is now one of those intensely golden sunsets which kindles the whole horizon into one blaze of glory, and makes the water another sky. The lake lay in rosy or golden streaks, save where white-winged vessels glided hither and thither, like so many spirits, and little golden stars twinkled through the glow, and looked down at themselves as they trembled in the water" (226).

The painterly qualities of antislavery writing provided a powerful means of directing readerly experience. Verbal landscapes, for instance, could help to shape the reader's impressions of regional identity, as political agendas were translated into competing ways of representing the national terrain. Or, natural settings and natural events, particularly when highly visually textured, could frame or stimulate a character's experience—evoking memories, eliciting feelings, presenting opportunities—in ways that the reader could identify with, thus establishing what I have called a circuit of shared meaning. And the "look" of nature in a literary work would communicate particular ideas about the natural order and, at one remove, about the moral or supernatural order suffusing it; in antislavery pastoral, love and freedom imbue physical nature with beauty and bounty; in antipastoral, greed and oppression manifest as natural decay and pestilence, or as deceptive gaudiness.

Yet the pictorial mode, when connected to race, had the negative potential of reducing human identity to little more than pictures—as Stowe's comment about "the negro character" implies, and as her actual representation of many of the African Americans in *Uncle Tom's Cabin* attests. For many Anglo-American writers, including those of relatively "enlightened" sensibilities, the impulse to portray nonwhites as just another part of the picturesque scenery apparently proved irresistible. To take just one example, consider the influential art critic James Jackson Jarves's description of Tahiti: "A dense belt of green waving palms and rich tomano-trees, with varied hues of tropical flowers and fruits, interspersed with native huts, bound shores, indented with quiet bays and coral-formed channels. . . . Amid all this, graceful canoes lightly shoot, their dark-skinned but brightly-apparelled crews gaily contrasting with their snowy-white sails. Such a spectacle gives the perfect repose of beauty. All is in keeping with the lovely whole. Less would injure, and more distract the scene. Has artist ever given this?"[56] The native Tahitians, rendered in a few quick brush strokes, fill Jarves's need for a primitive pigment in his pastoral scene, but only if drained of human complexity or independent agency.

As if in response to such simplification, some slave narrators figured their own lives as a kind of extended, narrativized portrait, in which word-pictures express three-dimensional emotion rather than mere physical appearance. The North Carolinian fugitive Lunsford Lane, for instance, takes stock of his past by dipping into an emotional palette: "I need not say, what the reader has already seen, that my life so far had been one of joy succeeding sorrow, and sorrow following joy; of hope, of despair, of bright prospects, of gloom; and of as many hues as ever appear on the varied sky, from the black of midnight, or the deep brown of a tempest, to the bright warm glow of a clear noon day."[57] Frederick Douglass, in a Byronic moment, makes an interesting distinction, writing in *My Bondage and My Freedom* that "[a]nguish and grief, like darkness and rain, may be described, but joy and gladness, like the rainbow of promise, defy alike the pen and pencil" (205). At the end of *Incidents in the Life of a Slave Girl*, Harriet Jacobs also blends these two pigments: "[T]he retrospection [of life in slavery] is not altogether without solace; for with those gloomy recollections come tender memories of my good old grandmother, like light, fleecy clouds floating over a dark and troubled sea."[58] In each case, the narrator shifts registers from feeling to vision, rendering emotional states as a painter would, and treating the entire life, as in Equiano's *Interesting Narrative*, as an object of retrospective visual contemplation, as a landscape, or skyscape, of memory. The painterly style has more than decorative significance, of course. It underlines the coherence and dignity of the slave's life and, in a manner that we have traced as far back as Phillis Wheatley, conveys the narrator's cultured aesthetic and affective responsiveness to the natural world. This technique works, moreover, to associate narrator and nature, thus authenticating the slave's emotional life by detaching it from the purely social. And most importantly, although the narrators are objects of our sight, they appear as undeniably human subjects; our vision is directed away from their skin color and toward their inner experience, a potential point of readerly identification.

In profound yet subtle ways, then, did the visual culture of the antebellum United States, with its new technologies, its expanding media markets, and its growing middle class, influence the country's perceptions of black-white relations and the future place of African Americans in the national experiment. Next to polemical rhetoric, visual images—in museums, homes, periodicals, and the "word-pictures" of literature—helped shape public attitudes toward race and slavery, and those that used the natural world as either backdrop or primary subject, as in landscape, yielded elaborate configurations of meaning. Drawing on different aesthetic traditions—luminism, pastoral, georgic, the picturesque, and the sublime—these images also encoded contemporary epistemic and ideological trends. Although constrained by such concepts as "beauty" or "harmony," and although invested in nature as a realm of common feeling, they nonetheless reveal within them the profoundly disruptive forces of racial and cultural conflict. They form part of the story of the struggle over human bondage that deserves continued attention.

I wish to be able to make a picture that shall be graphic & true to nature in its details.
HARRIET BEECHER STOWE to Frederick Douglass, July 1851

What I propose is intended simply to prepare men for the work of getting an honest living—not out of dishonest men—but out of an honest earth.
FREDERICK DOUGLASS to Stowe, March 1853

What Douglass is really, time will show—I trust that he will make no further additions to the already unfortunate controversial literature of the cause. Silence in this case will be eminently—golden.
STOWE to William Lloyd Garrison, December 1853

CHAPTER SIX

Revisiting, Reliving, Reforming

THUS FAR, the only full-length slave narrative we have examined in depth has been that of Olaudah Equiano, whose *Interesting Narrative*, with its recounting of both worldly and spiritual emancipation, helped define the genre for the nineteenth century. Between 1787 and the 1850s, however, the slave narrative evolved considerably, reflecting a new diversity of rhetorical technique, thematic emphasis, and social perspective. As the American literary marketplace responded to (and helped generate) the public's interest in the experience of slaves, a number of fictionalized variants appeared, such as Richard Hildreth's *The Slave; or, Memoirs of Archy Moore* (1836) or Emily Pierson's *Jamie Parker, the Fugitive* (1851). Moreover, many works, even if not billed as autobiographical testimony, included substantial material imagining the African American or slave perspective, such as Robert Montgomery Bird's

Sheppard Lee (1836). The riches of this literary terrain—particularly the scores of slave narratives published during the antebellum years—are still coming to light, having received woefully little scholarly attention, either in their own right or for how they contextualize the major slave narratives and novels of slavery.

This chapter focuses on two of the preeminent literary figures operating on that terrain—Harriet Beecher Stowe and Frederick Douglass—and on their complex reimagining of the genre in *Dred: A Tale of the Great Dismal Swamp* (1856) and *My Bondage and My Freedom* (1855). In both, concepts and images of nature play a much more central, unruly, and fertile role than in the authors' iconic, first-published works, *Uncle Tom's Cabin* (1851–52) and *Narrative of the Life of Frederick Douglass* (1845), and this evolution in literary expression, I will argue, reflected the changing character of each writer's racial politics during a period of deteriorating sectional conflict. Complicating matters, Stowe's and Douglass's racial politics were shifting not only in relation to enormously difficult political circumstances, but also in relation to each other. In contrast to the 1830s and 1840s, when black and white antislavery activists or writers enjoyed only sporadic contact and coordination, the 1850s witnessed increasingly close (although by no means perfectly harmonious) partnerships among them. In certain specific incidents, such as the Shadrach Minkins or Anthony Burns fugitive slave cases, black and white antislavery activists joined together to take direct action.[1] In a broader sense, the antislavery movement had simply matured, and the increasing independence of African American activists stimulated a wide-ranging reassessment of both political strategies and personal relationships.[2] For Stowe and Douglass, whose first works had made them famous, this entailed a heightened familiarity with each other, with each other's writings, and with intellectual perspectives they had not fully considered before. It also meant a reexamination of how their writing related to the goals of the antislavery movement and to their own aspirations as authors. As Robert Levine, Joan Hedrick, and others have argued, Stowe and Douglass during the 1850s were actively, and interactively, engaged in a personal and professional navigation of the racial politics of abolition.[3] In the process, they consciously and creatively tapped into the increasingly rich representational deposits formed by the intersection of natural science and natural aesthetics.

The breakthroughs that *Dred* and *My Bondage and My Freedom* represented politically—the former more militant, the latter more communal—entailed innovation aesthetically, as both authors pushed beyond the comparatively inert treatment of the natural world in *Uncle Tom's Cabin* and the 1845 *Narrative*, and in mainstream antislavery polemical rhetoric. When Stowe and Douglass first got into print, their shared imperative was to have readers conjure up in imagination the cruelty and violence intrinsic to the slave system. In antislavery literature, this effort often devolved into a straightforward moral geography opposing northern freedom and southern sin—a strategy that could disrupt the philosophical and emotional underpinnings of southern pastoral, but at the cost of simplifying psychological and cultural reality. In *Dred* and *My Bondage and My Freedom*, as they penetrated more deeply into the intellectual problems posed by the symbolic richness of the natural world, Stowe and Douglass came to engage a broader set of relations between nature and human life. Although economic and religious blind spots still mar each work, both authors ingeniously link racial identity to the scientific, aesthetic, and spiritual vocabularies of nature that history had made available to them.

Stowe, in her flawed, sprawling, yet energetic tale of a North Carolina plantation in decline, and of a militant slave leader who leads a maroon community in the Great Dismal Swamp, imagines a principle of creative destructiveness in the natural world that works to philosophically authorize slave rebellion and violence. This theme dramatically complicates the work's treatment of pastoral, the power of which Stowe acknowledges, but which she also renders as inadequate to the challenge of reconceptualizing race in America. Yet Stowe treats the natural world in terms drawn principally from philosophy and literary tradition, and while she does define character through nature, it remains essentially disconnected from psychological concerns. In *My Bondage and My Freedom*, by contrast, the natural world appears not simply as land to be worked or a domain of natural liberty, but as an emotionally charged, ambiguously formative, source of individual and familial identity. Surprisingly,

Douglass comes to express a more passionate belief than Stowe in the regenerative power of nature—surprising, because his enslavement had involved an enforced working of nature, and because mainstream Western racial ideology had defined African-descended people as "of" nature. As Douglass experienced it, nature represented bounty and beauty, authority and authenticity, danger and indifference, and all these qualities were bound up with his senses of belonging, responsibility, artistry, and freedom. What he works toward, in his second autobiography, is a vision of the liberating communal power of nature, of African American rootedness on the land, and for this reason *My Bondage and My Freedom* stands as a very different kind of contribution than the 1845 *Narrative* to African American literary history.

Both Stowe and Douglass were creatively invested in the geography of slavery—in the literal places of freedom or servitude, and in the dynamics of flight, marronage, and recapture. This dimension of their work did not arise ex nihilo, but from the family of geographic themes that had evolved in the slave narrative genre more broadly. Let us begin there.

The Geography of the Slave Narrative

The American slave narrative's unique social power had much to do with its dialogical relation to other cultural and literary forms—the domestic novel, the captivity narrative, the spiritual autobiography—but it is much more engaged than we have appreciated with matters of geography: with spatial relation, physical climate, and human interaction with the environment. As these narratives explore the related problems of mobility, rootedness, and social identity that slaves had to confront, geographic motifs and concepts work to link individual emotional and moral conflicts to broader cultural and racial issues. In the process, aesthetic questions become literal problems; landscapes, both built and natural, appear less as objects of contemplation than as sites of physical escape, renegotiated power, and communal survival. The consistent narrative and phenomenological dynamic, however, involves the remove to nature, and the possibility of a revitalized connection to the social world, and the essential questions have to do with *where* the individual will be able to find both bodily and mental freedom, both freedom and community, both familial rootedness and the opportunity for personal mobility. Slave narratives make clear that these are not abstract matters but deeply connected to the cultural and psychological relationships between human beings and the natural environment.

Simple as it may seem, the unifying narrative structure of the genre involves the movement of a human being from place to place: from plantation to swamp, from town to town, from South to North, from native land to foreign lands. Psychologically and communally, of course, such relocations were anything but simple. They invariably entailed disruption, but they also represented opportunities; they mingled freedom and pain in unpredictable ways; they entailed complex problems of social commitment, emotional upheaval, individual survival, and altered relations to the natural world. Frequently we find multiple removes within a single narrative, cumulative testimony to the terrible precariousness of a life not legally recognized. We also find motifs or structures of circularity. At times the circle takes literal and geographic form, as a narrator returns to the place of birth or childhood; in other cases the return is figurative or projected, a renewed commitment to the land and family left behind. This circularity will become essential to the mature social perspective of *My Bondage and My Freedom*.

Almost all slave narratives open with an account of the place of youth. Ordinarily the place is either African, as in narratives depicting tribal life before a kidnapping or sale, or southern, as in narratives depicting slave life at a plantation or estate. The first sentence often specifies the place ("I was born in Virginia, in 1832, near Charlottesville, in the beautiful valley of the Rivanna river"), and the opening pages often give us scenes of everyday life in that place.[4] Autobiography naturally calls for such an account, but in the slave narrative the treatment of an originary locale seems unusually consistent in its early positioning in the text and unusually significant for the adult narrator's self-representation.

This phenomenon expresses the strong relation between slavery and the land, between social condition and geographic happenstance. One is born not only into a family but also into a place, and in the antebellum United States place determined status de jure (according to the laws of the state) and de facto (according to the local form of slavery). More importantly, the emphasis on originary place also reflects the particular traumas that slave children endured—those of an intrusion into or violation of the geographic home, and of dangerous exposure, to the elements and to white violence. At the same time, as in the case of Olaudah Equiano, it conveys nothing more and nothing less than the adult narrator's feeling of dislocation from the scenes of his or her childhood, scenes that may in fact be remembered with great fondness. Wayne Franklin and Michael Steiner have written that "early memories of the land are lodged in our minds [and] deeply influence the course of our lives. The terrain of late childhood is especially potent, nurturing the developing intellect and dwelling in adult memory as a guiding image of coherence."[5] Significantly, it is also in late childhood that a slave narrator's shocking initiation into racial consciousness usually occurs, on the discovery of the brutal principle of "white over black." Psychologically, then, the *locus juvenilis* stands forth in sharp complexity. A place of violence and savagery, it yet evokes a longing for rootedness and family, and for an innocence or psychic harmony from which the narrator has since fallen into the dismal awareness of personal and cultural fragmentation.[6]

It also helps to explain the vexed relationship to home characterizing most American slave narratives that begin in the South. Here, the image of an ancestral African past has given way to the image of the plantation, which substitutes, despite everything, for a lost collective history, and which represents the symbolic locus *par excellence* of the intimate geographics of slave life. It epitomizes what Philip Fisher calls "damaged social space," where secrecy, power, and violence reign, as opposed to the democratic values of transparency and equality.[7] On the plantation, slaves had to navigate a hierarchical and unpredictable environment, where the arrangement of physical structures and natural space expressed an elaborate complex of power relationships and emotional realities.[8] The unavoidable lessons of agricultural slavery (and to a lesser extent of domestic servitude) were that the mastery of human beings thrived on the mastery of space; that overseers oversaw both the slaves and the terrain; and that the white regime enforced obedience not only by direct violence but also by restricting both mobility and spatial privacy. In both *Dred* and *My Bondage and My Freedom*, successful slave resistance entails an undermining of this spatialized, racialized form of control.

For power circulated in more covert ways as well, with an ebb and flow through the plantation's various nooks and crannies. In particular, the meeting places, secret paths, and personal refuges that slave communities evolved represented improvisational responses to a rigidly controlled environment, a form of collective rebellious chaos that worked to undermine the planter's territorial order. Many is the narrative in which a slave hides in the woods or between crop rows, swims downstream to elude the hounds, confers surreptitiously with other slaves to share information or resources, or travels unobserved, to and fro, via clandestine routes. Moses Grandy, for example, tells of his sister Tamar's escaping from slave speculators and returning to her family, but having to conceal herself. Living in the forest "in a den she made for herself," she "sometimes ventured down to [her] mother's hut, where she was hid in a hollow under the floor." In order to visit her, "we tied pieces of wood or bundles of rags to our feet that no track might be made."[9] The power conferred by secret hideouts and paths is the power of individual safety, of knowledge and communication, and of communal survival. Spatial mobility and sequestration also enable plotting, with the crucial psychological uplift that such plotting provides.

To achieve freedom, of course, a slave had to leave the plantation behind, and this departure—particularly when effected in the late teens or early twenties—was bound to be a fraught event emotionally (as a wrenching event of passage and severance) and morally (in its suggestions of self-interest at the expense of the slave community). Notwithstanding its violence and its terrors, the plantation was also, frequently, the place of youth and family. It was still "home" for many slave narrators, still native land that could be possessed in spirit and memory if not in law or in fact. As suggested by a number of postbellum narratives, a child's experience of the plantation could include a profound attachment to the natural environment and a happy belief, justified or not, that into this world the destructive forces of life had not yet intruded.[10] For that reason, in many narratives escape represents not simply a culmination but the initial arc of a longer journey.

Significantly, the actual attempt at escaping, or the escape itself, often follows a prefatory remove to a space in nature, where the narrator girds for the decision and comes to a fuller understanding of the meanings of the contemplated flight. During this remove, the narrator's experience of the immediate natural environment has affective, ethical, and ideological force—or more precisely, the affective and the ideological converge at a point of ethical decisiveness. In the first instance, the natural scene provides crucial emotional and spiritual strengthening at the threshold of the momentous event. Before her own escape, for example, Harriet Jacobs visits the burial site of her parents:

> A calmer, more beautiful day never came down out of Heaven. . . . The graveyard was in the woods, and twilight was coming on. Nothing broke the death-like stillness of the scene. For more than ten years I had frequented this spot, but never had it seemed to me so sacred as now. A black stump, at the head of my mother's grave, was all that remained of a tree my father had planted. His grave was marked by a wooden board, bearing his name, the letters of which were nearly obliterated. I knelt down and kissed them, and poured forth a prayer to God for guidance and support in the perilous step I was about to take. As I passed the wreck of the old meeting house . . . I seemed to hear my father's voice come from it, bidding me not to tarry till I reached freedom or the grave. I rushed on with renovated hopes. My trust in God had been strengthened by that prayer among the graves.[11]

That this scene mingles the natural and the cultural so fluidly suggests that the psychological power of nature here depends on the temporariness and instrumentality of the remove, on the fact that the narrator is not fleeing *to* nature, but drawing on nature as means of shifting her emotional relation to a vicious cultural reality. Jacobs describes an inner liberation—from fear, from self-doubt, and perhaps from filial guilt—that in a very real sense makes possible her physical escape from bondage. Our understanding of geography in the slave narrative needs to take into account such moments, for they reveal how natural spaces and environments can have fundamental importance to people's self-conceptions, decisions, and lives.

This individual dynamic parallels the formation of African American maroon communities, in which slaves banded together for mutual survival. In both cases, the simple fact of physical distance from slave territory increases the power of narrators or maroons to resist the oppressive culture they fled. If we understand marronage broadly, as "all those ways in which what is seen as African survives the corrupting degradation of colonial and postcolonial domination by the Babylon of economic, ecological, and social exploitation," we can regard individual removes as nuclei for the emergence of broader maroon societies, which both reflect and nurture the spirit of escape that motivates fugitive narrators.[12] The maroon community that Stowe imagines in *Dred*, for instance, in the "fastnesses of nature" that "bid defiance to all human effort either to penetrate or subdue" (275), represents a kind of collective remove from white society, an imperfectly secure geographic space in which new forms of racial consciousness and social relation can emerge.

For slave narrators who flee altogether (to the North, Canada, the British Isles), geography matters in a direct and elemental way, for the fugitive's knowledge of the surrounding terrain meant nothing less than survival. The drama of this passage through dangerous terrain appeared in the woodprints that accompanied many narratives, and in illustrations in such popular periodicals as *Frank Leslie's Illustrated Newspaper*. By the time of the Civil War, the scene of a slave or group of slaves making their way through the wilderness had become, next to the auction block, perhaps the preeminent image of the iconography of American slavery, reaching its artistic zenith in Eastman Johnson's *A Ride for Liberty—The Fugitive Slaves* (1862) and Thomas Moran's *Slave Hunt, Dismal Swamp, Virginia* (1863). These paintings and illustrations tend to be much more action-oriented and kinetic than the racial landscapes considered in chapter 5; they imagine nature less as a comfortable (or pastoral) setting, than as a place of openness and transition through which the slave passes, almost allegorically, from bondage to freedom. As in the era's paintings of westward progress, with their covered wagons, receding trails, and distant vistas, the illustrations of slave flight represent the experience in nature as transitory and purposeful. They thus lend additional narrative force to the text, bringing to the fore its characteristic themes of progress, motion, and struggle. Moreover, in the natural setting, the cultural relation between blacks and whites, or slaves and masters, can seem upended, neutralized, arbitrary. Whereas pastoral landscapes—settled, cultivated, tame—can serve to direct our attention away from social inequality and conflict, wild landscapes in which fugitives and hunters compete against one another more closely resemble arenas, where the natural law of free development is put to the test.

The vital importance of navigating successfully through dangerous terrain helps to explain why some narratives seem so extraordinarily, even unnecessarily, attentive to physical details of the local environment, and to matters of distance, direction, and spatial relation.[13] Such conscientiousness seems motivated less by a desire to share with an imagined readership the methods and routes of escape than by the impulse to communicate something of the narrator's craftiness, or geographic fitness, as we might term it—their quintessentially *human* ability to adapt to, survive in, even master a given environment. That fitness, crucially, is mental as well as physical. It depends on not only bodily but also emotional stamina, and cognitively it involves the mind's apperception, processing, and retention of important features of the landscape. During a fugitive slave's passage through unknown or unfamiliar territory, the sensory, analytical, and memory-making functions of the mind all cooperate in generating interior representations of the external world. These psychological correlatives to perceived or experienced landscapes form a kind of interior cartography that is continually checked and rechecked against the manifold reality of the natural environment, and revised accordingly. In framing the issue this way, I do not mean to advance a constructivist model of human cognition, in which mental "maps" are divorced from externality, but to emphasize the practical outer-directed and problem-solving capacities of the mind as it confronts its environment. It is a question, in Edward Reed's formulation, of trying to understand "how organisms make their way in the world, not how a world is made inside of organisms."[14] In this dynamic linking mind and world organically, the sense of sight figures centrally, in that it enables the mind to move from a merely sensory present to an abstract or imagined future, and as Hans Jonas concludes, "is thus a major factor in the higher freedom of the self-moving animal."[15]

This perspective helps illuminate scenes or passages through which a seasoned reader might otherwise skim, regarding them perhaps as generic or tangential. As James Williams, for example, recounts his escape from the Deep South, one can see his geographic imagination at work as it responds to the visual information provided by the natural world:

> I looked up to see the North star, which I supposed still before me. But I sought it in vain in all that quarter of the heavens. A dreadful thought came over me that I had been travelling out of my way. I turned round and saw the North star, which had been shining directly upon my back. I then knew that I had been travelling away from freedom, and towards the place of my captivity, ever since I left the woods into which I had been pursued on the 21st, five day [*sic*] before. Oh, the keen and bitter agony of that moment! I sat down on the decaying trunk of a fallen tree, and wept like a child. Exhausted in mind and body, nature came at last to my relief, and I fell asleep upon the log. When I awoke it was still dark. I rose and nerved myself for another effort at freedom. Taking the North star for my guide, I tuned upon my track, and left once more the dreaded frontiers of Alabama behind me. The next night, after crossing a considerable river, I came to a large road crossing the one on which I travelled, and which seemed to lead more directly towards the North.[16]

What stands out here is the high degree of subjectivity that imbues Williams's representation of place, and the close, almost intimate, connection between mind and world as Williams negotiates the evidence of his senses and calibrates his movements. As in other narratives, Williams's imagination is oriented less toward cartographically objectivizing or dominating the land than toward recreating, in language, the experience of navigating an unfamiliar landscape. In this subjectivization of landscape he illustrates, albeit in passing, Rick Van Noy's observation that words enable "literary cartographers" "to express how they were changed by their places, how the interior landscape they came with . . . had to be adjusted to what was really there, and to what took *place* there."[17]

Such passages alert us to the connection between geographic consciousness and the exercise of individual agency in the pursuit of freedom. They illustrate, in the most vivid possible way, three of the defining properties of agency that Eleanor Gibson identifies as retrospectivity, prospectivity, and flexibility.[18] In the mind's confrontation with the natural world—a confrontation that appears throughout the slave narrative genre—past experience forms the backdrop for action in the present, imagined or intended outcomes motivate specific decisions, and a multiplicity of means enables a creative response to fluid situations. For a fugitive slave—while running, hiding, moving, backtracking—all such decisions and actions necessarily take place in a shifting, unpredictable geographic context. Representations of temporal and spatial awareness, then, affirm the problem-solving capacities of the mind under the most difficult circumstances: an affirmation particularly important for a nineteenth-century audience not predisposed to hold a high opinion of the mental capacities of African or African American narrators.

The relation between the great variety of relatively "minor" slave narratives and *Dred* and *My Bondage and My Freedom* resembles the "reconstructive" dynamic described by David Reynolds in *Beneath the American Renaissance*, in which canonical literary works adapt, transform, and intensify the cultural materials available in their "socioliterary milieu." "[E]ach thematic strand in the major texts," Reynolds writes, "can be traced backward into a tremendous body of submerged works that have previously been hidden from view."[19] As I have suggested, the tremendous diversity of antebellum slave narratives represents a still untapped reservoir of literary and cultural knowledge, and it formed the enabling context for the innovations achieved by Stowe and Douglass as they sought to deepen their treatment of the natural world and its psychological and racial significance.

From the Garden to the Swamp: Harriet Beecher Stowe

In the heady years following the publication of *Uncle Tom's Cabin*, Stowe, newly famous and increasingly wealthy, undertook something of a self-education in the realities of slavery, expanding her knowledge of the institution, of those who had escaped from it, and of its tentacular reach into American life. As the sectional crisis intensified—due in large part to the novel's agitative effect on public opinion in both North and South—Stowe felt moved to follow up with another ambitious novel as a contribution to the cause of abolition, beginning work on *Dred: A Tale of the Great Dismal Swamp* in late 1855.

After decades in the critical wilderness, Stowe's "second antislavery novel," as some have called it, began to receive its scholarly due in the 1990s, and is now close to securing its place in the Stowe canon, if not in the national imagination. Readers of *Dred* have concentrated, in particular, on Stowe's more mature understanding of American racial politics, an understanding that both political events and Stowe's growing familiarity with African American activists and texts helped to foster. In the 1856 novel, Stowe scales back from the sentimental solutions and monolithic scriptural interpretation offered in *Uncle Tom's Cabin*, shows greater respect for rationality and militancy in addition to martyrdom and feeling, and incorporates more, and more-nuanced, African American perspectives. As the novel's subtitle suggests, moreover, Stowe has expanded her treatment of the natural environment; not a cabin but a swamp now represents the text's primary moral locus. Stowe's discursive and imagistic passages on nature, however, go far beyond the trappings and atmospherics of an outdoor setting; they are, in fact, integral to *Dred's* more aggressive racial politics specifically and to its philosophical core more broadly. Functioning primarily as stage scenery in *Uncle Tom's Cabin*, the natural world in *Dred* both directly influences the novel's narrative structure and informs Stowe's representation of racial identity and historical progress.

In representing nature in *Uncle Tom's Cabin*, Stowe generally adhered to a familiar pattern of dichotomies: realism versus romanticism, virtuous interiors versus the masculine market and public sphere, northern pastoral versus southern degeneracy. In the process, however, her natural imagery works to obscure the unsavory complexities of American economic life. Stowe intends to indict southern slavery without giving a wholesale endorsement to northern wage labor, and to propose a different model—a feminine domestic economy—as the ideal alternative. But in celebrating a kind of nonwage, precapitalist, self-sufficient labor system, *Uncle Tom's Cabin* subtly diverts attention from the interdependency of the American home and the American market, and therefore of the different regions of the country. Scholarship on *Uncle Tom's Cabin*, in turn, has often abetted this tendency, examining what transpires in the home or the public sphere but giving short shrift to the novel's natural settings and natural commodities, and thereby reproducing the illusory, obfuscatory dichotomy between interior and exterior. When Lori Merish, for instance, writes that "the home in Stowe's writings is marked off from the street, a space of neglect and cruelty," and "from the factory, a space in which objects and bodies are used methodically for economic gain," we might add that it is also marked off from the natural world, but depends on the acquisition and utilization of natural goods *as enabled by* the market.[20] Viewed carefully, the novel's domestic and natural environments communicate across a permeable barrier, with nature providing both the raw material for a habitable interior space and the symbolic material for a civilized home. Both the pastoral scene and the domestic home, with its "harmonious and orderly system," depend on a highly processed, ersatz version of the natural world, drained of anything that might disturb or tarnish a person's experience of it.[21] And that includes cotton.

When we see Rachel Halliday's muslin handkerchief and her table's "snowy cloth" (120), the "snowy cap" (135) of the hypothetical northern housewife, the "white window-curtains" (176) of the Quaker settlement, the white dress that St. Clare's mother "always wore" (195), Aunt Dorcas's "clear muslin cap" (331), and the "snowy cloth" of Eliza's dinner table in Canada—when we see, in short, the matriarchal home literally draped in cotton fabric, it virtually forces the conclusion that the domain of King Cotton has reached even into the "virtuous" female sphere, and that Stowe has overlooked the deep connection between slave-based agriculture and the ideal middle-class domicile. And these cotton products provide but one example of the interdependence of home and market. By midcentury, the decently appointed American interior—with its furniture, its *objets d'art*, its sentimental novels—increasingly required a manufacturing economy of scale, since the traditional artisanal economy could no longer meet the demands of a rapidly growing nation. Domestic ideology, in short, depended on resource consumption, and this traffic between the home and outside world depended on the commerce between North and South, whose economic systems, though defined in stark opposition to one another in both proslavery and antislavery rhetoric, actually formed a single, if heterogeneous, national economy. Even as Stowe's sentimental economy, then, resists the masculine economy of street and factory and plantation, it subtly if unwittingly shields its own implication in the history of American economic development. While Stowe reveals many of the cruel realities of slavery, *Uncle Tom's Cabin* stands as an object lesson in how sentimentalizing the natural world, or separating it, as in a centrifuge, into aesthetic antinomies, can provide rhetorical traction at the high cost of a richer understanding of cultural practice.

It is precisely such an understanding that Stowe works toward in *Dred*, which devotes much more attention to the relationships between the social and natural terrains that she describes. The two major plantations, the poor white and free black settlements on their outskirts, and the belt of forest and swampland running along the North Carolina border, form the principal coordinates of the novel's moral cartography.[22] As in the antebellum slave narrative, which consistently thematized the psychological and social importance of geographic space, Stowe locates social relations within a charged geographical context that enables her to argue forcefully from nature to culture—that is, to turn to an ostensibly objective realm of being in order to reorient her reader's perception of the subjective and cultural phenomena of the plantation South.

Much more consistently and dramatically than in *Uncle Tom's Cabin*, Stowe describes human or social behavior in terms drawn from the natural world. She frequently defines individual characters by the intensity of their relationship to the natural world, aligning spiritual wisdom with a perception of the patterns and processes of nature. Strikingly, the novel actually celebrates a spirituality that, while not exactly incompatible with orthodox Christianity, often resembles natural theology, and in certain places approaches animism or transcendentalism. The heroine Nina Gordon, for instance, who at one point describes herself as "almost a tree-worshipper," experiences moments of transcendental communion while reading with the elderly servant Tiff in his garden: "the world that [God] created seemed to whisper to her in every pulsation of its air, in every breath of its flowers, in the fanning of its winds, 'He still liveth, and he loveth thee.'"[23] Tiff himself, with his "peculiar gifts over animal creation," can draw out "the birds and squirrels from the coverts of the forest" (558). Such passages—and they are legion—forward two important aims. They endow Stowe's "good-hearted" characters with insight into the truths of nature, truths rooted in divinity and therefore invariably and manifestly opposed to subjection and vice. In subtler fashion, the natural religion of the slaves or free blacks implies an emotional sensitivity to aesthetic beauty that signals—as it had in antislavery literature since the eighteenth century—the African American capacity for or achievement of civilization. Thus Stowe pictures Dred's eyes as "fixed in revery on the moving tree-tops as they waved in the golden blue," and suggests that "[t]here were elements in him which might, under other circumstances, have made him a poet" (557). Being human, and being cultured, from this perspective, means being alive to the pastoral ideal.

At the most basic level, the pastoral ethic of *Dred* envisions a state of harmony in visible nature that embodies the inner principle of order that natural law and natural rights theory had always presupposed. Stowe, however, departs from standard antislavery pastoral rhetoric in several crucial respects. First, she avoids the simplified opposition of northern beauty and southern vice so characteristic of abolitionist prose. Rather than portraying differentiated natural settings as a means of assessing or defining the moral condition of particular locations, as she did in *Uncle Tom's Cabin*, Stowe defines the pastoral in *Dred* not by region but by interiority. In addition, the novel's pastoral displays a greater self-consciousness on Stowe's part; certainly, antislavery writers employed the pastoral deliberately, but Stowe takes pains to explore its mechanisms and its history, to illustrate that pastoral exists in a perpetual give-and-take with other discourses and other realities. Most importantly, she draws on contemporary scientific thought in articulating a vision of natural order that lies beyond the scope of traditional pastoralism.

Within her broader unifying polemic of demonstrating African American capacity and arguing against the naturalness of slavery, Stowe creates a dialectic between two visions of the natural world, the rejuvenating and the terrifying, that helps to structure her treatment of the social world. The pastoral, as always, depends on separating nature into these two broad aesthetic categories and then suppressing those aspects of nature that ill comport with emotional comfort. Thus the hero, Edward Clayton, feels regenerated in the woods, where "birds sung, waters danced and warbled, flowers bloomed, and everything in nature was abundant, and festive, and joyous" (473). But this is a far cry from the "wild and desolate swamp" (631) that Stowe later describes, from the "tiger in the human breast that delights in violence and blood" (626), and certainly from the "miasma and animalculae" that cause the outbreak of cholera that eventually carries off the ill-fated Nina Gordon. Such images of violence and disease are the stuff of theodicy; they represent the natural evils it undertakes to explain as temporary or even instrumental elements in providential design. As chapter 3 suggested, the explanatory role of traditional theodicy was both challenged and invigorated during this period by scientific narratives of upward ascent, and by literary Romanticism, which provided images of pure felicity unimplicated in knotty sectarian or theological disputes. In response arose a kind of natural theodicy that envisioned the emergence of good through the very workings of natural process, and which characteristically pictured a state of goodness in terms or images drawn from the pastoral tradition. In *Dred*, Stowe displays a remarkable awareness of this function of pastoral, yet also of the fragility of the imagined vision of "peace, love, joy, order, and harmony," in David Barrow's words. During a conversation with Anne Clayton, Nina recalls her childhood reading of "Gesner's Idyls," a book of pastoral poems, in which "there was no labor, and no trouble, and no dirt, and no care" and sighs that "I have never got over wanting it since!" (409). (The book is Salomon Gessner's *Idyllen* (1756), written in German and translated into several English editions in the early years of the nineteenth century.) Anne's reply is extraordinarily revealing, and extraordinarily modern, as if Virginia Woolf or Doris Lessing were speaking: "[W]hat constant fight we have to maintain for order and beauty! . . . [I]t's really a mystery to me what a constant downward tendency there is to everything—how everything is gravitating back, as you may say, into disorder. . . . [E]verything attacks you when you set out to attain it—flies, cockroaches, ants, mosquitoes!" (409–10). From this perspective, not only pastoral but all human achievement trembles on the precipice, perpetually threatened by disruptive, entropic forces. The pastoral, Stowe suggests, simply represents the *ne plus ultra* of our human capacity for creating pleasant scenarios and then believing in them, for imagining, at least temporarily, the banishment of pain, mortality, and evil from life. Its artificiality inheres in the very nature of the pastoral: a laboriously wrought fantasy of otium, an ivied arbor that cannot keep out the insects.

Reading *Dred* in light of Anne's comments foregrounds Stowe's active interest in the philosophical and social meanings of order and chaos. The novel abounds with imagery of stability and upheaval, structure and confusion, law and lawlessness. In part, this ominous imagery helps to convey Stowe's premonition that the United States hovered on the verge of even greater violence than the country had already seen. Against that prospect, the pastoral vision of Nina and her companions would seem to promise a zone of ideal order, undisturbed or unsullied by the chaos of cholera, bloodshed, and hatred. Edward's blueprint for enlightened plantation management—aimed toward the education and ultimately the emancipation of the slaves—represents an alternative to the moonlight-and-magnolias variety of southern pastoral, and is built around principles of right order. At Magnolia Grove, he encourages the slaves to be "consistently orderly and cleanly," and has implemented "certain rules for the order and well-being of the plantation" (396). The future health of society, he suggests, will depend on the well-governed transition from ignorance to knowledge, barbarism to civility, chaos to order.

Yet Edward Clayton is no Harriet Beecher Stowe, and his condescending, if well-intentioned, efforts at reform show little of the author's sympathy for the energies he plans to discipline and harness. Moving beyond not only Clayton's liberalism, but also the problematic liberalism of *Uncle Tom's Cabin*, Stowe imagines a form of creative destructiveness that philosophically underwrites *Dred*'s more aggressive racial politics. For she recognizes that there can exist malignant kinds of order, in the form of race- and class-based hierarchies, along with productive kinds of chaos, in the form of challenges to repressive structures and systems. Thus the lawyer Mr. Jekyl opposes religious instruction for slaves on the grounds that it would lead to the "end of all order"

(218), while Nina, in describing a run-down old estate, imagines that the slaves "have a general glorification in the chaos" (205). In order to evaluate the relative worth of law and lawlessness in the social world, however, Stowe must turn to the ostensibly objective realm of nature as a standard. She therefore creates a parallel dynamic of order and chaos in the animal and plant kingdoms, counterposing images of predictability and of overexuberance in the development of natural forms. The former tend to have a religious inflection. "How inflexibly and terribly regular are all [God's] laws!" Clayton exclaims, noting that fire, wind, and snow all "have a crushing regularity in their movements" (337). At the same time, however, he expresses an admiration for the "shocking, unsightly growths" in the woods, for the "briers running riot over trees, and sometimes choking and killing them." Telling Nina that she "would have well-trimmed trees and velvet turf," Clayton declares that he loves the "briers, dead limbs, and all, for their very savage freedom" (328). Stowe's point, here as elsewhere, is that the progressive growth of organisms, according to the natural law of free development, will inevitably and inexorably overcome all obstacles, manmade or otherwise, like ivy climbing a stone wall, or cholera, which "seems to spurn all laws" (437), sweeping mysteriously from place to place. Yet she is *not* suggesting that these forms of growth are foreign to, or a threat to, the providential design, for their manifest chaos conceals deeper principles of order that express the divine will. They are destructive, certainly, but creatively so, and their end is the defeat of stagnation and the overthrow of organized injustice. "Nothing is fixed," says Clayton, "that isn't fixed in right. God and nature fight against evil" (581).

The dialectic of order and chaos in *Dred* provides a means of imagining racial and social development within a larger philosophical context, and enables Stowe to authorize a specific political position through reference to the supposedly apolitical, transcendent principles of nature. While in *Uncle Tom's Cabin* Stowe defines heroism not as the overt resistance of George Harris but as the Christian patience of Uncle Tom, in *Dred* she forecasts a course of African American racial growth that will naturally (i.e., inevitably, and with the sanction of divine and natural law) produce resistance to malignant hierarchies. As proslavery writers had naturalized bondage through various appeals to scientific race theory, and to the "natural" constitution of an extended family, so Stowe naturalizes militant resistance by associating it with the operations of the natural world. For that reason Dred's mystically close relationship to nature involves not only a spiritual or aesthetic appreciation of the birds and the brooks, but an affinity with the powerful, frightening forces of nature that threaten to overwhelm civilization as presently constituted. For Dred, as for Nat Turner, the natural world is a place rich with occult meaning (sometimes "strange hieroglyphics would be written upon the leaves" [277]) and revolutionary guidance ("as if he had been a dark spirit of the tempest, he shouted and exulted" [357]).

Stowe's representation of African American militancy, however, raises serious problems, for she continues to traffic in the kind of racial essentialism that vitiated the liberalism of *Uncle Tom's Cabin*. While intended, no doubt, as a flattering commentary on African American capacity, her description of the "savage perfection of the natural organs" of Dred, and the alertness of his "sensuous organization" that resembles the "certainty of instinctive discrimination which belongs to animals" (354–55), recycles the old primitivism and discourse of black animality that writers such as Douglass had to work against in order to claim full membership in a "modern" capitalist society. Yet the racial essentialism in *Dred* plays a crucial role in Stowe's effort to *redefine* racial identity and to challenge her contemporary readers' perceptions of the historical course of "civilization." Associating the "vital powers" of African-descended peoples with emotional freedom, and the routinized labor and excessive propriety of white society with psychological repression,[24] Stowe suggests not simply that whites should seek the same wellspring of feeling within themselves, but that the bottled-up anger and passion and hate among slaves and free blacks will eventually sweep away all efforts at containment, with dire consequences for American society. If, as Ronald Takaki has argued, American economic and technological development in the nineteenth century entailed a systematic repression of the passional, irrational side of human life; and if white males justified the subordination of women and minorities under the new bureaucratic industrial order by associating them with "natural" qualities needing repression; then Stowe's celebration of the "fiery soil of a tropical heart" must be understood as more than run-of-the-mill racialism.[25] Gail Bederman has shown that late in the century, when the internal stability of the United States was not in doubt, white men could imagine drawing on "primitive energies" as a way of reclaiming manliness and forwarding "civilization."[26] In the 1850s, however, with civil war looming, Stowe and others imagined that the hitherto-contained energy of African Americans had the potential to disrupt if not actually destroy the edifice of American civilization.

Yet while the prospect in *Dred* of a racial uprising as inexorable as kudzu portends ill things for the *national* order, Stowe's vision of *racial* development is fundamentally optimistic in that it posits the impossibility of stasis and the inevitability of "progress." "The Ethiopian race is a slow-growing plant, like the aloe," intones Edward Clayton, "but I hope, some of these days, they'll come into flower; and I think, if they ever do, the blossoming will be gorgeous" (420). As with Emerson's concept of "providential biology," and as with the natural law of free development, the emergence of new natural and biological orderings, though chaotic relative to present orderings, will overturn all unholy structures in furtherance of the divine plan. The novel's primitivist strain, then, rather than fantasizing an escape into the past, underlies a progressivist ethos that echoes contemporary discourses of proto-Darwinist developmental science. Situating her literary tale of the Great Dismal Swamp within a larger narrative of organismal growth and racial upheaval, Stowe locates *that* narrative, in turn, within a supernatural teleology by which the violence and apparent randomness of social processes embody deeper principles of the divine order.

The pastoral tradition in *Dred* therefore represents but part of a larger method of comprehending the natural world and what it means for human society and consciousness. A glimpse of paradise, infinitely peaceful, the green world of the imagination lives unriven by black and white, unbesplattered by red blood; in the pastoral vision, an embracing natural unity transcends and obliterates human difference, while a rich natural bounty obviates the causes of human conflict. Yet that ideal, Stowe suggests, forms a closed system: static, growthless, even stagnant—at least in its literary form. She turns, then, to another kind of utopianism, one that recognizes the necessity and celebrates the vigor of difference and conflict, by subsuming these conditions to a narrative of ascent that possesses the authority of both natural science and revealed religion. In this way, Stowe's representation of nature in *Dred* surpasses the relatively simple pastoral and antipastoral strategies characteristic of mainstream abolitionist literature. Nonetheless, her intellectualized treatment of the natural world lacks the power that the pastoral can achieve in autobiography. Although the semiotics of nature animate Stowe's portrayal of her characters' lives, desires, thoughts—in a word, their identities—both the pastoral and the scientific discourses in *Dred* remain essentially unconnected to personal memory or to familial bonds. We must turn to Douglass to see how these emotional and communal meanings of natural imagery come to the fore.

Oxen and Sweet Potatoes: Douglass on the Land

Although the 1845 *Narrative of the Life of Frederick Douglass* still commands more attention by scholars and more of the space on course syllabi, *My Bondage and My Freedom* has slowly gained recognition as the more full-bodied, if not the more influential, autobiography. It certainly deserves greater attention, not only on its own terms as a remarkable work of life writing, but because of its complex intertextual relation to the 1845 *Narrative*, which helps us understand Douglass's evolving sense of self and his attitude toward American racial politics. Readers of *My Bondage and My Freedom* have remarked Douglass's more-nuanced treatment of slave resistance and revolutionary ideology; his weightier emphasis on home, on the female community, and on his responsibility to translate individual achievement into social activism; his more mature sense of the interdependence of North and South; and his sharpened ambition toward embodying and articulating a representative American story.[27] Just as Stowe's maturation as an author involved a willingness to reexamine her earlier assumptions, so Douglass's reworking of the *Narrative* reflected a coming-to-terms with his younger self and his relation to both African American and Anglo-American culture. If the *Narrative* amounts to an African American jeremiad in the sense that it insists on the rightness of elemental American values, represented by the hardworking, freedom-loving people of the North, while lamenting the perversion or destruction of those values in the South, *My Bondage and My Freedom* offers a more complicated analysis of life in the United States.[28] In the process, Douglass reconceptualized the role of the natural environment in his and his cultures' (plural) experience, coming to see the natural world, both symbolically and literally, as the foundation for a revitalized African American community.

As a revision of an earlier slave narrative, and perforce a reflection on the slave narrative form, *My Bondage and My Freedom* evinces the greater imaginative freedom and assertiveness we can identify in African American literature of the 1850s—and this freedom enables Douglass's re-envisioning of his own relationship to the natural world. In particular, his adaptation of the American pastoral and georgic traditions signals his determination to turn the language and symbols of the United States against its mythologized self-image, and thereby to assert his independence not only from the South, but from the expectations of northerners as well. Throughout, Douglass exercises what Eric Sundquist calls "his capacity to break through and critique the discourses of subordination that are imposed upon him, whether by northern abolitionists or later readers," and, we might add, by literary convention.[29] The sophistication and power of Douglass's representation of nature in *My Bondage and My Freedom* owe much to his increasingly independent engagement with rhetorical tradition, and to the changed sense of self that this independence emblematized.

It should be stressed at the outset, however, that Douglass's representation of nature in *My Bondage and My Freedom* displays the range of ambivalence and contradiction we can expect of an author actively in the process of coming to terms with his life. As a former agricultural slave living in a northern city, committed to national economic progress, well versed in the major work of Romanticism, and nostalgic for the pleasures of a rural childhood, Douglass was bound to view nature in complex terms. Yet out of this complexity several related patterns emerge. Employing, when the occasion calls for it, a similar set of pastoral and antipastoral images and discourses as *Uncle Tom's Cabin* and the abolitionist press, Douglass presents nature as a realm that transcends human difference and conflict even as it symbolizes divergent regional identities. In this transcendence, nature possesses an authority that social forms and practices do not, and it imparts that authority to those who successfully associate themselves with "natural" principles. Most importantly, Douglass begins to link the reconstruction of a viable black community to the georgic ideal, offering a vision of African American life in which cultural health depends on the spiritual and psychological sustenance of nature. Yet Douglass also links communal uplift to an economic system and religious worldview that, as we have seen repeatedly throughout this study, runs against the grain of the pastoral and agrarian traditions he invokes.

The author of the 1855 autobiography presents himself as a man who has learned important lessons about how to see the world, both literally and symbolically. Recalling the fateful day when his grandmother escorted him to the Lloyd plantation, and when he in his fear had mistaken logs and stumps for wild beasts, Douglass writes that "[t]hus early I learned that the point from which a thing is viewed is of some importance" (35). Similarly, after recounting the paranoia of the slaves who conspire to run away from Mr. Freeland's plantation and imagine that Mr. Freeland can read their faces, he writes that "[m]en seldom see themselves as others see them" (169–70). These passages express a contemplative detachment, more philosophical than the 1845 *Narrative*, that elevates their significance above their immediate context and invites us to consider them as paradigmatic statements of a hard-won *weltanschauung*. They both associate the faculty of sight with wisdom, and yet warn of the influence of subjectivity, suggesting that the meaning of an object (or person, or event) depends on one's peculiar angle of vision, and that "we have no means of correcting these colored and distorting lenses which we are," as Emerson put it in "Experience."[30] Yet for both authors, subjectivity implies opportunity as well as limitation, as to perceive something's or someone's essential quiddity requires a kind of internal moral adjustment or refocusing.

In that spirit, the author of *My Bondage and My Freedom* also presents himself as a man who has learned something about the central place of community and of women in African American life. These two forms of wisdom—one philosophical, one deeply personal—come together in a remarkable passage early in the autobiography that suggests how introspection and retrospection can lead to a new understanding of both human family and racial identity. Having described slavery's destructive influence on families and lamented the absence of his father and mother, Douglass refers the reader to, of all things, a famous text of racial science. "There is in '*Prichard's Natural History of Man*,' the head of a figure—on page 157—the features of which so resemble those of my mother, that I often recur to it with something of the feeling which I suppose others experience when looking upon the pictures of dear departed ones" (38–39). This passage, which had prompted James McCune Smith to praise Douglass's "almost marvelous feats of recollection of forms and outlines" (22), reminds us that Douglass had published his essay "The Claims of the Negro Ethnologically Considered" the previous year (1854), and suggests that James Cowles Prichard's *Natural History* played an important role in Douglass's thinking about racial science.[31] Especially striking, however, is the use he makes of Prichard here, mingling science, emotion, and memory in such a way as to illustrate the living human reality behind the claims of racial theory. Through Douglass's emotional response and his imaginative specification, the picture of the anonymous woman actually serves to counteract the notion of the impersonal, average specimen on which racial taxonomies were based.

Douglass describes his relation to his absent mother in primarily visual terms: "The side view of her face is imaged on my memory," he continues, "and I take few steps in life, without feeling her presence; but the image is mute, and I have no striking words of her's [*sic*] treasured up" (41–42). This emphasis on her visual image is significant because it reflects an understanding of how the mind stores and remembers emotionally charged information. In *The Emotions and the Will*, published the same year as *My Bondage and My Freedom*, Alexander Bain suggested that the faculty of sight, by virtue of the mind's power to recall visual images more intensely than other sense data, plays a unique role in emotional memory:

> Cohering trains and aggregates of the Sensations of Sight make, more than any other thing, perhaps more than all other things put together, the material of thought, memory, and imagination. . . . [The] process of employing one sense as a substitute for others, avails itself principally of vision, the most retentive of them all. Thus it is that objects thought of on account of their taste or smell, are actually conceived under their visual aspect. The image of a rose dwells in the mind as a visual picture, and in a very inferior degree as a perpetuated impression of a sweet odour.

Bain then links this psychophysiological phenomenon to a person's emotional life, which is nourished by the visual memories the mind retains: "Intense affections have a like influence in sustaining the ideal presence of their subject."[32] For Douglass, then, the portrait in Prichard's *Natural History* triggers a whole range of experiential associations that have both racial significance, since they register the history of a family in slavery, and human significance, since they involve such elemental matters as sensation, recollection, and filial love. In this passing moment, Douglass has begun to instruct his reader in (as Stowe might put it) the right way of feeling—through the right way of looking. He has also inaugurated an important theme in the autobiography: the unavoidable human question of how to view the past and its significance for the present and future.

Douglass's pervasive interest in vision, like Emerson's, took form in a larger intellectual context. In particular, during the antebellum period the faculty of sight got connected to broader debates about human origins and development. Most accounts presented the eye as a physiological marvel too complex to be accounted for by natural forces. "[A]s you ascend in the scale of organization," wrote the conservative doctor John Augustine Smith, in arguing against Robert Chambers's protoevolutionary *Vestiges of the Natural History of Creation*, "in addition to this general improvement [the nervous system], one distinct organ of sense after another is conferred—the window of the mind, the eye, being the last."[33] In 1860, Asa Gray, the principal American champion of Darwin's ideas, acknowledged that the eye presented a formidable challenge for evolutionary theory: "Think of such an organ as the eye, that most perfect of optical instruments, as so produced in the lower animals and perfected in the higher! A friend of ours, who accepts the new doctrine, confesses that for a long while a cold chill came over him whenever he thought of the eye."[34] Whether regarded as the product of evolutionary development, however, or of special creation, humanity's most sophisticated organ was almost universally taken as evidence of the species' superiority or chosen status. Visual experience, therefore, becomes a sign of common humanity, and the range of subjective response that sight stimulates becomes an expression of one's full humanness.

In a very real sense, then, Douglass's famous observation that in order "to make a contented slave" it is "necessary to darken his moral and mental vision" (194) refers not only to the enforcement of ignorance, but to the literal forms of visual deprivation that slaves experienced. More explicitly than other slave narratives, Douglass makes clear that the faculty of sight enabled the formulation of plans of escape, the identification of possibilities and opportunities, and, as the natural historians had argued, the full development of higher reason and abstract thought. On the Lloyd plantation, young Frederick is fascinated by a windmill ("always a commanding object to a child's eye" [46]) and a sloop; he writes that they were "full of thoughts and ideas. A child cannot well look at such objects without *thinking*" (46, original emphasis). What he thinks of, naturally, though he does not immediately say so, is the freedom of motion that these objects imply, a freedom embodied in and enabled by the movement of wind and water. On the plantation, sight confers knowledge and power; seeing is living, and being seen can mean discipline or death. On the slave "breaker" Edward Covey's farm, a perpetual dynamic of surveillance and concealment reigns, with Covey hiding behind trees and in bushes and "watching every movement of the slaves!" (134). The threat of surveillance applies as well to the reading of countenances, since slaveholders watch "with skilled and practiced eyes, and have learned to read, with great accuracy, the state of mind and heart of the slave, through his sable face" (169).

The motif of vision in *My Bondage and My Freedom* leads us into critical issues involving Douglass's experience of nature and of the plantation, and from there to his reimagining of the American landscape. Like the slave narrative tradition more broadly, Douglass's treatment of the southern plantation thematizes the ideological and phenomenological importance of spatial relationships, the emotionally fraught nature of the *locus juvenilis*, and the complexity of geographic consciousness. Compared to the 1845 *Narrative*, Douglass's second autobiography devotes much more space to his experience of the South's natural and built environments, directing our attention to the spatial relationships between buildings, gardens, and fields, and consistently investing places, or the relative positioning of places, with psychological and social significance.

Beyond lending texture to his portrait of slave life, this strategy allows Douglass to explore how a turn to nature can provide an opportunity for escape from a vicious culture, and for psychic restoration. In expanding on the famous scene of his confrontation with Covey, for example, Douglass greatly heightens the importance of the natural remove to his fateful ethical decision. Hiding in the woods surrounding Covey's farm, two days before actually beating Covey in a fistfight, Douglass suddenly switches from past to present tense, as if, like Equiano recalling his mother's graveside oblations, he conjures up the experience as he writes: "I am in the wood, buried in its somber gloom, and hushed in it; solemn silence; hid from all human eyes; shut in with nature and nature's God, and absent from all human contrivances. Here was a good place to pray; to pray for help for deliverance—a prayer I had often made before" (144–45). In the simplest sense, this passage illustrates the dynamic of visual surveillance and concealment that governed relations on the plantation. But the interlude takes on greater meaning as the natural world prompts Douglass, hidden from *all* human eyes, to reevaluate the cultural world, and to prepare for a renewed, more critical, and more productive engagement with it. Echoing the Declaration of Independence in the phrase "nature and nature's God," Douglass shows that he can claim for himself the sacred symbols of American history, and he does so in a way that links the principles of freedom and devotion with the natural world. Only in this natural cathedral, free of "all human contrivances," does Douglass believe his prayers may be heard. Here, true Christianity—as opposed to the "sham religion which everywhere prevailed"—embraces God, nature and supplicant in one mutually sustaining relationship. But this transcendental moment, reminiscent of Emerson's transparent eyeball apotheosis in *Nature*, is neither indefinitely sustainable nor sufficient in itself. Douglass tries to pray, but finds that faith has abandoned him. He reflects on his condition as a slave ("What had I done, what had my parents done, that such a life as this should be mine?"). He emerges from the woods when fellow slave Sandy Jenkins happens by, and despite religious misgivings, accepts the "magical" root that Sandy offers as protection. Newly rebellious in his "backslidden" state, Douglass resolves to stand up to Covey, and after defeating him physically and morally, he writes that the fight "brought up my Baltimore dreams [of freedom] . . . and inspired me with a renewed determination to be A FREEMAN." Then follows the abstract principle: "A man, without force, is without the essential dignity of humanity. Human nature is so constituted, that it cannot *honor* a helpless man, although it can *pity* him."[35] The remove to nature, in short, is temporary and imperfect, because the human world continues to impinge on Douglass's consciousness. The woods act as a kind of spiritual and emotional restorative, but cannot relieve him of his human responsibilities, and thus herald a return to culture—to antebellum Maryland culture—rather than an abandonment or repudiation of it.

If the psychology of the autobiography, particularly in the first half, plays out primarily on what we might call the microgeography of the plantation landscape, its politics operate on a broader geographic canvas, with national and regional identities getting reworked and redefined. These rhetorical terrains, however, are complementary and interconnected, for the cultural ambiguities and emotional ambivalences that Douglass experiences on the plantation imbue, on a larger scale, his relation to the different regions of the United States. Significantly, the woodprints introducing each section of the autobiography, "Life as a Slave" and "Life as a Freeman," present a national moral geography familiar from antislavery propaganda. Conveying in dramatic visual terms the work's narrative trajectory of ascent, or Douglass's move northward from the hell of slavery to the comparative heaven of freedom, these woodprints subtly condition our interpretation of the text and frame several of its core themes: the superiority of the northern economic system to the southern, the contrast of southern license and northern freedom, slavery's stunting of the natural development of the nation, the gulf between the harmony of northern town life and the inhumanity of southern plantation life. These themes are simplifications, of course, but Douglass does get a fair amount of mileage from them, turning on occasion to the familiar antipastoral strategy of denigrating the southern environment, with the "worn-out, sandy, desert-like appearance of its soil" and the "prevalence of ague and fever" (27), or having others do it for him, as when he quotes the famously lurid picture Whittier paints of the South in "The Farewell of a Virginia Slave Mother to her Daughters, Sold into Southern Bondage."

Yet even as he critiques the slave system, Douglass's treatment of the natural world of the South proves more nuanced than the woodprints might imply. His description of the Big House at the Lloyd plantation, for instance, emphasizes abundance rather than deficiency, voracious gluttony rather than disease, as the world's natural bounty is inexorably "caught in this huge family net":

> The table groans under the heavy and blood-bought luxuries gathered with painstaking care, at home and abroad. Fields, forests, rivers and seas, are made tributary here. . . . Here, appetite, not food, is the great *desideratum.* Fish, flesh and fowl, are here in profusion. . . . The teeming riches of the Chesapeake bay, its rock, perch, drums, crocus, trout, oysters, crabs, and terrapin, are drawn hither to adorn the glittering table of the great house. . . . Nor are the fruits of the earth forgotten or neglected. . . . The tender asparagus, the succulent celery, and the delicate cauliflower; egg plants, beets, lettuce, parsnips, peas, and French beans, early and late; radishes, cantelopes, melons of all kinds; the fruits and flowers of all climes and of all descriptions, from the hardy apple of the north, to the lemon and orange of the south, culminated at this point. (70)

Here, the grotesque material reality of southern "pastoral" disrupts Fitzhugh's romantic image of the slaveholding family by making vivid the dynamic of greedy consumption and racial exclusion. The whites, through the labor of others, seem to have fulfilled their biblical grant to dominion over the natural world, but in satanic fashion, reducing its "riches" to commodities and status symbols that satisfy their appetite not for food, but for power. And the plantation's "beautiful lawn, very neatly trimmed, and watched with the greatest care" (47), so similar to the "velvet turf" (328) in *Dred*, suggests an almost fetishistic desire for control. Both the exactitude and the extravagance, of course, are made possible through the exploitation of "blood-bought" human beings, as the economics of slavery draws plants, animals and slaves indiscriminately into the plantation's maw. This is an antipastoral passage not because the desire for oysters and asparagus is intrinsically immoral, but because the plantation embodies excess and exploitation—and we might even term it "antigeorgic" since the plantation is not self-sufficient but parasitic.

More broadly, the pastoral ethic of *My Bondage and My Freedom* calls into question not only the practices of the South, but also the values of the whole country. In his famous letter to William Lloyd Garrison, composed en route to England and republished in *My Bondage and My Freedom*, Douglass invokes and then immediately subverts the national pastoral ideal:

> In thinking of America, I sometimes find myself admiring her bright blue sky, her grand old woods, her fertile fields, her beautiful rivers, her mighty lakes, and star-crowned mountains. But my rapture is soon checked, my joy is soon turned to mourning. When I remember that all is cursed with the infernal spirit of slaveholding, robbery, and wrong; when I remember that with the waters of her noblest rivers, the tears of my brethren are borne to the ocean, disregarded and forgotten, and that her most fertile fields drink daily of the warm blood of my outraged sisters; I am filled with unutterable loathing, and led to reproach myself that anything could fall from my lips in praise of such a land. America will not allow her children to love her. (225)

Linking natural plenty to racial domination and violence, Douglass voices with remarkable force the awful marriage of beauty and agony faced by an oppressed people living in nature's nation. "*All* is cursed" with the blight of slavery; the whole of "America" has outcast her children. This broader moral prospect, compared with the *Narrative*, seems almost the literal result of viewing his country from a seaborne ship, as if geographic removal allows Douglass's vision to take in the whole American expanse, its "New World littorals that are / mirage and myth and actual shore."[36] The wider scope of the indictment, and the charged language in which he casts it, suggests that Douglass means to connect not only the southern fields with the blood of his enslaved people, but the systematic violation of African Americans with the systemic pollution of the natural world. In such a land, he seems to ask, what should be the attitude of an African American who admires the natural beauty of his country, and yet who legally ranks no higher than the timber or the hogs bound for market? Can there be spiritual solace in a natural world whose "beautiful rivers" flow with African blood and whose "bright blue sky" canopies a theater of pain?

The answer to this second question appears to be a qualified "yes," but standing between Douglass and the innocent pastoral felicity he longs for are the twinned obstacles of racial division and relentless time, for he could find pure spiritual solace in nature only as a child and unaware of the system of slavery that would drastically reshape his relationship to his environment. Recapturing that solace requires some kind of return to an earlier time, an earlier consciousness, when he and his "brethren" and "sisters" could take an uncorrupted pleasure in the world around them. This personal significance of the pastoral ideal—tied up as it is with loss and memory and desire—dramatically distinguishes Douglass's treatment of nature in *My Bondage and My Freedom* from essentially propagandistic antislavery literature, including his earlier autobiography, *Uncle Tom's Cabin*, and even *Dred*.

In a world of dehumanizing bondage, Douglass seeks (or says he sought) refuge in the bosom of nature. A number of important passages in the early chapters, entirely absent from the *Narrative*, help to establish the more nostalgic mood of *My Bondage and My Freedom* and render nature a vital part of the child's world.[37] It is the paradoxical privilege of the slave boy, for instance, that, unconstrained by the expectations of proper behavior that hamper the white child, he can "roll in the dust, or play in the mud, as best suits him, and in the veriest of freedom. . . .

His days, when the weather is warm, are spent in the pure, open air, and in the bright sunshine" (32). As a child, Douglass enjoys the freedom to enact "all the strange antics and freaks of horses, dogs, pigs, and barn-door fowls, *without in any manner compromising his dignity*" (31, emphasis added). As a young man, however, Douglass finds that his innocent, carefree relationship to nature has been corrupted by slavery and by a heightened self-consciousness. "The tops of the stately poplars were often covered with the red-winged black-birds, making all nature vocal with the joyous life and beauty of their wild, warbling notes. These all belonged to me, as well as to Col. Edward Lloyd, and *for a time* I greatly enjoyed them" (48, emphasis added). The language of possession in this passage underlines the contrast between the purely materialistic use to which Lloyd puts nature, and the more aesthetic, spiritual responsiveness of the young Douglass. And its wistful close suggests that Douglass the adult author longs to return to the enjoyment he felt as a child. When he writes that America "will not allow her children to love her," he speaks on both metaphorical and literal levels, imagining a kind of collective orphanhood whose pain includes the separation of children from their innocent consciousness of the natural world.

Douglass's fall into adult consciousness, like that of Equiano, echoes an earlier fall, and the narrative's theme of dispossession echoes the Christian myth and one of its defining paradoxes: a simultaneous belief in humankind's alienation from, yet superiority to, nature, and an abiding desire for a more perfect union with the natural world. In Douglass's eyes as in Christian tradition, the fate of humankind is to work in the world, to have to struggle for survival in nature as a consequence of the original expulsion from Eden. Since Douglass knew this struggle only too well, his longing for a prelapsarian state of harmony does not easily translate—as it does for Edward Clayton with his blooming flowers and warbling waters—into transcendental rapture in the natural world. Symptomatically, the text divides between a romanticized, even spiritualized nature and a fallen, hellish nature reminiscent of Stowe's "loathsome" water moccasin. This tension registers both Douglass's experience as a slave who has had to work the fields under a lash and his recognition that the natural world offers far more than that experience.

It captures his engagement with the languages of pastoral and georgic as a self-conscious adult writer, his understanding of the often brutal realities that underlie the human relation to nature, and his remembrance of a childhood in which the natural world seemed to reflect and embody his own innocence. Ultimately, it expresses his ambivalent relationship to a natural environment he loves but cannot imaginatively separate from his life as a slave.

This ambivalence helps to explain Douglass's coexisting desires to draw spiritual sustenance from nature and to master it. At numerous places in *My Bondage and My Freedom*, he imagines the conflict between humans and nature on both psychological and practical levels, sometimes representing the environment as a hostile, threatening realm, and sometimes describing his urge to control it. This latter feeling, significantly, draws on (and surely reinforces) not only an anthropocentric religious ethos, but also the economic values of the culture in which Douglass was seeking to rise as a free man. It breaks forth explicitly as Douglass struggles to control the intractable oxen on Covey's farm, a scene whose humor cannot hide a darker significance: "I now saw, in my situation, several points of similarity with that of the oxen. They were property, so was I; they were to be broken, so was I. Covey was to break me, I was to break them; break and be broken—such is life" (132). He seems to have but two choices: either be ranked with the beasts, or in the effort to demonstrate his humanity, show his capacity to break the beasts, to rise above the natural world and by dominating it assume his rightful place in human society. Douglass had already made this point the previous year in "The Claims of the Negro Ethnologically Considered," where he argued that one of the defining activities of the human being is to change and improve the environment, and that the African, no less than the European, satisfies this criterion: "You may see him yoke the oxen, harness the horse, and hold the plow. . . . The horse bears him on his back—admits his mastery and dominion."[38] The idea that superiority to animals defines humanness reappears in *Das Kapital*, in a discussion of the conditions necessary for the creation of surplus value, one of which is a normally functioning system of labor. "Under slavery," Marx writes, "the worker is distinguishable only as *instrumentum vocale* from an animal, which is *instrumentum semi-vocale*, and from a lifeless implement, which is *instrumentum mutum*. But he himself takes care to let both beast and implement feel that he is none of them, but rather a human being. He gives himself the satisfaction of knowing that he is different by treating the one with brutality and damaging the other *con amore*."[39] The disdain of the slave for both animal and machine, Marx suggests, is both a consequence of his status under the system and a contributing factor to that system's productive inefficiency; capitalism, by contrast, translates labor into value with comparatively less material waste (though at the cost, of course, of alienating the individual worker from his labor by depriving him of much of the value that results from it). Douglass's experience with the oxen, then, represents a loss of time, talent, and energy that, multiplied many times over the years, will drag the South down morally and economically. In this much, at least, Marx and Douglass would agree. Douglass does not, however, embrace the Marxist critique of capitalism (or, of course, the southern critique, à la Fitzhugh), and we should therefore measure his spiritual and aesthetic relationship to nature against the economic suppositions or inclinations of the text.

Douglass's economic liberalism, expressed most visibly in his allegiance to the free-labor system and the doctrine of American progress, flows from two core beliefs regarding "natural" hierarchies: first, that human beings are superior to the nonhuman world; and second, that no individual human being can claim a "natural" superiority to any other (even though Douglass does allow for hierarchies of class and culture). For Douglass, spiritual liberty logically underwrites an individual's economic liberty to work, strive, and compete in a democratically structured, meritocratic market system. Although *My Bondage and My Freedom*, therefore, sustains a broader critique of American society than did the *Narrative*, it does not bring capitalist philosophy into its sights. "Capitalist progress had its human costs," writes Waldo Martin, "but the relevant question was whether it was worth those costs. Notwithstanding his humanitarianism, Douglass accepted the economic system without questioning its human costs to the point where the system itself might be found irretrievably flawed."[40] Indeed, Douglass's portrayal of the northern economic system, where "everything went on as smoothly as the works of a well adjusted machine" (210), and where "everything was done here with a scrupulous regard to economy, both in regard to men and things, time and strength" (211), downplays the problems and abuses that many writers—including abolitionists—recognized. This reflects, on one level, the slave narrator's characteristic determination to contrast the indolence and decadence bred by slavery with the industrious values of the free market, and to set the stage for his own fruitful participation in the American experiment. It also suggests, however, that Douglass's adult priorities include a utilitarian approach to nature at odds with his lingering fondness for the woods and creeks of his youth. From this perspective, economic liberalism and pastoral felicity represent two irreconcilable lines of thought in *My Bondage and My Freedom*—one realistic, the other sentimental; one forward looking, the other nostalgic.

Yet Douglass's concept of individualism, and the economic liberalism it sustains, has matured markedly since the *Narrative*. The individual, Douglass now suggests, is always embedded in a social context, always, like the figures in Eastman Johnson's *Negro Life at the South*, defined by relation to family and community. Indeed, Douglass's greater emphasis in *My Bondage and My Freedom* on the commonalities of human nature goes hand in hand with his imagining of communal life as a central force in both the secular and spiritual salvation of individuals. In the 1845 *Narrative*, Douglass asserted his "manhood" through sheer force of example, presenting himself as a Promethean hero who managed to pull himself out of slavery through his own wits and force of will. In the revised autobiography, a more chastened Douglass makes clear the central roles that others played in his escape and stresses his new determination to give something of himself back to the African American community. This communal orientation of *My Bondage and My Freedom* finds its formal counterpart in the work's narrative trajectory, which extends that of the first autobiography by projecting Douglass's return to the South—metaphorically, by working on behalf of those people still enslaved, and literally as well, if and when slavery fell. Douglass, anticipating the southward pull of many postbellum slave narratives, had already written that most African Americans would remain in the South if they could live free, given their attachment to their families there and to the land itself. Maryland's "geography, climate, fertility, and products," he wrote in an open letter to Thomas Auld, "are such as to make it a very desirable abode for any man." More importantly, it is in the South that the community resides: "We want to live in the land of our birth, and to lay our bones by the side of our fathers; and nothing short of an intense love of personal freedom keeps us from the south."[41] These references to the natural environment of the South bring us, as they do Douglass, full circle, for they gather together the themes of family, economics, and sectional allegiance so central to the work's ethical vision.

My Bondage and My Freedom does not theoretically elaborate the relationship between community and the natural environment, but it makes a critical initial move by showing how a writer can conceive of nature as a restorative psychological and spiritual force. In his opening chapter, Douglass pays tribute to his grandmother in a way that calls to mind such later writers as Zora Neale Hurston and Alice Walker. Grandma Betty's sense of identity and her reputation among the other slaves are based largely on her sustaining relationship to the natural world:

> Her "good luck" was owing to the exceeding care which she took in preventing the succulent root [the sweet potato] from getting bruised in the digging, and in placing it beyond the reach of frost, by actually burying it under the heart of her cabin during the winter months. In the time of planting sweet potatoes, "Grandmother Betty," as she was familiarly called, was sent for in all directions, simply to place the seedling potatoes in the hills; for superstition had it, that if "Grandmamma Betty but touches them at planting, they will be sure to grow and flourish." (28–29)

His grandmother's gardening has a somewhat different meaning from that of Uncle Tom's garden; it has more to do with the process of cultivating nature than with the displayed results. And like the African American woman in *Eel Spearing at Setauket*, Grandma Betty is "somewhat famous for her good fortune in taking the fishes" (28). But while Mount's character is defined for the viewer primarily by her relation to the boy, Douglass establishes his grandmother's identity according to her relations to her family and to other slaves. She is a matriarchal figure who represents a source of strength in her profound relationship to nature, but that relationship, crucially, is economically viable and communally oriented rather than naively romantic or solipsistic. In that sense the figure of Douglass's grandmother unifies the work's pastoral and georgic strains, embodying both the idealism and emotional sweetness of the former and the outer-directed, practical, and realistic qualities of the latter.

We can also see her as representing the pastoral mood as described by Paul Alpers, who argues that the ethical core of pastoral involves the ability of the socially dispossessed to find their "strength relative to the world," and to do so by ameliorating loss, grief, and injustice through the forms of communal bonding that pastoral envisions. Though concerned primarily with Renaissance literature, Alpers's argument has deep relevance for the pastoral ethic in African American literature. He emphasizes the mode's emotional and social dimensions:

> The literary conception of the shepherd's strength relative to his world explains why pastoral is so "conventional" a form: as opposed to epic and tragedy, with their ideas of heroic autonomy and isolation, it takes human life to be inherently a matter of common plights and common pleasures. Pastoral poetry represents these plights and these pleasures as shared and accepted, but it avoids naiveté and sentimentality because its usages retain an awareness of their conditions—the limitations that are seen to define, in the literal sense, any life, and their intensification in situations of separation and loss that can and must be dealt with, but are not to be denied or overcome.[42]

This perspective provides a way of linking two of the major lines of revision that Douglass undertook in writing *My Bondage and My Freedom*: its expanded attention to the natural world of his youth and its heightened emphasis on the African American community. In projecting a return—even if metaphorical, even if in the indefinite future—to both his immediate family and his larger African American family, Douglass develops a pastoral theme by which individual loss is salved by communal love, and pride redeemed by responsibility. What he works toward is partly the mythical, innocent pastoralism of his childhood, which can be recovered only in literature and memory, and partly a pastoral that is mature and chastened, that acknowledges "human life to be inherently a matter of common plights and common pleasures."

In *My Bondage and My Freedom*, then, we can identify the stirrings of a vital theme in the African American literary tradition: the view of rural folk culture as a source of strength and a form of shared historical rootedness. It makes sense, of course, that many slave narratives, and many texts rooted in the genre, would celebrate life in the North, with the comparatively greater economic freedoms there. Yet the tradition also registers a deep ambivalence about the social undertow of urban capitalism and its erosive effect on communal life. During the twelve years of Reconstruction, and in the difficult decades to follow, a growing number of slave narratives projected the survival or reconstruction of a viable African American community not only in the North, or in Canada, but on southern land as well. Later, this would become a foundational theme in such major works as W. E. B. Du Bois's *The Souls of Black Folk* and Jean Toomer's *Cane*. Since a fugitive or former slave's achievement of freedom depended literally on a physical departure from the South, it entailed a separation both from the land and from the people left behind, and these two forms of severance, I believe, intertwined more deeply than we have recognized. In his reflections on the importance of locatedness in human life, the geographer Yi-Fu Tuan has suggested that "[p]lace and culture can be viewed as a creative adaptation to the myriad individual human experiences of fragility and transience, aloneness and indifference."[43] It is both lament and determination in the face of such "fragility and transience" that we hear, for instance, in William Troy's appeal against the potential indifference of his audience, an appeal figuring a kind of second diaspora:

> My reader, we have many . . . bereaved mothers of the South in Canada, and all over the United States of America. We meet with hundreds of such cases,—living "Rachels, weeping for their children, who will not be comforted because they are not." There are Jacobs who will go in sorrow to their graves—thousands of pilgrims wandering through forest and swamp, or hid in clefts of the rocks,—there are breaking hearts and fettered limbs—and, in the name of God, we ask the Christian world to rise and help the bondman.[44]

The growing effort to imagine a renewed Southern black community reflected both a desire to overcome the cultural and emotional deracination implied by individual mobility, and the experiential bonds between a narrator and the natural environment of his or her youth. It took the form of a projected or actual return to the place of origin, to the *locus juvenilis*, where a communal racial identity could grow and assert itself, and expressed an elemental desire for rootedness in the land. This southward pull in some narratives, therefore, including *My Bondage and My Freedom*, reminds us that the more-familiar urban and northern orientation of much African American literature should be measured against a countervailing desire for stability on southern soil.

The practical and legal obstacles to reclaiming southern land as homeland were less important, perhaps, than imaginative reclamation, for, as Lawrence Buell has observed, "whatever the conventions of ownership, place is more deeply a matter of belonging than of possession."[45] Yet the formidable emotional complexities of such belonging, or "place-connectedness," arise from the fact that the land of the South bears the impress of a terrible history, of generations of slaves mingled with the earth. The soil itself is like a palimpsest of the dead, many layered, written on with blood, and rich from the accumulation of bodies, experiences, and memories. Such is the power of the poem, "The Blood of the Slave," with which Peter Randolph opened his 1855 narrative:

> The blood of the slave cries unto God from the ground, and it calls loudly for vengeance on his adversaries.
> The blood of the slave cries unto God from the rice swamps.
> The blood of the slave cries unto God from the cotton plantations.
> The blood of the slave cries unto God from the tobacco farms.
> The blood of the slave cries unto God from the sugar fields.
> The blood of the slave cries unto God from the corn fields.[46]

Here as elsewhere, cultural memory is figured in terms of natural place, as burial in the ancestral ground—yet as premature burial, for the call of the unquiet dead resembles the return of the collective or historical unconscious that refuses entombment. It is that call, for reconstitution as well as retribution, that links the dead and the living, the past and the future, in narratives that seek a restoration of the African American community not only in the cities of the North but on the fields of the South.

Rather than the abandonment of place, therefore, the possibility such accounts raise is that of repairing damaged social space through the cultivation of a free community on the land—through an assertion, drawing on Philip Fisher's formulation, of narrative's compositional power, both aesthetic and political, against the smashing, *decompositional* forces of violence and social trauma. A mode of resistance ultimately more constructive than rhetorical condemnation, the slave narrative's imaginative reinvention of southern landscape enables the gradual reshaping of geographic place to meet the psychic and practical needs of individuals and communities. The desire to return to "Georgie land" in Parker's plantation song suggests reoccupation more than capitulation, and the final image is not one of dying alone, but of *living* and dying—and it is that livingness, in all its forms, that will underlie the establishment of a vital free community in the place of slavery. While the pastoral and georgic impulses in early African American literature register a real ambivalence, in light of southern agricultural history, they nonetheless represent a form of place-connectedness that emphasizes humankind's organic connection to the land and the sustaining power of familiar locales, despite or because of their witness to human suffering.

Only in passing, then, does the representation of nature of *My Bondage and My Freedom* invoke the binary of southern vice and northern virtue that antislavery pastoral so often employed. On deeper levels, it is complicated and energized by a number of issues that distinguish this autobiography from the first. The loss of pastoral innocence is attributed not just to the South, but to all of America, and more personally to the realities, inevitable or not, of growing up. As Douglass does mature, distances of time and space separate him from the songbirds and green fields of his youth, and from the innocence that allowed him to enjoy nature free from the bonds of self-consciousness. One reaction is to romanticize his early experience of the natural world—partly through the mischief of Mnemosyne and partly through the deliberateness of literary convention—both of which imply removal, detachment. At the same time, Douglass comes to espouse economic and religious views that problematize the work's treatment of nature, as suggested by the reference to "superstition" in his tribute to his grandmother, by his condescension toward a fellow slave's belief in conjure, and by his admiration for the glittering scenes of New York. Nonetheless, in its vision of the spiritual and psychological balm that nature can represent, and in its association of the natural world with a restored human community, *My Bondage and My Freedom* encouraged the development of a broader tradition of representing nature in African American literature. Douglass did not resolve, or perhaps even perceive, the tension between economics, religion, and natural beauty in his work, but he laid out the critical problems and avenues of thought for later authors—from Charles Chesnutt to Ntozake Shange—to grapple with. In the end, his most important contribution was to envision fundamental connections between his search for community and the organic wholeness of a natural world unpolluted by slavery. Inseparable from his past, and lived in memory, Douglass's pastoral ideal is more widely linked to the African American community that he seeks to recover at some point in the future.

In the postbellum years, particularly before the demise of the Freedmen's Bureau and the end of Reconstruction, practical opportunities presented themselves. In an 1873 speech to the Tennessee Colored Agricultural and Mechanical Association, Douglass—anticipating some of the rhetoric of Booker T. Washington—hailed agriculture as integral to both the past and the future of African Americans. Telling his audience that "[i]t is pleasant to know that in color, form, and features, we are related to the first successful tillers of the soil," Douglass described agriculture "as a refuge for the oppressed. The grand old earth has no prejudices against race, color, or previous condition of servitude, but flings open her ample breast to all who will come to her for succor and relief."[47] This vision of racial renewal through attachment to the land was problematic, of course, but also sustaining, and we can see it beginning to emerge in Douglass's earliest memories of his life as a young boy on a plantation in Maryland.

EPILOGUE

Shadows of Green

DECADES IN THE MAKING, the antislavery movement took shape as people once far-flung or loosely assembled, who deemed slavery an affront to God, a violation of nature, or simply a threat to white society, began to coalesce around a set of identifiable rhetorics and strategies. Necessarily, they worked from the discourses that history had made available to them, and I have sought to improve our understanding of how they did so. In the eighteenth century, Christian humanitarianism and natural rights theory represented two primary lexica, the latter a more secular cousin to the former, by which people could express the belief that human bondage contravened a transcendent moral code. As the terms of the debate changed, however, and as Western societies themselves changed, the conceptual and discursive field of antislavery literature evolved accordingly. Anthropology and natural history presented both challenges, primarily in the theorization of racial hierarchies, and opportunities, primarily in the emergence of new, optimistic ways of conceiving of biological and social progress. At the same time, old and new aesthetic traditions of representing nature, especially pastoral, provided fruitful avenues of attack against slavery, through emotionally compelling images of natural felicity, of an outward beauty that symbolized the spiritual equality and liberty that natural rights theory (at least as popularly understood) had championed. Despite their important differences, scientific and pastoral thought shared an idealism, a utopian core, that promised to bring humanity closer to the perfection imagined to exist in nature, whether in its physical laws or in its aesthetic purity. Although one person's utopia might be another's hell, the rhetorical advantage, or simple emotional power, of an idealistic vision of the world proved an indispensable element of antislavery literature.

Yet individual psychology and political propaganda rarely mesh neatly, and the expression through natural imagery of such themes as beauty, violence, liberty, memory, and community proved as problematic as they were fruitful. The transatlantic and antebellum struggles over the meaning of race and the future of slavery touched not only on matters of political governance but on fundamental issues of human experience. It found expression, therefore, in unexpected areas of cultural endeavor and, often, in seemingly apolitical forms in which imagistic strategies and psychological dynamics took precedence over the ideological and the polemical. From the insects that feed on the slave in *Letters from an American Farmer* to the blackbirds that young Frederick Douglass envies, from the manufacturing colony that Equiano envisions for Sierra Leone to the damp recesses of Stowe's Great Dismal Swamp, and from Walker's nascent pan-Africanism to Emerson's fugitive amalgamationism, antislavery authors wrestled with such essential problems as biology, money, time, and nationalism (to name only four) that the issue of slavery generated. We rarely hear these writers speaking with one voice, but recurring patterns of thought, and a certain common timbre, remind us that the chorus they formed, on the basis of a shared opposition to human bondage, did draw on a defined intellectual and ideological heritage.

In recovering that heritage, and in reconstructing how writers of quite different backgrounds came to terms with racial slavery and represented it in their work, I have had a number of subplots in mind. A principal one involves the tensions, problems, and limitations within liberal or humanitarian rhetoric. While calling attention to the imperfections of social criticism, however, I do not mean to deny or underestimate the political efficacy of oppositional texts. After all, any articulated ideology that moves from marginal to hegemonic status (such as the belief that slavery is wrong and must be constitutionally prohibited) cannot become influential in the modern public sphere absent its dissemination through the available media. Yet we have come to realize that the circulations of social power in any culture operate in complex ways, rarely conforming to predictable dynamics of centrifugal and centripetal flow. Discourse that operates radically in one sphere, can, intentionally or not, be conservative in another, in the sense of protecting one interest in the status quo while challenging another, or promoting changes that might end up structurally if not formally reproducing what was meant to be reformed in the first place.

In the case of antislavery, the well-intentioned effort to bring an end to one egregious form of labor exploitation led many writers or activists to commit themselves to another economic system that, by the end of the century, had produced its own severe abuses requiring extensive government intervention. This system—industrial capitalism—also proved increasingly antithetical to the pastoral ethic that antislavery writers had found so useful, and so genuinely compelling, over the years. Other " nonliberal" voices can also be heard: Stowe's racial stereotyping, Equiano's overseeing of a plantation among the Mosquito Indians, Crèvecoeur's opposition to the American Revolution, among others. Such observations, however, amount less to a criticism of individual writers or of abolition in general than to a recognition of the inevitable horizons that delimit a movement's perception of its place in and contribution to the broader sweep of history. It is also a recognition of the perpetual dialectic between idealism and realism in public affairs, of the tendency, even within the most morally passionate movement, to enter into certain impure or unsavory alignments in the interest of achieving a greater eventual good: a political theodicy, we might say, or a street-level version of *realpolitik*. It should be stressed that this is not necessarily a conscious matter; even the most uncompromising, self-righteous social critics can unwittingly implicate themselves in trends or forces that run against the grain of what they stand for.

What this perspective really describes is the luxury of historical retrospect, whereby actors on the stage of human affairs appear more or less "radical" based on a subsequent course of events that was by no means foreordained but that seems to ratify the triumph of particular beliefs and ideologies. It's not even that the winners write the history, as the adage has it, but that the hapless survivors do, and when we say that a historical figure or movement embodied enlightened, progressive ideas, we are not only expressing our own values, but often also operating on the assumption that the route to the present was less contingent than it appears, that it was somehow fated, or natural. This assumption informs, for instance, the argument that capitalism inevitably defeated communism, or the more recent claim that democratic values will inevitably triumph over "Islamofascism" because they more closely express "human nature." Maybe so: The rise or fall of particular ideologies certainly has much to do with how effectively they satisfy widespread human needs. But when the host of contingencies grows too numerous or complex to comprehend, the temptation to chalk it all up to a transcendent order—nature, fate, God—that *manifests* itself through history can become irresistible.

Yet irrespective of the ontological truth of deterministic theories of history, we can never step back and take a cosmic view of the relation between worldly event and transcendent order, for history unfolds perpetually, and its future unfoldings do not yield themselves up to human sight. "Progressive" or "reactionary" movements, from this perspective, should be considered as such only in relation to each other, and to the configurations of power that they confronted in a particular historical context. In the case of antislavery writers, this allows us to appreciate what was genuinely oppositional in their work without losing sight of their various investments in the status quo and without having to cast them in a glorious historical drama whose plot follows the inexorable triumph of liberal economic and social values.

Which might help to illuminate the deeper motivations behind this book. Although focused on a particular historical period, and on a limited number of historical actors, *Shades of Green* has been impelled by more than strictly intellectual and disciplinary considerations. Certainly, conceptual relationships and representational patterns form the grist of my argument, but the larger importance of the material, as I see it, involves its ability to shed light on enduring ethical and social problems. During the period in question—the early national and antebellum phases of American history—some of the central challenges we face today regarding race and the environment emerged in their broad original outlines, and the literature that responded to those challenges has much to teach us about the ideological and psychological dimensions of that struggle. The terrible reality of slavery raised difficult and divisive questions that have lost none their relevance or force: What is race? What is the human being? Where will we ground our sense of moral order? And the debates surrounding these questions were shot through with the language of natural science and natural beauty: What distinguishes human beings from animals? To what natural laws are we beholden? Can we reconcile the beauty of nature with its violence and apparent chaos? Since then, these problems have not gone away, but have taken on new forms and attached themselves to different political and cultural realities. The struggle over the meaning of evolution, for example, has grown more popular and more complex, but little has changed in its fierceness or its felt significance; the science of race has yielded to the combined pressure exerted by philosophers, cultural anthropologists, and geneticists, but race persists as a dominant concept with very real force; the preoccupation with the contours of "humanness" has morphed into a "posthumanist" anxiety about the rise of various biotechnologies and the seemingly relentless severing of human beings from the natural environment. And amidst all, horribly, the practices of slavery and forced labor persist as a global phenomenon which may be illegal, but which has scarcely abated in its number of victims.

In returning to a period of American history, then, during which writings on race and the natural world proved so instrumental in shaping our social reality, I have been particularly interested in those authors and artists who showed how nature and racial identity could be reconceptualized. The ethical and the activist dimensions of this rethinking figure centrally here because they help us understand the connection between ideological struggle and individual psychology. As an increasingly organized and influential social movement drawing on natural science and environmental questions to advance its moral positions, American antislavery has much to say to us today about how the language of nature can help to provide cultural legitimation for a controversial political program. And as writers who may have condemned slavery, but were only tangentially connected to the abolitionist movement, and who tended to put intellectual exploration ahead of rhetorical consistency, the major authors taken up here show how profoundly, unpredictably, and energetically nature enters into the most vital areas of human experience.

Throughout the period described by this study, the abiding theme that linked antislavery writers together was unity, or the quest for wholeness in the face of division and fragmentation. Yet unity is frequently chimerical, multiplicity richly valuable, and the literature of race and slavery proves most compelling when it recognizes this. Committed to lofty ideals in a fallen world, antislavery writers brought a religious intensity to their search for forms of harmony that transcended human conflict. At the same time, they brought the limitations and flaws of humanity to their work—and often possessed the wisdom to see those limitations and flaws in themselves. Visions of wholeness, that is, were seen through earthly eyes. Insisting on the biological unity of the human family, humanitarian authors were not above trafficking in the language of biological racial difference. Willing to shed blood for the sake of the Union, they were fiercely sectional loyalists; a number, in the early years, advocated northern secession themselves. The fragmentation of the diaspora led some to imagine an originary, recoverable wholeness in Africa, but repatriation, voluntary or otherwise, seemed to many to entail only further displacement. Amid all, these authors turned to nature as the transcendent standard of order and goodness, convinced or hopeful that scientific inquiry would reveal not chaos but purpose, and invested in a pastoralism dedicated to the proposition that the apotheosis of nature's design was the marriage of liberty and harmony. That this marriage remained, remains, unconsummated redounds not in the slightest to the antislavery commitment. For many felt, if we give the word "union" the fullest possible signification, that it is, in the words of the botanist Asa Gray, "better to suffer in devotion to the Union than prosper in petty fragments."[1]

In his poem "Slaves Among Blades of Grass," Yusef Komunyakaa captures something of the mystery, the mandala of violence and beauty, that I have tried to describe:

> The Amazon ants dispatch
> Scouts armed with mandibles
> Sharp as sabers. They return
> To drum each other's heads
>
> With antennae & then send out
> Columns of warriors to surround a nest
> & abduct pupae. As if made for battle,
> With jaws so deadly they can't feed
>
> Themselves, they possess slaves.
> New blades of grass beaded with water
> Light a sub-kingdom beneath
> Shadowed footsteps where the sky
>
> Meets indiscernible green of river
> & jungle, in this terrain
> Where a world is dismantled
> To make something else look whole.[2]

That "something else," so evocatively undefined, is what the authors taken up here, each in his or her own way, had the faith to envision and the wisdom to question.

Notes

Introduction: Nature, Race, Culture

1. Herman Melville, *Typee: A Peep at Polynesian Life* (New York: Penguin, 1996), 224.

2. Peter Coates, *Nature: Western Attitudes since Ancient Times* (Cambridge: Polity Press, 1998); John Torrance, ed., *The Concept of Nature* (Oxford: Clarendon Press, 1992); Kate Soper, *What Is Nature?* (Oxford: Blackwell, 1995); Neil Evernden, *The Social Creation of Nature* (Baltimore: Johns Hopkins University Press, 1992); Keith Thomas, *Man and the Natural World: A History of the Modern Sensibility* (New York: Pantheon Books, 1983); Raymond Williams, "Nature," in *Keywords: A Vocabulary of Culture and Society*, ed. Raymond Williams (New York: Oxford University Press, 1976).

3. Arthur Riss has recently argued that modern liberal thought must continue to recognize this instability, rather than uncritically assume the essential reality and integrity of "the person," and that the crucial ethical questions are

those "about who controls the terms that establish this conceptual category and what are the effects of such an account." *Race, Slavery, and Liberalism in Nineteenth-Century American Literature* (Cambridge: Cambridge University Press, 2006), 23.

4. The term "racial project" comes from Michael Omi and Howard Winant, *Racial Formation in the United States: From the 1960s to the 1980s* (New York: Routledge and Kegan Paul, 1986). Defining racial formation as "the sociohistorical process by which racial categories are created, inhabited, transformed, and destroyed," Omi and Winant write that this process involves "historically situated projects in which human bodies and social structures are represented and organized." In turn, such a "racial project" is "simultaneously an interpretation, representation, or explanation of racial dynamics, and an effort to reorganize and redistribute resources along particular racial lines" (56–57). Race is thus ideational and constitutive, a product of the imagination, an apparition arising from representational systems, and a source and arena of tangible struggle. This perspective accords with many other recent studies of race, including Naomi Zack, *Philosophy of Science and Race* (New York: Routledge, 2002); Paul Gilroy, *Against Race: Imagining Political Culture beyond the Color Line* (Cambridge, Mass.: Harvard University Press, 2000); and Philip Yale Nicholson, *Who Do We Think We Are? Race and Nation in the Modern World* (Armonk, N.Y.: M. E. Sharpe, 1999).

5. Recent critical studies of abolitionism that concern themselves with its rhetorical strategies and their relation to public opinion, but do not consider the importance of natural imagery or natural philosophy, include Timothy Patrick McCarthy and John Stauffer, *Prophets of Protest: Reconsidering the History of American Abolitionism* (New York: New Press, 2006); Robert Fanuzzi, *Abolition's Public Sphere* (Minneapolis: University of Minnesota Press, 2003); Michael Bennett, *Democratic Discourses: The Radical Abolition Movement and Antebellum American Literature* (New Brunswick, N.J.: Rutgers University Press, 2005); and Jacqueline Bacon, *The Humblest May Stand Forth: Rhetoric, Empowerment, and Abolition* (Columbia: University of South Carolina Press, 2002).

6. Indeed, some cultural historians have seen the antislavery movement as forwarding, or virtually presiding over, the nation's transition to an even more oppressive, because insidiously self-effacing, labor regime—that of laissez-faire market capitalism. See Ronald G. Walters, *The Antislavery Appeal: American Abolitionism after 1830 (Baltimore: Johns Hopkins University Press, 1976)* chap. 7; Seymour Drescher, *Capitalism and Antislavery: British Mobilization*

in Comparative Perspective (Basingstoke, Hampshire, England: Macmillan, 1986); David Brion Davis, *The Problem of Slavery in the Age of Revolution, 1770–1823* (Ithaca, N.Y.: Cornell University Press, 1975); David Brion Davis, *Slavery and Human Progress* (New York: Oxford University Press, 1984); Ronald Takaki, *Iron Cages: Race and Culture in Nineteenth-Century America* (New York: Oxford University Press, 1990), esp. chaps. 4 and 6; and John Ashworth, *Slavery, Capitalism, and Politics in the Antebellum Republic*, vol. 1, *Commerce and Compromise, 1820–1850* (Cambridge: Cambridge University Press, 1995), esp. chap. 3.

7. Lorraine Daston and Fernando Vidal, eds., *The Moral Authority of Nature* (Chicago: University of Chicago Press, 2004), 2, 8, 9.

8. Anthony Benezet, *Some Historical Account of Guinea* (Philadelphia, 1771), 15. Thomas Gray, *The Confessions of Nat Turner* (Baltimore, 1831), 10, 11; Frederick Douglass, *My Bondage and My Freedom* (1855; reprint, University of Illinois Press, 1987), 38–39; George Lunt, "An Address Delivered before the Massachusetts Horticultural Society, on the Dedication of Horticultural Hall, May 15, 1845" (Boston, 1845), 6; Paul Henri Thiry, Baron d'Holbach, *Good Sense: or, Natural Ideas Opposed to Supernatural*, 3rd ed. (New York, 1831), 30, 35; Anonymous, *The Tales of Peter Parley about Africa*, rev. ed. (Philadelphia, 1848), 116.

9. Dana Phillips, *The Truth of Ecology: Nature, Culture, and Literature in America* (New York: Oxford University Press, 2003), 30.

10. Jonathan Levin, "Forum on Literatures of the Environment," *PMLA* 114, no. 5 (October 1999), 1098.

11. Robert Young, *Colonial Desire: Hybridity in Theory, Culture, and Race* (New York: Routledge, 1995), 54.

12. One line of antiracist thought, Peter Wade has suggested, is "to argue that 'nature' is a more flexible domain than is commonly thought and that, especially when it comes to human nature, it is itself a cultural process, rather than a domain opposed to 'culture'" (*Race, Nature and Culture: An Anthropological Perspective* [London: Pluto Press, 2002], 110–11). Similarly, Donald S. Moore, Jake Kosek, and Anand Pandian have written that "[t]heir sense of universality both makes race and nature continually available for naïve rediscovery and continually obscures the historical conditions that make and remake them. Because race and nature always seem to precede history, they can be taken again and again as the very substrate on which myriad social truths are built" (*Race, Nature, and the Politics of Difference* [Durham, N.C.: Duke University Press 2003], 4).

13. Steven Pinker has offered this succinct definition: "The mind is a system of organs of computation, designed by natural selection to solve the kinds of problems our ancestors faced in their foraging way of life, in particular, understanding and outmaneuvering objects, animals, plants, and other people" (*How the Mind Works* [New York: Norton, 1997], 21). Edward Reed has written that evolutionary psychology (or what he calls "ecological psychology") "sees human beings as no more—and no less—than one special way in which animals have evolved to encounter their environment," and in identifying distinctive human characteristics, "psychologists should be more interested in modes of life than in heredity or essences." In that sense, he argues, "much of our success comes from a collectivization of efforts after value and meaning, or what we like to call culture and technology" (*Encountering the World: Toward an Ecological Psychology* [Oxford: Oxford University Press, 1996], 112, 113).

14. There has been a veritable torrent of scholarship in this area over the last decade. Recent works of significant merit include John Zeisel, *Inquiry by Design: Environment/Behavior/Neuroscience in Architecture, Interiors, Landscape, and Planning*, rev. ed. (New York: Norton, 2006); Susan Clayton and Susan Opotow, eds., *Identity and the Natural Environment: The Psychological Significance of Nature* (Cambridge, Mass.: MIT Press, 2003); Carolyn Saari, *The Environment: Its Role in Psychosocial Functioning and Psychotherapy* (New York: Columbia University Press, 2002); and Andrew J. Weigert, *Self, Interaction, and Natural Environment: Refocusing Our Eyesight* (Buffalo: SUNY Press, 1997).

15. The work of geographer Yi-Fu Tuan has been especially influential in this respect; see in particular *Space and Place: The Perspective of Experience* (Minneapolis: University of Minnesota Press, 1977) and *Topophilia: A Study of Environmental Perceptions, Attitudes, and Values* (Englewood Cliffs, N.J.: Prentice-Hall, 1974). Also important are Winifred Gallagher, *The Power of Place: How Our Surroundings Shape Our Thoughts, Emotions, and Actions* (New York: Poseidon Press, 1993) and Gaston Bachelard, *The Poetics of Space* (Boston: Beacon Press, 1994; originally published as *La poétique de l'espace* [Paris: Presses universitaires de France, 1958]).

16. Pinker, *How the Mind Works*, 32.

17. For a survey of the core criticisms, see Hillary Rose and Steven Rose, eds., *Alas, Poor Darwin: Arguments Against Evolutionary Psychology* (New York: Harmony Books, 2000).

18. Reed, *Encountering the World*, 171, 188. In a similar vein, Pinker rejects the customary binary between heredity and environment and maintains that

learning "is made possible by innate machinery designed to do the learning" (*How the Mind Works*, 33).

19. The experiential dimensions of racial identity are foregrounded in Linda Martin Alcoff, *Visible Identities: Race, Gender, and the Self* (New York: Oxford University Press, 2006). Also see Paula M. L. Moya and Michael R. Hames-Garcia, eds., *Reclaiming Identity: Realist Theory and the Predicament of Postmodernism* (Berkeley: University of California Press, 2000).

20. This latter claim is supported by the work of modern social scientists who have examined racial differences in attitudes toward various natural environments. See Rachel Kaplan and Stephen Kaplan, *The Experience of Nature: A Psychological Perspective* (Cambridge: Cambridge University Press, 1989); Cassandra Y. Johnson, Patrick M. Horan, and William Pepper, "Race, Rural Residence, and Wildland Visitation: Examining the Influence of Sociocultural Meaning," *Rural Sociology* 62, no. 1 (Spring 1997): 89–110, 106; and Eric Jay Dolin, "Black American Attitudes toward Wildlife," *Journal of Environmental Education* 20, no. 1 (1988): 17–21.

21. Particularly influential here have been Alfred Schutz, *Phenomenology of the Social World*, trans. George Walsh and Frederick Lehnert (Evanston, Ill.: Northwestern University Press, 1967); Hans Jonas, *The Phenomenon of Life: Toward a Philosophical Biology* (New York: Harper and Row, 1966; Evanston, Ill.: Northwestern University Press, 2001); Maurice Natanson, *The Erotic Bird: Phenomenology in Literature* (Princeton: Princeton University Press, 1998); Maurice Natanson, *Phenomenology, Role, and Reason: Essays on the Coherence and Deformation of Social Reality* (Springfield, Ill.: Charles C. Thomas, 1974); and David Carr, *The Paradox of Subjectivity: The Self in the Transcendental Tradition* (New York: Oxford University Press, 1999).

22. Explorations of the connections between phenomenology and environmentalism have formed a fruitful area of endeavor; recent important studies include David Abram, *The Spell of the Sensuous: Perception and Language in a More-Than-Human World* (New York: Pantheon Books, 1996); Edward S. Casey, *Getting Back into Place: Toward a Renewed Understanding of the Place-World* (Bloomington: Indiana University Press, 1993); and Bruce V. Foltz, *Inhabiting the Earth: Heidegger, Environmental Ethics, and the Metaphysics of Nature* (Atlantic Highlands, N.J.: Humanities Press, 1995). Work in race and phenomenology has been less extensive, but nonetheless very useful. The fullest treatment is Charles Johnson, *Being and Race: Black Writing since 1970* (Bloomington: Indiana University Press, 1988). More recently see Kenneth Danziger Knies, "The Idea of Post-European Science: An Essay on Phenomenol-

ogy and Africana Studies," in *Not Only the Master's Tools: African-American Studies in Theory and Practice*, ed. Lewis R. Gordon and Jane Anna Gordon (Boulder, Colo.: Paradigm, 2006); Bettina G. Bergo, "Roulez! il n'y a rien à voir or, 'Seeing white' from Phenomenology to Psychoanalysis and Back," in *White on White/Black on Black*, ed. George Yancy (Lanham: Rowman and Littlefield, 2005); Paget Henry, "Whiteness and Africana Phenomenology," in *What White Looks Like: African-American Philosophers on the Whiteness Question*, ed. George Yancy (New York: Routledge, 2004); and Cynthia Willett, "The Social Element: A Phenomenology of Racialized Space and the Limits of Liberalism," in *Racism in Mind*, ed. Michael P. Levine and Tamas Pataki (Ithaca, N.Y.: Cornell University Press, 2004).

23. E[lias] L[yman] Magoon, "Scenery and Mind," from *The Home Book of the Picturesque: or American Scenery, Art, and Literature* (New York: Putnam, 1852), 8, 16.

24. Navigating the distinction between these two kinds of experience has a long philosophical tradition, but in the past twenty years or so, scholars have begun taking the aesthetic potential of nature more seriously in its own right. See Allen Carlson, *Aesthetics and the Natural Environment: The Appreciation of Nature, Art and Architecture* (London: Routledge, 2000); Ronald Hepburn, *The Reach of the Aesthetic: Essays on Art and Nature* (Aldershot and Burlington: Ashgate, 2001); and Emily Brady, *Aesthetics of the Natural Environment* (Tuscaloosa: University of Alabama Press, 2003), esp. chap. 3.

25. This is the position taken by, among others, Holmes Rolston in "Does Aesthetic Appreciation of Landscapes Need to Be Science-Based?" *British Journal of Aesthetics* 35, no. 4 (1995), and "Aesthetic Experience in Forests," *Journal of Aesthetics and Art Criticism* 56, no. 2 (1998); Marcia Eaton in *Merit, Aesthetic and Ethical* (Oxford: Oxford University Press, 2001); and Allen Carlson in *Aesthetics and the Natural Environment.*

26. See Ronald Hepburn, "Landscape and Metaphysical Imagination," *Environmental Values* 5 (1996); Ronald Hepburn, "Trivial and Serious in Aesthetic Appreciation of Nature," in *Landscape, Natural Beauty and the Arts*, ed. Salim Kemal and Ivan Gaskell (Cambridge: Cambridge University Press, 1993); Arnold Berleant, *Aesthetics of Environment* (Philadelphia: Temple University Press, 1992); Noël Carroll, "Being Moved by Nature: Between Religion and Natural History," in *Landscape, Natural Beauty and the Arts*, ed. Kemal and Gaskell; and Stan Godlovitch, "Icebreakers: Environmentalism and Natural Aesthetics," *Journal of Applied Philosophy* 11, no. 1 (1994).

27. From *Critique of Judgement* (1790), First Part ("Critique of Aesthetic Judgement"), Section 1 ("Analytic of Aesthetic Judgement"), Book 1 ("Analytic

of the Beautiful") second moment ("Of the Judgement of Taste: Moment of Quantity"), ss 8 and ss 9.

28. See Joseph Carroll, "The Deep Structure of Literary Representations," *Evolution and Human Behavior* 20 (1999): 159–73; G. Currie, "Realism of Character and the Value of Fiction," in *Aesthetics and Ethics*, ed. J. Levinson (Cambridge: Cambridge University Press, 1998); and Joseph Carroll, *Evolution and Literary Theory* (Columbia: University of Missouri Press, 1995).

29. Michael P. Clark, ed., *Revenge of the Aesthetic: The Place of Literature in Theory Today* (Berkeley: University of California Press, 2000).

30. See, for example, Emory Elliott, Lou Freitas Caton, and Jeffrey Rhyne, eds., *Aesthetics in a Multicultural Age* (New York: Oxford University Press, 2002) and Isobel Armstrong, *The Radical Aesthetic* (New York: Blackwell, 2000).

31. See Ian Hunter, "Aesthetics and Cultural Studies," in *Cultural Studies*, ed. Lawrence Grossberg, Cary Nelson, and Paula Treichler (New York: Routledge, 1992) and Paul Gilmore, "Romantic Electricity, or the Materiality of Aesthetics," *American Literature* 76, no. 3 (September 2004).

32. Michael P. Clark, "Introduction," *Revenge of the Aesthetic*, 17; Christopher Castiglia and Russ Castronovo, "A 'Hive of Subtlety': Aesthetics and the End(s) of Cultural Studies," *American Literature* 76, no. 3 (2004): 423–35, 428–29.

33. Maurice Natanson, *The Erotic Bird: Phenomenology in Literature* (Princeton: Princeton University Press, 1998), 28, 13, 19.

34. Alfred Schutz, *Collected Papers*, vol. 1: *The Problem of Social Reality* (The Hague: Martinus Nihjoff, 1962), 75.

35. See also Mikel Dufrenne's pioneering work *The Phenomenology of Aesthetic Experience*, trans. Edward Casey (Evanston, Ill.: Northwestern University Press, 1973; originally published 1967).

36. In Neil Evernden's succinct formulation, "Science and art are merely different ways of giving form to nature" (*Social Creation of Nature*, 60). See also Jonathan Smith, *Charles Darwin and Victorian Visual Culture* (Cambridge: Cambridge University Press, 2006); James W. McAllister, *Beauty and Revolution in Science* (Ithaca, N.Y.: Cornell University Press, 1996); and Subrahmanyan Chandrasekhar, *Truth and Beauty: Aesthetics and Motivations in Science* (Chicago: University of Chicago Press, 1987).

37. See, for example, Noah Heringman, ed., *Romantic Science: The Literary Forms of Natural History* (Albany: SUNY Press, 2003); Lynn L. Merrill, *The Romance of Victorian Natural History* (New York: Oxford University Press, 1989); and Rebecca Bailey Bedell, *The Anatomy of Nature: Geology and Amer-*

ican Landscape Painting, 1825–1875 (Princeton: Princeton University Press, 2001).

38. Stephen Rosendale, *The Greening of Literary Scholarship: Literature, Theory, and the Environment* (Iowa City: University of Iowa Press, 2002); Karla Armbruster and Kathleen R. Wallace, eds., *Beyond Nature Writing: Expanding the Boundaries of Ecocriticism* (Charlottesville: University Press of Virginia, 2001). See Elizabeth Dodd, "Letter," *PMLA* 114, no. 5 (October 1999): 1094–95; and Paul Tidwell, "The Blackness of the Whale: Nature in Recent African-American Writing" (MLA 1994 Roundtable Discussion on Nature and Environmental Writing).

39. Kimberly K. Smith, *African American Environmental Thought: Foundations* (Lawrence: University of Kansas Press, 2007); Dianne D. Glave and Mark Stoll, eds., *To Love the Wind and the Rain: African Americans and Environmental History* (Pittsburgh: University of Pittsburgh Press, 2005).

Chapter 1. Nature, Civilization, and the Progress of Antislavery Philosophy

1. Carey McIntosh, *The Evolution of English Prose, 1700–1800: Style, Politeness, and Print Culture* (Cambridge: Cambridge University Press, 1998); Paul Keen, *The Crisis of Literature in the 1790s: Print Culture and the Public Sphere* (Cambridge: Cambridge University Press, 1999); Andrew Varney, *Eighteenth-Century Writers in Their World: A Mighty Maze* (New York: Palgrave Macmillan, 1999); Margaret J. M. Ezell, *Social Authorship and the Advent of Print* (Baltimore: Johns Hopkins University Press, 1999).

2. Important recent studies include David Brion Davis, *Inhuman Bondage: The Rise and Fall of Slavery in the New World* (New York: Oxford University Press, 2006); Steven M. Wise, *Though the Heavens May Fall: The Landmark Trial That Led to the End of Human Slavery* (Cambridge, Mass.: Da Capo Press, 2005); Adam Hochschild, *Bury the Chains: Prophets and Rebels in the Fight to Free an Empire's Slaves* (New York: Houghton Mifflin, 2005); Herbert S. Klein, *The Atlantic Slave Trade* (Cambridge: Cambridge University Press, 1999); and Hugh Thomas, *The Slave Trade: The Story of the Atlantic Slave Trade, 1440–1870* (New York: Simon and Schuster, 1997).

3. The term "representational affordances" draws on Edward Reed's theory of evolutionary psychology, in which affordances, including both resources and information, create selection pressures on individual organisms. By representational affordances, then, I refer to the almost infinite variety of tropes, motifs, images, narrative structures, and abstract concepts present or articulated in

the world of visual, textual, and even verbal discourse. These form the raw material that can be shaped to promote certain policies, values, or worldviews, in virtually any medium of communication: literature, painting, propaganda, conversation. See Edward Reed, *Encountering the World: Toward an Ecological Psychology* (Oxford: Oxford University Press, 1996).

4. Philip Gould, in *Barbaric Traffic: Commerce and Antislavery in the Eighteenth-Century Atlantic World* (Cambridge, Mass.: Harvard University Press, 2003), argues that antislavery writers invoked standards of "civilized" trade and Christian manners in attacking the "barbarous" traffic in human beings, thereby intervening (though not simplistically) on behalf of capitalist commerce. Srinivas Aravamudan, in *Tropicopolitans: Colonialism and Agency, 1688–1804* (Durham, N.C.: Duke University Press, 1999), investigates the various processes and compromises by which colonized subjects were able to seize agency in defining themselves and their relation to metropolitan values. Seymour Drescher, in *The Mighty Experiment: Free Labor versus Slavery in British Emancipation* (Oxford: Oxford University Press, 2002), examines the impact of the social sciences on the debates over race and slavery. Brycchan Carey, *British Abolitionism and the Rhetoric of Sensibility: Writing, Sentiment, and Slavery, 1760–1807* (New York: Palgrave Macmillan, 2005). Helen Thomas, in *Romanticism and Slave Narratives: Transatlantic Testimonies* (Cambridge: Cambridge University Press, 2000), argues that a Protestant "discourse of the spirit," in both abolitionist rhetoric and black autobiography, "provided an effective process of self-consciousness and self-authorising which challenged conceptual boundaries between 'selves' and racial 'others'" (13).

5. John Hepburn, *The American defence of the Christian golden rule, or An essay to prove the unlawfulness of making slaves of men* (New York?, 1715), preface; Elihu Coleman, *A testimony against that antichristian practice of making slaves of men* (Boston, 1733), 14.

6. James Otis, *The Rights of the British Colonies Asserted and Proved* (Boston: Edes and Gill, 1764), 30, 31.

7. James Ramsay, *An Essay on the Treatment and Conversion of African Slaves in the British Sugar Colonies* (London, 1784), in *Slavery, Abolition, and Emancipation: Writings in the British Romantic Period*, ed. Peter J. Kitson, Debbie Lee, et al. (London: Pickering and Chatto, 1999), 2:5, 8, 7, 7, 12, 10–11.

8. James Ramsay, *An Essay on the Treatment and Conversion of African Slaves*, 15–16, 16–17.

9. See Wolfgang Lefèvre, *Between Leibniz, Newton, and Kant: Philosophy and Science in the Eighteenth Century* (Dordrecht, Netherlands: Kluwer

Academic Publishers, 2001); Abraham Wolf, *A History of Science, Technology, and Philosophy in the Eighteenth Century*, 2nd rev. ed. (Gloucester: Peter Smith, 1968); Gerd Buchdahl, *The Image of Newton and Locke in the Age of Reason* (London: Sheed and Ward, 1961); and Harry Woolf's still-compelling general study, *The Transits of Venus: A Study of Eighteenth-Century Science* (Princeton, N.J.: Princeton University Press, 1959).

10. On the details and implications of Carolus Linnaeus's *System Naturae* (1735), see Wolf, *A History of Science*, 426–32 and 460–62; Alice Dickinson, *Carl Linnaeus: Pioneer of Modern Botany* (New York: F. Watts, 1967); and James L. Larson, *Interpreting Nature: The Science of Living Form from Linnaeus to Kant* (Baltimore: Johns Hopkins University Press, 1994).

11. In the first edition of the work, Blumenbach posited four major racial categories (Caucasian, American, Ethiopian, Mongolian), adding a fifth (Malay) to his second edition of 1881, and thereby inaugurating the racial schema that quickly became dominant in Western racial theory.

12. See Roxann Wheeler, *The Complexion of Race: Categories of Difference in Eighteenth-Century British Culture* (Philadelphia: University of Pennsylvania Press, 2000); Nicholas Hudson, "From 'Nation' to 'Race': The Origins of Racial Classification in Eighteenth-Century Thought," *Eighteenth-Century Studies* 29 (1996): 247–64; David Lloyd, "Race Under Representation," *Oxford Literary Review* 13 (1991), 62–94; Michael Banton, *Racial Theories* (Cambridge: Cambridge University Press, 1987); Stephen Jay Gould, *The Mismeasure of Man* (New York: Norton, 1981).

13. Edward Long, *History of Jamaica*, 3 vols. (London, 1774); Lord Kames, *Sketches of the History of Man* (1774). Kames denied the unity of the human species and suggested that God later introduced racial distinctions in order to prepare different races for dispersion. A later proponent of the theory was Charles White, in *Account of the Regular Gradation of Man* (1799). For standard accounts of the racial debate in the late eighteenth century, see William Stanton, *The Leopard's Spots: Scientific Attitudes Toward Race in America* (Chicago: University of Chicago Press, 1960), chaps. 1 and 2, and Thomas F. Gossett, *Race: The History of an Idea in America* (New York: Oxford University Press, 1963), chap. 3.

14. Bruce Dain, *A Hideous Monster of the Mind: American Race Theory in the Early Republic* (Cambridge, Mass.: Harvard University Press, 2002).

15. Johann Reinhold Forster, *Observations Made During a Voyage Round the World* (London, 1778), in Kitson, Lee, et al., *Slavery, Abolition, and Emancipation*, 8:26–27.

16. Thomas Clarkson, *An essay on the slavery and commerce of the human*

species, particularly the African, translated from a Latin dissertation (London, 1786), 187–88, 188, 190–91.

17. Theodore Parsons and Eliphalet Pearson, *A Forensic Dispute on the Legality of Enslaving the Africans Held at the Public Commencement in Cambridge, New-England, July 21st, 1773. By Two Candidates for the Bachelor's Degree* (Boston, 1773), 3–4, 5, 26, 31, 36, 35, 36, 37–38. It is not entirely clear which polygenist "attempts" Parsons is referring to, given that their debate occurred before the publication of Long's and Kames's 1774 works, although he may have Hume in mind.

18. Prince Saunders, "An Address Delivered at Bethel Church, Philadelphia . . . Before the Pennsylvania Augustine Society, for the Education of People of Colour" (Philadelphia, 1818), in *Early Negro Writing*, ed. Dorothy Porter (Baltimore: Black Classic Press, 1971), 90. Whipper, "Address Delivered in Wesley Church," ibid., 114; Hamilton, "Oration Delivered in the African Zion Church," ibid., 101.

19. Edward Long, *The history of Jamaica; or, General survey of the antient and modern state of that island: with reflections on its situation, settlements* (London, 1774), in Kitson, Lee, et al., *Slavery, Abolition, and Emancipation*, 8:5.

20. "Copy of a Letter from Benjamin Banneker to the Secretary of State, with his Answer" (Philadelphia: Daniel Lawrence, 1792), 4, 8, 9, 9.

21. Benjamin Banneker, *Banneker's almanac, for the year 1795: . . . Containing, (besides every thing necessary in an almanac,) an account of the yellow fever, lately prevalent in Philadelphia, with the number of those who died, from the first of August till the ninth of November, 1793* (Philadelphia, 1794), 1.

22. Joseph Corr, "Address Delivered before the Humane Mechanics' Society," in Porter, *Early Negro Writing*, 149–50.

23. Anonymous, "The Sons of Africans," in Porter, *Early Negro Writing*, 13.

24. Ron Eglash has outlined the possibility of African philosophical influence on Banneker's mathematical thinking; see "The African Heritage of Benjamin Banneker," *Social Studies of Science* 27, no. 2 (April 1997), 307–15.

25. Neil Evernden, *The Social Creation of Nature* (Baltimore: Johns Hopkins University Press, 1992), 85.

26. Evernden, *The Social Creation of Nature*, 86–87.

27. Michel Foucault, *The Order of Things: An Archaeology of the Human Sciences* (New York: Vintage Books, 1994), 353.

28. See Philip Curtin, *The Image of Africa: British Ideas and Action, 1780–1850* (Madison: University of Wisconsin Press, 1984), esp. chap. 2.

29. Anthony Benezet, *Some historical account of Guinea: its situation, pro-*

duce, and the general disposition of its inhabitants: with an inquiry into the rise and progress of the slave-trade, its nature and lamentable effects (Philadelphia: J. Cruikshank, 1771).

30. Benezet's sources include Jean Barbot, *A New and Accurate Description of the Coasts of Guinea* (London, 1705); Michel Adanson, *Histoire naturelle du Sénégal* (Paris, 1757; English translation, *A Voyage to Senegal, the Isle of Goree, and the River Gambia*, London, 1759); Willem Bosman, *A New and Accurate Description of the Coast of Guinea* (English translation, London, 1705); Thomas Phillips, *A Journal of a Voyage Made in the* Hannibal, *1694* (London, 1746); Francis Moore, *Travels into the Inland Parts of Africa* (London, 1738); William Smith, *A New Voyage to Guinea. . . .* (1744); William Snelgrave, *A New Account of Some Parts of Guinea and the Slave Trade. . . .* (1754); and Thomas Astley, publisher, *A New General Collection of Voyages and Travels*, 4 vols. (London, 1745–1747).

31. Henry Smeathman to J. C. Lettsom, October 19, 1782, in *The Works of John Fothergill, M.D.* (1784), ed. J. C. Lettsom, quoted in Curtin, *Image of Africa*, 59–60.

32. John Wesley, *Thoughts upon Slavery* (Philadelphia, 1774), 9.

33. Anonymous, "The Negro," *The General Magazine and Impartial Review* 1 (Baltimore, June 1798), 15.

34. Benezet, *Some Historical Account of Guinea*, 15–16, 28, 28–29, 31.

35. Benezet, *Some Historical Account of Guinea*, 63, 89, 86, 88, 133, 64, 74, 132–37, 143–44, 144.

36. Hannah More, "Slavery, a Poem," in Kitson, Lee, et al., *Slavery, Abolition and Emancipation: Writings in the British Romantic Period*, vol. 4 (Verse), ed. Alan Richardson (London: Pickering and Chatto, 1999), 114; William Cowper, "The Negro's Complaint," ibid., 75.

37. Long, *The History of Jamaica*, 5.

38. Edmund Burke, *A Philosophical Inquiry into the Origin of our Ideas of the Sublime and Beautiful*, in *A Philosophical Inquiry into the Origin of our Ideas of the Sublime and Beautiful and Other Pre-Revolutionary Writings*, ed. David Womersley (New York: Penguin Books, 1998), 101.

39. Immanuel Kant, *Critique of Judgment*, trans. Werner Pluhar (Indianapolis: Hackett, 1987), 65–95.

40. See Paul Guyer, *Kant and the Experience of Freedom: Essays on Aesthetics and Morality* (Cambridge: Cambridge University Press, 1996), 36–37.

41. Rachel Crawford, *Poetry, Enclosure, and the Vernacular Landscape, 1700–1830* (Cambridge: Cambridge University Press, 2002); John Goodridge,

Rural Life in Eighteenth-Century English Poetry (Cambridge: Cambridge University Press, 1995); Richard Feingold, *Nature and Society: Later Eighteenth-Century Uses of the Pastoral and the Georgic* (New Brunswick, N.J.: Rutgers University Press, 1978); Lore Metzger, *One Foot in Eden: Modes of Pastoral in Romantic Poetry* (Chapel Hill: University of North Carolina Press, 1986).

42. Jean-Jacques Rousseau, *A Discourse on the Moral Effects of the Arts and Sciences*, in *The Social Contract and Discourses*, ed. J. H. Brumfitt, John C. Hall, and P. D. Jimack; trans. G. D. H. Cole (London: J. M. Dent, 1993), 15.

43. Edgar Allan Poe, "Sonnet—to Science" (1829), in *Complete Poems*, ed. Thomas Ollive Mabbott (Urbana: University of Illinois Press, 2000), 90.

44. William Lisle Bowles, "The African," in Kitson, Lee, et al., *Slavery, Abolition, and Emancipation*, 4:193–94.

45. Phillis Wheatley, "On Imagination" (1773), in *The Collected Works of Phillis Wheatley*, ed. John C. Shields (New York: Oxford University Press, 1988), 65–68, 66–67, 65, 66, 67, 66.

46. From the *Critique of Judgment* 5:353–54, quoted in Guyer, *Kant and the Experience of Freedom*, 108–9.

47. Immanuel Kant, *Observations on the Feeling of the Beautiful and the Sublime* (1764), section 4.

48. Henri Grégoire, *De la littérature des Nègres, ou, Recherches sur leurs facultés intellectuelles*, trans. Thomas Cassirer and Jean-François Brière (Amherst: University of Massachusetts Press, 1996), 107.

49. Ignatius Sancho to John Meheux, October 17, 1779, in *Letters of the Late Ignatius Sancho, an African*, ed. Vincent Carretta (New York: Penguin, 1998), 184. Carretta suggests that "A—r—bn—s" is probably Sancho's mangled reference to Auburn, the eponymous town of Oliver Goldsmith's "The Deserted Village" (1770).

50. Paul Shepard, *Man in the Landscape: A Historic View of the Esthetics of Nature* (New York: Alfred A. Knopf, 1967), 24.

Chapter 2. Narrative, Temporality, and the International Traveler

1. Bryce Traister, "Criminal Correspondence: Loyalism, Espionage and Crèvecoeur," *Early American Literature* 37, no. 3 (2002): 469–96; Grantland S. Rice, "Crevècoeur and the Politics of Authorship in Republican America," *Early American Literature* 28, no. 2 (1993): 91–119.

2. Quoted in Rose Marie Cutting, *John and William Bartram, William Byrd II, and St. John de Crèvecoeur: A Reference Guide* (Boston: G. K. Hall, 1976), 107.

3. In perhaps the archetypal comment of this sort, Thomas Philbrick maintains that "*Letters* follows a downward arc of the dream gone sour." (*St. John de Crèvecoeur* [New York: Twayne, 1970], 88) In a similar vein, James Machor writes that Letter IX "foreshadows the mood and theme of the last letter in which the farmer's pastoral dream is revealed as a fiction" ("The Garden City in America: Crèvecoeur's Letters and the Urban-Pastoral Context," *American Studies* 23, no. 2 [1982]: 69–83, 80). More recently, see Traister, "Criminal Correspondence," 482; John D. Cox, *Traveling South: Travel Narratives and the Construction of an American Identity* (Athens: University of Georgia Press, 2005), 41, 38; and N. C. Krishnarani, "The Narrative Technique in Crèvecoeur's *Letters from an American Farmer*: A Manipulation of Form and Voice," *Indian Journal of American Studies* 27, no. 2 (1997): 21–23.

4. See H. L. Bourdin and S. T. Williams, "The Unpublished Manuscripts of Crèvecoeur," *Studies in Philology* 22, no. 4 (1925): 425–32; and H. L. Bourdin, "The Crèvecoeur Manuscripts," preface to *Sketches of Eighteenth-Century America; More "Letters from an American Farmer,"* ed. H. L. Bourdin, Ralph H. Gabriel, and Stanley T. Williams (New Haven, Conn.: Yale University Press, 1925). As Dennis Moore has demonstrated in his 1995 scholarly edition of Crèvecoeur's unpublished manuscripts, Bourdin, Gabriel, and Williams introduced serious editorial distortions into the texts by retitling essays, rearranging material, omitting passages and entire pieces, and misreading Crèvecoeur's handwriting. (*More Letters from the American Farmer: An Edition of the Essays in English Left Unpublished by Crèvecoeur.* [Athens: University of Georgia Press, 1995], xiv–xviii).

5. It is unclear whether Crèvecoeur was directly familiar with Lockean theory, but we know that he read Montesquieu and Rousseau, and Dennis Moore makes a strong case for his familiarity with Voltaire, all of whom read Locke. See the sketch "Landskapes," in Moore, *More Letters from the American Farmer*, 264; and David J. Carlson, "Farmer versus Lawyer: Crèvecoeur's *Letters* and the Liberal Subject," *Early American Literature* 38, no. 2 (2003): 257–79.

6. Timothy Sweet, *American Georgics: Economy and Environment in Early American Literature* (Philadelphia: University of Pennsylvania Press, 2002), 5, 6.

7. Thomas Jefferson, *Notes on the State of Virginia* (London, 1787), ed. William Peden (Chapel Hill: University of North Carolina Press, 1972; orig. repr. 1955). For an enduringly useful statement of the freehold ideal, see Chester Eisinger, "The Freehold Concept in Eighteenth-Century American Letters," *William and Mary Quarterly* 3rd ser., vol. 4 (1947).

8. Joel R. Kehler, "Crèvecoeur's Farmer James: A Reappraisal," *Essays in Literature* 3 (1976): 206–13, 210.

9. See, for example, Robert P. Winston, "'Strange Order of Things!': The Journey to Chaos in Letters from an American Farmer," *Early American Literature* 19, no. 3 (Winter 1984–85): 249–67; James C. Mohr, "Calculated Disillusionment: Crèvecoeur's *Letters* Reconsidered," *South Atlantic Quarterly* 69 (1970): 354–63; and Elayne Antler Rapping, "Theory and Experience in Crèvecoeur's America," *American Quarterly* 19 (1967): 707–18.

10. Daniel Boorstin, *The Lost World of Thomas Jefferson* (Boston: Beacon Press, 1948), 44, 149.

11. In the unpublished "Fifth Letter," Crèvecoeur wrote: "[T]hus one species of Evil is ballanced by another, thus the fury of one Element is repressed by the Power of y' other, in the Midst of this great this astonishing Équipoyse Man struggles and Lives [*sic*]" (Moore, *More Letters from the American Farmer*, 48).

12. Crèvecoeur also hints at the advantages of black labor in "Thoughts of an American Farmer on Various Rural Subjects" and "7th Letter—Description of Various Implèments," both in Moore, *More Letters from the American Farmer.*

13. According to Bernard Chevignard, Crèvecoeur's scientific nationalism accelerated after the 1782 publication of *Letters*: "As French Consul, Crèvecoeur made himself the bard of American ingenuity and the enthusiastic diffuser of its new techniques." Thus in the 1784 and 1787 editions, "St. John's point of view is very clear. Americans, far from 'degenerating,' are at the peak of scientific progress. Before him, James had been more modest." (*Saint John de Crèvecoeur: "Letters from an American Farmer" et "Lettres d'un Cultivateur Américain" Genèse d'une Oeuvre Franco-américaine.* Thèse présentée pour l'obtention du doctorat ès lettres. Tome 1–3. Lille: Universite de Lille [1989], tome 3, 28–29, 29).

14. The Russian visitor to John Bartram, describing the Queen of Sweden's admiration for the famous botanist, asks whether it is surprising "to see a princess, fond of useful knowledge, descend sometimes from the throne to walk in the gardens of Linnaeus?" (188). Bartram responds in kind: after learning "Latin enough to understand Linnaeus . . . I began to botanize all over my farm" (189).

15. On Crèvecoeur's other comments on intermixture in the originally unpublished essays, see Moore, *More Letters from the American Farmer*, 150, 183, 190, 195.

16. Pamela Regis, *Describing Early America: Bartram, Jefferson, Crève-*

coeur, and the Rhetoric of Natural History (DeKalb: Northern Illinois University Press, 1992), 24.

17. If Crèvecoeur drew on the *Histoire Philosophique et Politique* for his description of Charles Town, he significantly raised the volume on Raynal's rather bland description of the city: "People say it is well constructed, agreeably built, and fortified with adequate regularity. The considerable fortunes that the union and the opening of commerce drew forth must have influenced morals. Of all the cities in North America, it is in Charles Town that one finds the most luxurious commodities" (quoted in Chevignard, tome 3, 227).

18. From "Thoughts of an American Farmer on Various Rural Subjects," in Moore, *More Letters from the American Farmer*, 25.

19. Michel Serres, *The Natural Contract* (Ann Arbor: University of Michigan Press, 1995), 38.

20. Neil Evernden, *The Social Creation of Nature* (Baltimore: Johns Hopkins University Press, 1992), 108, 121.

21. In "Ant Hill-Town," the narrator has a similar reaction to a thunderstorm: "[E]ven the approach of a Thunderstorm, tho' so dreaded by the Generality of Mankind how solemn how awfull, what reverence does it not Inspire us with, Nature seems Angry [yes but it is] for our Good" (Moore, *More Letters from the American Farmer*, 117).

22. David Carr, *Time, Narrative, and History* (Bloomington: Indiana University Press, 1986), 75–76, 183.

23. G. I. Jones, "Time and Oral Tradition," *Journal of African History* 6, no. 2 (1965): 153–60; Kwasi Wiredu, "How not to compare African traditional thought with Western thought," chap. 3 of Wiredu, *Philosophy and an African Culture* (Cambridge: Cambridge University Press, 1980); Robin Horton, "Tradition and Modernity Revisited," in *Rationality and Relativism*, ed. Martin Hollis and Steven Lukes (Oxford: Basil Blackwell, 1982): 201–60; and Kwame Gyeke, *An Essay on African Philosophical Thought: The Akan Conceptual Scheme* (Cambridge: Cambridge University Press, 1987), part 1.

24. Vincent Carretta, *Equiano the African: Biography of a Self-Made Man* (Athens: University of Georgia Press, 2005). Carretta originally offered his hypothesis in "Olaudah Equiano or Gustavus Vassa? New Light on an Eighteenth-Century Question of Identity," *Slavery and Abolition* 20, no. 3 (December 1999): 96–105.

25. An early skeptic was S. E. Ogude in "Facts into Fiction: Equiano's Narrative Reconsidered," *Research in African Literatures* 13, no. 1 (Spring 1982): 31–43.

26. It also helps to explain various unsatisfactory efforts to identify the precise location of Equiano's home "Essaka," including G. I. Jones, "Olaudah Equiano of the Niger Ibo," in *Africa Remembered: Narratives by West Africans from the Era of the Slave Trade*, ed. Philip Curtin (Madison: University of Wisconsin Press, 1967): 60–69; and Catherine Obianju Acholonu, "The Home of Olaudah Equiano: A Linguistic and Anthropological Search, " *Journal of Commonwealth Literature* 22, no. 1 (1987): 5–16.

27. Carretta, "Olaudah Equiano or Gustavus Vassa?" 97. Also see Ogude, "Facts into Fiction," 36–37.

28. See Christopher J. Berry, *Social Theory of the Scottish Enlightenment* (Edinburgh: Edinburgh University Press, 1997), 54–71.

29. This admittedly abbreviated characterization of Christian conceptions of time and history draws primarily on S. G. F. Brandon, "The Deification of Time," in *The Study of Time: Proceedings of the First Conference of the International Society for the Study of Time*, ed. J. T. Fraser et al. (Berlin: Springer-Verlag, 1972): 370–82; Stephen Jay Gould, *Time's Arrow, Time's Cycle: Myth and Metaphor in the Discovery of Geological Time* (Cambridge, Mass.: Harvard University Press, 1987); Mircea Eliade, *Cosmos and History: The Myth of the Eternal Return*, trans. Willard R. Trask (New York: Harper, 1959); and Paolo Rossi, *The Dark Abyss of Time: The History of the Earth and the History of Nations from Hooke to Vico*, trans. Lydia G. Cochrane (Chicago: University of Chicago Press, 1984).

30. Already apparent in Rousseau's romantic portrait of the unrecoverable innocence of "natural man," and full-blown by the time of Friedrich Hegel's *Phenomenology of Spirit*, this strain in Western philosophy has proved remarkably durable. Eliade, for example, presents "archaic" ontology as deliberately disconnected from an "objective" temporal reality, based on "these societies' will to refuse concrete time, their hostility toward every attempt at autonomous 'history,' that is, at history not regulated by archetypes" (*Cosmos and History*, xi). Similarly, Claude Levi-Strauss has claimed that "[t]he characteristic feature of the savage mind is its timelessness," which takes the form of an epistemology that is "discontinuous and analogical" and that represents reality as a simultaneity rather than sequence of images (*The Savage Mind (Pensée Sauvage)* [Chicago: University of Chicago Press, 1966], 263).

31. Equiano knew William Snelgrave's *A New Account of Some Parts of Guinea and the Slave Trade . . .* (1754), Michel Adanson's *A Voyage to Senegal, the Isle of Goree, and the River Gambia . . .* (1759), Henry Smeathman's *Plan of a Settlement to Be Made near Sierra Leone* (1786), John Matthews's *A Voy-*

age to the River Sierra-Leone, on the Coast of Africa (1788), James Stanfield's *Observations on a Voyage to the Coast of Africa* (1788), and Anthony Benezet's *Some Historical Account of Guinea* (1788). Smeathman's and Matthews's reports become particularly relevant toward the end of Equiano's *Narrative*, where he envisions a new relation between Britain and Africa based on the model of Sierra Leone. Of the Stanfield and Benezet texts, the latter is more important for Equiano's purposes (he tells his reader in a footnote to "See Benezet's Account of Guinea throughout").

32. *The Interesting Narrative of the Life of Olaudah Equiano, or Gustavus Vassa, the African, Written by Himself* (London, 1787), ed. Vincent Carretta (New York: Penguin, 1995), 44.

33. See Mazi Elechukwu Nnadibuagha Njaka, *Igbo Political Culture* (Evanston, Ill.: Northwestern University Press, 1974), 28–49; Adiele Eberechukwu Afigbo, *Ropes of Sand: Studies in Igbo History and Culture* (Ibadan: University Press in association with Oxford University Press, 1981); and William R. Bascom, *Ifa Divination: Communication between Gods and Men in West Africa* (Bloomington: Indiana University Press, 1969).

34. Austin J. Shelton, *The Igbo-Igala Borderland: Religion and Social Control in Indigenous African Colonialism* (Albany: State University of New York Press, 1971), 30, 31.

35. Eliade, *Cosmos and History*, 35.

36. John Marrant, *Narrative of the Lord's Wonderful Dealings with John Marrant, a Black* (1785), 68–69; James Gronniosaw, *A Narrative of the Most Remarkable Particulars in the Life of James Albert Ukawsaw Gronniosaw, an African Prince, as Related by Himself* (1772; American ed. 1774), 45.

37. "A commercial Intercourse with Africa," he wrote in a letter to Charles Jenkinson, Baron of Hawkesbury and president of the Board of Trade, "opens an inexhaustible Source of Wealth to the manufacturing Interest of Great Britain; and to all which the Slave Trade is a physical Obstruction. . . . The Population, Bowels, and Surface of Africa abound in valuable and useful Returns; the hidden treasuries of Countries will be brought to Light and into Circulation" (Equiano to Lord Hawkesbury, in *Interesting Narrative*, appendix E, 333–34).

38. Pierra Nora, "Between Memory and History: *Les Lieux de Mémoire*," *Representations* 26 (Spring 1989): 7–25, 13.

39. See W. Jeffrey Bolster, *Black Jacks: African American Seamen in the Age of Sail* (Cambridge, Mass.: Harvard University Press, 1997), esp. chaps. 2, 3, and 4; and, in a more theoretical vein, Paul Gilroy, *The Black Atlantic: Modernity and Double Consciousness* (Cambridge, Mass.: Harvard University Press,

1993), esp. chaps. 1 and 2. Both works emphasize the relative permeability of cultural and racial boundaries as experienced at sea as opposed to land.

40. An authoritative account of the undertaking is Christopher Fyfe's *A History of Sierra Leone* (London: Oxford University Press, 1962). See also Seymour Drescher, *Capitalism and Antislavery: British Mobilization in Comparative Perspective* (Hampshire, England: Macmillan, 1986), chap. 4, and Philip Curtin, *The Image of Africa: British Ideas and Action, 1780–1850* (Madison: University of Wisconsin Press, 1984), 114–16. On Equiano's involvement with Sierra Leone, see Stephen J. Braidwood, *Black Poor and White Philanthropists: London's Black Poor and the Foundation of the Sierra Leone Settlement 1786–1791* (Liverpool: Liverpool University Press, 1994); Keith Sandiford, *Measuring the Moment: Strategies of Protest in Eighteenth-Century Afro-English Writing* (Selinsgrove, Penn.: Susquehanna University Press, 1988), 142–45, and Paul Edwards's introduction to his 1996 edition of the *Narrative* (London: Dawsons, 1969), v–lxxii. More recently see Cassandra Pybus, *Epic Journeys of Freedom: Runaway Slaves of the American Revolution and Their Global Quest for Liberty* (Boston: Beacon Press, 2006), esp. chaps. 9 and 11.

41. Carretta, introduction to *Interesting Narrative*, xxviii.

Chapter 3. Natural Evil and Human Development

1. William Ellery Channing, "The Present Age: An Address Delivered Before the Mercantile Library Company of Philadelphia" (1841), in *The Works of William Ellery Channing, DD*, 10th ed. (Boston: George G. Channing, 1849), 6:147–82, 168, 169.

2. See Alice Dana Adams, *The Neglected Period of Anti-Slavery in America, 1808–1831* (Gloucester, Mass.: P. Smith, 1964; orig. 1908), chaps. 2 and 3.

3. David Barrow, *Involuntary, unmerited, perpetual, absolute, hereditary slavery, examined on the principles of nature, reason, justice, policy, and scripture* (Lexington, Ky.: D. and C. Bradford, 1808), 9, 10, 11.

4. John Campbell, *Negro-Mania: Being an examination of the falsely assumed equality of the various races of men* (Philadelphia, 1851), 199, 322, 323, 324, 331.

5. Edward J. Pringle, *Slavery in the Southern States* (Cambridge, Mass.: J. Bartlett, 1852), 20.

6. "It is good for us to have been under the rod, when we are led to a clear discovery of our sins, and a cordial acknowledgment of the divine justice and wisdom in our chastisement" (Anonymous, *Sanctified Afflictions*, 3rd ed. [Andover, Mass., 1822], 4).

7. This thumbnail sketch of the essential elements of mainstream theodicy draws on John Hick, *Evil and the God of Love* (New York: Harper and Row, 1966); Alvin Plantinga, *God, Freedom, and Evil* (New York: Harper and Row, 1974); and Richard Swinburne, *Providence and the Problem of Evil* (Oxford: Clarendon Press, 1998), 4–5).

8. Horace Bushnell, *Nature and the Supernatural, as together constituting the one system of God* (New York, 1858), 64, 169, 187, 192, 222.

9. Sacvan Bercovitch, *The American Jeremiad* (Madison: University of Wisconsin Press, 1978).

10. Richard Forrer, *Theodicies in Conflict: A Dilemma in Puritan Ethics and Nineteenth-Century American Literature* (Westport, Conn.: Greenwood Press, 1986), 75.

11. Nathan O. Hatch, *The Democratization of American Christianity* (New Haven, Conn.: Yale University Press, 1989); Jon Butler, *Awash in a Sea of Faith: Christianizing the American People* (Cambridge, Mass.: Harvard University Press, 1990).

12. Matthews, Donald G. "The Second Great Awakening as an Organizing Process, 1780–1830: An Hypothesis," *American Quarterly* 21 (1969): 23–43.

13. Thomas Branagan, *The beauties of philanthropy; or, The moral likeness of God delineated, in miniature being an intellectual mirror for the dignified clergy, as well as the subordinate laiety . . .* 2nd ed. (Philadelphia: Joseph Rakestraw, 1808), 199, 358–59, 361, 363.

14. L.M., *The Devil let loose; or, A wonderful instance of the goodness of God. In a letter from a gentleman in South-Carolina to his friend in Annapolis* (New York, 1805), 24.

15. *The First Annual Report of the African Education and Civilization Society. Presented at their annual meeting, held on Friday, May 8th, 1846. With the address of Rev. E. L. Magoon, of Richmond, Va.* (New York, 1846), 8, 4, 15.

16. D[avid] T[homas] Ansted, *Scenery, Science and Art* (London, 1854), 309.

17. Lee Rust Brown, *The Emerson Museum: Practical Romanticism and the Pursuit of the Whole* (Cambridge, Mass.: Harvard University Press, 1997), 139.

18. Robert V. Bruce, *The Launching of Modern American Science* (New York: Knopf, 1987); George H. Daniels, "The Process of Professionalization in American Science: The Emergent Period, 1820–1860," in *Science in America since 1820*, ed. Nathan Reingold (New York: Science History Publications, 1976; orig. 1967); George H. Daniels, *American Science in the Age of Jackson*

(New York: Columbia University Press, 1968); Donald Zochert, "Science and the Common Man in Ante-Bellum America," in Reingold, *Science in America since 1820*.

19. Edward Everett, "On the Importance of Scientific Knowledge to Practical Men, and on the Encouragements to Its Pursuit," in *Orations and Speeches on Various Occasions*, 2nd ed. (Boston: Little and Brown, 1850), 1:246–82, 264.

20. Benjamin Silliman, "Introductory Remarks," *American Journal of Science* 1, no. 1 (1818): 8.

21. William H. Furness, *Nature and Christianity. A Dudleian lecture delivered to the chapel of the University at Cambridge* (Boston, 1847), 5.

22. Dov Ospovat, *The Development of Darwin's Theory: Natural History, Natural Theology, and Natural Selection, 1838–1859* (Cambridge: Cambridge University Press, 1981), 2–3.

23. Bushnell, *Nature and the Supernatural*, 83. This was a consistent line of thought in early nineteenth-century natural philosophy. For just two examples, see Rev. I. G. Burkhard, *Elementary or Fundamental Principles of the Philosophy of Natural History . . . Trans. from the German by Charles Smith* (New York, 1804): "There is not perhaps a single species of animated beings whose existence depends not, more or less, upon the death and destruction of others" (199); and George Combe, *The constitution of man considered in relation to external objects*, 3rd American ed. (Boston, 1834): "Destructiveness [is] used as a means, under the guidance of Benevolence and Justice, to arrive at an end in harmony with the moral sentiments and intellect" (15).

24. Hans W. Frei, *The Eclipse of Biblical Narrative: A Study in Eighteenth and Nineteenth Century Hermeneutics* (New Haven, Conn.: Yale University Press, 1974), esp. chaps. 5–7; Jerry Wayne Brown, *The Rise of Biblical Criticism in America, 1800–1870: The New England Scholars* (Middletown, Conn.: Wesleyan University Press, 1969); Karin E. Gedge, *Without Benefit of Clergy: Women and the Pastoral Relationship in Nineteenth-Century American Culture* (New York: Oxford University Press, 2003); Ira L. Mandelker, *Religion, Society, and Utopia in Nineteenth-Century America* (Amherst: University of Massachusetts Press, 1984); Ann Douglas, *The Feminization of American Culture* (New York: Knopf, 1977).

25. See Theodore Bozeman, *Protestants in an Age of Science: The Baconian Ideal and Antebellum American Religious Thought* (Chapel Hill: University of North Carolina Press, 1977) and Herbert Hovenkamp, *Science and Religion in America, 1800–1860* (Philadelphia: University of Pennsylvania Press, 1978).

26. Bushnell, *Nature and the Supernatural*, 18.

27. Channing, "The Present Age," 153, 154, 168, 168–69, 169, 170.

28. Hugh Miller, *The Foot-Prints of the Creator; or, The Asterolepis of Stromness* (Cincinnati, 1851, repr. from the 3rd London ed.; orig. London 1849), 54.

29. N[athan] C[ovington] Brooks, *Matter, Instinct, Mind: Their Nature and Relations. The closing lecture of the second annual course of lectures before the Maryland Institute of Education* (Baltimore, 1843), 27, 33, 36, 6.

30. Paul Henri Thiry, Baron d'Holbach, *Good Sense; or, Natural Ideas Opposed to Supernatural*, 3rd ed. (New York, 1831; originally published in Amsterdam in 1772 as *Bon Sens, on idées naturelles opposees aux idées surnaturelles*), 59–60; D'Holbach, *The System of Nature: or, Laws of the Moral and Physical World*, trans. H. D. Robinson (Boston, 1853; originally published in London in 1770 as *Le Système de la nature*, 2 vols.), 44, 45.

31. Robert Jameson, *Narrative of discovery and adventure in Africa: from the earliest ages to the present time: with illustrations of the geology, mineralogy, and zoology* (New York, 1831), 19.

32. William Coleman, *Georges Cuvier, Zoologist: A Study in the History of Evolution Theory* (Cambridge, Mass.: Harvard University Press, 1964); Toby A. Appel, *The Cuvier-Geoffroy Debate: French Biology in the Decades Before Darwin* (New York: Oxford University Press, 1987), esp. chap. 3.

33. On the general intellectual climate and specific issues of pre-Darwinian evolutionary science see, in addition to Ospovat, Pietro Corsi, *The Age of Lamarck: Evolutionary Theories in France, 1790–1834* (Berkeley: University of California Press, 1988) and Appel, *The Cuvier-Geoffroy Debate.*

34. Hans Jonas, "Philosophical Aspects of Darwinism," in *The Phenomenon of Life: Toward a Philosophical Biology* (Evanston, Ill.: Northwestern University Press, 2001; orig. 1966), 46, 46, 49, 49.

35. Stephen Jay Gould, *The Structure of Evolutionary Theory* (Cambridge, Mass.: Belknap Press of Harvard University Press, 2002); Ernst Mayr, *What Evolution Is* (New York: Basic Books, 2001); and Elisabeth A. Lloyd, *The Structure and Confirmation of Evolutionary Theory* (Princeton, N.J.: Princeton University Press, 1994).

36. See James A. Secord, *Victorian Sensation: The Extraordinary Publication, Reception, and Secret Authorship of Vestiges of the Natural History of Creation* (Chicago: University of Chicago Press, 2003).

37. Gillian Beer, *Darwin's Plots: Evolutionary Narrative in Darwin, George Eliot, and Nineteenth-Century Fiction* (New York: Routledge, 1983); George Levine, *Darwin and the Novelists: Patterns of Science in Victorian Fiction* (Cambridge, Mass.: Harvard University Press, 1988); Bert Bender, *The De-*

scent of Love: Darwin and the Theory of Sexual Selection in American Fiction, 1871–1926 (Philadelphia: University of Pennsylvania Press, 1996); Joseph Carroll, *Evolution and Literary Theory* (Columbia: University of Missouri Press, 1995); Joseph Carroll, *Literary Darwinism: Evolution, Human Nature, and Literature* (New York: Routledge, 2004); and Jonathan Gottschall and David Sloan Wilson, eds., *The Literary Animal: Evolution and the Nature of Narrative* (Evanston, Ill.: Northwestern University Press, 2005).

38. George Gliddon, "The Monogenists and the Polygenists," in *Indigenous races of the earth; or, New chapters of ethnological inquiry; including monographs on special departments of philology, iconography, cranioscopy, palaeontology, pathology, archaeology, comparative geography, and natural history* (Philadelphia, 1857), 448; Nott, *Indigenous Races of the Earth* (Philadelphia, 1857), 361.

39. Stephen Jay Gould, *The Mismeasure of Man* (New York: Norton, 1981), chap. 2.

40. J. H. Guenebault, *Natural History of the Negro Race* (Charleston, 1837), v, vi, 1.

41. Henry Clarke Wright, *Anthropology; or, The science of man: in its bearing on war and slavery, and on arguments from the Bible, marriage, God, death, retribution, atonement and government, in support of these, and other social wrongs* (Cincinnati, 1850), 5.

42. See Seymour Drescher, *The Mighty Experiment: Free Labor versus Slavery in British Emancipation* (Oxford: Oxford University Press, 2002).

43. James Russell Lowell, "Ethnology" (February 1, 1849), in *The Anti-Slavery Papers of James Russell Lowell* (New York: Negro Universities Press, 1969; orig. Houghton Mifflin, 1902), 2:29, 28.

44. Frederick Douglass, *The Claims of the Negro Ethnologically Considered: An Address, Before the Literary Societies of Western Reserve College, at Commencement, July 12, 1854*, in *The Frederick Douglass Papers*, series 1, *Speeches, Debates, and Interviews*, vol. 2, *1847–1854*, ed. John W. Blassingame (New Haven, Conn.: Yale University Press, 1982), 502, 503, 504, 509, 505, 507.

45. Douglass, *The Claims of the Negro Ethnologically Considered*, 522.

46. George W. Bassett, *Slavery examined by the light of nature. Sermon preached by Rev. Geo. W. Bassett, at the Congregational Church, Washington D.C., Sunday, February 28, 1858* (Washington, D.C.?, 1858), 4.

47. Wright, *Anthropology*, 11.

48. Ospovat, *The Development of Darwin's Theory*, 18.

49. William Ellery Channing, *Slavery* (1835), in *Against Slavery: An Abolitionist Reader*, ed. Mason Lowance (New York: Penguin, 2000), 183.

50. Frederick A. Rauch, *Psychology; or, A view of the human soul: including anthropology* (New York, 1840), 64.

51. J[ermain] W[esley] Loguen, *The Rev. J. W. Loguen, as a Slave and as a Freeman. A Narrative of Real Life* (Syracuse, N.Y., 1859), 179.

52. Loguen, *Rev. J. W. Loguen*, 176.

53. John Brown, *Slave Life in Georgia: A Narrative of the Life, Sufferings, and Escape of John Brown, a Fugitive Slave, Now in England*, ed. Louis Alexis Chamerovzow, (London, 1855), 3.

54. Loguen's mother suffers a beating, which, "while it checked the growth of the sympathies and virtues of artless childhood . . . awakened and strengthened animal energies, which under better influences had ever slept." Later, "Jarm's spirit quickly developed into manhood. The sense of servitude and danger which bent his soul and body to degrading forms, passed away, and he stood erect in the manly proportions of his nature" (J. W. Loguen, *Rev. J. W. Loguen*, 16, 20, 180).

55. John Greenleaf Whittier, "Hymn, Written for the meeting of the Anti-Slavery Society, at Chatham Street Chapel, New York, held on the 4th of the seventh month, 1834," in *Songs of Labor, and Other Poems* (Boston: Ticknor, 1850).

56. Whittier, "The Farewell of a Virginia Slave Mother to Her Daughters Sold into Southern Bondage," in *Songs of Labor.*

57. John Pendleton Kennedy, *Swallow Barn; or, A Sojourn in the Old Dominion* (Philadelphia, 1832), 2:55.

58. See Joel Williamson, *New People: Miscegenation and Mulattoes in the United States* (New York: Free Press, 1980); Suzanne Bost, *Mulattas and Mestizas: Representing Mixed Identities in the Americas, 1850–2000* (University of Georgia Press, 2003); Werner Sollors, *Interracialism: Black-White Intermarriage in American History, Literature, and Law* (Oxford: Oxford University Press, 2000); and Elise Lemire, *"Miscegenation": Making Race in America* (Philadelphia: University of Pennsylvania Press, 2002).

59. Anonymous, *Civilis to the United States and the world: The rights of man* (U.S., 1849?), 4–5.

60. William Wells Brown, for example, in a disturbing moment of essentialist reasoning, wrote that "the black race has, to some extent, become refined by intercourse and commingling of blood with the Anglo-Saxon, so that they feel more sensitively the separations of families, sundering of ties and other cruelties which are inseparable from the system." ("Speech Delivered at the Horticultural

Hall, West Chester, Penn., 23 Oct. 1854," printed in the *National Anti-Slavery Standard* [November 4, 1854], in *The Black Abolitionist Papers*, vol. 4, *The United States 1847–1858*, ed. C. Peter Ripley [Chapel Hill: University of North Carolina Press, 1991], 245–55, 247.)

61. Thomas Smyth, *The unity of the human races: proved to be the doctrine of Scripture, reason, and science. With a review of the present position and theory of Professor Agassiz* (New York, 1850), 301–2.

62. James McCune Smith, January 20, 1855, editorial published in *Frederick Douglass' Paper*, January 26, 1855, in *Black Abolitionist Papers*, vol. 4, 259–65, 259, 261.

63. Samuel E. Cornish, June 30, 1838, editorial in the *Colored American* (New York), in *The Black Abolitionist Papers*, vol. 3, *The United States 1830–1846*, ed. C. Peter Ripley (Chapel Hill: University of North Carolina Press, 1991), 272–74, 272.

64. "Have been thinking amalgamation would be a speedy way of extinguishing the black race & this process is going bravely on [in the] South." (Union surgeon George Martin Trowbrige to wife, February 22, 1864 [Bentley Historical Library, University of Michigan]).

65. James McCune Smith to Horace Greeley, January 29, 1844, reprinted in the *National Anti-Slavery Standard* (New York), February 8, April 18, 1844, in *Black Abolitionist Papers*, vol. 3, 430–41.

66. Ebenezer Baldwin, *Observations on the physical, intellectual, and moral qualities of our colored population: With remarks on the subject of emancipation and colonization* (New Haven, Conn., 1834), 44. See also D. T. Ansted: "the coloured race disappears, not by absorption into the white, but by a process of absolute extinction." (D. T. Ansted, *Scenery, science and art*, 307.)

67. Anonymous, *Spermaceti for Inward Bruises, with prescriptions from the saddle-bags of Drs. Franklin and Jefferson, revised and amended for the use of modern politico, theologico, valetudinarians* (Syracuse, N.Y., 1851), 25, 26.

68. Paul Goodman, *Of One Blood: Abolitionism and the Origins of Racial Equality* (Berkeley: University of California Press, 1998), xix, xx.

Chapter 4. Nations of Blood

1. Ronald G. Walters, *The Antislavery Appeal: American Abolitionism after 1830* (Baltimore: Johns Hopkins University Press, 1976), chap. 8.

2. In 1850, the corresponding statistics were 3.2 million and 13.9 percent; in 1860 they were 3.95 million and 12.7 percent (U.S. Department of Commerce, Bureau of the Census).

3. Ralph Waldo Emerson, "Address to the Citizens of Concord on the Fugi-

tive Slave Law," in *Emerson's Antislavery Writings*, ed. Len Gougeon and Joel Myerson (New Haven: Yale University Press, 1995), 67. Hereafter cited in text as *EAW*.

4. The African American experience during the early national period is finally beginning to receive the scholarly attention it deserves. Important recent works include Gary B. Nash, *The Forgotten Fifth: African Americans in the Age of Revolution* (Cambridge, Mass.: Harvard University Press, 2006), esp. chap. 3; Simon Schama, *Rough Crossings: Britain, the Slaves and the American Revolution* (New York: Ecco, 2006); Patrick Rael, *Black Identity and Black Protest in the Antebellum North* (Chapel Hill: University of North Carolina Press, 2002); Eddie S. Glaude Jr., *Exodus! Race, Religion, and Nation in Early Nineteenth-Century Black America* (Chicago: University of Chicago Press, 2000), esp. part 1; and James Oliver Horton and Lois E. Horton, *In Hope of Liberty: Culture, Community and Protest among Northern Free Blacks, 1700–1860* (New York: Oxford University Press, 1997), esp. chaps. 6–10.

5. John Ashworth argues that "it is not too much to say that behind every event in the history of the sectional controversy, lurked the consequences of black resistance to slavery" (*Slavery, Capitalism, and Politics in the Antebellum Republic* [Cambridge: Cambridge University Press, 1995], 1:6). Also see Merton Dillon, *Slavery Attacked: Southern Slaves and Their Allies, 1619–1865* (Baton Rouge: Louisiana State University Press, 1990), esp. chaps. 6 and 7.

6. Robert Alexander Young, *The Ethiopian Manifesto: Issued in Defence of the Black Man's Rights in the Scale of Universal Freedom* (New York, 1829), in *The Ideological Origins of Black Nationalism*, ed. Sterling Stuckey (Boston: Beacon Press, 1972), 35, 37.

7. Thomas Gray, *The Confessions of Nat Turner* (Baltimore, 1831), 10.

8. Frantz Fanon, *Black Skin, White Masks*, trans. Charles Lam Markmann (New York: Grove Press, 1967), 11.

9. Ian Finseth, "David Walker, Nature's Nation, and Early African American Separatism," *Mississippi Quarterly* 54, no. 3 (Summer 2001): 337–62.

10. See William H. Pease and Jane H. Pease, "Walker's Appeal Comes to Charleston: A Note and Documents," *Journal of Negro History* 59 (1974): 287–92; Sean Wilentz, introduction to *David Walker's Appeal, in four Articles; together with a preamble, to the Coloured Citizens of the World, but in particular, and very expressly, to those of the United States of America*, ed. Sean Wilentz (New York: Hill and Wang, 1995; orig. 1829), xiv–xv; and Clement Eaton, "A Dangerous Pamphlet in the Old South," *Journal of Southern History* 2 (1936): 323–34.

11. Peter Hinks, *To Awaken My Afflicted Brethren: David Walker and the Problem of Antebellum Slave Resistance* (University Park: Pennsylvania State University Press, 1996).

12. Wilentz, *David Walker's Appeal*, 1. Subsequent page references appear in parentheses.

13. William Watkins, *An Address Delivered Before the Moral Reform Society*, in *Early Negro Writing, 1760–1837*, ed. Dorothy Porter (Baltimore: Black Classic Press, 1995; orig. 1971), 160.

14. John Ernest, *Liberation Historiography: African American Writers and the Challenge of History, 1794–1861* (Chapel Hill: University of North Carolina Press, 2004), 41, 42. A condensed version of the argument is John Ernest, "Liberation Historiography: African-American Historians before the Civil War," *American Literary History* 14, no. 3 (Fall 2002): 413–43.

15. See Scott Trafton, *Egypt Land: Race and Nineteenth-Century American Egyptomania* (Durham, N.C.: Duke University Press, 2004), esp. chap. 1.

16. Sterling Stuckey, *Slave Culture: Nationalist Theory and the Foundations of Black America* (New York: Oxford University Press, 1987), 131.

17. David Walker, "Address Delivered before the General Colored Association at Boston," in Wilentz, *David Walker's Appeal*, appendix 1, 83. This address, which previews many of the themes and arguments of the *Appeal*, was given on December 19, 1828, shortly before Walker began writing his major work.

18. Martin Delany, "Sound the Alarm," published in *The North Star*, January 12, 1849, in *Martin R. Delany: A Documentary Reader*, ed. Robert S. Levine (Chapel Hill: University of North Carolina Press, 2003), 142.

19. Martin Delany to Frederick Douglass, April 20, 1848, published in the *North Star*, May 12, 1848, in Levine, *Martin R. Delany: A Documentary Reader*, 91.

20. Martin Delany to Frederick Douglass, February 24, 1849, published in the *North Star*, March 9, 1849, in Levine, *Martin R. Delany: A Documentary Reader*, 133–34.

21. Robert Levine, *Martin Delany, Frederick Douglass, and the Politics of Representative Identity* (Chapel Hill: University of North Carolina Press, 1997), esp. chap. 2.

22. Delany's racial politics have generated considerable critical controversy. See Tunde Adeleke, *Without Regard for Race: The Other Martin Robison Delany* (Jackson: University of Mississippi Press, 2003), chap. 2; Cyril E. Griffith, *The African Dream: Martin R. Delany and the Emergence of Pan-African Thought* (University Park: Pennsylvania State University Press, 1975); Dorothy Sterling,

The Making of an Afro-American: Martin Robison Delany 1812–1885 (Garden City, N.Y.: Doubleday, 1971); and Victor Ullman, *Martin R. Delany: The Beginnings of Black Nationalism* (Boston: Beacon Press, 1971).

23. Basil Davidson, *The Black Man's Burden: Africa and the Curse of the Nation-State* (New York: Times Books, 1992), 43.

24. Page numbers refer to *Blake; or, The huts of America, a novel* (Boston: Beacon Press, 1970). Floyd J. Miller's editorial note explains the text's byzantine publication history.

25. Jeffory A. Clymer, "Martin Delany's *Blake* and the Transnational Politics of Property," *American Literary History* 15, no. 4 (Winter 2003): 709–31.

26. T. Douglas Doyle, "'Standing Still to See the Salvation': Paralyzed Resistance in Delany's *Blake*," *MAWA Review* 11, no. 2 (December 1996): 89–93.

27. Eric Sundquist, *To Wake the Nations: Race in the Making of American Literature* (Cambridge, Mass.: Harvard University Press, 1993), 220.

28. Levine, *Martin Delany, Frederick Douglass, and the Politics of Representative Identity*, 216, 216.

29. Martin Delany, *Official Report of the Niger Valley Exploring Party*, in *Search for a Place: Black Separatism and Africa, 1860 [by] M. R. Delany and Robert Campbell*, ed. Howard H. Bell (Ann Arbor: University of Michigan Press, 1969), 111, 121.

30. From "The Young American" (1844), in *Ralph Waldo Emerson: Essays and Lectures*, ed. Joel Porte (New York: Library of America, 1983), 213, hereafter cited as *EL*.

31. Gustaaf Van Cromphout, for example, separates Emerson's "ethical thinking" from the "confines" of his actual life, concentrating instead on its "intrinsic" quiddity (*Emerson's Ethics* [Columbia: University of Missouri Press, 1999], 5). Susan Sutton Smith and Harrison Hayford write that dramatic historical events "made it seem imperative [to Emerson] for the scholar to leave his 'honied thought' and take an active public stand on the side of the right" (foreword to *Journals and Miscellaneous Notebooks of Ralph Waldo Emerson*, ed. Ralph H. Orth [Cambridge, Mass.: Harvard University Press, 1978], 14:xiv, hereafter cited as *JMN*). The most uncompromising formulation is probably that of John Carlos Rowe, who asserts flatly that Emerson's "transcendentalism" and his activism proved simply "incompatible" (*At Emerson's Tomb: The Politics of Classic American Literature* [New York: Columbia University Press, 1997], 21).

32. Philip Nicoloff traces this side of Emerson's racial thought primarily to his reading of Johann von Herder's *Outlines of a Philosophy of the History of Man* (1800) and Victor Cousin's *Cours de Philosophie* (1829). See *Emerson on*

Race and History: An Examination of English Traits (New York: Columbia University Press, 1961).

33. Journal U 135, *JMN* 9:77. The passage is repeated, almost verbatim, in Notebook S Salvage, 133, in *The Topical Notebooks of Ralph Waldo Emerson*, ed. Susan Sutton Smith (Columbia: University of Missouri Press, 1990), 3:119–20, hereafter cited as *TN*.

34. Journal CD 92, *JMN* 10:100; Journal D 85, *JMN* 7:59.

35. Notebook Naturalist 120, *TN* 1:50. Variant appears in Journal HO 185, *JMN* 13:261 (late 1853 or early 1854); reappears in "Literature," from *English Traits* (1856), and "Poetry and Imagination" (1872). Here Emerson echoes similar claims in the more philosophically oriented scientific texts of his day; for instance, he owned and notated Peter Mark Roget's *Animal and Vegetable Physiology* (Philadelphia, 1836), in which Roget writes, "By knowing the general tendencies of analogous formations, we can sometimes recognise designs that are but faintly indicated, and trace the links which connect them with more general laws" (2nd ed., 1839, 38). Also: "To regard any of the beings in the creation as isolated from the rest, would be to take a very narrow and a false view of their condition; for all are connected by mutual relations" (50).

36. Journal GO 140, *JMN* 13:87 (late 1852 to early 1853). Variant appears in Notebook EO 83, *TN* 1:71 (probably 1853 or 1854); used later in "Fate," in *The Complete Works of Ralph Waldo Emerson*, ed. Edward Waldo Emerson (Boston: Houghton Mifflin, 1903–04), 6:36, hereafter cited as *CW*.

37. Emerson transcribed the following passage, for instance, from Richard Owen's *Paleontology; or, A Systematic Study of Extinct Animals and Their Geological Relations* (1860): "Palaeontology [*sic*] teaches, as regards the various forms of life which this planet has supported, that there has been 'an advance & progress in the main'" (Notebook Naturalist 107, *TN* 1:48).

38. Notebook Naturalist ii, *TN* 1:28.

39. Emerson's exposure to developmentalism, and to the ideas that scaffolded it, came primarily through the writings of Lorenz Oken (via John Bernhard Stallo's *General Principles of the Philosophy of Nature* [Boston, 1848]), Jean Baptiste Lamarck, Charles Lyell, John Pringle Nichol, Geoffroy de St. Hilaire, and Robert Chambers.

40. From *Nature* (*CW* 1:27) and "Fate" (*CW* 6:39).

41. Journal R 25, *JMN* 8:362. Notebook PH 10, *TN* 2:336 (italics indicate material that Emerson added after the initial entry, while strikethrough indicates material that he struck out).

42. Journal HO 285, *JMN* 13:288.

43. This passage, published in "Race," from *English Traits* (1856), *CW* 5:49, draws on a journal entry from August 1855 (Journal NO 283–84, *JMN* 7:466).

44. Journal HO 87 [late 1853], *JMN* 13:233.

45. The cited phrase is from Journal GH 5 (1847), *JMN* 10:131. Variations occur in Journal U 79, *JMN* 9:50 ("La nature aime les croisements. Fourier"), which is repeated in "Inspiration," *CW* 8:289; "Works and Days," *CW* 7:162 ("Nature loves to cross her stocks"); and "Powers and Laws of Thought," the first chapter of "Natural History of Intellect," *CW* 12:25–26 ("Nature loves mixtures").

46. Journal AB 107, *JMN* 10:45.

47. Gregg Crane, *Race, Citizenship, and Law in American Literature* (Cambridge: Cambridge University Press, 2002), 97–100.

48. Laura Dassow Walls, *Emerson's Life in Science: The Culture of Truth* (Ithaca, N.Y.: Cornell University Press, 2003), 184.

49. Journal O 23, *JMN* 9:365.

50. Journal V 18, *JMN* 9:104; Horace Bushnell, *Nature and the Supernatural, as together constituting the one system of God* (New York, 1858), 97; Journal E 204, *JMN* 7:393; Journal Y 119–20, *JMN* 9:299–300; James Elliot Cabot, *A Memoir of Ralph Waldo Emerson* (Boston: Houghton Mifflin, 1887), 2:789; *CW* 8:207.

51. Journal U 148–49, *JMN* 9:83.

52. Buell describes Emerson as an "intermittment nationalist at best" who "was formed and constrained by provincial and national allegiances but also strove mightily to overcome these" and who "for most of his life attached less intrinsic value to such allegiances than is usually thought" (*Emerson* [Cambridge, Mass.: Harvard University Press, 2003], 272, 4).

53. See, for example, Journal HO 93, *JMN* 13:234: "[W]hilst man is for eternity, for poetry, for love, yet he has a Greek, an English, an American career, which masks effectually the ulterior purpose from ordinary eyes. England is a coat." Also see Notebook S Salvage 133–34, *TN* 3:119–120: "Pedantry to estimate nations by census &c. Measure nations subjectively."

54. Journal CO 128–29, *JMN* 11:406.

55. David Theo Goldberg, "Liberalism's Limits: Carlyle and Mill on 'The Negro Question,'" in *Philosophers on Race: Critical Essays*, ed. Julie K. Ward and Tommy L. Lott (Oxford: Blackwell, 2002), 203.

56. Russ Castronovo, *Fathering the Nation: American Genealogies of Slavery and Freedom* (Berkeley: University of California, 1995), 9–10.

57. John Carlos Rowe, "Nineteenth-Century United States Literary Culture

and Transnationality," *PMLA* 118, no. 1 (January 2003): 78–89; Anita Patterson, *From Emerson to King: Democracy, Race, and the Politics of Protest* (New York: Oxford University Press, 1997); Christopher Newfield, *The Emerson Effect: Individualism and Submission in America* (Chicago: University of Chicago Press, 1996).

58. In 1845, after reading Chambers's protoevolutionary *Vestiges of the Natural History of Creation*, Emerson pondered whether the current stage of human development was merely transitional: "Well & it seems there is room for a better species of the genus Homo. [line break] The Caucasian is an arrested undertype" (Journal W 65, *JMN* 9:212). See Journal W 107, *JMN* 9:233: "We owe to every book that interests us one or two words. Thus to 'Vestiges of Creation' we owe 'arrested development.'" Emerson is actually questioning Chambers's conclusion that "the leading characters . . . of the various races of mankind, are simply representations of particular stages in the development of the highest or Caucasian type" (*Vestiges of the Natural History of Creation*, 307).

59. Rogers M. Smith, *Civic Ideals: Conflicting Visions of Citizenship in U.S. History* (New Haven: Yale University Press, 1997), 6, 471.

Chapter 5. Race in the Landscape

1. Harriet Beecher Stowe to Gamaliel Bailey, March 9, 1851, quoted in Joan Hedrick, *Harriet Beecher Stowe* (New York: Oxford University Press, 1995), 208. On the illustrations that accompanied the novel, see Julia Thomas, *Pictorial Victorians: The Inscription of Values in Word and Image* (Athens: Ohio University Press, 2004), chap. 1.

2. A Carolinian [Edward J. Pringle], *Slavery in the Southern States* (Cambridge, Mass., 1852), 1, 5.

3. Gwendolyn DuBois Shaw, *Portraits of a People: Picturing African Americans in the Nineteenth Century* (Seattle: University of Washington Press, 2006); Michael D. Harris, *Colored Pictures: Race and Visual Representation* (Chapel Hill: University of North Carolina Press, 2003), chap. 2; Geoff Quilley and Kay Dian Kriz, eds., *An Economy of Colour: Visual Culture and the Atlantic World, 1660–1830* (Manchester: Manchester University Press, 2003); Marcus Wood, *Blind Memory: Visual Representations of Slavery in England and America* (New York: Routledge, 2000), esp. chap. 3; and Albert Boime, *The Art of Exclusion: Representing Blacks in the Nineteenth Century* (Washington, D.C.: Smithsonian Institution Press, 1990).

4. W. J. T. Mitchell, ed., *Landscape and Power* (Chicago: University of Chicago Press, 1994); John Barrell, *The Dark Side of the Landscape: The Rural*

Poor in English Painting, 1730–1840 (Cambridge: Cambridge University Press, 1980); D. E. Cosgrove, *Social Formation and Symbolic Landscape* (London: Croom Helm, 1984).

5. Robert E. Abrams, *Landscape and Ideology in American Renaissance Literature: Topographies of Skepticism* (Cambridge: Cambridge University Press, 2004), 9, 14.

6. Mark Twain, *Adventures of Huckleberry Finn*, ed. Gerald Graff and James Phelan (New York: Bedford/St. Martin's, 2003), 125, 131.

7. From Mount's own *Catalogue of portraits and pictures painted by William Sidney Mount*, housed at the Suffolk Museum in Stony Brook, N.Y., quoted in *Painter of Rural America*, ed. Alfred Frankenstein (Washington, D.C.: H. K. Press, 1968), 37.

8. John Berger, "Painting and Time," in *The Sense of Sight* (New York: Vintage, 1993; orig. 1985), 209.

9. Charles Lanman, *Letters from a Landscape Painter* (Boston, 1845), 243.

10. Gaston Bachelard, *Water and Dreams: An Essay on the Imagination of Matter*, trans. Edith R. Farrell (Dallas: Pegasus Foundation, 1983), 23.

11. George Lunt, *An Address Delivered before the Massachusetts Horticultural Society, on the Dedication of Horticultural Hall, May 15, 1845* (Boston, 1845), 5–6.

12. Lunt, *An Address*, 11.

13. Hans Jonas, *The Phenomenon of Life: Toward a Philosophical Biology* (Evanston, Ill.: Northwestern University Press, 2001; orig. 1966), 147.

14. Thomas C. Upham, *Elements of mental philosophy, embracing the two departments of the intellect and the sensibilities*, 2 vols. (New York, 1843), 106.

15. Paul Shepard, *Man in the Landscape: A Historic View of the Esthetics of Nature* (New York: Knopf, 1967), 10.

16. Alexander Bain, *The Senses and the Intellect* (London, 1855), 448.

17. E[lias] L[yman] Magoon, "Scenery and Mind," in *The Home Book of the Picturesque; or, American Scenery, Art, and Literature* (New York, 1852), 3–4.

18. See Emily Brady, *Aesthetics of the Natural Environment* (Tuscaloosa: University of Alabama Press, 2003), esp. chap. 3.

19. Shepard, *Man in the Landscape*, 24.

20. Lunt, *An Address*, 7.

21. Ibid., 9–10.

22. "The Annual Report of the Library Company of Philadelphia for the Year 1998" (Philadelphia: Library Company of Philadelphia, 1999).

23. On the importance of "friendship albums" to the political and social culture of African American women during this period, see Erica R. Armstrong, "A Mental and Moral Feast: Reading, Writing, and Sentimentality in Black Philadelphia," *Journal of Women's History* 16, no. 1 (2004): 78–102.

24. James Thompson, "After the Fall: Class and Political Language in Britain, 1780–1900," *Historical Journal* 39, no. 3 (September 1996): 785–806; Margaret R. Somers, "The Narrative Constitution of Identity: A Relational and Network Approach," *Theory and Society* 23, no. 5 (October 1994): 605–49; Margaret R. Somers, "Narrativity, Narrative Identity, and Social Action: Rethinking English Working-Class Formation," *Social Science History* 16, no. 4 (1992): 591–630; George Steinmetz, "Reflections on the Role of Social Narratives in Working-Class Formation: Narrative Theory in the Social Sciences," *Social Science History* 16, no. 3 (1992): 489–516; and Rick Fantasia, *Cultures of Solidarity: Consciousness, Action, and Contemporary American Workers* (Berkeley: University of California Press, 1988), esp. part 1.

25. Many studies have shown us just how complex the lived experience of, and resistance to, this ideology proved to be. See, for example, Nancy Isenberg, *Sex and Citizenship in Antebellum America* (Chapel Hill: University of North Carolina Press, 1998), esp. chaps. 2, 5, and 6; Gillian Brown, *Domestic Individualism: Imagining Self in Nineteenth-Century America* (Berkeley: University of California Press, 1990), esp. chap. 2; Carroll Smith-Rosenberg, *Disorderly Conduct: Visions of Gender in Victorian America* (New York: Knopf, 1985), esp. part 2; Karen Halttunen, *Confidence Men and Painted Women: A Study of Middle-class Culture in America, 1830–1870* (New Haven: Yale University Press, 1982), esp. chaps. 3 and 4.

26. William Whipper, "Moral Reform—original," in Amy Cassey's personal album, housed at the Library Company of Philadelphia.

27. Ritchie Watson Jr., *Yeoman Versus Cavalier: The Old Southwest's Fictional Road to Rebellion* (Baton Rouge: Louisiana State University Press, 1993); Jan Bakker, *Pastoral in Antebellum Southern Romance* (Baton Rouge: Louisiana State University Press, 1989); Raimondo Luraghi, *The Rise and Fall of the Plantation South* (New York: New Viewpoints, 1978), esp. chaps. 5–7; and Lewis Simpson, *The Dispossessed Garden: Pastoral and History in Southern Literature* (Athens: University of Georgia Press, 1975).

28. William Lloyd Garrison, "Address," *Liberator* 8, no. 33 (August 17, 1838): 132.

29. Angela Miller, *The Empire of the Eye: Landscape Representation and American Cultural Politics, 1825–1875* (Ithaca, N.Y.: Cornell University Press, 1993), 210, 216.

30. Anthony Low, *The Georgic Revolution* (Princeton, N.J.: Princeton University Press, 1985), 12.

31. Beth Fowkes Tobin, *Colonizing Nature: The Tropics in British Arts and Letters, 1760–1820* (Philadelphia: University of Pennsylvania Press, 2005), chap. 1; Michael Collins, "Risk, Envy, and Fear in Sterling Brown's Georgics," *Callaloo* 21, no. 4 (Fall 1998): 950–67.

32. Frederick A. Rauch, *Psychology; or, A view of the human soul: including anthropology* (New York, 1840), 192.

33. Josef Pieper, *Leisure, the Basis of Culture*, trans. Alexander Dru (New York: New American Library, 1963), 26.

34. John Ashworth, *Slavery, Capitalism, and Politics in the Antebellum Republic* (Cambridge: Cambridge University Press, 1995), 114–21; Ira Berlin, *Many Thousands Gone: The First Two Centuries of Slavery in North America* (Cambridge, Mass.: Belknap Press of Harvard University Press, 1998), 11; and Eric Foner, *Free Soil, Free Labor, Free Men: The Ideology of the Republican Party before the Civil War* (New York: Oxford University Press, 1970), chap. 1.

35. Daniel T. Rodgers, *The Work Ethic in Industrial America, 1850–1920* (Chicago: University of Chicago Press, 1978), esp. chap. 1.

36. Quoted in Ashworth, *Slavery, Capitalism, and Politics in the Antebellum Republic*, 60.

37. See, for example, Frederick Law Olmsted, *The Cotton Kingdom: a traveller's observations on cotton and slavery in the American slave states; based upon three former volumes of journeys and investigations* (New York, 1861); Olmsted, *A journey in the seaboard slave states, with remarks on their economy* (New York, 1856); Richard Hildreth, *Despotism in America; or, An inquiry into the nature and results of the slave-holding system in the United States* (Boston, 1840); and C. G. Parsons, MD, *Inside View of Slavery; or, A Tour among the Planters* (Boston, 1855).

38. "Introduction," *Southern Agriculturist* 1, no. 1 (1828): 1, 2.

39. Rev. Dr. Manly, "An Address on Agriculture," *Southern Agriculturist* 2, no. 7 (July 1842), and James Hamilton, "An Address on the Agriculture and Husbandry of the South," *Southern Agriculturist* 4, no. 8 (August 1844).

40. Daniel Rodgers, "Republicanism: The Career of a Concept," *Journal of American History* 79, no. 1 (June 1992): 11–38, 31.

41. Thomas Kettell, *Southern Wealth and Northern Profits, as Exhibited in Statistical Facts and Official Figures: Showing the Necessity of Union to the Future Prosperity and Welfare of the Republic* (University: University of Alabama Press, 1965; orig.1860), 109.

42. The painting is privately owned and unavailable for reproduction, but it appears in Guy C. McElroy, *Facing History: The Black Image in American Art, 1710–1940* (San Francisco, Calif.: Bedford Arts; Washington, D.C.: Corcoran Gallery of Art, 1990).

43. David C. Miller, *Dark Eden: The Swamp in Nineteenth-Century American Culture* (Cambridge: Cambridge University Press, 1989), 8. Miller describes a shift in the meaning of swamp imagery during the 1850s, when the swamp "emerged as a metaphor of newly awakened unconscious mental processes" (3) and the "energy and intricacy of jungle vegetation tended to undermine [the] inherently moralizing conventions" (4) of Romantic iconography, stimulating a "reconfiguration of notions of the self and its relation to the body politic" (10).

44. A short article that does address the question of race is Kenneth T. Reed, "Washington Irving and the Negro," *Negro American Literature Forum* 4, no. 2 (July 1970): 43–44.

45. The concept of the Manichean binary is not a modern invention. "[B]lack is the color of mourning," wrote Frederick Rauch in 1840, "because it extinguishes all other colors; white is the color of innocence, because it is the general ground for all colors. Black and white mixed, form gray, the color of resignation, fear, uneasiness and twilight. Hence nearly all nations represent good beings in white, evil spirits in black, and ghosts in gray" (*Psychology; or, A view of the human soul: including anthropology* [New York, 1840], 190). Mechal Sobel links this color symbolism to the subconscious; see *Teach Me Dreams: Search for Self in the Revolutionary Era* (Princeton, N.J.: Princeton University Press, 2000), 39. More recently, Sarah Burns has connected it to the gothic tradition; see *Painting the Dark Side: Art and the Gothic Imagination in Nineteenth-Century America* (Berkeley: University of California Press, 2006), 120–25.

46. Thomas Jefferson to Roger C. Weightman, June 24, 1826, in *The Works of Thomas Jefferson*, ed. Paul Leicester Ford (New York: Knickerbocker Press, 1904), 10:391–92.

47. See Ann Fabian, *Card Sharps and Bucket Shops: Gambling in Nineteenth-Century America* (New York: Routledge, 1999), chap. 3.

48. This observation draws on John Berger's discussion of the significance of suits at the turn of the twentieth century, which, he argues, "far from disguising the social class of those who wore them, underlined and emphasised it" ("The Suit and the Photograph," in *About Looking* [New York: Vintage, 1991; orig. 1980], 34–35, 39).

49. George Fitzhugh, *Cannibals All! or, Slaves without Masters* (Richmond, 1857), ed. C. Vann Woodward (Cambridge, Mass.: Belknap Press of Harvard University Press, 1988; orig. 1960), 193, 36, 194.

50. John Davis, "Eastman Johnson's 'Negro Life at the South' and Urban Slavery in Washington, D.C.," *The Art Bulletin* 80, no. 1 (March 1998): 67–92.

51. Martha Griffith Browne, *Autobiography of a Female Slave* (New York, 1857), 120.

52. John Brown and Louis Alexis Chamerovzow, *Slave Life in Georgia: A Narrative of the Life, Sufferings, and Escape of John Brown, a Fugitive Slave, Now in England* (London, 1855), 208.

53. Booker T. Washington, *Up From Slavery*, ed. William L. Andrews (New York: Norton, 1996), 44–45.

54. John Bender, although concerned specifically with Spenser, provides a helpful definition: "[P]oetry is pictorial not when its formal organization reminds us of a painting or drawing, but when its relationship to our experience of the visual world is analogous to the relationship of the visual arts to that world" (*Spenser and Literary Pictorialism* [Princeton, N.J.: Princeton University Press, 1972], 24). See also Karl Kroeber and William Walling, eds., *Images of Romanticism: Visual and Verbal Affinities* (New Haven, Conn.: Yale University Press, 1978).

55. Marianna Torgovnick, *The Visual Arts, Pictorialism, and the Novel: James, Lawrence, and Woolf* (Princeton, N.J.: Princeton University Press, 1985), 19, 23.

56. James Jackson Jarves, *Art-hints. Architecture, sculpture, and painting* (New York, 1855), 132–33.

57. Lunsford Lane, *The Narrative of Lunsford Lane, Formerly of Raleigh, N.C. Embracing an Account of His Early Life, the Redemption by Purchase of Himself and Family from Slavery, and His Banishment from the Place of His Birth for the Crime of Wearing a Colored Skin. Published by Himself* (Boston, 1842), 36–37.

58. Harriet Jacobs, *Incidents in the Life of a Slave Girl, Written by Herself* (Boston, 1861), 303.

Chapter 6. Revisiting, Reliving, Reforming

1. Albert J. Von Frank, *The Trials of Anthony Burns: Freedom and Slavery in Emerson's Boston* (Cambridge, Mass.: Harvard University Press, 1998); and Gary Collison, *Shadrach Minkins: From Fugitive Slave to Citizen* (Cambridge, Mass.: Harvard University Press, 1997).

2. See Bruce Laurie, *Beyond Garrison: Antislavery and Social Reform* (Cambridge: Cambridge University Press, 2005); and John Stauffer, *The Black Hearts of Men: Radical Abolitionists and the Transformation of Race* (Cambridge, Mass.: Harvard University Press, 2004).

3. Robert Levine, *Martin Delany, Frederick Douglass, and the Politics of Representative Identity* (Chapel Hill: University of North Carolina Press, 1997), chap. 4; Joan Hedrick, *Harriet Beecher Stowe: A Life* (New York: Oxford University Press, 1994), chaps. 19–21; Robert S. Levine, "*Uncle Tom's Cabin* in *Frederick Douglass' Paper*: An Analysis of Reception," *American Literature* 64, no. 1 (March 1992): 71–93; Robert B. Stepto, "Sharing the Thunder: The Literary Exchanges of Harriet Beecher Stowe, Henry Bibb, and Frederick Douglass," in *New Essays on Uncle Tom's Cabin*, ed. Eric J. Sundquist (Cambridge: Cambridge University Press, 1986), 135–53; and Eric J. Sundquist, "Slavery, Revolution, and the American Renaissance," in *The American Renaissance Reconsidered*, ed. Walter Benn Michaels and Donald Pease (Baltimore: Johns Hopkins University Press, 1985).

4. Louis Hughes, *Thirty Years a Slave: From Bondage to Freedom: The Institution of Slavery as Seen on the Plantation and in the Home of the Planter* (Milwaukee: South Side Printing, 1897) 5.

5. Wayne Franklin and Michael Steiner, eds., *Mapping American Culture* (Iowa City: University of Iowa Press, 1992), 5.

6. My perspective on geography and childhood draws on work that emphasizes the formative psychological significance of actual natural scenes and experiences, particularly in response to conditions of social trauma and in continuity with the later development of adult consciousness. See Stephen R. Kellert, "Experiencing Nature: Affective, Cognitive, and Evaluative Development in Children," in *Children and Nature: Psychological, Sociocultural, and Evolutionary Investigations*, ed. Peter H. Kahn Jr. (Cambridge, Mass.: MIT Press, 2002); Gary Paul Nabhan and Stephen Trimble, *The Geography of Childhood: Why Children Need Wild Places* (Boston: Beacon Press, 1994); Edith Cobb, *The Ecology of Imagination in Childhood* (New York: Columbia University Press, 1977); and Louise Chawla, *Spots of Time: Manifold Ways of Being in Nature in Childhood* (Cambridge, Mass.: MIT Press, 2002).

7. Philip Fisher, *Still the New World: American Literature in a Culture of Creative Destruction* (Cambridge, Mass.: Harvard University Press, 1999).

8. See Michael Vlach, *Back of the Big House: The Architecture of Plantation Slavery* (Chapel Hill: University of North Carolina Press, 1993) and Theresa Singleton, *The Archaeology of Slavery and Plantation Life* (Orlando: Academic Press, 1985).

9. Moses Grandy, *Narrative of the Life of Moses Grandy; Late a Slave in the United States of America* (London, 1843), in *North Carolina Slave Narratives*, ed. William L. Andrews et al. (Chapel Hill: University of North Carolina Press, 2003), 176.

10. See, for example, Thomas Jones, *The Experience of Rev. Thomas H. Jones, Who Was a Slave for Forty-Three Years* (New Bedford, Conn., 1885), 211; and Annie Burton, *Memories of Childhood's Slavery Days* (Boston, 1909), 3.

11. Harriet Jacobs, *Incidents in the Life of a Slave Girl, Written by Herself* (Boston, 1861), ed. Jean Fagan Yellin (Cambridge, Mass.: Harvard University Press, 1987), 90–91.

12. Erin Mackie, "Welcome the Outlaw: Pirates, Maroons, and Caribbean Countercultures," *Cultural Critique* 59 (Winter 2005), 44.

13. See, for example, Henry Bibb, *Narrative of the Life and Adventures of Henry Bibb, an American Slave, Written by Himself* (New York, 1849), 159–61, and Moses Roper, *A Narrative of the Adventures and Escape of Moses Roper, from American Slavery* (Philadelphia, 1838), in *North Carolina Slave Narratives*, ed. William L. Andrews et al. (Chapel Hill: University of North Carolina Press, 2003), 63–66.

14. Edward Reed, *Encountering the World: Toward an Ecological Psychology* (New York: Oxford University Press, 1996), 10–11.

15. Hans Jonas, "The Nobility of Sight," in *The Phenomenon of Life: Toward a Philosophical Biology* (Evanston, Ill.: Northwestern University Press, 2001; orig. 1966), 145. See also Jonas's essay "Image-Making and the Freedom of Man" in the same work.

16. James Williams, *Narrative of James Williams, an American Slave, Who Was for Several Years a Driver on a Cotton Plantation in Alabama* (New York: American Anti-Slavery Society; Boston: Isaac Knapp, 1838), 92–93.

17. Rick Van Noy, *Surveying the Interior: Literary Cartographers and the Sense of Place* (Reno: University of Nevada Press, 2003), 4.

18. Eleanor J. Gibson, "Has Psychology a Future?" *Psychological Science* 5, no. 2 (March 1994): 69–76.

19. David Reynolds, *Beneath the American Renaissance: The Subversive Imagination in the Age of Emerson and Melville* (Cambridge, Mass.: Harvard University Press, 1988), 561, 564.

20. Lori Merish, "Sentimental Consumption: Harriet Beecher Stowe and the Aesthetics of Middle-Class Ownership," *American Literary History* 8, no. 1 (Spring 1996), 12.

21. Harriet Beecher Stowe, *Uncle Tom's Cabin*, ed. Elizabeth Ammons (New York: Norton, 1993; orig. 1851–52), 179.

22. See Maria Karafilis, "Democratic Space in Harriet Beecher Stowe's *Dred*," *Arizona Quarterly* 55, no. 3 (Autumn 1999), 23–49.

23. Harriet Beecher Stowe, *Dred: A Tale of the Great Dismal Swamp*, ed. Judie Newman (Edinburgh: Edinburgh University Press, 1999; orig. 1856), 161, 438.

24. "When this oriental seed [religious enthusiasm], an exotic among us, is planted back in the fiery soil of a tropical heart, it bursts forth with an incalculable ardor of growth" (277). For whites, by contrast, the "first impulse is to forbid everything that would not be proper" (317).

25. Ronald Takaki, *Iron Cages: Race and Culture in Nineteenth-Century America* (New York: Oxford University Press, 1990), esp. chaps. 6 and 7.

26. Gail Bederman, *Manliness and Civilization: A Cultural History of Gender and Race in the United States, 1880–1917* (Chicago: University of Chicago Press, 1995).

27. Aside from numerous articles on these issues, the important discussions in book-length studies include William L. Andrews, *To Tell a Free Story: The First Century of Afro-American Autobiography, 1760–1865* (Urbana: University of Illinois Press, 1986), esp. 214–39; Eric Sundquist, *To Wake the Nations: Race in the Making of American Literature* (Cambridge, Mass.: Harvard University Press, 1993), 83–92; Levine, *Martin Delany, Frederick Douglass, and the Politics of Representative Identity*, chap. 3; and David Leverenz, *Manhood in the American Renaissance* (Ithaca, N.Y.: Cornell University Press, 1989).

28. On the relation of the *Narrative* to the jeremiad genre, see Andrews, *To Tell a Free Story*, 123–38.

29. Sundquist, *To Wake the Nations*, 87. A less optimistic perspective is given in Wilson J. Moses, "Writing Freely? Frederick Douglass and the Constraints of Racialized Writing," in *Frederick Douglass: New Literary and Historical Essays*, ed. Eric J. Sundquist (Cambridge: Cambridge University Press, 1990), 66–83.

30. Ralph Waldo Emerson, "Experience," from *Essays: Second Series*, in *Emerson: Essays and Lectures*, ed. Joel Porte (New York: Library of America, 1983), 487.

31. James Cowles Prichard (1786–1848), one of the leading champions of monogenesis, was influenced by the German anatomist J. F. Blumenbach (1752–1840), who in his later career sharply moderated his initial polygenist conclusions regarding racial differentiation and defended the reputation of African-descended people. See also Michael A. Chaney, "Picturing the Mother, Claiming Egypt: *My Bondage and My Freedom* as Auto(bio)ethnography," *African American Review* 35, no. 3 (Fall 2001): 391–408.

32. Alexander Bain, *The Senses and the Intellect* (London, 1855), 349, 350.

33. John Augustine Smith, *Prelections on some of the more important subjects connected with the moral & physical science, in opposition to phrenology, materialism, atheism, and the principles advanced by the author of the Vestiges of Creation, and deducing the true criterion of moral propriety from the instinctive ruling of the moral sense* (New York, 1853), 282. Likewise, Thomas Upham maintained that the complexity of the eye "must be to a candid and reflecting mind a most powerful argument in proof of the existence and goodness of the Supreme Being" (*Elements of mental philosophy, embracing the two departments of the intellect and the sensibilities*, 2 vols. [New York, 1843], 1:106).

34. Asa Gray, *Darwiniana: Essays and Reviews Pertaining to Darwinism* (New York, 1876), 127. The chapter from which this quote is taken—"Natural Selection not Inconsistent with Natural Theology"—was first printed in the *Atlantic Monthly* in July 1860.

35. Douglass, *My Bondage and My Freedom*, 144–51.

36. Robert Hayden, "Middle Passage," in *Angle of Ascent* (New York: Liveright, 1975).

37. Lawrence Buell writes that *My Bondage and My Freedom* "emphasize[s] [Douglass's] love of countryside to a much greater degree than his format permitted him to do in his earlier *Narrative*, and thereby . . . dramatize[s] further the sense of the slave's exclusion from his rightful estate" (*The Environmental Imagination* [Cambridge, Mass.: Harvard University Press, 1995], 44).

38. Douglass, *Claims of the Negro Ethnologically Considered: An Address, Before the Literary Societies of Western Reserve College, at Commencement, July 12, 1854*, in *The Frederick Douglass Papers*, series 1, *Speeches, Debates, and Interviews*, vol. 2, *1847–1854*, ed. John W. Blassingame (New Haven, Conn.: Yale University Press, 1982), 480.

39. Karl Marx, *Capital: A Critique of Political Economy*, ed. Ernest Mandel, trans. Ben Fowkes (London: Penguin Books, 1976), 1:303–4. The capitalist, Marx writes, "has bought the use of the labour-power for a definite period, and he insists on his rights. . . . [A]ll wasteful consumption of raw material or instruments of labour is strictly forbidden, because what is wasted in this way represents a superfluous expenditure of quantities of objectified labour, labour that does not count in the product or enter into its value" (303).

40. Waldo Martin, *The Mind of Frederick Douglass* (Chapel Hill: University of North Carolina Press, 1984), 211. On Douglass's views of capitalism and social mobility, also see Benjamin Quarles, *Frederick Douglass* (New York: Atheneum, 1968); and Peter Walker, *Moral Choices: Memory, Desire, and*

Imagination in Nineteenth-Century American Abolition (Baton Rouge: Louisiana State University Press, 1978), chap. 8.

41. Frederick Douglass, "Letter to His Old Master," appendix to *My Bondage and My Freedom*, 267. Originally published in the *North Star* in 1848 as "To My Old Master, Thomas Auld."

42. Paul Alpers, *What Is Pastoral?* (Chicago: University of Chicago Press, 1996), 93.

43. Yi-Fu Tuan, "Place and Culture: Analeptic for Individuality and the World's Indifference," in Franklin and Steiner, *Mapping American Culture*, 44.

44. William Troy, *Hair-breadth Escapes from Slavery to Freedom* (Manchester, UK, 1861), 105–6.

45. Lawrence Buell, *Writing for an Endangered World: Literature, Culture, and Environment in the U.S. and Beyond* (Cambridge, Mass.: Harvard University Press, 2001), 78.

46. Peter Randolph, *Sketches of Slave Life; or, Illustrations of the "Peculiar Institution"* (Boston, 1855), 5. The poem has four more lines, in which the blood of the slaves cries from "the whipping-post," "the auction-block," "the gallows," and "the hunting-dogs that run down the poor fugitive." See also Martha Griffith Browne, *Autobiography of a Female Slave* (New York, 1857): "From the distant rice-fields and sugar plantations of the fervid South, comes a frantic wail from the wronged, injured, and oh, how innocent African! Hear it; hear that cry, Christians of the North, let it ring in your ears with its fearful agony!" (401).

47. Frederick Douglass, *Address Delivered by Hon. Frederick Douglass at the Third Annual Fair of the Tennessee Colored Agricultural and Mechanical Association on Thursday, September 18, 1873, at Nashville, Tennessee* (Washington, D.C., 1873), 7, 9–10.

Epilogue: Shadows of Green

1. Asa Gray to George Engelmann, January 25, 1861, in *Letters of Asa Gray*, ed. Jane Loring Gray (Boston: Houghton Mifflin, 1893), 2:467.

2. Yusef Komunyakaa, "Slaves Among Blades of Grass," *Nation* 269, no. 1 (July 5, 1999): 31.

Index